International and Comparative Business

International and Comparative Business

Foundations of Political Economies

Leo McCann

Los Angeles | London | New Delhi
Singapore | Washington DC

Los Angeles | London | New Delhi
Singapore | Washington DC

SAGE Publications Ltd
1 Oliver's Yard
55 City Road
London EC1Y 1SP

SAGE Publications Inc.
2455 Teller Road
Thousand Oaks, California 91320

SAGE Publications India Pvt Ltd
B 1/I 1 Mohan Cooperative Industrial Area
Mathura Road
New Delhi 110 044

SAGE Publications Asia-Pacific Pte Ltd
3 Church Street
#10-04 Samsung Hub
Singapore 049483

Editor: Matthew Waters
Editorial assistant: Nina Smith
Production editor: Sarah Cooke
Copyeditor: Jeremy Toynbee
Proofreader: Katherine Haw
Marketing manager: Alison Borg
Cover design: Lisa Harper
Typeset by: C&M Digitals (P) Ltd, Chennai, India
Printed in Great Britain by Henry Ling Limited, at the Dorset Press, Dorchester, DT1 1HD

MIX
Paper from responsible sources
FSC www.fsc.org FSC™ C013985

First published in 2014

Library of Congress Control Number: 2013936836

British Library Cataloguing in Publication data

A catalogue record for this book is available from the British Library

ISBN 978–1-4129–4875–3
ISBN 978–1-4129–4876–0 (pbk)

For Ruby and Max

Contents

About the Author

Dr Leo McCann is Senior Lecturer in International and Comparative Management at Manchester Business School. His research and teaching focuses on the impacts of large-scale economic change on work and organization across numerous countries. He has written many articles on the subject of the international transformation of white-collar work in journals such as *Journal of Management Studies, Human Relations*, and *Organization Studies*. He is the co-author of *Managing in the Modern Corporation* (Cambridge University Press, 2009). His research draws on the paradigms of sociology of work, varieties of capitalism, and political economy, exploring how large-scale 'global' transformations are translated through national institutional structures with often profound effects on the everyday lives of organizations, managers, workers and citizens. The present volume is his first textbook, based on over a decade of experience teaching and researching comparative capitalism, globalization, and the restructuring of organizations and work.

Prologue

Tōkaidō Shinkansen, approaching Shin-Ōsaka station, Japan

The carriage is a picture of calm. There is barely any noticeable vibration or rocking as the train slides along its dedicated high-speed tracks. The electric hum of the engines is muted and unobtrusive. Somehow it is even pleasing to the ear, contributing to a sense of forward flow. This is high-speed travel as art form. The intense light and sound of Japanese urban life cannot penetrate the cocoon. Instead the neon and concrete flashing past the windows serve as a colourful backdrop. Many passengers have pulled the sun-shutters down to block it completely. The train is quiet, tidy, clean and spacious. The interior colour scheme of dull whites, silvers and pastels is impeccably neat and tidy. The whole scene is beautifully organized but dull, somehow empty and clinical.

The old-fashioned uniform and extremely polite bowing of the ticket inspector hints at traditional notions of hierarchy, stability and authority. He has probably been employed by Japan Rail all of his working life. The passengers are quiet and orderly. Cellular phone networks work well, meaning there is no need for passengers to speak loudly or repeatedly call back when the signal drops. In fact, when they do talk, they move into the vestibule area, speaking in hushed tones, covering their mouths so as not to create undue noise. There's even a Silence Car, in which not only are calls forbidden, but so is talking to other passengers and the public address system is switched off. Many of the passengers are men in suits – the 'salarymen' rank and file of giant Japanese corporations and public bureaucracies. Several of them are asleep, slumped into reclining chairs; an indication of the uncompromising pace, intensity and length of Japanese office days. If they need a boost they could purchase a drink from the young saleswoman who wears an old-fashioned apron tied with a bow and calls out her items for sale in a sing-song, exaggeratedly girlish manner.

***

East Midlands Trains Liverpool–Norwich service, arriving at Manchester Oxford Road, UK

The carriage overflows with humanity. The old, ugly train's diesel engines grumble, vibrate and belch filthy fumes. The service seems to be running around 10 minutes late but there is no announcement or apology. The outside of the train looks odd. It is made of four carriages – the front two feature the new colour-scheme of maroon and gold but the trailing section is coloured green and blue. The muddled colour schemes point to the frequent changes of train companies that have operated this franchise. Neither of the colour schemes match the uniforms of the staff. The catering staff uniform bears the slogan 'Innovation' but there is scant evidence of newness or invention in the products on offer. Besides, the overcrowding is so severe that the trolley cannot advance down the train and it remains rooted at one end. People talk loudly into mobile phones, which regularly cut out as the network coverage fades. There is a lot of noise. There is also a tremendous mix of ethnicities and an apparently broad gender balance; several women are making business calls, tapping on laptops, checking emails. Many passengers appear to be international migrants, such as the dozens of Chinese students travelling between the several university cities on the line.

***

This book is about international comparisons. The public transport systems of different nations are a common point of comparison, often made very negatively in Britain's case.[1] My simple comparison of two train journeys would be a grossly unfair one if I tried to generalize from it. Many other services in Britain are far better than this particular line, including some that run on upgraded, high-speed electric lines. Many services in Japan are notoriously overcrowded, and the speed and comfort of the local services at the bottom of Japan's hierarchy of train transport compare poorly to those of the Shinkansen at its summit. The Shinkansen has been a symbol of Japanese modernity for many years (Hood 2006). Some of the trains have been emblazoned with the slogan 'AMBITIOUS JAPAN!' across the cars (in English). This train system is widely regarded as a phenomenal success, and one that reflects well on the country and the various government bureaucracies and domestic industrial giant firms that planned, built and run it. Japanese railways

[1] A recent study by the UK's independent rail travel watchdog found that, on average, UK rail fares were 50% more expensive than for similar journeys in European nations, 'GB rail fares more than Europe', *BBC News*, 19 February 2009, http://news.bbc.co.uk/1/hi/uk/7897903.stm. Accessed 4 July 2013.

have a reputation as being possibly the best managed, most safely operated and most heavily used systems in the world.

A brief comparison of the Japanese and British railways raises dozens of broader questions. Questions that might probe beneath the shiny surface in Japan and reflect other angles on both the Japanese train system and the socio-economic system that brought it into being. For example, is its operator, JR Tōkai (Central Japan Railway Company), a profitable, well-run company? Would it even matter if JR Tōkai was losing money or is it more important that it provides a 'world-class' public service? Passenger tickets for the Shinkansen are notoriously expensive – is this service available to all citizens or can only the rich afford to use it? Does the speed, reliability and availability of the line mean some sort of efficiency gains for businesses? Or are Japanese executives too heavily focused on the importance of face-to-face contact, meaning that the Shinkansen simply enables them to make lots of rather pointless, long-distance journeys? Are there any ways in which the UK's much-derided train system could emulate Japanese practice? Should the UK government, for example, finally bite the bullet and spend billions of pounds on new high-speed rail links rather than expanding environmentally damaging airports and roads? These are almost impossible questions to answer unequivocally as they depend on subjective judgements, not just about how to make profits, but also political and social judgements about what makes a 'good society'.

The UK rail system is highly fragmented following privatization and there have been major conflicts between the various players in a complex arrangement of train operating companies, banks (who own the rolling stock) and the not-for-profit company that owns and runs the infrastructure. This messy system has been widely criticized, not least for it possibly being responsible for a series of tragic fatal accidents during the period shortly after the change (Law and Mol 2002). The sector has been massively underfunded for decades, leading to a lack of investment in new trains and signalling systems. It suffers from chronic overcrowding in many urban areas, some services struggle with reliability and tickets are also very expensive. The slow decline of the industry reflects the general malaise of British manufacturing; dozens of production and maintenance companies, based in traditional rail manufacturing towns such as Doncaster and Crewe have shrunk to almost nothing. There is now very little train-building industry left in the country, and what remains (the former British Rail Engineering Limited facility at Derby) has been through several overseas takeovers and is currently owned by Bombardier of Canada. Many of the existing trains that were built by British firms are gradually running down towards decommissioning, and all new trains are built by international contractors, such as Alstom of France, Siemens of Germany or even Hitachi of Japan. One might argue that the physical, infrastructural, manufacturing side of rail transport now lies outside of the UK's core expertise, which represents a complete turnaround since the glory days of UK industry when pioneering engineering achievements took place. Today the UK is at cutting edge of finance, rather than mechanical engineering - a world leader in services rather than industry. Although its train-building industry is now a pale shadow of its former self, the UK boasts the world's biggest train museum, the National Railway Museum at York. There is clearly only one winner in a comparison of the UK's and Japan's rail infrastructure. One might also say in the UK's defence that it has moved on into other sectors, being more flexible and responsive to change. This brief vignette has also hinted that the UK is a more open, less controlled, society than Japan with more diverse ethnic and gender representation in its workplaces.

Acknowledgements

I would like to thank all at SAGE for their support and immense patience in waiting for me to deliver this manuscript. Particular thanks go to Matthew Waters and Nina Smith for seeing the book through to its final stages, and to Delia Alfonso-Martinez for showing such enthusiasm for my original idea all those years ago. At the University of Manchester, I gratefully acknowledge the support and collegiality of fellow members of the People, Management and Organizations division and the Organization and Society group at Manchester Business School. It is a pleasure to work in an environment with such a strong research culture. I would also like to extend my thanks to students on my comparative management course BMAN22000 (especially those who provided feedback on chapters in progress, such as Henry Ludlam and Diane Pallardy). I wish these bright and enthusiastic students all the best for the future, and I hope that at least some of them find the book useful. Lastly, I would like to thank my family and my wife Kate for always being there for me.

The author and publishers wish to thank the following authors and the following publishers who have kindly given permission for the use of copyright material.

- For Anthem Press for reproduction of Table 6.1 from Chang, H-J., (2003) *Kicking Away the Ladder: Policies and Institutions of Economic Development in Historical Perspective*, page 104.
- For Cambridge University Press for the reproduction of Exhibit 3.2 from Hassard, J., McCann, L., and Morris, J., (2009) *Managing in the Modern Corporation*, page 131; for the adaptation and reproduction of Table 11.4 from Mouer, R., and Kawanishi, H., (2005) *A Sociology of Work in Japan*, page 234; for excerpts from Palm, G., (1977) *The Flight from Work*, pages 61, 61, and 74.
- For Council on Foreign Relations, Inc, for excerpt from Bissell, R., (1951) 'The Impact of Rearmament on the World Economy', *Foreign Affairs*, 29(3), April 1951.

- For Little, Brown Book Group for excerpt from Johnson, C., (2002) 'Blowback: The Costs and Consequences of American Empire', pages 155–6.
- For The MIT Press for reproduction of Table 10.2 from Naughton, Barry., *The Chinese Economy: Transitions and Growth*, Figure on page 63 © 2006 Massachusetts Institute of Technology, by permission of The MIT Press.
- For Oxford University Press for the reproduction of Figure 1.2 from Hall, P.A., and Soskice, D., eds., (2001) *Varieties of Capitalism*, page 19; for the reproduction of Table 4.1 from Crafts, N.F.R., and Woodward, N.W.C. eds., (1991) *The British Economy Since 1945*, page 10; for excerpt from Wacquant, L., (2004) *Body & Soul: Notebooks of an Apprentice Boxer*, page 19; for reproduction of Table 9.2 from Panagariya, A., (2008) *India: The Emerging Giant*, page 37; for excerpt from Mokyr, J., (1990) *The Lever of Riches*, page 233; for excerpt from Dore, R., (2000) *Stock Market Capitalism: Welfare Capitalism, Japan and Germany versus the Anglo-Saxons*, pages 116–118.
- For Perseus Books Group, for excerpt from Andreev-Khomiakov, G.M., (1997) *Bitter Waters: Live and Work in Stalin's Russia*, pages 82–3.
- For Random House, Inc, for excerpt from INDIA UNBOUND by Gurcharan Das, copyright © 2000 by Gurcharan Das. Used by permission of Alfred A. Knopf, a division of Random House, Inc. Any third party use of this material, outside of this publication, is prohibited. Interested parties must apply directly to Random House, Inc. for permission.
- For Random House, UK, for adaptation and reproduction of Table 1.1 from Hutton, W., (1995) *The State We're In*, page 282.
- For University of California Press for excerpt from Ogasawara, Y., (1998) *Office Ladies and Salaried Men: Power, Gender, and Work in Japanese Companies*, page 39.
- For University of Chicago press for excerpt from Dudley, K.M. (1994), *End of the Line: Lost Jobs, New Lives in Postindustrial America*, page 1.
- For Verso Books for excerpt from Boltanski, L., and Chiapello, E. (2005) *The New Spirit of Capitalism*, page 231–2.

ONE Introducing the Field

Chapter objectives

- To introduce readers to the field of study known as 'varieties of capitalism' (VoC), showing that even as the world economy is becoming more interconnected and 'globalized', it still tolerates wide differences in national 'models' of capitalism
- To lay out the four main aims of the book
- To introduce the two general characterizations of types of 'models' of capitalism that exist in the world: namely 'liberal market economies' (LMEs) versus 'coordinated market economies' (CMEs)
- To introduce the ideas of globalization and VoC as powerful yet contested concepts

Introduction: a global economy, but made of many 'varieties of capitalism'

We are increasingly told by politicians, think tanks, academic experts, businesspeople and the media that we live in a 'global' economy. People the world over live and work in a globalized economy of dramatic and intense change, in which products and services are increasingly designed, produced, delivered and consumed across almost all territories of the world, and in which financial and physical transactions cross borders at dizzying speed. Multinational corporations, such as McDonald's, Unilever, Toyota, Tata or Siemens, market their products and services to almost all corners of the world, and a global labour market for employee 'talent' has emerged within which companies compete to recruit the 'best and the brightest' graduates regardless of their country of origin. 'World class' corporations claim to be genuinely global companies – although they have a headquarters somewhere in the world they detach themselves from their traditional national moorings as they try to attract global consumers, investors and employees. 'Global' seems to have superseded 'national' as any attempts by governments to develop distinctly national economic plans or industrial policies seem doomed to failure. Traditionally national 'ways of doing business' have 'converged' into an ephemeral 'world best practice' as the seemingly 'universal' norms of global capitalism take over.

This is what we are told. But is it true? This book agrees that the world economy is changing, and is in many ways becoming more internationally interconnected than ever before. But it also demonstrates that many profound differences remain in how business (and capitalism more generally) operates across many regions of the world. This is true even across highly advanced economies, such as Japan, the USA, France, Britain, Germany or the Nordic economies, and the book suggests that national traditions of business are likely to remain very significant. The book introduces readers to a large and influential set of literatures that explains economic action not in terms of detached, 'global' norms but as framed, enabled and constrained by complex, historically produced and contemporaneously reproduced local and national institutions. These institutions form essential 'rules of the game' that allow capitalism to work yet also continue to structure it and reproduce it in quite different forms. There remain powerful forms of national difference in supposedly 'global' business in terms of how companies are financed, who they do business with, how they recruit, train and retain staff, their interaction with unions and other forms of employee representation (such as German-style Works Councils), how they develop and deploy technology and how they restructure when facing financial trouble.

Just because the world is (arguably) getting more integrated and globalized, this does not necessarily mean that economic action and firm behaviour is becoming more similar. Rather than the somewhat simplistic assertion of a 'convergence' in economic behaviour under globalization, a large and powerful literature points to continued 'divergence' and the maintenance of difference (Amable 2003; Coates 2000, 2002; Dore 2000; Hall and Soskice 2001, Morgan et al. 2010; Whitley 1999; Wood and Demirbag 2012). These authors have developed and contributed to the influential 'varieties of capitalism' (VoC) or 'national business systems' (NBS) literatures, which focus on the production and reproduction of the institutions that make up national economies. This literature teaches us that countries develop distinct 'models' of economic behaviour, which clearly change over time but in doing so retain certain fundamental features even under the pressures of globalization and convergence (Coates 2000; Steinmo 2010).

This book aims to explore and describe this globalizing world economy, but it does so by paying close attention to historical and contemporary differences in national 'models' of capitalism. It aims to build on the insights of VoC, noting this body of work as a powerful corrective to the often overblown globalization and convergence theories. It does this by exploring a large literature on a range of countries, discussing the historical development of each country's economic 'model' and the ways in which each 'model' has changed, adapted and perhaps been eroded by domestic and global forces of competition and transformation. Much of the VoC and NBS literature is very abstract, technical and detached. Many readers, while attracted to the logic of the argument that there remains many distinct systems of capitalism, become frustrated by this abstraction and by the absence of detail on how and why these systems have formed. This book aims to make a contribution to these debates by paying closer attention to distinct country-based research in each chapter, by focusing in depth on how each major country 'model' really operates, in terms of finance and corporate governance, government institutions and macroeconomic policy, and at more micro levels – the level of management, work and organization. In doing so, it tries to project a more 'human face' onto discussion of VoC.

The book has four main aims:

- The first is to explore the theoretical background to debates on VoC and NBS, pointing out why these debates are crucial to a thorough and realistic appraisal of the world economy, and why it is important to note the wide diversity in socio-economic models that persist amid 'globalization.'
- The second is to provide detail on the historical development and contemporary reproduction of national models or systems of capitalism. It covers all of the world's major economies, moving from West to East through chapters exploring the USA, the UK, France, Germany, the Nordic economies, Russia, India, China and Japan. The book will focus on country-specific literature in order to build up a clear and detailed picture of the domestic and international forces that have helped shape these distinct models over time.
- The third is to show how these country models have changed in recent decades. Clearly globalization and convergence are real forces at some level. 'Neoliberal' economic theory and concepts of 'global best practice' in management, finance and government policy have spread across all manner of national business systems, and countries, firms and institutions demonstrably do change and adapt, especially when previously secure and economically successful models run into

trouble following recessions or financial crises. Governments initiate reform policies that open up their economies to international trade and inward investment, and companies restructure themselves so that they better conform to (typically Anglo-American) forms of 'best practice' as they try to remain competitive. The chapters will show that (at a very general level) all of the nations have been through three very broad phases in the development of their own version of capitalism. These phases are: (1) an early period of growth in which 'wild' and unregulated forms of liberal capitalism emerge, often involving considerable social turmoil; (2) a period of 'organized' capitalism in which the rougher edges of capitalism are smoothed over by government regulations and the emergence of bureaucratic management structures in firms, which constitute more established 'rules of the game' and typically result in a more egalitarian distribution of wealth; and (3) a period up to today of 'disorganized capitalism' (Lash and Urry 1987), characterized by intensified international economic relations, widespread organizational restructuring, and a return to higher levels of income inequality. These three phases are similar to what Boltanski and Chiapello call the first, second and third 'spirits' of capitalism (Boltanski and Chiapello 2005). Throughout each of these phases, however, each of these countries has retained distinct institutional elements that means that notions of *national* varieties of capitalism still remain sensible and accurate.

- Finally, it tries to insert more of a discussion of morality and ethics into the typically rather technical discussions of models of capitalism. Much of the VoC literature has rather little to say about which models are the most morally defensible or socially attractive. Some write of the various strengths and weaknesses in national innovation systems and the ways in which various national models tend to specialize in different industrial and service sectors (Hall and Soskice 2001) but these analyses are often problematic. Supposedly strong and effective models can act in ways that confound expectations. What appears to be an effective or dominant model in one era can falter in the next. Change can be unpredictable and can often occur in some of the last places you expect to see it. The book will largely stay away from debates about the economic effectiveness of models, but will try to provide some insights into the relative strengths and weaknesses of the models in a moral and ethical sense. Recent years have seen many important economies struggle severely with the impact of financial crashes, unemployment, social dislocation, poverty, joblessness, even hopelessness. In such a context, which of the models seems the most morally defensible? The book will ask which – if any – of these various systems of capitalism approximate most closely to a model of a 'good society' – especially when it comes to their relative levels of income inequality, or workplace democracy, or employee dignity.

VoC literature places a great deal of emphasis on the existence of differing economic and social *institutions* that operate in different nations. These institutions (such as national laws and historical and cultural customs and practices) serve to structure the ways in which businesses, organizations and people operate (Scott 2008a). Institutions set the 'rules of the game' for capitalism, and these rules can differ significantly across difference regions of the world (North 1991). As the prologue has suggested, Japanese institutions seem better at supporting train-building industry and infrastructure than British institutions. In contrast, the UK's institutions might be better at supporting the development and running of museums or other service-based firms. Institutions therefore assist the smooth development of certain economic forms, but also serve to inhibit or restrict the development of others.

This introductory chapter proceeds in five further sections. First, it outlines one of the main ways of distinguishing and categorizing different varieties of capitalism, explaining what is meant by so-called *liberal market economies* or LMEs (such as the UK) and *coordinated market economies* or CMEs (such as Japan). The chapter moves on to explore the debate between the VoC approach and another major (perhaps dominant) area of literature, that of globalization theory. Thereafter a discussion ensues about the disturbing and traumatic economic crises that seem to have become a common feature to all economic systems in recent years. In that section, I will briefly explore the extent to which all 'varieties' of capitalism were caught up in the 2007–8 subprime mortgage crisis, and the extent to which this crisis may have discredited or disrupted the previously dominant ideology of neoliberalism and the LME model. A very brief section then explains the main motivations for writing this book, which aims to help the reader understand the value of this field of study. The chapter closes by highlighting the complex, contested and very unresolved nature of the field of international and comparative business.

Introducing the two main 'models' of capitalism: liberal market economies versus coordinated market economies

VoC authors have made many different attempts to describe, clarify and categorize the competing socio-economic systems that exist across the world. One of the simplest and widest-used frameworks was that developed by Hall and Soskice (2001), in a very widely cited text that seems to have had a labelling effect on the field of study – *Varieties of Capitalism*.[1] In their interpretation countries that operate LMEs are compared to countries operating CMEs.[2]

LMEs are highly open, highly globalized economies with traditions of minimal governmental interference and light regulation, and in which short-term stock market movements are of crucial importance in both explaining firm behaviour and motivating top management. Large firms operating in such a climate tend to be owned by a large and very diverse range of shareholders, which exercise considerable pressure on top management to ensure that the company is acting in the interests of owners by delivering 'shareholder value'. These pressures are often short-term and the management of firms in LMEs often engage in dramatic and radical organizational change (such as downsizing and cost-cutting) in order to maintain high stock prices and dividends. Employment and careers inside LME firms can be insecure, and workers tend to have limited say in the operation of their work and in the running of the company. LME firms often radically reinvent themselves to stay 'ahead of the game' exiting quickly from industry sectors that appear to be non-value-creating, and entering new areas, such as in the so-called 'new economy' era in the 1990s when IT and internet companies (especially in the USA) boomed in value. The word 'liberal' in this context refers to the freedoms the system grants for business; implying limited state involvement in the economy and the absence of heavy regulation. Under these systems firms also tend to be less cooperative with each other than they may be in other economic systems. This feature is particularly clear in the USA that has especially tight anti-trust legislation.[3] LMEs are also known as 'Anglo-Saxon economies' or 'stock market capitalism'. The classic examples are the USA and UK, which are well

[1] There may be others, but the earliest use of the exact phrase 'varieties of capitalism' that I have come across was in Thomas McCraw's textbook *Creating Modern Capitalism* (1997a: 11–12).

[2] There have been many different versions on this theme, often using different language to describe either the same things or the same idea with a slightly different regional or philosophical emphasis. The LME model is regularly labelled 'Anglo-Saxon capitalism', 'stock market capitalism', the 'Anglo-American model' or 'neoliberal capitalism'. The CME model is variously called 'alliance capitalism', the 'social-market economy', 'welfare capitalism' or 'non-liberal capitalism'. Other theorists have proposed more than two versions of capitalism suggesting for example six (Whitley 1999) or five (Amable 2003) distinct models that do not always correspond neatly to the individual boundaries of nation states. For a deeper discussion see Chapter 2.

[3] Anti-trust legislation refers to laws that are designed to encourage more open competition and to break up monopolies and cartels.

known as 'business friendly' environments, especially since the enactment of 'neoliberal' economic reforms begun under US President Ronald Reagan and UK Prime Minister Margaret Thatcher in the 1980s.[4]

In contrast, there are the CMEs. The most widely used examples of CMEs are Germany and Japan. These countries have tended to progress down different economic routes from the LMEs for numerous reasons, not least of which is the almost total rebuilding of their economies after the Second World War. As the 'coordinated' title suggests, these countries exhibit a much-increased role for inter-firm interaction and cooperation, such as the formation of large business groups. 'Coordination' also refers to firms' close interactions with various institutions of government (Hall and Soskice 2001: 8–9). The post-war rebuilding of Germany and Japan, which involved considerable state intervention, direction and ownership of industry, has often led to the CME model being associated with the concept of the 'developmental state' (Johnson 1982; Wade 2003). Ownership of large companies in CMEs tends to be much more concentrated, with more committed owners who are invested for the longer term and are relatively unconcerned with short-term movements in share price. Sometimes these owners are families, sometimes they are large and conservative banks, sometimes they are other companies who are fellow members of business groups which have traditionally collaborated with one another. The absence of a 'shareholder value logic' means the CME firms are typically understood to be able to plan and invest for longer time horizons than their counterparts in LMEs. This tends to mean that careers in CME firms are more stable and long-term (even 'jobs for life') and that employees have stronger forms of representation and involvement in their work and in the strategy of their companies. This can also mean, however that CMEs are conservative and slow-moving environments, in which radical changes and innovations are relatively rare. A good example might be the Japanese economy's slow and indecisive response to its major financial crisis of the 1990s.

There are many facets through which the differences between these kinds of national economy are compared and examined. These include the banking and finance systems of the countries (to what extent nations' economies are open to financial risk-taking), their education and training systems (what kinds of skills are generated and retained by firms and by educational institutions) and the innovation systems of these nations (how firms in these countries develop and apply new ideas and technologies). Many authors have presented

[4] For an excellent introduction to the notion of 'neoliberalism' see Steger and Roy (2010).

these comparisons in tabulated form. An early and fairly straightforward example is provided by Will Hutton (1995: 282). Hutton does not use the terminology of LMEs and CMEs and he outlines four distinct VoCs rather than just two. However, clearly under his explanation the US and British systems are similar in many ways and could be grouped together as LMEs, as could the German and Japanese models as CMEs.

Table 1.1, along with many others like it that feature regularly in the VoC literature, demonstrates that LMEs and CMEs exhibit different sub-features. According to Hutton (1995: 283), these sub-features interlock and become mutually re-enforcing. This concept is known as *complementarity* in the VoC literature. As he explains:

> In Britain, profit-maximising firms that give the building of market share a low priority have to be run autocratically in order to produce the kind of shareholder returns that the financial system demands – and that in turn has consequences for the way the labour market is run: the less committed the financial system, the less the firms are able to offer lifetime employment and the less willing they are to undertake training. (1995: 283).

Hutton's table indicates that under the UK version of capitalism the financial system is 'uncommitted' and 'marketised', which means that short-term, share-driven financial demands on firms dominate, to the extent that UK firms struggle to develop a long-term focus on human or physical capital. Conversely, for Japan, the table indicates that the financial system of that country is 'personal' and 'committed', meaning that large Japanese firms have long-term, trusted relationships with banks, which provide them with long-term finance on relatively soft terms. This enables Japanese firms to invest for the long run in technology, industry and in lifetime employment for skilled staff. To use Japanese parlance, the relationships between banks and firms in the UK are *dorai* (dry - meaning reserved, rational, instrumental and arms-length) whereas in Japan the relationships between banks and firms are *uetto* (wet - meaning personal, sentimental and trusting).

Large firms operating under LME or CME conditions are affected by these national institutions in different ways, developing different forms of competencies and weaknesses accordingly. Other, much more complicated comparisons of economies and their subsystems are made by other authors and some of these will be discussed in Chapter 2. Hall and Soskice argue very convincingly that these different institutional practices 'are not distributed randomly across nations' (2001: 18). Instead, one can see clear clustering effects that delineate liberal from CMEs. They provide several figures that illustrate clear general effects of the different economic models (Hall and Soskice 2001: 19, 42–3). Figure 1.1 plots stock market capitalization (the market value of stock market listed domestic

Table 1.1 A comparative overview of broad models of capitalism

Characteristic	American capitalism	Japanese capitalism	European social market	British capitalism
Basic principle				
Dominant factor of production	capital	labour	partnership	capital
'Public' tradition	medium	high	high	low
Centralisation	Low	medium	medium	high
Reliance on price-mediated markets	high	low	medium	arms-length
Supply relations	arms-length price-driven	close enduring	bureaucracy planned	price-driven
Industrial groups	partial, defence, etc.	very high	high	low
Extent privatised	high	high	medium	high
Financial system				
Market structure	anonymous securitised	personal committed	bureaucracy committed	uncommitted marketised
Banking system	advanced marketised regional	traditional regulated concentrated	traditional regulated regional	advanced marketised centralised
Stock market	v. important	unimportant	unimportant	v. important
Required returns	high	low	medium	high
Labour market				
Job security	low	high	high	low
Labour mobility	high	low	medium	medium
Labour/ management	adversarial	cooperative	cooperative	adversarial
Pay differential	large	small	medium	large
Turnover	high	low	medium	medium
Skills	medium	high	high	poor
Union structure	sector-based	firm-based	industry-wide	craft
Strength	low	low	high	low
The firm				
Main goal	profits	market share stable jobs	market share	profits
Role top manager	boss-king autocratic	consensus	fulfilment consensus	boss-king hierarchy
Social overheads	low	low	high	medium, down

(Continued)

Table 1.1 (Continued)

Characteristic	American capitalism	Japanese capitalism	European social market	British capitalism
Welfare system				
Basic principle	liberal	corporatist	corporatist social democracy	mixed
Universal transfers	low	medium	high	medium, down
Means-testing	high	medium	low	medium, up
Degree education tiered by class	high	medium	medium	high
Private welfare	high	medium	low	medium, up
Government policies				
Role of government	limited adversarial	extensive cooperative	encompassing	strong adversarial
Openness to trade	quite open	least open	quite open	open
Industrial policy	little	high	high	non-existent
Top income tax	low	low	high	medium

Source: adapted from Hutton (1995: 282). By permission of Random House, UK.

companies as a percentage of the nation's GDP) against the strictness of the countries' labour laws (to what extent laws protect and support employees, such as statutory redundancy compensation and maternity leave). This graph shows two distinct clusters with CMEs grouped together in the top left-hand corner, demonstrating that they share strict labour laws and that the stock market value of their firms is somewhat moderate relative to the size of their economies (in other words, in a typical CME the stock market is generally less important relative to the rest of the economy). The LMEs, in contrast, are grouped in the bottom right-hand corner of the graph, suggesting low levels of employment protection and high stock market value of firms relative to the GDP of these economies (meaning that the trading of stocks and shares makes up a central part of economy as a whole). This indicates that stock market capitalism (the LME model) is associated with short-term employment practices, reflecting its open, flexible, fast-moving tendencies.

Hall and Soskice (2001) go on to describe the industry sector specializing effects of these societies. They argue that the VoC approach can explain many features of contemporary economic organization. Patent application data, for example, shows that the USA tends to specialize in

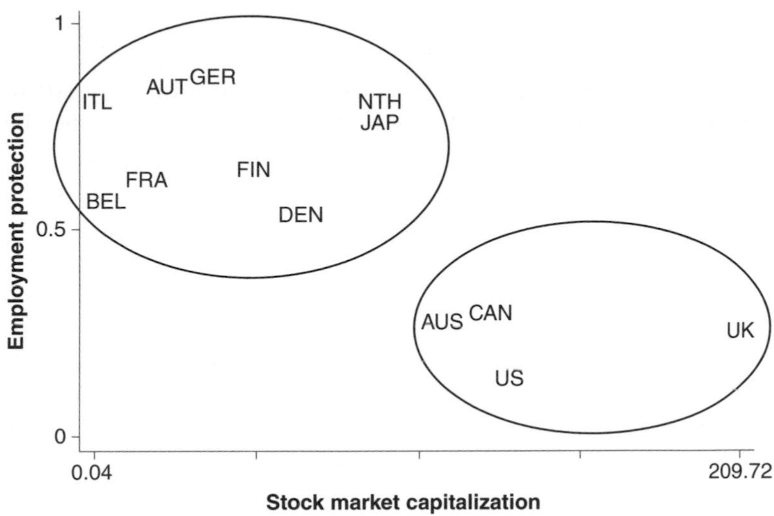

Figure 1.1 Institutions across sub-spheres of the political economy

Note: Employment protection refers to the index of employment protection developed by Estevez-Abe, Iversen, and Soskice in *Varities of Capitalism*. Stock market capitalization is the market value of listed domestic companies as a percentage of GDP.

Source: Hall and Soskice (2001: 19). By permission of Oxford University Press.

highly fluid and flexible industries in which radical innovations and sudden breaks with the past are common, such as the biotechnology and IT sectors, whereas Germany has tended to focus on industries in which longer-term, cumulative, incremental innovations are required, such as machine tools, transport industries and engines. Hall and Soskice therefore powerfully demonstrate the importance of differences in country models. National economies are structured differently and tend to specialize in different industries and services, just like the UK and Japan railways example in the prologue.

Aside from these macro-level comparisons that crop up frequently in the literature, there are numerous other ways in which VoC authors make valid and important points. While many of the features of different nations can be compared in terms of their difference by degrees of quantity, there are is also much to learn about national and region differences on a more qualitative level. For example, the German business historian Sigurt Vitols has written extensively on the nature of various nations' banking systems, showing that the fundaments of German, Japanese and North American financial structures developed along quite different lines from each other since the 1929 Wall Street Crash and 1930s Great Depression (Vitols 2001). Similar comparative historical analyses have been undertaken by the contributors to Streeck and Yamamura's (2001) book *The Origins of Nonliberal Capitalism*.

An appreciation of historical differences in the national institutional rules of the game remains centrally important to a serious and detailed understanding of how the global economy functions. However, VoC authors need to be sensitive to the ways in which all economies are subject to change and destabilization. The historical formation and contemporary reproduction of national versions of capitalism are powerful, but there is also very strong evidence to suggest that global and domestic pressures for change and convergence are very real. The debate between a 'VoC' position, which tends to emphasize the continued diversity of country models, and between a 'globalization' position, which emphasizes dramatic change, disruption and convergence of systems, is the subject of the next section.

One economy or many? Globalization theory versus international and comparative business approaches

Although international comparisons of economies, work and organization have been central to much economic analysis for many years, the specific rise of the VoC literature can probably be traced back to 1991 and the dramatic and, to many, unexpected collapse of the USSR. With the demise of state socialism, many authors rushed in to proclaim the power, inevitability and success of globalization. Globalization was described as a set of processes that were bringing about a new world order, involving much closer economic, social and political linkages between nations. The end of the USSR was both one of the drivers of globalization and one of its end-results. Political theorist Mary Kaldor suggested that with the collapse of the Berlin Wall, 'the last barrier to globalization was removed'.[5]

Globalization arguments are therefore often associated with the concept of *convergence* – the notion that economic and business practices are becoming more similar as the physical, economic, political and cultural distances between regions and countries fade away. It could be reasonably assumed that business practice across the world, once very different and based on unique historical traditions, might be becoming more uniform as the boundaries between nations are disrupted or, to use the language of bestselling globalization author Thomas Friedman (2006), as the world is 'flattened' by economic and technological change.

However, many regard such a view as simplistic, politically motivated and superficial. The VoC (Hall and Soskice 2001) and NBS (Whitley 1999)

[5] 'The New Ideas that Freed Europe', *The Independent*, 22 October 1999.

literatures emerged as a powerful counterweight to mainstream globalization arguments, such as those of Friedman and many others. An early statement of the anti-convergence position was laid down by the French author Michel Albert in his widely cited book *Capitalism Against Capitalism* (1993). This was one of the first works to claim that the demise of the USSR entailed the emergence of a new era in which competition would not be between capitalism and communism, but between many versions of capitalism. The VoC approach has since the late 1990s become a major growth area in academic analysis. It has tended to argue strongly that convergence towards a singular form of 'global best practice' is exaggerated or mythological. Although processes of globalization themselves may be largely real, different nations still demonstrate quite different forms of economic and business practice, and we can expect these differences to remain powerful for the foreseeable future.

VoC authors base a lot of their arguments on the ideas advanced by authors in the field of *institutional theory* or *institutional economics*. These authors (one of the most famous being Douglass North [1981, 1991]) have long argued that the now mainstream, neoliberal view of economic behaviour - based on abstract, universal and to a large degree mathematic 'laws' of supply and demand - is inaccurate because it fails to note that economic behaviour takes place within a larger set of *social* features. These social features are often labelled *institutions*, defined as 'the rules by which the economic game is played and the beliefs that generate these rules and people's adherence to them' (Mokyr 2009: 7). These rules and beliefs include customs, laws and ideologies, some of which are official and explicit, whereas others are informal and implicit. In other words all kinds of economic behaviour taken by individuals, firms and governments are not free-floating and universal phenomena but are *embedded* into the institutions of particular societies.[6] This idea is part of the bedrock of VoC analysis - social institutions have powerful structuring effects on national economies, and these are not being dissolved by the supposedly homogenizing effects of globalization.

A closely related idea to this is the concept of *path-dependence*. This notion has also been widely adopted in the VoC literature. This idea, which has been written on extensively by the economist W. Brian Arthur, suggests that history has a very powerful influence on current events. Choices taken in the past affect the choices available to people now and in the future. Certain features of national economies have become established, long-term systems that are unlikely to change. They have become 'locked-in' to the system, and actors have to live with these features, whether advantageous or otherwise. An excellent example of lock-in is the QWERTY keyboard layout. As Arthur (1989)

[6] On the concept of 'embeddedness' see Granovetter (1985).

explains, the earliest typewriters were liable to jam if their operators typed too fast. Therefore, the inventor of the first typewriter in 1874 Christopher Scholes came up with a partial solution to this problem with what became known as the QWERTY layout. Although this arrangement is logically confusing, the system became standardized with the success of the typewriter. A 'lock-in' effect took hold, whereby even though the keyboard layout is illogical and difficult to learn, it is now pretty much commercially impossible to produce computer keyboards and laptops with different, more straightforward, layouts (David 1986). If typewriters or computers were invented at a later point in history, with the supporting technology that would have allowed them to perform quickly without malfunction, then the world would have had a better system on which to build for the future. But unfortunately, as the path-dependence idea suggests, the world is awkward and stubbornly refuses to work this way.

Path-dependent action has entailed the development of all kinds of sub-optimal, strange and seemingly illogical organizational forms, but given the path-dependent context, this is fully understandable and logical (see, for example, David Stark's [1995] work on the development of confusing and compromised forms of capitalism in the former communist societies after the collapse of the USSR). Ideas such as path-dependence, lock-in and institutional configurations over time demonstrate that economic action and decision making are not as logical, 'rational' and as 'self-interested' as mainstream thought would like to suggest, but are instead deeply and intimately connected with social and 'non-economic' structures and actions, such as political compromises between actors with limited options and bound by unequal power relations. Moreover, it also suggests that the world economic system actually tolerates a wide array of different practices that exist because of historical accident rather than by rational design, and that they are likely to stay.

Globalization theorists and mainstream business media usually project a much simpler but largely superficial (and politicized) viewpoint of markets and action. Publications such as *The Economist, Financial Times, Fortune*, *Business Week* or *Forbes* usually present the straightforward view that the world is built in the image of Anglo-Saxon economies. They seem to suggest that if something differs from the LME model it must somehow be wrong, anomalous, backward and likely to be changed soon to reflect more 'normal' (read 'Western') practice. Mainstream academic textbooks on international business/international management tend to share this tone (such as the multi-million selling Hill [2008]). For example *The Economist* produced a special report on the Japanese economy in November 2007.[7] While it contained plenty of

[7] 'Japan's hybrid model of capitalism', *The Economist*, 29 November 2007.

detail and some interesting ideas, its approach – like many other neoliberal publications – was condescending towards Japan. Western literature on Japan (and other powerful non-Western nations such as Korea and China) often contains a subtext that their economic successes have somehow been improperly earned. US literature can also sometimes be highly critical of co-ordinated models, such as the various modes of European social-market capitalism. For example work by Bailey, Farrell and colleagues (as cited in Baumol et al. 2007: 214) advocates a string of neoliberal reforms (such as 'reduce barriers to hiring and firing of employees') that would 'wake up' Europe. Arguments like these are somewhat patronizing and highly questionable, especially as they were made on the eve of the subprime-mortgages relative financial crash of 2007–8 which has its roots in the USA.[8]

The VoC approach thus builds a much more detailed and diverse picture of the world economy than the globalized image created by mainstream neoliberalism; a picture that suggests that there are viable alternatives to Anglo-Saxon neoliberal economic models and that differences in economic and organizational structures are not 'wrong', inefficient, anomalous or backward, but can be just as efficient and rational as the more business-friendly structures of LMEs.

Yet the VoC literature has many weaknesses of its own. I will turn to these in more detail in Chapter 2, but for now it is worth paying attention to a very important issue at the outset. A major problem with the VoC literature is that it tends to focus almost exclusively on the richest Organisation for Economic Co-operation and Development (OECD) nations, essentially just six to eight or so countries in a world of more than 200 nations. This clearly is a problem, and it is one I return to in Chapter 2. Another possible weakness is the political agnosticism of many VoC authors. They spend a lot of time comparing and defining the differences in institutional forms in the abstract, but the more concrete social and political issues inherent in these discussions often fall away. What exactly is the point of all this comparison? We can establish that things are different in Japan from in USA, but why does this matter? I have heard frequent complaints around these issues among students and academics reading VoC literature.

In response to the first complaint this book will attempt to cover a wide range of countries, including some that have mostly remained outside of attempts to categorize and compare varieties of capitalism – most notably Russia, India and China. The book tries to do this by consulting

[8] Diana Farrell was writing while at the US consultancy McKinsey, so perhaps had an interest in popularizing neoliberal reforms. Elsewhere she expresses frustration at the slowness at which multinationals have embraced offshoring's possibilities for 'value creation' (Farrell et al. 2006).

a wide range of in-depth country-specific literature in addition to the more general comparative work that tends to take place at a higher level of abstraction. In doing so – and this relates to the second complaint mentioned above – this book will discuss some of the political and social features of different versions of capitalism, discussing not just economic and managerial outcomes, but ethical, political and human ones. Recently more attention has started to be paid in the macro-level literature to issues of environmental degradation, the quality of working life and general human well-being. Some economists have started to suggest that economic growth should not be the sole indicator of national success, but that other 'non-economic' factors should be considered such as the 'happiness' of its citizens (Layard et al 2006). These factors could be used to judge the comparative performance of different versions of capitalism. The new economics foundation (a liberal British think tank, published a report on 24 January 2009 in which the UK sat a very disappointing 15th out of 22 countries as regards indicators of social well-being (new economics foundation 2009: 22). This is a very poor outcome given that the UK is the fifth largest economy in the world. Other countries with smaller economies appear to perform much better on the social well-being index, such as Denmark (in first place) and Spain (in third). A thoroughgoing international comparison of these issues was provided in a provocative book by the UK epidemiologists Wilkinson and Pickett (2009), *The Spirit Level*. Their argument is that differences in financial and social inequality have serious effects; the more unequal the society, the worse it performs. VoC literature clearly has something potentially important to say to these debates on inequality and the socio-economic performance of various economic models.

Indeed there already exists a very wide and detailed literature on precisely these issues – those that the VoC literature often ignores. There are, for example, some fascinating sociological studies of various regions of the world being confronted by socio-economic upheavals. For example, Kathryn Marie Dudley's (1994) book *The End of the Line* is a classic study of the de-industrializing US city of Kenosha, Wisconsin. It articulates the subjective arguments, experiences and aspirations of different types of people as they confront the probable shutdown of the Chrysler plant in the city. Obviously car workers and the United Auto Workers union are deeply threatened by these developments and they do all they can to save the plant, including attempting to sue Chrysler top management. But others, such as property developers and town planners, had quite different views about the city and the region's future, and are secretly pleased that the well-paid autoworkers will soon be in search of new employment, and that their trade union which had 'artificially' defended them for so long has been defeated. While the factory was in turmoil, someone somewhere was making plans for Kenosha. Such stories of disruption that unhinge and confuse traditional structures are central to capitalism given its incessant drive for change and adaptation.

A key issue here is the level of analysis that the observer wants to take. It is common to talk of three levels of analysis, macro (the global 'big picture'), meso (the level of national institutions) and micro (the behaviour of firms). VoC tends operate at the meso-level. My view is that the meso-level needs to be closer connected to the micro, where the clearer impacts of these system effects can be noted; their effects in terms of firm behaviour and regional development, and their costs and benefits to people who live and work in those firms and regions. My main motivation for writing this book was to provide an accessible introductory text for this field of study, but also to look critically at its weaknesses. The central VoC argument - that the world economy tolerates a very wide array of business systems - is extremely powerful. However, I suggest that VoC could benefit from closer connection to political concerns, and to other traditions of writing that have more human, personal detail on what these socio-economic systems might mean for employees and citizens. This is especially true when one considers the problems that can occur when systems and models break down and change, as we shall explore further in the next section.

Are all forms of capitalism 'in crisis'? What is the 'best' model?

In September 2008 the shocking collapse of the US investment bank Lehman Brothers triggered intense panic in world financial markets. By the end of the year it had become clear that the subprime financial crisis that first emerged in the summer of 2007 was an extremely serious problem. This is important for this book for at least two reasons. First, it revealed how closely interlocked the different economies of the world are. Although this crash is rooted in the easy credit and lax regulation of the US model, the problem rapidly spread to other economies. In fact, it was not simply about 'spreading'; many of the other models were already implicated in this system, notably France, Germany and even Japan - countries that were supposed to be much more risk-averse, and bank-led rather than the high-risk, capital-market led USA. Second, countries nevertheless experienced this crisis differently, and their reactions to the crisis often differed. This issue of policy reactions to the crisis was most clearly demonstrated when President Sarkozy of France and Chancellor Merkel of Germany spoke of the need to develop a 'more moral capitalism' on the eve of a G20 meeting in

January 2009, suggesting the continued influence of a 'social-market' capitalism.[9] Britain's Prime Minister Gordon Brown warned against excessive re-regulation – a typically Anglo-Saxon reaction.

The crisis stimulated a major growth in introspection and discussion of the nature of capitalism, and especially of neoliberalism, which had become so dominant since the 1980s.[10] The world of comment is awash with discussion about what capitalism is, how it works, how it fails (especially in its neoliberal variant), how fair it is, to what degree it should be regulated and how it might be changed. Although subprime is simply the latest in a string of financial crises (Japanese crisis 1990, Nordic crisis 1991, Asian crisis 1997, Russian crisis 1998, US dotcom crisis 2000–1), it is by far the most disastrous of recent years, probably the worst since the Wall Street Crash of 1929. Some have predicted an economic recession as deep and as long as the Great Depression of the 1930s and as Barack Obama was inaugurated as the new President of the USA in January 2009, many discussed the need for him to announce a New Deal as significant as Franklin D. Roosevelt's original version in the 1930s.

Capitalism has always been prone to crisis periods. However, it is becoming concerning how regular these events are becoming. Frank Partnoy (2003), in one of several insider exposés of the sharp realities of financial trading, describes in close detail how the pressures for rapid financial growth result in the development of all kinds of weird and wonderful new financial instruments, just like the mortgage-backed securities and collateralized debt obligations that were behind subprime. These products are near-impossible to understand, value accurately or regulate effectively. This point was made by the legendary US investor Warren Buffet, in his 2003 letter to Berkshire Hathaway shareholders, when he described such high-risk derivatives as 'weapons of financial mass destruction'.[11] But there will always be the temptation, even the compulsion, for financial traders to invent new products such as these in the future. The producers of new financial instruments are unavoidably one step ahead of the regulators, like computer hackers or software pirates. Insider exposés such as Partnoy's, while probably sensationalized,

---

[9] 'Sarkozy and Merkel Tell US that Europe Will Lead Way Towards "Moral" Capitalism', *Guardian*, 8 January 2009.

[10] Such was the level of turbulence the UK's *Financial Times* ran a series of articles from March 2008 onwards entitled 'The Future of Capitalism'. Martin Wolf, who just two years prior had proclaimed in the pages of the *Financial Times* that globalization had 'won the day', was a regular contributor to the 'future of capitalism' series. 'Seed of its Own Destruction', *Financial Times*, 8 March 2008; 'Forces for Globalization Win the Day', *Financial Times*, 12 September 2006.

[11] 'Buffett Warns on Investment "Time Bomb"', BBC News, 4 March 2003.

paint a terrifying picture of a lack of overall control of the financial markets. The Marxist author Jack Barnes, vilified as laughably behind the times by most observers, predicted the crash very well in 2005, describing a 'giant debt bubble built up by finance capital over nearly two decades' (2005: 134). He went on to ask:

> How sound are the institutions that stood behind all the forms of fictitious capital ...? The pricking of the housing bubble will have substantial consequences for the entire capitalist financial system. Banks and other lenders slice up mortgages they've issued, package them according to risk, and then sell them to big, government-backed financial institutions such as ... Fannie Mae and Freddie Mac. (2005: 135, 138–9)

With these criticisms in mind, it seems difficult to accept the mainstream, textbook, explanation of how economics functions, with its emphasis on equilibrium and rational self-interest. Part of the reason the growing subprime turmoil was ignored until it was too late was that a broader narrative was constructed by the investment community around the idea that stock markets, hedge funds, private equity and investment banks were not high-risk activities in need of some kind of regulation, but as 'providing liquidity' in the markets. A broader sense of contentment about financial market-driven capitalism was installed, and few eyes were looking in the places where signs of trouble might be found. Complacency in the supposedly 'self-correcting' nature of markets and with neoliberal ideas that government intervention and regulation must be 'minimal' and 'restrained' surely played some role in allowing the crash to occur. This provides another good reason to be sceptical of the view that all economies should follow the Anglo-Saxon 'best practice' of LMEs.

As the crisis deepened, other scandals started to reveal themselves, including the largest financial loss in French history at Société Générale (€ 4.9 billion) and the Bernard Madoff 'pyramid' scandal in the USA (a US$65 billion fraud). 2008 was the worst year for the UK's FTSE 100 index of leading shares since 1984, and the worst in New York's Dow Jones since 1931.[12] Estimates of total subprime losses amount to the horrendous figure of US$379 billion.[13]

It would be overplaying it to suggest that the neoliberal model is dead following subprime, but it is probably fair to say that confidence it has been shaken dramatically, and that the mainstream view appears less convincing than it has at since the early 1980s. Alan Greenspan, the long-serving former chairman of the US Federal Reserve (the central

[12] 'FTSE 100 Index Has its Worst Year', *BBC News*, 31 December 2008.

[13] 'Subprime Losses Top $379 Billion on Balance-Sheet', Bloomberg, 19 May 2008.

bank of the USA, and to some degree therefore, the world) was considered an economic policy genius by thousands of observers. Neoliberal economic policy was strongly advocated by the US economic establishment, and vigorously promoted by think tanks such as the American Enterprise Institute, the Heritage Foundation and the Cato Institute. It was widely regarded as the right policy choice - right up until the subprime crisis hit.

It is hard to 'future-proof' ones' theories and arguments given how quickly things can change (Dicken 2007: 547). Many VoC analysts have suffered from this problem, with Japan being probably the best example; it was hugely praised as a superior form of capitalism in the 1970s and 1980s then damned in the 1990s. Just as there are markets for products, markets for services and markets for corporate control, there are also markets for ideas - all have boom and bust cycles. It is very hard to disentangle the various elements of the theories in order to explain success, failure and changes of firm strategy and business environments. Literature on the world economy (whether in the VoC school or elsewhere) incorporates many different approaches involving a wide array of academic disciplines and political persuasions. Analysts write for different audiences, who have read, debated, accepted and rejected different ideas about the nature of things. As I explain below, this book attempts to plot some sort of a logical course through this complexity, to describe and explain to the reader the various versions of capitalist organization that exist throughout the major economies, and to suggest areas where we can possibly understand them better.

The need to study the foundations of political economies: the rationale behind this book

I have taught courses on international capitalism for over 10 years at the University of Manchester, and I have always been struck by the absence of a suitable textbook for any of these courses. This puzzled me as the paradigms of VoC were becoming very influential during this time. This book tries to address two areas of shortage: first, the general lack of textbooks available that give due attention to the differing institutional systems and socio-economic traditions of countries and their major firms and, second, the need for a counterweight to the highly optimistic, ethnocentric and prescriptive material usually provided in international management/international business textbooks.

The book attempts to achieve its first aim by supplying in-depth coverage of a number of different countries, mostly by introducing established academic studies of these regions and the make-up and behaviour of firms based in and across these territories. Wherever possible, I will try to critically engage with several diverse literatures, encouraging the reader to reflect on the usefulness of these academic texts for their comparative understanding of different national business systems.

As for the second aim, the book will set out a more critical angle by showing that, contrary to the viewpoints of mainstream business and management textbooks, there is actually no 'one best way' for states and firms to behave in terms of regulation, finance, employment and strategy. Rather, the world economy features a wide range of different systems and philosophies. The book will argue that the powerful philosophy of neoliberalism - in the ascendant since the 1980s - has led to significant wealth creation, but at substantial costs as regards social inequality, the removal of employment security and the intensification of working life, not to mention sustained poverty in the majority of the world's regions. Furthermore, corporate restructuring, intended to make firms more flexible, 'lean', profitable and accountable to shareholders, has involved job cuts and pay freezes for thousands of staff (alongside skyrocketing salaries and bonuses for top management), while typically delivering modest financial results (Lazonick 2005; McCann et al. 2004). This critical angle will be employed in relation to discussions around giant firms' finance, innovation and labour systems, with the main emphasis on management, organization, work and employment, in order to provide readers with an idea of the realities of working life in the giant firms of different countries.

Conclusion: plotting a path through complexity

In taking this critical approach, the book will try to also provide adequate coverage of the enormous complexity of contemporary international capitalism. In much of the analysis of VoC, the emphasis is laid on national institutions and national influences. Moreover mainstream textbook understandings of these 'national' models are often based on misleading stereotypes (McCormick 2007). Thinking of firms as Japanese or German or American can be a trap (Smith 2005). Dan Coffey, an expert on the international car industry, notes the unhelpful 'tacit assumptions ... about "national" - British, Japanese and German manufacturing attributes' (2006: 10). The reality, certainly when concerning sophisticated, high-value goods such as automobiles, is considerably more complex, involving firm-level, local, regional and trans-regional relationships and competencies. Although the Toyota Camry might be a 'Japanese' car, if one is purchased in the USA most of its assembly would have been performed in the USA, using American labour. So a Camry owner is in some sense 'buying American'. The supply chains that feed into car production are enormously internationalized. Many parts of the vehicle, some of its electronics, for example, are likely to be sourced from China. Its design team would have been drawn from many countries (mostly Japan, but increasingly highly skilled design work is being performed in remote, lower-cost regions [see Manning et al. 2008]). Moreover, company ownership is often tangled and confusing. Mazda, for example, is clearly a 'Japanese' brand, but for many years over 33% of Mazda's stock was owned by Ford meaning that the profits (or loss) from the sale of each Mazda contributed in some way to the balance sheet of a US multinational.[14] To complicate matters yet further the same car model is often given a different name in different countries and certain types of car are available in some countries but not in others (Maxton and Wormald 2004: 15–16).

In other industries such as consumer electronics there is even more complexity, due to the existence of complex webs of OEM ('original equipment manufacture') outsourcing which are largely invisible to the end-user. For example, a Samsung flat-screen LCD television purchased in Europe would almost certainly have been built in Slovakia, not Korea. In fact, the television might have had had little to do with Samsung at all, besides having a Samsung badge attached to the front, and Samsung branding placed into the labelling, packaging and instruction manual. The television could be identical in almost every respect to one produced under a different brand via OEM. This is even more likely for smaller, less design-sensitive parts of the product that were bundled with the TV package such as the remote control or the cabling.

This complexity is one of the key problems this book confronts. The closer one gets to the operations of firms and to the products and services that they offer, the more blurred the boundaries between systems and country models appear to be. The VoC literature in its various guises is often at great pains to classify and compare different 'national models'. The most instantly recognizable one is Hall and Soskice's (2001) binary division between LMEs and CMEs. But this works only at the most general level of abstraction. While there are certain truths in this basic two-way division (for example the USA pretty much 'works' as an LME and Japan 'works' as a CME), it fails to account for the complexities of multinational firms, or for the great variety of firm operation within Japan or the USA. Several analysts have got beyond the most simplistic categorizations by examining firm-level governance and competencies (Whitley 2007). But here confusion

[14] In light of its very serious financial difficulties in recent years, Ford sold 20% of this stake in 2008. At the time of writing it owns 13.4% of the company and no longer has overall management control.

creeps in pretty quickly, because, with each insertion of further details or riders, the simplicity of the model rapidly disappears into a mass of confusing and complex multi-layered concepts. Whitley's analysis, for example, moves well beyond Hall and Soskice's two basic version of capitalism, and instead posits as many as six distinct models of capitalism, each cross-cut by four different groups of 'key institutional features'. But still this struggles to account clearly for the kind of product market complexity actually offered by multinational firms as described just above.

If the reader is keen to carry on beyond this chapter then he or she is simply going to have to confront this problem. Rather than hiding this away, I state from the outset that the VoC field contains a lot of shortcomings. I cannot hope to remedy them, but I aim to introduce and explain this field of research, and try to offer some clarity. It is in this spirit of inquiry that I start the main analysis of the book, beginning in Chapter 2 with a much more in-depth introduction and discussion of some of the key theories of the VoC school.

Further reading

Hall, P.A., and Soskice, D., eds, (2001) *Varieties of Capitalism: The Institutional Foundations of Comparative Advantage*, Oxford: Oxford University Press.

This book contains a mine of information on the subject, and is an essential reference point for anyone interested in this field. However, like so many of the major texts on VoC it is an edited collection of chapters written by several different authors. Many of the chapters are pitched at quite a high level of abstraction, and some of the heavy theoretical detail and jargon can be off-putting. However, several of the chapters reward close reading. The editors Hall and Soskice do an excellent job of outlining just how complex the subject area is in their long introductory chapter. Elsewhere in the book, the chapters by Thelen on different industrial relations regimes throughout the world and Hancké on the liberalization of the French economy are very useful.

Dore, R., (2000) *Stock Market Capitalism: Welfare Capitalism: Japan and Germany Versus the Anglo-Saxons*, Oxford: Oxford University Press.

(Continued)

(Continued)

Ronald Dore is not really a VoC theorist. He is one of the world's foremost Japan specialists who has spent his career studying the country's economic, political and social systems in great detail. His work has always contained a strong comparative element, going back as far as one of the early classics of comparative industrial relations *British Factory–Japanese Factory* (1973), where the UK's General Electric Company is discussed in detail alongside Japan's Hitachi. His work provides some tremendous detail on the anthropological nature of Japanese workplaces and he is very convincing in his description of how Japanese managers and workers tend to think and act. He is rather weaker on the theory side, which in itself points up a problem with VoC literature - the closer you get to studying any one nation, the harder it gets to engage in the kinds of abstract, macro- or meso-level comparisons. This book usefully discusses the concept of 'financialization' and it also contains some helpful material on recent economic changes in Germany.

Coates, D., (2000) *Models of Capitalism: Growth and Stagnation in the Modern Era*, Cambridge: Polity.

This is a very wide-ranging and ambitious book that deals with many different kinds of debates and literatures. It mostly focuses on the Anglo-Saxon, Japanese, German and Swedish economies, and it describes the different institutional forms and histories of each of these models. Coates focuses in particular on the relative strength of trade unions and the labour movement in each of the countries and the quality of these nations' educational systems. This is a much more politically charged book than most in the 'varieties' literature, and is therefore quite different in tone and aim from works such as Hall and Soskice. He also covers globalization in some depth and discusses the deeper, structural limitations and contradictions that he claims are inherent within capitalism in all its different forms.

TWO Theorizing Varieties of Capitalism

Chapter objectives

- To explore in more depth the concepts and claims associated with the VoC approach to studying international and comparative business
- To discuss how and why the VoC paradigm emerged
- To explore the strengths and weaknesses of the paradigm for our understanding of the complexities of the contemporary world economy
- To outline the approach taken to studying the countries in the chapters to follow

The varieties of capitalism writings did not spring from a vacuum. As with all concepts and approaches there is a range of theories that have influenced the development of new (or recycled) concepts. Over time certain core concepts begin to coalesce and are repeated, until some sort of body of knowledge or 'school of thought' eventually becomes established. For VoC, this seemed to happen by around the early 2000s, but the wider concepts upon which this school draws have much longer histories. This chapter explores the core ideas and concepts of VoC literature in an attempt to sketch its aims and underlying assumptions. This is done in order to try to improve the clarity of what can be an abstract and difficult field of knowledge. In so doing, the chapter moves on to discuss critiques of VoC, identifying several weaknesses and limitations in the approach. The chapter concludes by showing that although there are some problems with many formulations of VoC the overall question of the diversity and reform of world capitalism is hugely important and potentially a fascinating field of study. The chapter begins by discussing some of the earliest formulations of the broad question of the diversity of modern capitalism.

Exploring the emergence of VoC

Most authors have Michel Albert's *Capitalisme contre Capitalisme* as the first point of reference for the emergence of VoC. (The first English translation is Albert [1993].) Albert begins by describing two great victories for capitalism: the recent dominance of neoliberal economics spearheaded by Reagan and Thatcher in the USA and the UK (1980s), and the collapse of state socialism in Eastern Europe and the USSR (1989–91). Albert notes the dramatic successes of capitalism but notes that, for all the triumphalism, debate and controversy will continue over which models of capitalism are the most economically efficient and socially acceptable. *Capitalism Against Capitalism* was a successful book that was translated into 19 languages. Albert is very much a product of the French economic system, and it is no surprise that his book defends continental European models and attacks Anglo-Saxon approaches. He served as the head of the Commissariat générale du Plan (Plan Commission) from 1976–1981, which formulated five year plans for economic progress in the grand style of French socialist-inspired long-term planning (see Chapter 5). He was president of the insurance firm Assurances Générale de France in 1982, before becoming a member of the Monetary Committee of the Bank of France in 1994.

Parts of the book are now dated but the text is put together in a very engaging and politically charged style. In common with many French observers, he is unhappy with the general ways in which the European Union project is turning out – not as a federation or 'superstate' that its early supporters had envisaged, but as a much looser grouping, with the neoliberal, globalizing goal of the European common market as its central theme. The overtly political tone differentiates Albert's writing significantly from the rather drier academic work in VoC that was to follow. Albert spends large parts of the text discussing very wide issues about what kind of society we might want; what is a civilized, dignified kind of life? How will the least fortunate in society be protected and which models of capitalism are best able to deliver not only economic growth, but also human dignity and social welfare? Later work, such as Hall and Soskice (2001) and Whitley (1999), tend to focus on narrower, much less philosophical, issues such as firm performance and industrial specialization.

Although Albert is often the first reference point for VoC, his writings are part of a long tradition of comparative international work.

Broadly speaking this is the field of *political economy*. Usually housed in university departments of politics rather than economics or business schools, political economy as a subject is concerned with how wealth is created and distributed across societies in an increasingly internationalized world. It draws on a wide range of disciplinary approaches. Much of it is Marxist in orientation and mostly it challenges the arguments of the now-conventional neoliberalism. Political economy has, to a large extent, been pushed to the margins by the ascendancy of neoliberal and financial economics, which have become dominant in public policy circles and the private sector (Coates 2005). As the name suggests, it merges economic with political discussions in ways that are somewhat reminiscent of a much older, multi-disciplinary, approach to understanding economic life, rather than the narrow, abstract, highly stylized and mathematical approach of today's neoliberal economics. Political economy authors often use the technique of comparing practice across nations in order to make their arguments. Much of it contains implicit and explicitly moral arguments about how economies might be more justly organized. There is hence a very long and distinguished history of precursor literature to books such as Albert's, and this book could not possibly manage to cover them successfully. It will, however, mention several of the most important contributions to this field in the hope of pointing to some common themes surrounding the comparative study of capitalism.

There are many other kinds of literature that discuss varieties of capitalism without self-consciously contributing to the body of literature on political economy or VoC. One of the most important is Michael Porter's (1990) work on international competitiveness, which puts forward some clear (and very influential) ideas about how countries and regions can maximize their competitive potential in a globalized economy. Porter makes implicit and explicit judgements about the effectiveness of different countries' and regions' policies. A similar, older, more academic text in political economy is Zysman's (1983) *Governments, Markets, and Growth*, in which he reviews the different industrial policies of the richest nations, drawing attention in particular to their institutional structuring and path-dependence. Going back to the 1960s, a very well-respected academic work is Andrew Shonfield's (1965) *Modern Capitalism*. This is another book that advocates French-style long-range planning, and a more organized, seemingly more rational version of capitalism than the chaotic short-termism that seemed to be holding back the UK. Many interdisciplinary texts have explored the complex and diverse ways in which organizational ideas and trends (such as the largely American ideas of scientific management and human relations, see Chapter 3), became established unevenly across different nations (Bendix 1956; Djelic 1998; Ellwood 2012; Guillen 1994). Going further back, the pioneering political economy writings of Karl Polanyi (1944) helped lay the ground for the later development of institutional approaches to studying economic action (see below).

Although all of these texts contain important ideas, the growth of the globalization paradigm has threatened the premise that nations and governments can 'chose' from a range of existing 'models'. Politicians increasingly argue that their hands are tied as regards the economy and that the very concept of a national industrial policy that might govern the economy has been made obsolete by the dramatic spread of global market forces and international competition. This is actually highly debatable, and a rereading of classic texts such as Shonfield and Zysman, is interesting as they predate globalization theory and have a much wider appreciation of the distinct possibilities for variation in economic action, and for government to steer it. Even if we accept the reality of global market forces, all countries have their own systems and models that adapt to changes in their own ways (Steinmo 2010). This implies that political choices to select, emulate or defend at least certain elements of country 'models' remain relevant.

With this theme of choices in mind, there have been many texts about differences in world capitalism that sit at the more 'popular' end of the publishing spectrum. These often have clear political arguments to make, with their authors clearly favouring certain models over others. For example Will Hutton, the director of the UK's Work Foundation, and former editor of the Labour Party-supporting newspaper *The Observer* wrote two major books, *The State We're In* (1995) and *The World We're In* (2002). Both strongly support European, rather than US, capitalism arguing that the UK is politically, institutionally and ethically more similar to Europe than it is to the USA.

Popular texts often have a 'favourite' model in mind. This can cause difficulties when economic times change. Shonfield and Hutton struggle (as does Albert) with the 1990s slowdown of Germany, France and Japan and the simultaneous resurgence of the USA. In fact, much VoC-related literature in the 2000s became increasingly strident it its critique of European and Japanese capitalism, and what became known in certain circles as 'Eurosclerosis' (see Baumol et al. 2007: 199–200; Eichengreen 2007: 414–423).

Popular and academic texts often use the rhetorical device of creating lists of 'good' and 'bad' elements of the competing systems. Take a look at Exhibit 2.1 opposite, in which comparisons are made between portions of what Bailey et al. and Ishihara have to say about European and American capitalism. It is interesting to note how these lists basically mirror one another and that the value (or otherwise) of the situations they highlight basically come down to unspoken theoretical, moral, and political underpinnings and assumptions that lie beneath the texts.

Exhibit 2.1 Opposing visions of a 'good' economy: a Japanese view of America, and an American view of Europe

A summary of some of Shintaro Isihara's views on how the USA should reform its economy (Ishihara 1991: 130–137)

- Restrain speculative investment by corporations and channel capital into productive sectors.
- Adopt measures to prevent speculative investment. For example, consider taxes and other disincentives to discourage hostile takeovers.
- Curb leveraged buyouts.
- Raise the minimum wage.
- Encourage management to have a long-run perspective.
- Discard the short-term, quick-profits mentality and follow a far-sighted strategy in plant and equipment investment.
- Adopt a new management philosophy that stresses labour-management cooperation, anticipation of consumer needs, quality control, and technology and production processes.
- Consider measures, including legislation, to alter the disdain in management circles for hands-on manufacturing experience and bias in favour of financial or legal expertise.
- Re-evaluate the labor contract system and consider adoption of lifetime employment.
- Create loyalty and commitment to the company through extensive benefits and recreational programmes and facilities.
- Reconsider the terms of employment, root and branch, and provide security against layoffs, for example, to foster labor-management cooperation.
- Recognize that a corporation is privately owned but also a public entity with obligations to its employees and the public.
- Study tax measures to limit the huge bonuses paid to corporate executives.

* * *

A summary of various points made by Bailey, Kirkegaard, and Farrell on how Europe should reform its economy (as cited in Baumol et al. 2007: 214).

- Abandon policies for promotion of 'national champions'.
- Open EU markets to global competition.
- Improve the market for corporate control by eliminating artificial barriers to efficiency-enhancing mergers and acquisitions.
- Substantially reduce barriers to hiring and firing of employees.
- Require companies to provide reasonable compensation for laid-off workers, but only at moderate and predictable levels that do not discourage workers from looking for new jobs.
- Limit government benefits for unemployed workers in size and duration, but pair them with a new 'wage insurance' program to cushion the impact of accepting a new job with lower pay.
- Cut marginal tax rates on low- and middle-income workers.
- Reform government health programs by introducing more marketlike incentives for performance.

As we can see above, on the one hand, the Japanese nationalist politician Ishihara manages to take something of a 'high road' in praising the long-term, patient capital of the Japanese financial system, which allows its firms to develop world-class manufacturing capacity. Not only this, Japan is said to be an 'employee-favouring' system, in which workers enjoy considerable protection from layoffs or arbitrary treatment. Ishihara's is then essentially a 'win–win' argument, asserting that both labour and management can benefit from what is a more efficient, profitable and humane work system. This kind of argument is echoed by the later emergence in the USA of the 'high-performance work systems' literature (Appelbaum et al. 2000; see also Chapter 3). On the other hand, Bailey, an American consultant working for McKinsey, argues that free markets offer the solution to all economic conundrums, proposing for example the introduction of 'flexible' labour markets that give managers the freedom to hire and fire 'at will'. The two visions are polar opposites of one another and while presented as rational, 'best practice' options, in reality they are highly subjective assertions of politicized positions.

Another important book in a more 'popular' rather than 'academic' mould is Lester Thurow's (1992) *Head to Head*, in which he explores the various strengths and weakness of American, European and Japanese economic systems. Interestingly, he traces the beginning of the proto-VoC literature not to Albert but to George C. Lodge of Harvard Business School and his 1991 text *Perestroika for America* (1992: 32). Another popular book is Yergin and Stanislaw's (2002) *The Commanding Heights*, a journalistic account of the political processes whereby a series of important nations (including Russia, India and China) have come to accept neoliberal restructuring of their economies. For Yergin and Stanislaw (as with Albert beforehand) the collapse of the USSR is the point at which the levees holding back the floodwaters of marketization and competitive capitalism finally break. Many authors have written critically on this theme, such as Steger (2005) and Frank (2000), describing the neoliberal faith in untrammelled market forces as 'market fundamentalism'.

Interestingly, although national economies have been flooded by the tsunami of market globalism, all have changed in different ways, enabled and constrained by the various configurations of their own institutions (Perraton and Clift 2004). Some of these institutions serve as bulwarks against the incursion of alien or unwanted neoliberal changes, such as group company 'blockholdings' in Japan and Germany that insulate corporations from hostile takeovers or leveraged buyouts. 'Market fundamentalism' does exist of course, but this does not mean that every nation slavishly falls into line to rapidly adopt its concepts and policies. National economies are almost certainly becoming increasingly globally integrated, and are abandoning some of the forms of stability and predictability of their post-war 'managed' or 'organized' forms of capitalism. However, as business systems change there are always elements of continuity. Moreover, change is often taken on in the most superficial and reluctant way in order to do the minimum currently required so as to postpone further, more substantial, reforms (Dore 2000; Steinmo 2010).

Another very important, and highly academic, book that is in some way a precursor to the VoC literature is Lash and Urry's (1987) *The End of Organized Capitalism*. This book argues that national models of capitalism, while remaining distinct, have all recently gone through processes of change and disruption, and all have increasingly abandoned their earlier post-war 'organized' models of capitalism. They have moved since the 1980s into a more flexible, fast-moving and disruptive era of financially driven globalization and hyper-competition. Lash and Urry note that the form of 'disorganized capitalism' that emerges from each countries' reforms in the 1980s is strongly structured by the specifics of their prior forms of *organized* capitalism. In their words: 'the greater the extent to which a nation's capitalism has ever been organized, the more slowly and hesitantly its capitalism, *ceteris paribus*, will disorganize' (Lash and Urry 1987: 7). This is a very powerful insight and readers will note the influence of this argument in the country chapters of the current book.

In making their points about the distinctiveness and resilience of national systems of capitalism, the VoC literature attempts to move beyond the journalistic reporting and the political rhetoric and prescription of the populists or consultants such as Bailey et al., Ishihara or Yergin and Stanislaw. It attempts to be more analytical, 'scientific' and less normative, especially when it uses path-dependence and institutional theory concepts. In doing so, however, it often eschews making predictions or even defending or attacking different models for fear of being proved wrong by changes in macroeconomic performance of different nations. For this reason, many find VoC writings to be frustratingly detached, apolitical and agnostic in their claims about which models are more ethical or morally defensible.

Having briefly introduced some of the background debates on VoC, the rest of the chapter analyses the value of the field in terms of the insight in provides into our understanding of contemporary capitalism across different regions of the world. Ultimately this book is supportive of the overall project of the VoC literature, but does not fully draw on the approach in the main body of the book. In chapters on the individual countries, I turn to the literatures of business and economic history, and industrial relations and workplace sociology, as the historical and contemporary foundations of each country's political economy is drawn out and examined. This, I believe, provides a more accessible and less abstract articulation of the historical stages through which national business systems have developed, stabilized and changed over time.

Assessing the core claims of VoC theory

VoC provides a strong foundation for understanding the diversity and complexity of capitalism across nations. Many VoC authors demonstrate that the different configurations of social institutions are not simply scattered randomly across countries, but are structured by clear path-dependent, embedded effects (Hall and Soskice 2001). While somewhat problematic because of their abstract nature, the various dimensions around which comparisons are made (such as the financial system, labour system, innovation system, cultural system and the state: see Whitley [1999]) are useful when it comes to understanding how and why these differences have historically been produced over time, and how and why they are likely to be reproduced both now and in the future. This kind of comparative approach is helpful as an 'ideal typical' framework upon which further research data can be placed in order to make detailed and rigorous comparisons of different social facts. Detailed comparison across the sub-dimensions of national business systems allows all kinds of secondary analyses and arguments to be made about the economic or social utility of these configurations.

VoC and NBS accounts of historical processes are most important in an era when we are assailed by the arguments about the 'inevitability' and 'irreversibility' of globalization, international competition, flexibility and free markets. VoC instead emphasizes that change in societies is essentially quite a slow process and that genuinely radical change is rare. This is a powerful insight. Radical changes rarely happen overnight, to either governments or firms (unless we are talking about very serious shocks such as wars, revolutions or total economic collapses). As any senior manager of a large organization will tell you, organization change is usually a slow, drawn-out, partial, contradictory, conflictive and painful process. Some valuable and detailed studies of historical processes and path-dependent economic development are provided by VoC authors, for example Vitols (2001) on the history of German, Japanese and American financial systems, and Djelic's (1998) important study on how the USA attempted to shape the post-war history of Europe in *Exporting the American Model*. These texts tie in closely with some major ideas in political economy and economic history such as the 'Timing of Industrialization' thesis (Gerschenkron 1962).

The idea of *complementarity* is central to VoC, interacting closely with the concepts of path-dependence and embeddedness, to create a powerful counterbalance to mainstream economistic views of how firms and societies work. Complementarity is an especially useful concept when it comes to demonstrating how resistant institutions, firms and economic actors can be to change. A genuine transformation of practice is very hard to enact in almost any organizational setting because of the interlocking and self-reinforcing nature of institutions. This is particularly true in highly coordinated nations, such as Japan and Germany, where most research tends to demonstrate an ambivalent situation of change in some areas but alongside general continuity (Dore 2000; Jacoby 2005).

Path-dependence will always be relevant given that a genuine convergence of business systems across the world looks unlikely. Although there is huge difficulty in explaining exactly *how* these institutions work (especially in terms of arguing which are the most relevant and powerful), the social institutions into which economic action are embedded are bound to be relevant to the structuring and change of national models of capitalism. It is an ongoing task to make our analysis of the institutions of capitalism more accurate, and VoC authors readily acknowledge that their 'models' and 'business systems' are ideal types that require clarification and qualification with research evidence.

Another large strength of VoC (but one not always built on in analysis) is its sensitivity to the endless possibilities for variation at local and national levels. Human societies and their economic actors are extraordinarily complex and diverse, from job-hopping Silicon Valley IT engineers (Barley and Kunda 2004 to devoted *chaebol* company men in Seoul (Amsden 1989). Any sensible analysis of the world economy has to take note of this variation. Potentially there is huge scope for close-up qualitative investigation of the subtleties and nuances of different economic action. Unfortunately, VoC's tendency towards abstraction and 'modelizing' has meant that much of the literature has turned its back on such an approach. Theoretically at least, with its focus on embeddedness, path-dependence and international variation, VoC is extremely well-placed to be able to comment on and contribute to such a nuanced understanding of the many diverse worlds of capitalism, as opposed to the dry, undersocialized and narrow numerical-mathematical approach of mainstream economics.

VoC authors basing their work in the broad tradition of institutional theories (see for example Granovetter 1985; Nee and Swedberg 2005; North 1991; Scott 2008a) are not reliant on the questionable neoclassical concept of the rational, self-interested, calculative *homo economicus*. There are many areas of research that have demonstrated that human actors are not as 'rational' in their decision making than economic theory tends to assume. Self-interested economic calculation is not the dominant reason behind economic or managerial decision making. People have to consider a much wider range of factors when conducting economic action. Economic action is embedded into wider social norms, many of which are not governed by rules of economic calculation, but rather by delicate social norms about 'acceptable' behaviour or social 'legitimacy' (DiMaggio and Powell 1983; Scott 2008a). By using the concepts of institutional norms, path-dependence and complementarity writers in the field of international and comparative business powerfully reject neoliberal assumptions about free markets and rational choice. Institutional theories argue that *markets are socially constructed*, suggesting that organizational actors often have fewer courses of action than they might think.

Vivien Schmidt's work on the UK, Germany and France (for example, Schmidt 2002), provides a good example of the ways in which supposedly 'global' norms such as shareholder value and the neoliberal rollback of welfare state regimes cannot be easily moved wholesale from the USA to Continental Europe. This is because the 'social market' European economies such as Germany and France are not welcoming institutional environments for such philosophies; powerful norms exist around what a firm's duty is to wider stakeholders, not just to the owners of shares. Welfare states are, to a degree, the product of complex post-war agreements and compromises that cannot be restructured without considerable conflict and debate. A more extreme example is the long and protracted process of opening up the economy of India to free markets and competition. The Congress Party of post-independence India held a significant commitment to socialism and a deep scepticism of markets. In such environments it typically requires a major a shock or crisis in order for radical moves to become acceptable and viable (Klein 2007; McCann 2013a). VoC provides us with a framework for understanding how and why various economic models stubbornly persist even in the face of supposedly unstoppable forces of 'global' change.

All of the above are the traditionally strengths of the VoC, institutional or NBS approaches to studying comparative business. However, these literatures also contain some significant weaknesses. In recent years a widening array of authors have pointed to some severe weakness in VoC theorizing. An exhaustive run-down of the criticisms appears in Hancké et al. (2008: 7). Some of the most important charges are that VoC is overly static and unable to account for socio-economic change, that 'within country' divergence is downplayed, that too few countries are selected for study, and that it is apolitical and blind to the intense conflicts over the future of the models (for various critiques see, for example, Allen 2004; Deeg and Jackson 2007; Kinderman 2005; Perraton and Clift 2004; Pontusson 2005; Smith 2005). The subprime crisis has also been troubling for VoC, as it exposed the weakness of this literature's understanding of the highly interconnected financial system that increasingly operates transnationally and over which national institutions seem to have negligible influence (Bruff and Horn 2012).

While VoC literature includes diverse and convincing accounts of institutional context, its explanation of institutions themselves can be vague and static, and can be particularly uncomfortable when trying to account for changes to these systems. The issue of change has historically been a difficult one for institutional theory, which tends to be more comfortable with describing continuity and social reproduction over time (Greenwood et al. 2002; Lawrence et al. 2009). We can identify various institutions and can see their historical path-dependent effects, but are these 'locked in' forever? When might they change and what would cause them to? In all of the countries described in this book, change has been a near-constant theme, even as national institutional forms provide continuity.

VoC also struggles to explain situations in which institutions seem to have no 'traction' such as when economic action within a nation departures from institutional norms (such as the rise of the low-budget, anti-union, 'hard-discounting' retail chain Aldi in Germany, see Wortmann 2004). The VoC and NBS literature tends not to include a distinct focus on work and workers and is pitched at abstract and macro/meso levels. There is arguably a need for a more humanized approach, drawing on research in workplace sociology and industrial relations (Barley and Kunda 2004; Doellgast 2012; Hassard et al. 2009), business and management history (Amatori and Colli 2011, Booth and Rowlinson 2006; Chandler 1977, 1990; McCraw 1997a; Mokyr 1990, 2009) and political economy (Bruff and Horn 2012; Chibber 2003; Perraton and Clift 2004; Wade 2003).

And if we are to fully understand changes to country models we also need to look rather more seriously at those calling for change, and the roles played by power and ideology in these political drives for reform (Clegg 2010; Clift 2012). This could involve unpacking and exploring the various forms of ideological and cultural practices that make up the 'totality' of socio-economic relations, the framing and structuring of what is possible and what is said to be 'world best practice' that all competitive firms and governments must emulate (McCann 2013a). These include management and organizational trends such as Fordism and corporate paternalism in the 19th and early 20th centuries, and Keynesian demand management and long-range planning as government policies in the 1930s through to the 1960s, before the onset of the neoliberal advance of the 1980s (Klein 2007). More recently, ideology plays a huge role in the promotion of so-called 'lean' systems (Liker and Morgan 2006) or 'value-based management' in the realm of corporate governance and performance management (Dore 2000). Institutional theory can often create the impression that institutions are fixed and immutable, but clearly they undergo change (and even erode to nothing or collapse suddenly), partly through various forms of emulation or 'isomorphism' transmitted through various actors such as professional bodies, transnational government regulations or by committed individuals who wish to change them, known as 'institutional entrepreneurs' (DiMaggio and Powell 1983; Lawrence et al. 2009; Scott 2008a, 2008b). Institutional change is intimately bound up in institutions themselves and is often pursued by powerful groups, such as professional associations, that 'tend' institutions or 'fields' (Greenwood et al. 2002). National socio-economic institutions can change as a result from pressures from within as well as from without. Conflict often breaks out over institutional maintenance or change, as different groups wish to see institutions maintained, changed or abolished.

A great example from the literature is Daniel Kinderman's (2005) argument about the mobilization of think tanks and employers' associations in a concerted 'offensive' against the traditionally employee-friendly German institutions. Such attacks are countered with resistance from other stakeholder groups such as trade unions, public sector employees or left-of-centre voters (Schmidt 2002) who are unconvinced about the reasons for jettisoning traditional structures and embracing supposedly 'world best practice'. Institutions are also formed and reformed out of intense political struggles, with none being more prominent than the Cold War standoff between capitalism and communism, which structured the second half of the 20th century. While the transformation of political economies is often slow and path-dependent, major shocks such as financial crises (such as India's almost total financial meltdown in 1991), and political collapses (such as the fall of the USSR in 1989–91), can induce rapid and unsettling changes (Klein 2007; McCann 2013a).

I realize I am proposing a large and varied menu of items to digest. I cannot hope to offer a full and complete description and explanation of all of these themes of institutional development, maintenance and change in the country chapters to follow. There will surely be important issues left out of the narrative due to my own limitations of knowledge and understanding, and because of lack of space. Some readers may find my approach frustratingly unclear because I refuse to lay out a simple set of measures along which I will compare the various paths that these country models have taken. I only offer the defence that there are no simple answers and that the best way to really understand differences and similarities in political economies is to throw oneself into the messy detail of each nation, rather than to assemble elegant but abstract comparative figures and models. Country 'systems' or 'models' are in reality very jumbled and unclear. I try to provide detailed historical narratives on the development, stabilization and change of national political economies. There are some clear commonalties in the broad 'directions of travel'; while each country sets out from different positions, each goes through three distinct phases of 'liberal' capitalism, 'organized' capitalism and 'disorganized' capitalism, in their own distinct ways (Boltanski and Chiapello 2005; Lash and Urry 1987). These broad paths are laid out in the country chapters that follow.

Conclusion

Despite the weaknesses of the approach, VoC is a very useful set of ideas. It seems true that even while exposed to (and contributing to) powerful forces of globalization, national business systems still retain some unmistakably 'national' (such as Japanese, American or German) structures and forms of behaviour, and that these features seem to be derived in no small part by social institutions that govern and reproduce the economic rules of the game in each society. The industrial and financial structures of many countries remain particularly divergent. Anthropologically, human behaviour in large firms across various nations can look and feel very dissimilar.

The VoC and NBS literatures make these points well. However, I believe that the different worlds of capitalism can be studied in much more interesting ways than by endless abstraction and comparative model-building. I have argued that it is perhaps more fruitful to turn to the disciplines of political economy, business history and sociology of work in examining capitalism across countries, and this is the approach that the book takes in the country-based chapters below. Rather than the development of general and all-encompassing models in the style of authors such as Whitley, Amable or Hall and Soskice, the book attempts to build up a picture from the ground, trying to gather interesting materials piece by piece. This will always be a work in progress, a patchwork approach, echoing the words of Erturk et al. of 'a mixed-methods approach to a capitalism of multiple logics and discrepancies where this is no simple linear relation between objectives, initiatives, practices, and outcomes' (2008: 37).

I am not searching for abstract 'laws' but I instead try to offer detailed *discussions* and *interpretations* of processes of the formation, establishment and transformation of major models of capitalism, exploring economic, political, ideological and ethical elements. I wholeheartedly agree with the approach of the French theorist Michel Beaud who writes:

> I was taught that capitalism is an economic system. I understood quickly enough that one could not reduce it to the economic dimension alone, and that it is necessary to take into account the social, ideological, political and ethical dimensions as well. Fundamentally, what we call 'capitalism' is inseparable from the societies and states with which it develops. (2001: 5)

The focus throughout the rest of the text will be on large firms, at the expense of small and medium-sized ones. I realize this is a major omission, yet it is an omission shared in the literature I am discussing. The diversity of capitalism in small and medium-sized enterprises (SMEs) is an area where new work is needed, but that is way beyond the scope of this book. The book also focuses pretty much exclusively on industrial and services firms, and has very little to say about agriculture. This sector is critical in development economics and some may object to this omission when historical development of nations is covered. My defence here is that this omission is again common in business history and in VoC literature, and that it is just too far outside of my competence to discuss it properly. The same also applies to the large literature on comparative welfare systems (exemplified by the work of Esping-Andersen [1990]), which is clearly relevant here but also omitted for reasons of space and clarity. Lastly, before we make headway into the country chapters, I make a few suggestions below of major works in VoC which readers may wish to consult and interpret.

Further reading

Albert, M., (1993) *Capitalism Against Capitalism*, London: Whurr.

Although this book is very much a product of its time, following hot on the heels of the collapse of state socialism in Eastern Europe, it is well worth reading as one of the first expositions of what eventually became known as the VoC literature. Unlike much of the writings that followed it is very accessible. It provides a very interesting discussion of many issues of relevance to the field (especially the much-neglected issues of geopolitical power and US hegemony), and offers a powerful left-of-centre critique of the Anglo-Saxon model that one might expect from a French author.

Amable, B., (2003) *The Diversity of Modern Capitalism*, Oxford: Oxford University Press.

This is an important addition to the VoC field, which leans heavily in the direction of theory and model-building. Ultimately Amable asserts the existence of five distinct models of capitalism, which build on 'Regulation School' arguments about distinct capitalist modes of production. This is a fairly technical, general and detached approach to the study of VoC, but it contains some important discussions about the value of these different economic and social systems.

Whitley, R., (2007) *Business Systems and Organizational Capabilities: The Institutional Structuring of Competitive Competences*, Oxford: Oxford University Press.

This is a complex and ambitious work that attempts to show how national 'dominant institutions' structure business action at firm level. In doing so, Whitley describes the scope for firms' business operations or their 'organizational capabilities', which are based on path-dependent and embedded social-economic configurations. His earlier *Divergent Capitalisms* (1999) lays out his own theoretical position, modelling six different 'business systems' which are similar in some ways to other authors' versions of capitalism. Whitley, however, attempts to show that the six systems do not map directly onto geographical regions, emphasizing instead the role of large firms' organizational capacities to act differently.

In addition there are several collections that reproduce dozens of important academic papers or book chapters on all aspects of VoC. Coates has edited a three-volume set *Models of Capitalism: Debating Strengths and Weaknesses* (2002), and Whitley a two-volume set *Competing Capitalisms* (2002). There is also the very useful *Debating Varieties of Capitalism: A Reader*, edited by Bob Hancké (2009).

THREE The USA: The World's Foremost Economic, Political and Military Power

Chapter objectives

- To provide brief background on the rapid growth of the USA from inauspicious beginnings to the world's only superpower
- To explore key concepts of the US business model through three main historical stages: the Gilded Age (19th to early 20th century), the era of managerial capitalism (1940s–1980s) and the stock market-fuelled rise of investor capitalism (1990s and beyond)
- To discuss the USA as a highly complex, multifaceted political environment of 50 states plus a powerful federal bureaucracy
- To describe the USA as simultaneously the world's most dominant economy, yet also a country facing some major problems such as market failure and widespread poverty

Introduction

The story of the USA's rise to economic, political and military preeminence is a remarkable one. It is all the more remarkable because it is so rarely described as such. Instead, in so many literatures on business, management, economics and politics, the idea of a dominant USA regularly emerges as if it were simply part of the natural order of things. The true story is quite different. What is now the USA grew from a small group of 13 British colonies to an independent state, to a dominant world power in fewer than 200 years. Its influence on the rest of the world is undeniably huge. The USA's surge to its position of world leadership represents a rapid shift in the balance of power away from Western Europe, a tectonic shift that happens rarely in world politics.

The USA has been the world's foremost economic power since at least the end of the Second World War. With its vast economic, cultural, political, social and military assets, the USA is able to influence most corners of the world in some way or another. This is expressed in the common saying 'when America sneezes the rest of the world catches a cold'. This was spectacularly demonstrated by the subprime crisis of 2007–8. It is hard to imagine another country where a collapse of its housing and mortgage system could bring about a global economic downturn. On a more positive note, the successes of US economic policies or management systems are also emulated all over the world. The huge success of the Silicon Valley 'model' in the 1990s is a key example. Central, regional and city governments all over the world have attempted to build 'science parks' or 'innovation hubs' in their attempts to copy California's IT success. Economic and social policy innovations emerging from North America are often emulated in Europe, Japan and the less developed countries. For example, the 'new public management' approach to cutting back on public spending while also supposedly improving public services delivery emerged in the USA, especially during the Clinton presidency (1993–2000).

At the level of corporate organization and management, the methods and philosophies developed by US firms are also closely copied and widely discussed. In fact, US authors have pretty much cornered the market for business bestseller books, from Peters and Waterman's (1982) *In Search of Excellence* to Jim Collins' (2001) *Good to Great*. Organizational change ideas, such as business process re-engineering, culture change and Six Sigma, were all originally developed in the USA, are used extensively at home and are exported to large firms the world over (Mills et al. 2009). A quick search on Google Scholar in March 2013 (note the US influence again) brought up an astonishing 18,791 citations for Prahalad and Hamel's (1990) article 'The Core Competence of the Corporation', from the *Harvard Business Review*. Their work has since been translated into dozens of languages (including Chinese). Both authors have owned consulting companies. The USA is also the birthplace of the MBA and of business school education. The world's first business school, the Wharton School at the University of Pennsylvania, was established in 1881. The first issue of *Harvard Business Review* was published in 1922, when many other countries' economies - Japan, Korea, India, China - were just starting on the road to industrial modernization. Many of the core textbooks used for university teaching across the world in disciplines such as economics, international business or accounting and finance are written by US authors.

More concretely, for decades the USA has effectively underwritten global capitalism, formally through the Bretton Woods currency exchange system up until its collapse in 1971, and informally through the undeniably huge power of the Federal Reserve Bank. The world financial system is still to a large extent underpinned by the US dollar (Albert 1993: 34–35). The US military is also massively powerful. The Pentagon currently has a budget of around 1.5 billion dollars *per day*.[1] There is also a large number of extremely powerful US private sector military contracting firms, such as Lockheed Martin, Raytheon, Boeing and General Dynamics. In 2009 the US military owned or rented 716 military bases across 30 countries of the world. (It also possesses certain facilities whose existence is not publicly disclosed).[2] In addition, over 1.4 million US troops are currently stationed in 158 states of the world.[3] There are around 203 nation states that are unambiguously recognized as such by the UN, so this represents a projection of military power that goes way beyond any seen in prior history. Many regard the USA, therefore, as a modern-day empire - probably the most powerful ever assembled (Johnson 2002, 2004).

This chapter unfolds in the following directions. Its primary task is to outline the historical development of US capitalism. It does this through three historical epochs: first the 'robber baron' phase of US capitalism; second, the New Deal era in which US capitalism was much more strongly regulated; and, third, the more recent age of investor capitalism, when many of the controls of the prior era were lifted. Overall, the US model is famous for free markets, few curbs on managerial prerogative and generally limited government intervention. Nevertheless, 'big government' has certainly not disappeared in the USA: the Federal budget for 2011 was set at over US$3.8 trillion, and the USA has struggled severely recently with budget deficits and large-scale government

[1] 'No More Monopoly Money, and Don't Ask for the Moon', *Guardian*, 2 February 2010.

[2] See the US Department of Defense *Base Structure Report*, 2009, available at: www.defense.gov/pubs/pdfs/2009Baseline.pdf.

[3] Although obviously the vast majority (1.16 million) are stationed in USA and its territories. PBS Frontline, TV series *Rumsfeld's War* companion website, http://www.pbs.org/wgbh/pages/frontline/shows/pentagon/maps/9.html.

borrowing.[4] The USA remains the number one economy in the world and, despite losing its foremost position in key industries such as cars and electronics, it is still a world-leader in many others, such as IT, software and aircraft manufacturing.

But all is not well in America. Despite its influence and success the country faces all kinds of challenges and concerns, some of which are extremely serious. Just as the USA is characterized by colossal wealth and power so also are many of its cities blighted by chronic poverty, crime, violence and drugs. Recent years have seen the collapse of traditional industries, enormous budget and trade deficits, financial crises, political scandals, weak levels of social provision and healthcare protection, and military overextension. Attending an American Sociological Association conference in Boston in 2008, I was struck by how many papers were devoted to the topic of the 'death of the American dream'. There is a long tradition of downbeat academic literature on the USA, such as Bluestone and Harrison's (1982) *The Deindustrialization of America* and *The Great U-Turn* (1988), in which the country is portrayed as unable to deal with its major structural problems, partly because the rich have become so much richer comparative to the rest of the nation that they do not feel moved to care too much about it. US sociologists Robert and Carolyn Perrucci's (2009) recent work *America at Risk* brilliantly updates this picture for the late 2000s. The unattainable nature of the American Dream is a major subtext to President Barack Obama's (2008) book *The Audacity of Hope*.

While obviously an attractive country for millions of immigrants and tourists, life in the USA for the poor can be a daily tragedy involving joblessness, or low pay and fragile employment. Many of the mainstream economics, business and management texts portray US companies and the US economy as idealized perfections when the real picture can be light years away. US society is riven with contradictions and, as we shall see below, this applies just as much to management, organization and economy as it does to social inequality and cultural representation. The reader is well advised to bear these contradictions in mind if he or she continues with the remainder of the chapter.

The emergence of the American powerhouse: rugged individualism and 'wild' capitalism

The US economy is typically regarded as the most liberal and open of all the major economies. The US has for many years championed free

[4] 'No More Monopoly Money, and Don't Ask for the Moon', *Guardian*, 2 February 2010.

markets and restrained government. Since the establishment of the country following its victory in the War of Independence (1775–1783) with Britain, US political leaders have been keen to distance themselves from Europe and from European traditions. The USA was conceived as a different kind of country from European nations, free from the autocratic rule of monarchs, with a strong separation of church and state and devolved political powers. In its early years, and totally unlike today, the Presidency was symbolic and rather weak compared to a much stronger Congress. The President has to some extent always been controlled by the 'checks and balances' of Congress, the Supreme Court and the Constitution, which were designed to protect ordinary citizens from arbitrary rule. In fact, the whole concept of governmental authority is questionable in America, probably more than in any other developed nation. Even today citizens often regard government power (especially federal government power) as inappropriate, wasteful and detached from the concerns of ordinary citizens. Many periods of US history have exhibited widespread scepticism about government being relevant or as offering a solution to anything.

Paradoxically, however, the USA has always had powerful forms of government. Since its earliest days, the US economy has been stimulated and supported by active government policies, especially by protectionist tariff policies (Eckes 1995). This point is rarely highlighted today. More often the US economy is simply considered neoliberal, and is portrayed as it if always has been neoliberal. The reality is quite different. The early political and economic leaders of the USA were fearful that their young nation would be swamped by imports from the older – and at the time much more powerful – European nations. George Washington's Treasury Secretary Alexander Hamilton was especially keen on infant industry protection policies that would allow US industry to grow behind protective barriers to imports. Subsequent presidents, in particular Abraham Lincoln, were also strong supporters of what became known as the 'American System' of infant industry protection, as opposed to the 'British System' of free trade (Chang 2003: 24–32; McCraw 1997b: 312–4). This sits in stark contrast to the neoliberal approach associated so strongly with the USA today and the pervasive US political ideology of limited government and 'free' trade.

While the New World was never a fully free market, it was certainly a diverse and rapidly growing one, attracting massive migration from many parts of the world, mostly from Europe, but also from as far away as China. Between 1850 and the First World War, around 55 million people left Europe for the USA (Rauchway 2008: 5). McCraw describes how America's population grew from 5.3 million in 1800 to 76 million in 1900. By 1890, '80 per cent of New York's citizens were immigrants or the children of immigrants, 87 per cent of Chicago's, and 84 per cent of Detroit's and Milwaukee's' (1997b: 307). The USA symbolized a radical shift away from Europe or Asia, where people could seek fortune and a new way of life based on their own hard work, not bogged down by traditional roles often imposed on them in feudal monarchies. Conditions for new arrivals were extremely harsh. Working weeks of 72 hours were common (McCraw 1997b: 315). Jobs were often dangerous. Industrial accidents claimed the lives of 22,000 railroad workers in the year 1889 (Zinn 2005: 256).

Further horror existed in the form of the slave trade and the brutal repression of Native Americans. Both are major parts of US development history (Zinn 2005: 1–38). For example McCraw (1997b: 305) notes that 10 million Africans were forcibly transported to the New World, with nearly 600,000 sent to areas that became part of the US (others were taken to Brazil or to Caribbean islands). Standard histories of US capitalism and US corporations tend not to mention slavery, which has to a large extent been written out of the business school history canon (Cooke 2003). The established story prefers to focus on entrepreneurs and the great (white) men of history. Cooke mentions that even Chandler, probably the world's pre-eminent historian of US business, gives slavery just three pages out of 500 in *The Visible Hand* (2003: 1900). Slavery on the plantations involved extremely heavy, backbreaking labour, under duress and in extremes of heat. Slaves were regularly beaten, whipped, raped and murdered. Although debatable, it is likely that a considerable part of the explanation for the economic success of US growth can be attributed to this brutal form of free, captive labour. Other nations were complicit in the slave trade, notably seafaring countries such as Britain. Not until 1865 at the end of the American Civil War were the 4 million slaves emancipated, and that was only the beginning of a much longer struggle for civil rights for black Americans, especially in the southern states (Payne 2001).

A central part of the rise to global dominance of the USA was its internal growth, notably its expansion westward. The Louisiana Purchase (from France) in 1803 increased the size of the nation by 828,000 square miles (a territory that encompasses about 14 of the current US states). The California Gold Rush of the 1850s sent thousands of people westward in search of their fortunes. Meanwhile industry and commerce continued to grow in stature and sophistication, covering ever more of the expanding US territory. Certain sectors became dominated by massive, mostly family-owned, organizations which came to be known as 'trusts'. The most important of these included Standard Oil, established by John D. Rockefeller, and the various railroad companies owned by Cornelius Vanderbilt. By some calculations, given the context of his time Rockefeller was the richest man who ever lived. The era of the trusts is often known as the 'Gilded Age', or the 'robber baron phase' of US capitalism. These companies were owned and run by the entrepreneurs who originally established them. Growing from fairly small beginnings some developed into huge business empires. As their economic power grew they were able to secure ever larger investments from financial houses who themselves were also organized along similar lines as family-owned trusts, notably JP Morgan (see Chernow 2010, and Exhibit 3.1).

Exhibit 3.1 The rise of industrial and financial capitalism in the USA

Thomas McCraw in *Creating Modern Capitalism* (1997a: 319–20) describes the early days of large-scale managerial hierarchies in industrial America, drawing an explicit link between organizational and military chains of command. As employee size grew, so did market capitalization and the power of investment bankers; from its early days US capitalism has been a form of financialized capitalism:

'The key management challenge here was an organizational one: how to fix authority and responsibility so that railroad firms could operate safely, efficiently, and profitably. For many years, railroads seemed simply too big to manage. In the 1840s, the largest factories in the United States were employing perhaps 800 people. But railroad companies quickly came to employ several thousand, and by the end of the nineteenth century a few employed over 100,000.

'The only precedent for managing such enterprises was the kind of organizational structure designed for the huge "citizen armies" of Europe that had fought the Napoleonic Wars. So, in the United States, many graduates of West Point began to gravitate toward work on the railroads. As engineers and managers, they adapted to their new setting the line-and-staff distinctions between types of assignments for military officers. [...]

'Before the 1880s, even the largest manufacturing firms seldom had been capitalized at more than $1 million. But by 1900, John D. Rockefeller's Standard Oil Company had grown into a multinational corporation capitalized at $122 million. By 1904, James B. Duke and his colleagues had built the American Tobacco Company into a behemoth capitalized at $500 million. And in 1901, when the financier J. Pierpont Morgan engineered a merger of leading steel firms, including the giant company built up by Andrew Carnegie, he capitalized the new United States Steel Corporation at $1.4 billion. At that time the nations' Gross National Product was about $21 billion. A similar deal done in the 1990s, expressed as the same proportion of GNP, would approach half a trillion dollars.'

(McCraw 1997a: 319–20)

Trusts developed close links with state and federal legislators, attempting to influence them to pass laws and policies that would favour their continued economic dominance, such as tariff barriers and lax regulation (Zinn 2005: 255, 258). (Many have observed that the recent development of Russia in the 1990s and 2000s after the collapse of the USSR had a similarly 'wild' nature to it, with Russian oligarchs akin to US robber barons in their power and unpopularity.) In the words of Chernow overwhelmingly powerful banks such as JP Morgan were 'insinuated into the power structure of many countries' (2010: xii). To be fair, many trusts also made massive charitable and philanthropic donations to schools, hospitals and universities.

Nonetheless, some would regard these donations as bribes (Zinn 2005: 254). Here Chernow describes how Standard Oil executive J.D. Archbold made regular, generous payments to US senators in return for favourable political treatment, such as Senator Matthew Quay of Pennsylvania 'who received $42,000 between 1898 and 1902' (2004: 548). At one time Archbold even wrote the following to his recipient in the Senate: 'Please ask for payments as needed from time to time, not all at once'. A US senator was once even placed directly onto Standard's payroll! (The issue of political donations, or 'campaign contributions' to use the contemporary phrase, is still a thorny one today.)

Much like the biggest transnational corporations today, the trusts were hugely powerful and highly unpopular among many. They were regularly criticized as undemocratic, rapacious and basically too powerful; able to crush competition by means fair and foul. This is an important point to make, because the USA is so often characterized as the most pro-business country in the world. This is essentially true, but there have always been powerful countervailing tendencies, including from the general public, which can be suspicious and resentful of companies that have grown too large.

Much of the finance for building these empires came from reinvesting their retained earnings (McCraw 1997b: 320). However, as the corporations grew in size, stock markets located across the USA grew rapidly in importance. In order to continue to grow, trusts had to make speculative forward investments, making the case to the banks that these investments will pay off handsomely in 5, 10 or 15 years' time. This was an early form of financially leveraged capitalism.

One of the most important industries of the industrial age was the railroads. During 1830s and 1840s, many railroad corporations were formed, and new tracks were laid down across the country linking cities and further assisting the growth of industry. Farms became more mechanized, supplying ever-larger amounts of produce to feed the rapidly growing urban populations. Joint-stock financing was particularly important for railroad building, as this industry required considerable up-front investment and took time to return a profit (McCraw 1997b: 318). New industrial innovations sprung up which occasionally allowed their inventors to develop new companies, some of which were to become hugely successful. Famous examples include James Duke's cigarette rolling machine, which eventually allowed Duke to form British American Tobacco (Zinn 2005: 254). The various firms that eventually merged into the mighty conglomerate General

Electric were originally built around Thomas Edison's ingenious electrical devices (Smith and Walter 2006: 57).

New and exciting ideas also emerged in the world of finance. The securities market grew massively on New York's Wall Street. This did not just involve the provision of investment stock for industry. It also involved investing purely for the purpose of creating more money itself. Staple commodities such as grain and iron were 'securitized' in the forms of bonds and shares, in which investors could purchase in the hope of rising prices. 'Futures contracts' for grain changed hands on the floor of the Chicago Board of Trade, which became the world's first dedicated futures and options exchange (McCraw 1997b: 335).[5] Bonds were also widely raised on European markets, especially for the purpose of US railroad building – the banks of London and Frankfurt became intimately connected with economic growth across the Atlantic (Chernow 2010: 30). At this stage the USA had an extremely decentralized banking system, with thousands of separate, independent banks across the states. Interstate banking was complicated by 1920s legislation, which meant that each of the states tended to develop banking corporations of their own (Smith and Walter 2006: 194). At this time the USA had no central bank, and therefore no overall government control over monetary policy. The US Federal Reserve Bank was finally re-established in 1917, but it remained a rather weak institution all at sea in a wide and diffuse economy. Financial crises struck in the years 1873, 1893, 1907 and 1919 (Zinn 2005: 242), but stock market fuelling of US capitalism (for industry and for purely financial investments) was to continue to grow in importance from that point on. It reached epic proportions during the so-called 'roaring Twenties', when things started to spiral out of control (see below).

As the industrial revolution gathered pace, the sophistication and complexity of the trusts and firms grew. Many started to adopt systems of vertical integration by which the company sought to include as many parts of the supply chain as possible under its direct ownership or control. For example, Ford Motor Company built its own steelmaking and glassmaking facilities at its massive River Rouge plant. Ford even owned a Brazilian rubber plantation (Grandin 2010). Major corporations of this time often acted like islands entire of themselves, as autonomous and autarkic as practicality would allow. Vertical integration aimed towards uninterrupted supply of raw materials and managerial control over the marketplace for commodities. It allowed company

[5] Options have also been traded for generations in many other financial centres, including Paris, London and Amsterdam. Mackenzie (2008: 119) notes that options on Dutch East India Company stock were traded in Amsterdam as far back as 1688.

managements to drive through efficiency and cost-savings measures by eliminating their exposure to external markets (Chandler 1977). It enabled massive economies of scale to grow. According to Zinn:

> Between the Civil War and 1900, steam and electricity replaced human muscle, iron replaced wood, and steel replaced iron (before the Bessemer process, iron was hardened into steel at the rate of 3 to 5 tons a day; now the same amount could be processed in 15 minutes). Machines could now drive steel tools. ... People and goods could move by railroad, propelled by steam along steel rails; by 1900 there were 193,000 miles of railroad. The telephone, the typewriter, and the adding machine speeded up the work of business. (2005: 253)

The growth of early US multinationals was heavily based around their export of new technologies such as Singer (sewing machines) and Industrial Harvester (agricultural machines) (Chandler 2006: 2). Between the Wall Street Crash and the rise of Japan in the 1970s, the USA became a dominant force in telecommunications and electronics industries, demonstrated, for example, by the power of giant, near-monopolistic organizations such as the RCA, General Electric, AT&T and Westinghouse.

The rapid growth of the USA also threw up new ideas about how business and management should be organized. The most famous of these new ideas was scientific management, the approach espoused by Frederick W. Taylor (1856–1915). Also known as Taylorism, scientific management is one of the most famous innovations in management thought. Essentially it argued for a radical division of 'thinking' work from 'doing' work, whereby white-collar managers and engineers 'scientifically' measured the 'one best way' to carry out work, and imposed these new systems and techniques on blue-collar workers who would have no say in the matter. According to Tamura:

> Taylor recommended that all aspects of work and time involved should be measured; on this basis, a formal document should be prepared for each task, and all details of standard operations documented for communication to relevant personnel. The aim was for operations planned by relevant managers and engineers to be transmitted without fail to all operatives on the shopfloor where manufacturing is carried out. Transmission of information in a written form means that precise operational details can be defined, and it also serves to emphasize the authority to control operations. (2006: 510)

In recent years the 'micromanaging' approach of Taylorism has been heavily criticized in that it encourages and reinforces a blue-collar–white-collar 'them and us' mentality. Mass standardization, while far from universally adopted, did influence major US companies (especially

Ford), which set the tone for the more bureaucratic, standardized, heavily controlling approach to management and organization that became the norm in the era of managerial capitalism (see below). In fact, so powerful is the idea of 'Fordism' that the term became shorthand for a whole period of history in Western capitalism, basically the 'golden age' of post-war growth from 1945–73.

There were several other major theories about organization and management that arose during this period. Perhaps the second most famous after Taylorism is what became known as the Human Relations School. This refers to a series of ground-breaking studies into the nature of management and work that took place at Western Electric's Hawthorne Works in southern Chicago in 1924–32. The researchers conducted numerous experiments designed to understand how the working environment affects worker efficiency and job satisfaction (Roethlisberger and Dickson 1939). Unfortunately, the onset of the Great Depression meant that these studies were cancelled. But an extraordinarily rich legacy of academic work emerged from Hawthorne, and much of it subsequently influenced the development of new techniques designed to humanize the workplace and to properly understand working life. While Taylorism/Fordism represented the regularity and standardization of the managerial capitalism era that came afterwards, the Human Relations School also prefigured its stability and paternalism.

None of the industrial developments of this time pursued peacefully or easily. There were huge amounts of industrial unrest during this, and other, periods of American economic growth. Zinn describes many rebellions by people who lived and laboured in appalling conditions: 'The new industrialism, the crowded cities, the long hours in the factories, the sudden economic crises leading to high prices and lost jobs, the lack of food and water, the freezing winters, the hot tenements in the summer, the epidemics of disease, the deaths of children – these led to sporadic reactions from the poor. ... Sometimes it was organized into demonstrations and strikes' (2005: 221). Trade unions were in their infancy, and were to become powerful rather later, especially after the Second World War.

Moreover, the more or less unchecked power of the trusts was starting to become a political problem. Trusts such as JP Morgan 'represented everything that had bothered Americans for a generation – factories thrown up helter-skelter across the landscape, brutal mergers, a carnival atmosphere on Wall Street that caused boomlets and busts in crazy, unending succession' (Chernow 2010: 147). Politicians were increasingly arguing that unregulated competition meant the stifling of competition. Towards the end of the 19th century some important pieces of legislation were passed by Congress in an attempt to rein in the trusts. The most important was the Sherman Antitrust Act 1890, which was an attempt to ban companies from forming cartels and artificially fixing prices. Its first major casualty was Standard Oil Corporation. A federal court in Illinois in 1907 found Standard guilty of violating fair competition practices, and ruled that the company must be broken up. Standard Oil of Indiana was fined the astronomical sum of US$29.24 million, with J.D. Rockefeller himself liable for around US$8 million The presiding judge 'called Standard no better than a common thief and castigated its lawyers for their "studied indolence"' (Chernow 2004: 541). In later years, major firms such as IBM were relentlessly pursued by government anti-trust lawsuits (Olegario 1997: 378–380).

Sherman was an effort to control capitalism, but only in so far as this control is enough to stimulate fair competition. US capitalism became somewhat more regulated, but the regulation was designed to stimulate competition further. In the US context, the state itself is not meant to be a central economic player (unlike in, for example, South Korea, Japan or France). Instead it is meant to be more of a rule-setter, sat on the sidelines of the economic game. It is important to bear in mind, however, that even though these trusts symbolize a wild form of unregulated US capitalism, the state was in fact often closely involved in economic growth. In fact, in many ways it helped the 'robber barons' build their empires by protecting US industry with import-prevention measures. Tariff barriers formed part of a major infant industry protection policy in the USA. Some of these tariffs were very heavy, making the import of foreign goods prohibitively expensive. The first tariffs were installed in 1816; '30 percent duties on iron products and 25 percent on cotton and woollen goods' (Eckes 1995: 52; see also Chang 2003: 17). The USA widely used tariffs from this period until the onset of the First World War.

The early days of US capitalism, therefore, were an odd mixture of government assistance to industry, and state and industry at war with each other. The wild era of US capitalism reached its zenith in the 1920s. Financial speculation, especially in company shares, started to be recklessly regarded as a no-lose investment, and was marketed as such by stockbrokers keen to invest money from companies and private investors. Stocks were purchased by hundreds of thousands of US citizens in the expectation of future earnings. Many thousands even borrowed money to invest in stocks – an extremely risky practice known as buying 'on margin'. Stock indices grew for six years straight, fuelling the view that one would lose out if he or she was not on this ride. Stock tickers were installed in public places such as barber shops and cafés. The late 1920s was one of the biggest ever examples of a speculative financial bubble; it ended in one of the world's worst crashes. No-one knows exactly what caused the panic selling that triggered the Wall Street Crash of 29 October 1929. But the crash when it came was devastating, ushering in a prolonged slump known as The Great Depression, which hit most parts of the world. Hundreds of banks failed. Billions of dollars in savings were lost. Millions lost their jobs and homes.

The story of how US capitalism became much more tightly controlled and regulated after the Crash is the topic of the next section.

The beast is tamed: the new traditions of US managerial capitalism

We have noted how regularly the US business system is described as the paradigmatic example of Anglo-Saxon capitalism, liberal market capitalism, neoliberalism or free market capitalism. There are obvious reasons why the USA is so often used as the clearest example of this model. The contemporary US economy includes limited regulation and a minimalist welfare state, weak unions, strong managerial prerogative and powerful anti-trust legislation. Recent decades have seen major processes of liberalization and privatization of the US economy. A comparatively high proportion of the US population invests in shares rather than low-risk savings accounts. The US has for many years been at the forefront of the shareholder activism movement, a key part of the logic of shareholder value.

But the US model of business did not always resemble the highly open, risky and leveraged system it is today. In fact, the reverse was almost the case in the years after The Great Depression until the 1980s. This was the era of managerial capitalism, and the rest of this section will describe and discuss its key features. Managerial capitalism exists in different versions across most of the world's advanced economies. In the UK it was evident in companies such as ICI or British Telecom before privatization. In Japan it still is a fairly accurate description of the kind of management systems currently in place which privilege long-term investments, length of service and seniority (see Chapter 11). In France a form of managerial capitalism is also to some extent still with us (see Chapter 5).

The New Deal refers to a policy approach whereby the government stepped in to modify, regulate and stimulate the economy when markets have failed. It emerged in the aftermath of the Wall Street Crash during the long presidency of Franklin D. Roosevelt (FDR) (1933–45). FDR usually occupies third place in opinion polls of the greatest US presidents of all time (behind only Lincoln and Washington). His popularity is well-justified; FDR's administrations were arguably responsible for building a powerful and durable structure of regulation into which US capitalism was embedded, for contributing a major role in the Allied Powers' victory in the Second World War and ultimately for laying the foundations for the long post-war economic boom that lies at the heart of the success of contemporary capitalism in the West.

Hundreds of new pieces of legislation were issued during the New Deal era, especially during the 'first hundred days' programme of Roosevelt's first term.[6] One of the most famous and enduring pieces of New Deal legislation was the Banking Act 1933, which included the famous Glass–Steagal provisions. This radically reformed the US banking industry, stipulating that banks be either depository banks or investment banks; only the latter were given the authority to engage in the riskiest forms of lending and speculation. One of the reasons the Great Depression was so savage was because there was no effective 'lender of last resort'; there was no larger financial institution that could bail out banks or companies when the wolves were at the door. FDR tried to solve this problem by strengthening the role of the Federal Reserve Bank. New Deal legislation also strengthened the position of ordinary working people; the National Labor Relations Board was formed providing the legal basis for trade union representation and dispute resolution; a system of industrial relations that was to last in more or less the same form until quite recently.

The New Deal also set an important precedent whereby the federal government increased hugely in size and influence. In some ways it laid the ground for the later New Frontier and Great Society programmes of later Democratic administrations of Kennedy and Johnson. Safeguards were put in to make the financial system, firms and households less vulnerable to downturns. Banks were much more heavily regulated (this regulation is very complex in the USA, as it takes place at state and federal level). Regulation of any kind was heavily resisted by the major players in high finance such as JP Morgan or by the New York stock exchange itself.[7]

---

[6] The phrase 'first one hundred days' has since gone into the business and management lexicon, referring to the vision that a new leader must have as he or she steps into a new management position. Change has to be instigated soon lest the window of opportunity be lost forever (Khurana 2004: 15). Important first one hundred days legislation included the Reconstruction Finance Corporation Act 1932, which allocated US$500m in aid to troubled banks and corporations (Rauchway 2008: 137).

[7] One such opponent of regulation was Richard Whitney, once the president of the New York Stock Exchange (1930–5), the man who made the famous stroll from JP Morgan on 23 Wall Street across the road to the Exchange to buy up steel stocks in an ultimately vain attempt to reassure investors and stop the 1929 crash. He argued fiercely against government intervention in economic matters. Whitney was later indicted of grand larceny and sentenced to 5 to 10 years in Sing Sing prison (Chernow 2010: 428).

Outside of direct government influence changes were afoot in the nature of the US firm. The 'robber baron' phase started to end as corporations outgrew their founders. Large firms of the 20th century (across the developed nations) were increasingly characterized by the division of ownership from control. Firms increasingly looked to capital markets for extra investment funding, so issued shares to private investors, thereby opening themselves to external ownership. Firm ownership shifted from entrepreneurs and their families to outside investors. Typically these investors bought securities in the company (stocks and shares) in return for a stake in the future earnings of the business, (usually realized in dividend payments or the increased value of their shareholding). Some shareholders also have voting rights, enabling them to attend annual general meetings and vote on senior managers' plans for the business. In theory, they can rebel against members of boards of directors, even ousting them if their records are especially poor.

The split of ownership and control encouraged the growth of large chains of middle management, who were entrusted by the new owners to run the company in the interests of the shareholders. The received wisdom is that senior managers, like most workers, are inherently self-interested and cannot be trusted to discharge their duties to shareholders without strong control systems being put into place. Managers also tended to have low expectations with regards to blue-collar worker commitment and behaviour. Their response was usually to issue clear work orders and exercise close monitoring of behaviour to ensure that these orders are effectively carried out. This approach is often labelled 'command and control', a phrase widely used in the military that gives an indication as to its meaning. Command and control is all about discipline, routine, clear (mostly downward) lines of communication, hierarchy and authority. Traditional management systems of the era (such as Taylorism and Fordism) rely on rigid divisions of labour, and US corporations became increasing productive and efficient, at the cost of being authoritarian workplaces with very limited discretion extended to blue collars or mid-level administrators.

The New Deal era eventually 'blurred into the war' (Rauchway 2008: 6). The USA formally entered the Second World War in December 1941. The war provided an enormous stimulus to American industry, especially for steel, vehicle, engine and aircraft manufacturers, which were suddenly flooded with orders from the Pentagon. Ford, General Motors (GM) and Boeing massively ramped-up their production capacity. Ultimately, the USA emerged in a stronger position after the war than any of the other major powers. It suffered approximately 295,000 deaths (civilian and military combined), amounting to around 0.4% of the population. This was considerably fewer than, for example, France

(810,000 and 1.9% of population); Japan (2.69 million and 3.6%); and Germany (6.85 million and 9.5%). The USSR lost around 22 million – about 11% of its population.[8] With the exception of Pearl Harbor, none of the fighting took place on US soil, meaning there was no destruction of cities and infrastructure that devastated Europe and Japan. After the war, the USA occupied Japan for eight years (see Chapter 11) and, through the Marshall Plan, provided US$13 billion of funding for the rebuilding of Europe (McMahon 2003: 30). There was a concerted attempt to remake Europe in the American image (Djelic 1998), although this was never fully achieved, with European and Japanese economies retaining important socio-economic features. Nevertheless the stage was set for the subsequent period of US dominance of world politics, and the Cold War standoff with the USSR.

The post-war boom was based around the standardization and stability of the managerial age. Managerial capitalism was most famously explored by the business historian Alfred Chandler Jr, especially in his highly influential text *The Visible Hand* (1977). What Chandler means by the visible hand is a set of forces different from the classical invisible hand of market forces. Whereas earlier times (such as the Gilded Age) were characterized by wild capitalism and individual entrepreneurs, the period from the New Deal onwards was about stability, collectivity and managed growth. Large firms became run by their tall ranks of salaried, professional, general managers, rather than by dominant entrepreneur-owners. Literature from the period includes classic books such as *The Organization Man* by Whyte (1960), C. Wright Mills' *White Collar* (1953) and *The Power Elite* (1959), and Melville Dalton's *Men Who Manage* (1959). Culturally, the references also extend to Sloan Wilson's novel *The Man in the Gray Flannel Suit* (1955/2005) and the current retrospective HBO television series *Mad Men* (2007–). Organizations of the time operated according to strict hierarchical procedures, almost like a military chain of command. Above the workers on the front line or the shop floor, there would typically be a blue-collar supervisor, then many levels of white-collar, non-unionized managers. There could be as many as 12 ranks of management between supervisor and the board of directors.

In the middle of the 20th century US firms became highly political, complex organizations, with numerous goals and diverse groups of stakeholders to keep happy. Economists and organizational scholars of the time such as March and Simon (1958) used terms such as 'satisficing behaviour' to describe how US firms were not primarily focused on

[8] These numbers are, of course, highly contentious estimates that differ across sources. I have taken the European and Soviet figures from Bullock (1991: 1086–1087), and the Japanese figures from (Choucri et al. 1992: 26), and Duus (1998: 249).

profit-making, but were prepared to be pragmatic, to act with patience and to work in concert with diverse groups of stakeholders. One even coined the term the 'soulful corporation' (Kaysen 1957: 314). Managerial capitalism was arguably less ruthless than what came before and after. Top managers focused on growth and acquisition, rather than shareholder value. Many US corporations went beyond vertical integration and began purchasing other companies in wholly unrelated fields (Lazonick 2005: 584). Large conglomerates were formed during the period, such as Litton Industries, which produced an array of goods from advanced weapons for the Pentagon to typewriters and microwave ovens (Byrne 1993: 379–390, 482–499). Teledyne Corporation at one time had over 100 lines of business, from dental products to tank engines. The strategy of internal development was famously described by Lazonick and O'Sullivan (2000) as 'retain and reinvest' rather than the approach of 'downsize and distribute' (which was to come later, see the following section).

Although often associated with managerial capitalism the fate of US conglomerates provided a prelude of things to come. The diversified, unrelated acquisitions made by firms such as Litton represented an early sign of the rising financial dominance of Wall Street, as the strategy of acquisition was increasingly enacted mostly to try to impress the investment community. Byrne (1993) describes how Litton top management became increasingly desperate to demonstrate to the investment banks, business media and stock rating agencies that big is beautiful, and that there was a sensible underlying strategy (or 'synergy') to its myriad acquisitions. But this confidence trick could not work forever and, in a fall from grace that presaged the disasters of Enron, Worldcom and Tyco over 40 years later, the bubble popped as confidence in the entire business model of conglomerates came to an end. Litton was dismissed as 'a numbers game'. A front cover of *Forbes* magazine in December 1968 became iconic – it featured a smashed window with the caption 'The Shattered Image of Litton Industries' (Byrne 1993).

One company that perhaps exemplifies the era of managerial capitalism more than any other was IBM. IBM has the nickname 'Big Blue'. Although the root of this term is foggy some believe it refers to the unofficial uniform of IBM 'men' – a dark blue suit, white shirt and dark tie. Highly respected companies, such as IBM, inculcated in its staff a similar image to those of public bureaucracies (such as the FBI where its employees, especially under J. Edgar Hoover, were expected to act and appear in a way which came to symbolize authority and respect). 'Company men' projected the same aloof and detached demeanour of their companies.

Managerial capitalism stood for routine, loyalty and submission. White-collar staff devoted their whole careers to one firm and tended not to entertain ideas about leaving for greener pastures. Why would a salaried manager want to leave? The paternalistic corporation of the period provided good pay, benefits, pensions and medical insurance (Jacoby 1997). Jobs were secure as long as staff remained loyal and worked to a satisfactory standard. General Motors built movie theatres and ball rooms for its workers. Although its work was backbreaking, dangerous, even poisonous, Kaiser Aluminium did its best to compensate its workers, by paying high wages and offering a very generous healthcare plan. Kaiser Aluminium's healthcare insurance system eventually morphed into Kaiser Permanente one of America's most powerful healthcare maintenance organizations (Kusnet 2008: 19).

The advantages of managerial capitalism did not accrue only to the college-educated white-collar staff. Trade unions were a powerful political force during this era, and unionized blue-collar workers also enjoyed job security and considerable benefits. They could start to afford to take on the trappings of middle-class life - a house in the suburbs, a car, a refrigerator, savings plans for sending the kids to college. Managerial capitalism delivered the American Dream to millions of households. Society was changing fast. In 1958, the world famous economist J.K. Galbraith published the first edition of *The Affluent Society*, an influential book about the prospects for an end to scarcity in advanced economies. Real incomes doubled during this period (McCraw 1997b: 342). Managerial capitalism (Chandler 1990) was the crucial ingredient of America's 'organized capitalism' (Lash and Urry 1987) or its 'second spirit of capitalism' (Boltanski and Chiapello 2005). According to Robert Presthus in his book *The Organizational Society*:

> Beginning about 1875, social, economic and political trends in the United States prepared the way for the 'organization society', characterized by large-scale bureaucratic institutions in virtually every social area. The master trends included the separation of ownership from management; increasing size and concentration in business; the decline of competition as financial resources required for entry in almost every sector became prohibitive; and the emergence of an employee society. (1979: 84)

Some companies were quick to note the changing society around them, realizing huge new potential for commercial gain. Alfred Sloan of GM was one of the most highly respected US executives of all time. He brought order to a complex, messy and failing GM, and helped bring about a revolution in corporate organizing and marketing techniques (McCraw and Tedlow 1997). Sloan positioned the wide range of GM vehicles according to which parts of the society could afford, or aspire to afford, them (this approach came to be known as 'market segmentation'). GM could even help customers move up by offering credit through General Motors Acceptance Corporation (GMAC), its finance division. Each of the main GM badges offered their own range of cars that went from basic to luxurious. GM customers could move upmarket as their income (and borrowing power) increased. Cars, like houses and clothes, became powerful status symbols.

> The 1950s and 1960s were truly the 'golden age' of American capitalism. There was tremendous optimism about continued growth.[9] Democratic presidents Kennedy and Johnson embarked on ambitious programmes of federal spending, allocating funds to improve transport, education, science, and, most famously in Kennedy's case, the space race (in 1961 he promised to put an American on the moon by 1969). (McCraw and Tedlow 1997: 292)

The USA was also at the forefront of the world's entertainment industry. Hollywood movie studios churned out thousands of films reaffirming the message of the US way of life as dynamic and luxurious.

Some believed that the industrial achievements of the managerial capitalist model were helping to spread advanced modernity all over the world. Convergence theorists, such as Clark Kerr et al. (1960), even argued at the time that Western capitalism and Soviet state socialism were becoming increasingly similar due to the use of advanced industrial and organizational technologies in both. The Cold War era (1945–91) was characterized by a dramatic standoff between the USA and the USSR. During the Cold War, the USSR and USA projected their (mirror) images as the more advanced nation, as a model for developing nations to emulate and become allied with. Flushed with success after World War Two, the USA built itself an infrastructure for world influence: the North Atlantic Treaty Organization (NATO) and its unofficial leadership roles in transnational political organizations, such as the IMF and the World Bank. Under the 'Bretton Woods' system of international currency exchange, the US dollar effectively became the world's reserve currency. The US military engaged in repeated interventions around the world as it attempted to demonstrate its credibility as the best hope for democracy and freedom in the world. Many of these were unsuccessful. By far the worst was the disastrous war in Vietnam (1959–75). Despite failures such as these, the USA ultimately emerged victorious from the Cold War as the USSR collapsed at century's end. The 20th century became known as 'the American Century' and managerial capitalism played a major part in it.

[9] At least among the more fortunate white citizens – for blacks there was still massive social and economic problems including an absence of civil rights (such as the right to vote) that whites enjoyed. The Civil Rights movement eventually won some major victories for African Americans in the 1960s, but blacks and Hispanics still to this day remain significantly over-represented in the poorest socio-economic groupings.

However, managerial capitalism was not without its critics. Scratch the surface and one could regularly see rough treatment by managers of those below them in the chain of command. Many staff lived in fear of their bosses, and secrecy, intimidation and public humiliation were widely used management tools (Starkey and McKinlay 1994). Systematic isolation of women and ethnic minorities were also rife in large organizations of the period. Women, where they worked at all, performed menial office work. Managerial capitalism rested on the assumption of a male 'breadwinner' and a female 'homemaker'. Major authors of the period such as Whyte (1960) and Mills (1953) criticized the micromanaging, brainwashing approach inherent in managerial capitalism.

Distinctions were clear in the age of managerial capitalism, especially between white-collar and blue-collar workers, who tend to occupy quite different parts of organizations, literally and figuratively. Blue-collar workers would traditionally toil away in unpleasant, demanding and dangerous factories, while the white-collar managers would reside in office blocks some distance away. Blue collars were typically heavily unionized and paid hourly or piece rates, whereas white collars received annual salaries, and were not generally recruited into unions. Management–labour relations were traditionally poor in this classical environment, marked by regular conflict and an absence of trust (Hamper 1992). To a large extent, this meant that US corporations were storing up major problems for the future.

As firms grew in size and complexity they often developed separate functions such as personnel, marketing and accounting, and these roles became institutionalized as the foundation of Western understandings of business subjects, as taught in MBA programmes. GM, while under the chairmanship of Alfred P. Sloan (1937–56) was the classic example of divisionalization. Sloan's ideas were widely adopted and taught as the foundations of effective management of large organizations. A grant from the Sloan Foundation led to the establishment of a business school at MIT (Sloan School of Management), adding further credibility to, and broadening the spread of, these concepts. (In the later era of 'investor capitalism' this 'silo culture' of people working in separate parts of the same organization came in for revision as observers questioned the efficiency of having so many divisions of people who are, after all, working for the same company and supposedly interested in achieving more or less the same results.)

Managerial capitalism, along with the post-war New Deal boom that spurned it, started to fall apart in the 1980s. In common with most of the OECD economies, the USA was deeply challenged by the 1973 oil crisis, which ushered in a period of retrenchment and decline, compounding the economic and social misery created by the Vietnam War. Detroit's obsession with 'gas-guzzler' vehicles began to look seriously misplaced as the price of oil spiked. Ford, GM and Chrysler were becoming outpaced by Japanese success in building smaller, more fuel-efficient, more reliable vehicles. Japanese-badged cars started to be built directly in the US by overseas branches of Mazda, Honda, Nissan, and Toyota, employing American workers using efficient Japanese management techniques (Adler 1992, Fucini and Fucini 1992). High-tech Japanese electronics factories sprung up in California (Milkman 1991). US capitalism started to turn away from industry and toward services, especially finance.

The 1970s and 1980s also saw renewed signs of strain in US industrial relations. Major strikes and sit-down protests erupted at, for example, Dodge Truck and GM Lordstown. These were frightening developments for the political elite, so much so that the Nixon administration commission the famous *Work in America* study (US Department of Health, Education and Welfare 1973) that recommended major reforms to make industrial work more humane (Granter 2009: 103–104; Kusnet 2008: 39). There was also a very serious banking crisis in the 1980s - what became known as the 'savings and loan' scandals, when many of the thousands of small banking operations around the USA became insolvent. Banks became 'hemmed in by government restrictions. ... banks watched helplessly as much of their business disappeared into the capital markets' (Smith and Walter 2006: 193).

During the era of managerial capitalism, there were none of the leveraged buyouts, junk bonds or derivatives that came to dominate US business. Wall Street had considerably less influence over managerial behaviour than in later times. However, as we shall see, when it came, the final dominance of finance over production was dramatic, effectively revolutionizing US and, to a certain extent, world capitalism.

From managerial to investor capitalism in the USA

The move from managerial capitalism to investor capitalism (Khurana 2004; Useem 1999), or from organized to disorganized capitalism (Lash and Urry 1987) is of massive importance. 'Investor capitalism' describes a new organizing paradigm for business that emerged in the USA around the mid-1980s and has become dominant there since, and widely copied elsewhere in the world. Investor capitalism has several important features that differ considerably from managerial capitalism. The most obvious change refers to a shift in the balance of power away from internal stakeholders within the firm (such as the ranks of salaried managers or long-term board members) towards investors outside of the firm (especially institutional investors such as pension funds or hedge fund managers). These investors typically demand higher returns on their investments, and have become increasingly strident in recent years, especially since the economic slowdown of the US model in the 1980s.

Changes in the banking system of the USA were highly significant throughout the 1990s. Commercial banks such as Citicorp and Bank of America rapidly expanded in scale, scope and centralization by aggressively taking over smaller banks around the country as the 'distress of the 1980s allowed many banks to get around legal restrictions on interstate banking' (Smith and Walter 2006: 194). After years of intense lobbying of Congress, the major commercial banks finally achieved the repeal of Glass–Steagal in 1999. This opened the door for a revolution in US banking as large banks were able to indulge in increasingly risky lending, and to further accelerate the trend whereby stock market prices became the only relevant touchstone for large firm performance.

The shift to investor capitalism was neatly encapsulated by Lazonick and O'Sullivan's (2000) famous paper in the journal *Economy and Society*. They describe how large firms moved from a 'retain and reinvest' strategy to one of 'downsize and distribute' (Lazonick and O'Sullivan 2000). Changes in the way firms were financed (such as the rise of major institutional investors) had fundamentally reordered large firms' priorities away from internal, insider governance and increasingly towards attempting to please outside investors. Firms paid far more attention to their investor relations and attempted to project an image whereby every action they take is designed to satisfied shareholders. This is called shareholder value logic, and its influence is hugely important in the USA and increasingly elsewhere. Froud et al. (2006) discuss how large conglomerates were 'unbundled' to make them look less complicated to the investment community: simpler, more agile, better focused.

The move from managerial capitalism towards investor capitalism, therefore, represents a concerted power shift away from managers and back towards owners (much like the robber-baron phase). Only this time, the owners were not individually wealthy families or the entrepreneurs, such as Carnegie, who originally started the firms. Nowadays the owners of capital are powerful institutional investors with sophisticated forms of influence over firm management. A related change is the rise of the private equity model, which represents a total collapse of managerial capitalism, as it explicitly values owners' interests well above those of any other stakeholders (Clark 2009).

By the end of the 1980s, the US financial scene was flooded with new and highly risky financial practices. Leveraged buyouts became common, whereby aggressive investors would secure high levels of debt from investment banks with which to buy ailing companies. The new owners would then ruthlessly restructure the firms (usually involving replacing the top executives and firing thousands of staff down the hierarchy), then sell the firms off quickly and at a profit (Byrne 1999). New financial instruments came into much wider circulation, especially high-risk options and futures. The falling cost and increasing power of IT systems allowed the development of 'day trading' in stocks and shares by personal investors. The inexorable rise of the internet fuelled great excitement about high-tech start-ups – the 'dotcoms' that were the harbinger of a so-called 'New Economy'. The USA had emerged from its 1980s slump and had repositioned itself at the forefront of the new high-tech frontier (Best 2001). Silicon Valley in California became a new centre of gravity for the US economy. High-tech experts such as web designers and software coders flitted from job to job instead of pursuing long careers in one bureaucratic firm such as IBM (Barley and Kunda 2004). There was huge investor interest in the new dotcoms, but for every success such as amazon or ebay, there were thousands of failures and poor investments. Some have argued that the new technology start-ups represented America's new 'robber barons'. Microsoft, for example, has been widely criticized for its abuse of temporary workers (Kusnet 2008: 97–149; Barley and Kunda 2004). Increasingly, top managers of US firms became dominated by personnel with backgrounds in finance and law, rather than those with direct specialism in the business, (such as engineers). The focus of the firms' operations became fixated on marketing and finance, often to the detriment of operations and engineering. IBM, for example, was split for many years between the designers and engineers and the marketers (Olegario 1997).

The growing power of pension funds and other institutional investors meant that it was they who seemed to pull the strings of major firms, as opposed to large boards of company lifers in the prior era. Unlike the era of managerial capitalism, finance was no longer the servant of firms. It became their master. Investor capitalism makes huge demands on large firms to demonstrate a coherent public narrative that impresses the financial community. A wide range of authors have recently argued that the scandals that erupted at Enron and WorldCom in 2001 (and at others such as Sunbeam under Al Dunlap [Byrne 1999; Smith and Walter 2006: 183]) were symptoms of a broader malaise. An excellent example of this argument is provided in Tillman and Indergaard's *Pump & Dump* (2005). Corporate America has come to rely too heavily on financialization, and has increasingly embraced risky, short-term lending and financial engineering rather than concentrating on the underlying value creation of the firm. Corporate strategy gets lost under a shroud of 'investor relations' marketing. Similar points are made by Smith and Walter (2006). Forms of 'narrative performance' artificially pump up the stock price while the underlying value of the firm can be problematic or non-existent (Froud et al. 2006). This explains both the boom in technology stocks in the so-called 'New Economy' era of the late 1990s, and the way they collapsed so quickly once the shine had rubbed off.

Politically, the state was retreating from active economic involvement. After the disasters of the Nixon era, the Republicans fought back strongly, occupying the White House from 1981 to 1993. Presidents Reagan (1981–9) and George H.W. Bush (1989–93) were big believers in 'restrained government', forcing through policies of liberalization, deregulation and privatization. The most dramatic episode of neoliberal attack on union power was Reagan's defeat of PATCO, the air traffic controllers' union in 1981, in which 11,345 striking workers were fired and then banned from federal service for life (Shostak 2006). Democratic President Bill Clinton (1993–2001), although less hostile to labour, continued many of the neoliberal policies of his Republican predecessors, famously declaring in his State of the Union address on 27 January 1996 that 'the era of Big Government is over'.[10]

Institutional changes in US capitalism were reflected in dramatic changes within large firms. More subtly, the culture of US firms changed, away from the paternalistic long-term stability of managerial capitalism and towards a much more aggressive, uncompromising form of work and organization, characterized by fast turnover of staff and senior management, a move away from seniority-based payment systems and stable career ladders, regular restructuring, and a culture of buzzwords and managerial fads such as 'business process re-engineering' or 'culture change' programmes (Willmott 1993).

Blue- and white-collar labour was fundamentally restructured during this time. A major trend was towards flattening the organizational hierarchy, and the increased use of temporaries and part-timers. The 'gray flannel suits' retreated into terminal decline. Although criticized for its rather 'loose' use of evidence, one of the most famous books on this subject is Richard Sennett's (1998) *The Corrosion of Character*, in which a long-term career melds into a series of detached and fragmented jobs. In Hassard et al.'s (2009) *Managing in the Modern Corporation*, managers in the USA and elsewhere are shown to be exposed to massive forces of destabilization. Organizational change was almost continual, and job security was reduced in a much more

[10] Having said this, the USA hypocritically continued with import tariffs at certain times, such as on Japanese cars, Korean steel and Chinese tyres, partly because congressmen and senators attempted to protect jobs in their home states.

intense 'performance culture', reinforced by statistical performance management systems and more forceful bonus regimes. One manager in a recruitment firm in the USA described how managers looked on aghast as an incoming senior executive announced that the firm was no longer going to be a family company: 'You could have heard a pin drop', she said (Hassard et al. 2009: 65).

Old job titles reminiscent of the New Deal era melted away. Hassard et al. (2009: 131) describe how at 'AutoCo', one of the US's largest car firms, the white-collar career structure used to range from point 9 to point 21 on an employment scale. This was replaced by the new structure of 'Leadership Levels' 1 to 6.

Exhibit 3.2 A leaner management structure for 'AutoCo'

Pre-1998 managerial levels	Post-1998 managerial levels
9. Superintendent	Leadership Level Six (LL6)
10. Superintendent (Large Area)	
11. Area Manager	LL5
12. Area Manager (Large Area)	
13. Assistant Plant Manager	LL4
14. Plant Manager	
15. Plant Manager (Large Plot)	LL3
16. Operations Manager	
17. Operations Manager	LL2
18. Operations Manager	
19. Top Management: Corporate Vice-President	
20. Top Management: Corporate Senior Vice-President	LL1
21. Top Management: Corporate Senior Vice-President	

(Hassard et al 2009: 131)

Such changes were in keeping with firms' attempts to demonstrate to Wall Street that they are lean and efficient, and not wasteful of shareholders' investments. Whole industries collapsed in the era of investor capitalism, as they could no longer demonstrate to the investment community that their business model was worth investing in. The US consumer electronics industry was one of the first to go in the 1980s. Alfred Chandler documents how RCA failed to keep pace with its Japanese competitors Sony and Matsushita, largely because the investor capitalism model could not generate sufficient funds for reinvestment in industrial innovations (Chandler 2006: 23–33). The US car industry started to suffer badly during this time, largely for the same reason, especially given that Japanese competitors were producing more reliable, more environmental-friendly vehicles using fewer, better-trained staff. Despite the problem being identified for decades, US carmakers seemed addicted to heavy-duty vehicles with poor fuel efficiency. For example Ford's F-series pickup truck was the bestselling car in US for 17 years (1991–2007), but was overtaken in 2008 not only by the Honda Civic, but also by Toyota's Corolla, Camry and Honda's Accord, dropping it into fifth place. Recent years have been nightmarish for the US carmakers, calling to mind their disastrous performance in the 1980s during Japan's initial boom. In the wake of the subprime crisis, GM posted losses of US$6 billion, and Chrysler was rescued by FIAT.[11] GM moved into bankruptcy protection, and emerged a radically slimmer firm, having closed its Hummer brand and sold SAAB to the Dutch firm Spyker. GM and Chrysler were both bailed out by Congress to the tune of US$17.4 billion in 2009.[12]

Industrial firms in general came to be viewed by the investment community as 'value destroyers', and stock analysts instructed investors to sell their stock in these 'sunset' sectors of the economy. The US steel industry struggled, as investment and employment collapsed in the 'rust belt' states of Pennsylvania and Indiana. The iconic Bethlehem Steel works (home of Taylor's famous pig-iron studies) closed in 2003. Critics started to point to an 'hourglass economy' whereby the solid, middle-range jobs protected by blue-collar unions (such as steel or carmaking) were rapidly disappearing, leaving a new band of super-rich at the top, a thinning middle, and a large rump of poorly paid service workers in dead-end jobs at the bottom (Appelbaum et al. 2003; Newman 2000).

Some employers, such as Southwest Airlines and Cisco Systems (Osterman et al. 2001) have taken the 'high road' as regards employment relations, upskilling their workforces and developing sophisticated forms of employee involvement as they adopt the much-vaunted 'High-Performance Work Systems' approach (Appelbaum et al. 2000). But elsewhere there has been a concerted employer offensive against the remnants the New Deal era. In many sectors, especially where deregulation has brought in new forms of cost competition, union membership has collapsed and wages have shrunk. Union density in the public sector is relatively strong at 36%, while in the private sector it has collapsed to just 7.5% of the workforce (Katz and Colvin 2011: 79). In trucking, for example, average real wages tumbled 30% between 1977–95 (Osterman et al. 2001: 66). In some areas, unions have retaliated. Ruth Milkman (2006) has written extensively on the revival of unions in California, which enjoyed considerable success in recruiting

[11] 'GM Loses $6bn Over Quarter as Sales Halve', *Guardian*, 7 May 2009.

[12] 'U.S. Lays Down Terms for Auto Bailout', *New York Times*, 30 March 2009.

and organizing migrant service workers, partly by using dramatic new techniques such as public protests and non-violent disruption.[13]

Amid the job loss and insecurity CEOs in corporate America received enormous salary increases and stock options. Osterman describes the Bacchanalian excess loaded onto the lucky few: 'CEO Chad Gifford obtained a sweet deal after selling Fleet to Bank of America: a $24.3 million severance bonus; $3.1 million in retirement income per year for life; a private jet that he can use for any purpose, including personal; and four tickets to fifteen Red Sox games per year for life' (2008: 130). Meanwhile US employers opened up new attacks on pensions (Monk 2009); new attacks on unions (Milkman 2006). American capitalism found itself a new ruthlessness.

Exhibit 3.3 Celebrity CEOs in the USA

Two quite different authors write about Lee Iacocca, one of the most famous business leaders of all time. Iacocca was famously sacked as President of Ford Motors, but went on to save Chrysler Motors from bankruptcy in the 1980s. Templar, a British author of management self-help books, provides a quotation from Iacocca about honesty and integrity:

> 'I have found that being honest is the best technique I can use. Right up front, tell people what you're trying to accomplish and what you're willing to sacrifice to accomplish it.'
>
> Lee Iacocca, President of Ford and Chrysler,
> as quoted in Templar (2005: 199)

Another quite different author, a sociologist researching the economically down-at-heel city of Kenosha, Wisconsin, opens her book with lines from a song about Iacocca written by disgruntled Chrysler workers:

Hey Lee

Hey, hey Lee, why did you lie?
Several thousand workers now left behind to die
They bust their backs for you, hard as they can
If your sales are down, don't blame Japan
And where is the worker's protection plan?
Hey, hey Lee, can't you make a stand?
So you turn your back and you walk away
Hey, hey Lee, that ain't the American way

(Dudley 1994: 1). By permission of University of Chicago Press.

[13] The most famous of these new union campaigns was the Service Employees' International Union (SEIU)'s 'Justice for Janitors' campaign, in which immigrant workers cleaning the high-end offices of banks, law firms and Hollywood movie agents won widespread union recognition and greatly improved wages and conditions. This iconic campaign was the subject of the movie *Bread and Roses*, directed by UK filmmaker Ken Loach (2000).

CEOs cashed in on the changing cultural signifiers of US business. Business and management success was supposedly created by top leaders' exciting 'visions' and 'values', no longer by soulless conformity to organizational norms. The selection of new CEOs for firms is arguably not an open labour market but a complex social ritual, dominated by the expectations created by Wall Street and the investor community. The new age of investor capitalism meant an end to the stuffy and conservative image of corporate America – all of a sudden big business was being made 'sexy' to the investment community and the general public (Khurana 2004: 51–80).

Lou Gerstner Jr, one such celebrity CEO, phased out the old-fashioned 'Big Blue' culture of IBM. His book *Who Says Elephants Can't Dance?* (2003) embodies the approach of mainstream US 'leadership' literature. Gerstner was an outsider, a Harvard MBA with no background in the industry but came in armed with a new vision and a contempt for traditional custom and practice. Formerly CEO of RJR Nabisco and American Express, Gerstner explains how he successfully 'changed the culture' of IBM from a process-driven, complex, messy structure, to a lean, customer-focused, streamlined organization (cutting 170,000 jobs in the process, see Olegario 1997: 384). Gerstner moved on to become chairman of Carlyle Group, one of the largest private equity partnerships in the world, with investors from over 150 countries. Carlyle pretty much encapsulates US investor capitalism and, like many others, lost out heavily in subprime-related bets in 2008.

In some ways, we have come full-circle – the new super-elite of US capitalism, the celebrity CEOs of Microsoft or IBM, or the lesser-known private equity partners, have wealth and power rivalling (perhaps surpassing) those of the robber barons of the Gilded Age. This new class also developed powerful belief systems of its own which have spread throughout much of the world; ideas about the so-called 'best practice' of lean, flexible, ruthless capitalism predicated on endless corporate change and restructuring.

Having said this, successful US companies do not always behave according to this new cultural script. Even within authors as mainstream as Collins (2001) and Peters and Waterman (1982), there is a critique of US business practice, and it is not at all clear what 'the US business model' actually is. There can be enormous variety in the structure, culture and capacities of US firms. A very detailed argument about this is provided by Jacoby (2005), who notes real diversity between his five case study companies, from a single-minded focus on financialization and shareholder value, to a product-led, insider-governed, traditionalist model as espoused by Collins (see Osterman et al. [2001], for a similar discussion of the diversity of corporate forms within America). Almond and Ferner (2006) also note significant variation in the makeup of US multinational corporations, and differences in how they conduct their overseas operations. We need to get away from our obsessions with country stereotypes (Coffey 2006). Although the overall structure of US business has clearly changed from one of stability and paternalism to one of ceaseless change, there still remains considerable within-country diversity in corporate models.

Questioning the future of the US model

Indeed the problem of within-country differences in capitalism is especially acute when it comes to the USA, which is a highly complex and diverse nation, embracing a wide range of economic and political forms. US firms draw from a range of different organizational influences (Jacoby 2005). Some retain long-term employment, engage with trade unions and have powerful systems of employee representation. Osterman (2008) also shows that some of the New Deal architecture remains in place in large firms, and that middle managers in his case study companies still have career ladders to climb, and remain deeply committed to their employers. Quite different pictures are available, such as Barley and Kunda's study of Silicon Valley (2004), where a radically flexible and short-term employment paradigm exists.

This diversity is also reflected in the USA's governing institutions. The USA operates a complex, plural system of government. There are 50 states, each with their own delegated powers and historical trajectories, and a powerful federal government. Conflict between state and federal branches of government is common in US politics. The Republican Party has often stood for a strengthening of 'states' rights' and a diminution of federal influence, especially under Reagan and Nixon. For the Democrats, in general, the federal system has usually been strengthened, such as the New Deal under FDR or Johnson's Great Society programme. The lawmaking powers of the 50 states mean that there is a possibility of 'a race to the bottom' whereby states compete for the attraction of businesses and jobs by offering the loosest possible regulation in their territories. Over 60% of the *Fortune 500* is incorporated in the tiny state of Delaware for this reason[14] (Smith and Walter 2006: 52).

[14] Figures from the state of Delaware official website: http://www.corp.delaware.gov/aboutagency.shtml.

While the US system is at the forefront of global change, the subprime crisis has generated tremendous criticisms of the American model. Many have suggested it has become 'tarnished' (Whitley 2009). The US car industry, so often an icon of US success, now signifies its decline and crisis. GM's was one of the most dramatic stories of corporate breakdown in decades. It emerged from Chapter 11 bankruptcy protection in 2009 a much smaller company, humbled by its failure and bailout. There were even suggestions that GM might be forced to move out of its iconic Renaissance Center headquarters in downtown Detroit. That once-proud city has become a picture book for industrial decline and poverty. Images of the Renaissance Center rising into the sky above rows of boarded-up houses seemed incongruous. Down on street level, welfare checks, drugs and violence became the only economy in town, a tragic story repeated across many US cities (see Simon and Burns' [2009] epic piece of reportage *The Corner*). Twenty years on, Michel Albert's critique of the US model remains apt:

> The land of opportunity, birthplace of Mickey Mouse and brave new world of space shuttles, Star Wars and leveraged buyouts is not the Eldorado some still imagine it to be.
>
> ...
>
> Polarization in America is by now a widespread, generalized phenomenon, thanks largely to the ultra-liberal policies of the Reagan administration. And it is not only the polarization of rich and poor, but of whole institutions: prestigious universities on the one hand, a public education system in tatters on the other; gleaming, modern hospitals and clinics in stark contrast to a bloated, obsolete medical infrastructure. (1993: 37–38, 44)

Income inequality is a desperately serious problem in the USA. So poor are some of its citizens that 'microfinance' techniques – usually employed in developing nations such as Bangladesh – have cropped up in US inner cities. Grameen Bank, the world's foremost 'peer-lending' bank, founded by Nobel Prize winner Mohammed Yunus in Bangladesh, has operations in America.[15] Such is the lack of prospects for 'the unbanked' in the USA (an estimated 28 million have no bank account[16]) that poverty-stricken communities cannot survive on welfare checks and food stamps alone, and become dominated by an informal, untaxed, criminal economy, especially the trade in hard

[15] http://www.grameenamerica.com, Yunus was awarded the Presidential Medal of Freedom by Obama in 2009.

[16] http://www.grameenamerica.com/About-Us/Grameen-America.html.

drugs. A study of drug users conducted in Baltimore, Maryland[17] found that 96% of the sample of 1,288 users were African American, 84% were homeless in the prior six months and only 23% held legal forms of employment (Sherman and Latkin 2002: 270). The authors note that the destruction of well-paying, unionized industrial jobs has hit African American men especially hard (2002: 267; see also Simon and Burns 2009: 67–68).

Exhibit 3.4 Poverty and deprivation in urban USA

Although the world's pre-eminent economic power, the USA has always grappled with severe problems of poverty and lack of opportunity. Even in Chicago, one of the world's major financial centres and the home of global industry and services multinationals such as Motorola and Manpower, sections of the city are blighted by poverty and social deprivation, and the infrastrcuture physically collapsing. In *Body & Soul: Notebooks of an Apprentice Boxer*, Loic Wacquant explores the subculture of a boxing gym in a rundown neighbourhood of Woodlawn; a place seemingly cut away from mainstream America, and where 'pandemic unemployment dooms half the men to idleness' (Wacquant 2004: 23).

'A few empirical indicators give a measure of the socioeconomic hardship and vulnerability visited upon the residents of Woodlawn. According to the 1980 census, a third of families lived below the official federal poverty line and the average annual household income of $10,500 amounted to barely half the citywide figure. The percentage of households recorded as female-headed had reached 60 percent (compared to 34 percent ten years earlier), the official unemployment rate was 20 percent (twice the city average after tripling over a decade), and fewer than one household in eight owned its home. Only 34 percent of adult women and 44 percent of adult men held a job; 61 percent of households had to rely in part or whole on support from public aid. [...] The neighbourhood no longer has a single high school or movie theater, library, or job training and placement facility. Despite the close proximity of one of the world's most reputed centers of medical innovation, the University of Chicago Hospital, infant mortality in Woodlawn is estimated at about 3 percent and *rising*, a figure almost three times the national average and exceeding that of many Third World countries.'

(Wacquant 2004: 19). By permission of Oxford University Press, USA.

Recent Gini coefficients demonstrate that the USA is one of the world's most unequal societies, and the divisions are getting starker. According to *Forbes* magazine, Gini in the USA in 2003 stood at 40.8, whereas in

[17] This city is the setting for the massively influential television drama *The Wire*, which graphically depicts the ongoing tragedy of the drugs economy in the city, the collapse of well-paying union jobs, and the general crisis in public administration.

France it was 32.7 and in Japan just 24.9.[18] With a relatively weak social safety net, corporate elites themselves attempt to offer some solutions, such as the Bill and Melinda Gates Foundation - much like Rockefeller's donations generations before (Chernow 2004: 320).

It is difficult to get away from the idea that the US system is built to champion individual rather than collective achievement. The same piece in *Forbes* went on to argue that inequality is a price worth paying if the system is liberal enough to allow the growth of so many self-made billionaires in the USA, following in the footsteps of Ford or Gates. It showed that the USA has 222 billionaires, by far the largest number in the world (the next biggest were Germany with 43, and Japan with 19).[19] Perhaps this is one of the reasons US business ideas are so influential, in that it plugs into a dream that is shared outside US borders - the dream of self-made success. This is one of the reasons why the nation has always attracted immigration in such massive numbers. It might be why many people around the world have a fondness for the USA despite its social problems and its all-too-frequent foreign policy interventions. The idea of America - 'the land of the free', a liberal democracy where anyone can become wealthy and can realize his or her dreams is a seductive one, and is a subtext to much of the mainstream US business literature, from *In Search of Excellence* (Peters and Waterman 1982) to Stephen Covey's (2004) *The 7 Habits of Highly Effective People*.

But how often are dreams actually realized? The short-termism and ruthlessness of the US system do seem to generate major economic and social problems. US investor capitalism is restless and chaotic; Hassard et al.'s work (2009: 72–73) describes the endless series of spinoffs, restructurings and new 'visions' where nothing is ever given the chance to work. President Obama famously 'declared war on Wall Street', in 2010, threatening to curb its powers and limit its reckless lending.[20] But will he really be able to reel in the excessive power of the financial markets in the face of a hostile and partisan Congress? Will his healthcare bill actually make a difference for poor Americans or is it too watered-down by special interest groups to be of any use? Will the US economy be forever overshadowed by the excessive debt and fiscal cliffs? One could argue that the US needs an injection of

---

[18] The Gini coefficient is a measure of overall income inequality, with 0 being perfect equality, and 100 (or 1 depending on how it is expressed) being perfect inequality. 'In Praise of Inequality', *Forbes*, 17 March 2003.

[19] 'In Praise of Inequality', *Forbes*, 17 March 2003.

[20] 'Barack Obama Declares War on Wall Street', *The Times*, 22 January 2010.

social democracy and re-regulation – much like the Sherman Act or Glass–Steagal – to make the USA and its firms less ruthless, more stable and more democratic. The Democratic Party needs to rally around a renewed vision of America. But can it manage this? Can it be radical enough? Or is it, too, in the pockets of the corporations and their lobby groups? Sociologists Perrucci and Perrucci argue for a 'Jobs for America' plan, whereby individual citizens can make contributions, matched by Congress and unions, to pay for job-creating infrastructure projects, or additional nurses and teachers (2009: 136–139). Such an idea sounds fanciful. But by introducing rhetorical suggestions such as these they powerfully make the point that perhaps the USA can do better than this? Can a renewed model of America be made more palatable to the rest of the world? Can the richest country on the planet be made more civilized, less unequal, more fit for ordinary people to live in?

Conclusion: the most influential model of all?

An enormous amount has been written on the US economy. The size of the US media, entertainment, education, and business publishing industries, the size of its economy, and its geopolitical reach have all contributed to making it the most influence model of all.

Although the US system has gone through different phases, (such as the Gilded Age, managerial capitalism and investor capitalism), it is probably correct to argue that the American system today is the most liberal of all the rich economies. There is a long tradition of scepticism about the effectiveness and legitimacy of 'big government', in the USA, and markets tend to be allowed wide scope, to such a degree that any talk of industrial policy or long range planning is 'taboo' (DiTomasso and Schweitzer 2013). This is not to say that the USA does not have a strong state. Although taxes are comparatively low by OECD standards, the myriad forms of US government are powerful and complex. Outside of the agriculture[21] and defence sectors, however, in normal times there is little in the way of CME-style government regulation and involvement in business. I say 'in normal times' because the subprime crisis of 2007 onwards has forced the US government to become more much

[21] The Department of Agriculture is the federal government's fifth biggest budget item, totalling US$146 billion in 2011, 'No More Monopoly Money and Don't Ask for the Moon', *Guardian*, 2 February 2010. The USA retains a very large farm sector, employing around 26 million people out of a total rural population of over 50 million according to 2008 Department of Agriculture figures. (The urban workforce is around 154 million out of an urban population of 254 million.) http://www.ers.usda.gov/StateFacts/US.htm.

involved in the day-to-day ownerships and control of the economy, with the US$800 billion fiscal stimulus plan in 2009 and several congressional bailouts of struggling firms.

Little is provided in the way of social protection for employees who lose their jobs and homes. While the two largest items on the US budget are health and human services (US$934 billion) and social security (US$789 billion)[22] the level and coverage of social protection provided by Medicare, Medicaid and social security are weak by European standards. Households in the USA are vulnerable to bankruptcy and mortgage foreclosure. Massive vulnerability and inequality are major drawbacks of the US system. Conversely, the liberal and flexible US model remains well-regarded around the world; the World Economic Forum's 'Global Competitiveness Report' usually places the USA at the very top of the list, its position tending to shuffle around between the Nordic nations for the top three or four places.[23] It is helpful therefore, to think of the USA as a high-risk economy; citizens have few backstops against poverty and failure, but arguably have more opportunities for wealth-creation in a liberal and flexible market with relatively limited taxation and few forms of government intervention. Despite widespread poverty (Newman 2000; Perrucci and Perrucci 2009), the USA remains comfortably the largest economy in the world, and has occupied this number one spot since the end of the Second World War.

The high-end of the US economy is dominated by service, 'knowledge' and financial sectors. Consulting, banking and insurance, advertising, publishing and IT provided the most obvious career choices for US graduates. Several US firms have also powerful positions in the hardware sector also, such as Intel and AMD in microprocessors. Products such as Apple's iPod and iPhone have been phenomenal recent successes in sectors where US producers have historically lost ground to Japanese and Korean manufacturers. (Of course, the designers and executives of the firm will mostly reside in the US, but the actual manufacturing of these goods takes place in cheaper Asian regions such as China and Vietnam.) West-coast IT firms such as Microsoft, Apple and Oracle in many ways exemplify the high-end of the US economy, as does the world of high finance (such as JP Morgan or Citibank). The US has dozens of great universities. The New Economy demonstrated the extraordinary dynamism but also the 'irrational exuberance' of US financial markets and the investment community as good money was thrown into bad investments. Nevertheless, the US remains at the forefront of

[22] 'No More Monopoly Money and Don't Ask for the Moon', *Guardian*, 2 February 2010.

[23] http://www.weforum.org/documents/GCR09/index.html.

the internet economy even if its physical infrastructure for broadband cabling far from ideal. (According to OECD figures, Japan and South Korea are way out in front as regards average broadband speeds available, with US lagging behind in 19th place in the world.[24])

However, outside of these service and IT sectors, the US economy faces uncertainty. Much of the job-creation in the last two decades in the USA has been at the low end of the labour market, such as cleaning, food preparation and security. Its recent record in generating manufacturing jobs is poor, and its industrial, transport and digital infrastructure are relatively weak. Its levels of environmental protection and uptake of green technology are also poor. According to a survey undertaken by the American Society of Civil Engineers in 2005 and reported by Perrucci and Perrucci (2009: 134–135), the USA scores a D+ for aviation infrastructure, C for bridges, D for energy, D+ for transit and D for schools. These are all areas that require sustained capital investment if they are to be maintained and upgraded, and the stock market obsession of US firms tends to turn attention away from these sectors.

Growing levels of inequality in US society are increasingly obvious and increasingly problematic. America represents a ruthless, restless form of capitalism, taking no prisoners and making few apologies. There is huge potential for successful business to generate massive profits and for their senior personnel and private investors to be very handsomely rewarded. These are the 'winners' in the US economic game. Sadly, the weak levels of social and labour protection, and the absence of a full public healthcare system,[25] also mean that the US system generates many millions of losers.

Further reading

There are numerous, massive literatures on all aspects of the US economic and political scene. This makes the job of picking out some really outstanding books quite difficult.

[24] Figures from OECD Broadband portal, www.oecd.org/sti/ict/broadband.

[25] The mostly private US healthcare system was rated 37th in the world (WHO 2000: 155). Currently an estimated 50 million Americans have no health insurance. 'Number of People Without Health Insurance Climbs', *CNN Money*, 13 September 2011. Around 90 million are officially in poverty or 'near poverty' (Perrucci and Perrucci 2009: 113–116).

Jacoby, S.M., (2005) *The Embedded Corporation: Corporate Governance and Employment Relations in Japan and the United States*, Princeton, NJ: Princeton University Press.

It is probably helpful to select a book that combines overall 'big picture' narrative of the US system with close-up details of employment, work and organization. A great recent book that takes this approach is Sanford Jacoby's (2005) *The Embedded Corporation*. This is a superbly detailed account of the corporate governance and employment systems of large US and Japanese firms. Jacoby demonstrates considerable diversity within the US cases, and does so in an admirably clear way, free of some of the theoretical and conceptual baggage which dogs so much of the VoC literature. This is highly recommended for readers who want a detailed and convincing account of the organizational philosophies and the anthropological 'feel' of contemporary Japanese and US companies.

Chandler, A.D., (1977a) *The Visible Hand: The Managerial Revolution in American Business*, Cambridge, MA: Harvard University Press.

This is the classic exposition of the era of managerial capitalism, which contains a mass of historical detail on the development of large US firms such as GM, DuPont and Sears Roebuck. All of the main issues are covered, such as the division of ownership from control, the rise of anti-trust legislation, and the emergence of vertical integration and economies of scale. This is a very major work, running to 608 pages!

McCraw, T., ed. (1997a) *Creating Modern Capitalism: How Entrepreneurs, Companies, and Countries Triumphed in Three Industrial Revolutions*, Cambridge, MA: Harvard University Press.

If Chandler is too off-putting, then Thomas McCraw's textbook is a superb place to go for more concise coverage of the development of large-scale capitalist firms. It is especially strong on the personalities involved, discussing the 'rugged individualism' of vital characters such as Ford, Sloan and the Watsons at IBM. It also has the added bonus of in-depth discussions of Japanese, British and German capitalism. It is a goldmine of detailed information.

(Continued)

(Continued)

Osterman, P., Kochan, T.A., Locke, R.M., and Piore, M.J., (2001) *Working in America: A Blueprint for a New Labour Market*, Cambridge, MA: MIT Press.

This book provides an excellent introduction to several important debates around the creation and destruction of jobs in America. It demonstrates that there is a wide variety of organizational forms in US corporations, from 'high-performance work systems' to 'low-road' anti-union firms. Useful information is provided on important US firms young and old, such as Kodak, Lucent Technologies, Cisco Systems and Southwest Airlines. The book also contains strong coverage of legacy of the New Deal, and the diverse ways in which US companies have moved away from it.

Khurana, R., (2004) *Searching for a Corporate Savior: The Irrational Quest for Charismatic CEOs*, Princeton, NJ: Princeton University Press.

In this highly readable and thought-provoking work, Khurana discusses the processes by which new CEOs are attracted and appointed to large US firms. He argues that this process is dominated by Wall Street's expectations, which distort and pervert decision-making processes and the labour market for executive talent. The book is, therefore, a powerful critique of investor capitalism. What is most interesting is that Khurana works at a highly mainstream and prestigious US business school (Harvard) and provides important forms of criticism from within the system.

FOUR The United Kingdom: A Problematic Triumph of Finance Over Industry

Chapter objectives

- To examine how the UK became one of the world's first industrialized nations, a primacy that ushered in a long period of economic superiority based on advanced engineering technology and the factory system
- To provide brief coverage of the imperial history of the UK, explaining the role it played in the establishment of the City of London as one of the world's foremost financial centres
- To describe how the end of the Second World War ushered in the long-run decline of Britain's international status, but also led to the development of a powerful and enduring welfare state in the UK, and a shift towards French-style state-led national economic policy
- To evaluate how and why the British form of state-managed capitalism failed in the 1980s, and to describe the highly liberalized and financialized economy that emerged amid its ruins
- Finally to discuss the economic and moral strengths and weaknesses of the British model; an economy that is highly open and flexible, but arguably 'unbalanced' given the dominance of services and the fragility of industry

Introduction

In the VoC and political economy literatures the UK is widely regarded as the major economy most similar to that of the USA. On many levels this is true. The UK has been at the forefront of world trends in globalization and liberalization for the last three decades. The financial heart of the City of London (often known as 'The City' or 'The Square Mile') is one of the world's most powerful financial centres, a position it has held for generations, inherited from the era when the British Empire dominated large swathes of world territory. In recent years the UK state has steadily retreated from day-to-day management of the economy. Neoliberalism has been a prominent feature of economic policy in the UK (as befits an LME), much more so than the CME approach of many of its European competitors such as France, Germany or the countries of Nordic Europe.

Conversely, it is vital to note that the UK is different from the USA in many fundamental ways. Alongside its highly liberal and financialized LME-type economy, the UK also possess a substantial welfare state, including the National Health Service (NHS), which at the time of writing (2013) employs around 1.3 million staff. The NHS's origins lie in the welfare state set up by the newly elected Labour government at the end of the Second World War (of which more below). It was designed to provide care 'free at the point of use' to anyone who requires it regardless of their ability to pay. Despite regular cutbacks, reforms, crises and bad press, the NHS remains a much-loved institution that performs vital work for patients every day. It is difficult to imagine such a free national system existing in the USA; attempts in 2009 by President Barack Obama to introduce a fairly minimal state-run health insurance system were met with hostility by many citizens in ways that most Western Europeans found unfathomable. It is important to bear in mind that the British and American models of capitalism, while usually grouped together as Anglo-Saxon or liberal capitalism, possess significant differences.

This chapter will explore the economy of Britain, noting its powerful industrial and imperial legacies. It will show that the UK system has gone through dramatic change, closely following the US story of the shift from managerial to investor capitalism, probably in a faster and deeper way than any of the other major nations. It will also note that, like America, there has been a strong feeling in the UK for decades that its once-proud industrial sector is in terminal decline, and that, amid great wealth at the top of UK society, there are deplorable problems with poverty, crime and deprivation (Davies 1998; Wilkinson and Pickett 2009). The UK – like the USA – also has a poor recent record when it comes to the creation of good quality, high-paying jobs (McGovern et al. 2004). The UK's large public sector seems also to be on the threshold of a major running-down, raising questions as to the sustainability of the entire UK business model.

The chapter begins with a brief historical overview of the rise of the UK as a major industrial and imperial power, discussing the radically new working environment ushered in by the age of the modern factory system. It will note several important developments, including the early rejection of economic protectionism and early embrace of international 'free' trade and investment. It will go on to explore the awkward and contested rise of 'organized capitalism' (Lash and Urry 1987) after the Second World War, as a kind of state-led managerial capitalism emerged, a system that was arguably closer to the French rather than the US model. This included a strong welfare state, powerful trade unions, extensive government regulation and a policy of state-owned 'national champions' in industry (such as British Steel and British Leyland Automobile Company). Much of this system collapsed in the 1980s, to be replaced by a new era of US-style investor capitalism, financialization and globalization. These changes have been extremely challenging for the nation and most of its population. The conclusion will discuss the economic and moral issues associated with the contemporary British model. How well is it facing up to the economic challenges of the 21st century? Can the UK be considered a 'good society?' Given economic crashes, government bailouts of the banks, public services cutbacks, substantial income inequality and widespread poverty and unemployment, what prospects (if any) exist for the growth of a more moral capitalism in the UK?

Empire, riches and poverty: the troubled history of a great power

Great Britain[1] was the first Western nation to industrialize on a massive, society-transforming scale (McCraw 1997b: 49). The changes that took place to political, economic and social life in Great Britain around the years 1760–1830 (known as the First Industrial Revolution) were radical, and set the tone for the establishment of modern, developed economies. This era saw the harnessing of water, steam and then coal in the generation of energy which enabled massive increases in the power and scale of industrial machinery. Crucially, it also led to the establishment of the

[1] In 1707, the Kingdoms of England (which already included Wales from 1535) and of Scotland were unified as the Kingdom of Great Britain (Great Britain). In 1801, the Kingdoms of Great Britain and of Ireland unified to form the United Kingdom of Great Britain and Ireland (the UK).

factory system as we know it today. Work organizations changed fundamentally, from small-scale operations employing two or three skilled workers in or near the home, to giant factories employing hundreds or even thousands of unskilled and low-skilled workers and machines.

Great Britain benefitted enormously from its long-standing status as an oceangoing nation (McCraw 1997b: 49), which opened the country to a wide array of trading partners, and also allowed it to project considerable military and colonial force. An abundance of cheap coal was also beneficial (Allen 2011: 14). British science and technology played major roles in the development of hundreds of industrial innovations (Mokyr 2009). An important example is the Watt steam engine developed in the mid-18th century, a hugely successful system that was widely used to power machinery in the newly established factories. As trade in industrially produced goods opened up around the country, British entrepreneurs and engineers developed new forms of transportation such as steam railways. What appears to be the first ever rail journey was taken in 1804, on Robert Trevithick's steam engine at the Pen-y-darren iron works near Merthyr Tydfil, south Wales. Probably the most famous British engineer was Isambard Kingdom Brunel (1806–1859), who designed the Great Western Railway, the Clifton Suspension Bridge and the SS *Great Britain*, the world's first propeller-driven oceangoing iron ship - at its time (1843) the largest ship ever built.

Cotton spinning technologies were progressively improved by refinements and innovations throughout the 18th century (Mokyr 2009: 128–129). Later industrial innovations included the Bessemer converter (1855), which radically simplified the process of steel manufacturing. Powerful and increasingly reliable textile manufacturing machines (such as those built by Platts of Oldham) were sold to firms in industrializing countries, such as Japan, or colonies, such as India (Mathias 1969: 414). In 1851, the Great Exhibition was held in London's Hyde Park, showcasing British (and foreign) industrial and scientific achievements. This event has worldwide historical significance as a crowning moment of Victorian Britain, attracting 6 million visitors from around the world (Botticelli 1997: 51). The centrepiece was the building in which the exhibition was itself housed, Joseph Paxton's magnificent The Crystal Palace. This radical and ambitious building (constructed largely from plate-glass, a recent invention, and iron) was widely referenced in literature of the era and beyond, for example by Russian intelligentsia (Berman 1982: 220). After the First Industrial Revolution, Great Britain's economic and technological might was the envy of the world. In 1870, one-half of the world's coal, 40% of the its steel, more than one-half of the world's pig iron, and almost half of its cotton cloth were produced in Britain. Great Britain produced well over one-third of the world's manufactured goods (Turner 1971: 3).

Industrialization was not only about technological and organizational achievements. It also meant urbanization, the rise of slums and the clustering of chronic poverty. Those attracted to work in the rapidly developing industrial centres, such as London, Glasgow, Manchester and Sheffield, often had no option but to live in appallingly cramped and unsanitary conditions (Mokyr 2009: 380–385). Frederick Engels famously wrote about this in *The Condition of the Working Class in England* (1887/1993) and, as Karl Marx lived in England from 1849 until his death in 1883, the economic might and social misery of the new British industrial system served as primary data for *The Communist Manifesto* and Volume One of *Capital*.[2] One passage of *Capital* describes young female textile workers that bears a striking resemblance to the dreadful work conditions of many textile or electronics workers in contemporary China, Indonesia or Vietnam (see Klein 2000: 195–229; also this volume, Chapter 10):

> These girls work, on average, 16½ hours without a break ..., and the flow of their failing 'labour-power' is maintained by occasional supplies of sherry, port or coffee. ... Mary Anne Walkley had worked uninterruptedly for 26½ hours, with sixty other girls, thirty in each room. The rooms measured only 1/3 of the necessary quantity of air, measured in cubic feet. At night the girls slept in pairs in the stifling holes into which a bedroom was divided by wooden partitions. ... Mary Anne Walkley fell ill on the Friday and died on Sunday. ... The doctor, a Mr Keys, called too late to the girl's deathbed, made his deposition to the coroner's jury in plain language: 'Mary Anne Walkley died from long hours of work in an overcrowded work-room, and a too small and badly ventilated bedroom.' (Marx 1867/1976: 364–365)

Great Britain had only the most limited and patchy forms of social support for those living in such poverty. What existed were the Poor Laws. Codified in the early 16th century, they lasted in modified form until Lloyd George's introduction of national insurance in 1911 and the establishment of much more extensive modern welfare state after the Second World War. By the 1830s, once the industrial revolution had more fully transformed the socio-economic landscape, the problem of urban poverty was addressed by new legislation. The New Poor Law 1834 centralized the poor relief system, drawing a notorious distinction between 'the deserving' and 'the undeserving' poor, and instituting the infamous workhouses, in which workhouse residents lived and laboured in brutal conditions.

Attitudes towards appalling poverty slowly changed. The more enlightened employers and sections of government applied pressure to

[2] Marx and Engels expected proletarian revolutions to take place in the most advanced industrial nations, such as Great Britain and Germany. As it turned out, the comparatively backward Russian Empire was the home of the first major revolution that most closely resembled Marxist theory (see Chapter 8).

reduce working hours in factories and mines (especially as regards child labour), with Factory Acts of the 19th century providing important, but far from comprehensive, measures to restrict the worst excesses (Mathias 1969: 202–203).[3] In common with other nations' periods of unregulated or 'robber-baron' capitalism, Great Britain established various charitable and philanthropic institutions, such as the 19th-century ragged schools, set up by philanthropists for the provision of education for children of the truly disadvantaged. Cheap, good quality housing was provided by, among others, George Peabody, a London-based American entrepreneur and financier (Chernow 2010: 14). Many Peabody Estates are still in use across London today, housing almost 50,000 tenants and owners.[4] Over time, more effective state provision of welfare started to emerge, such as National Insurance, which began in 1911 (Chang 2003: 103–106), but it lagged some way behind the most advanced developments elsewhere, such as in Germany, for example (see Chapter 6). The British economy historically and today reflects trends of great wealth and economic triumphs alongside severe poverty and social exclusion.

It is also important to bear in mind that Britain's robber-baron phase enjoyed considerable international reach from a very early age. A very significant part of British economic power was derived from its huge imperial might, enforced through its large and technologically advanced Royal Navy (Chang 2003: 21; see also Gamble 1994a: xiii). Elizabeth I (1558–1603) sent trade missions far and wide. The British East India Company has famously been described as the world's first multinational corporation (Robins 2006), given Crown backing to establish forcefully monopolistic trade relations with India. The Company played an instrumental role in breaking the long-standing situation in which the East (especially India and China) was the dominant trading partner in relation to the West (Robins 2006: 7). This early international influence in trade and projection of state power also served to develop the City of London into what it is today. While morally bankrupt, this imperial monopoly capitalism provided a strong base for the rapid accretion of British wealth.

Given this powerful international presence, the UK, more than any other developing nation, had good reasons to insist on the establishment of 'free' trade. British elites actually benefited from free trade; its economy was already heavily internationalized by then and was able to play key roles in international commerce (Reich 1991: 28). As an early industrializer, the UK had little need to protect its infant industries, and import tariffs were mostly abolished in 1846 (Botticelli 1997: 67). In contrast to almost every other nation that has industrialized, the role of the British

[3] It was not until 1878 that these laws and the system of official inspection fully applied to all workshop and factory trades (Mathias 1969: 204).

[4] http://www.peabody.org.uk/about-us/history.aspx.

state as a coordinator and 'pusher from above' of industrialization was remarkably limited (Mathias 1969: 4). The City of London was opposed to tariffs because British finance was so 'heavily concentrated in foreign investments' (Botticelli 1997: 67–68). In 1899, the UK was the world's number two exporter of manufactured goods after the USA, and by the beginning of the 20th century the nation imported huge quantities of food and raw materials. The UK also did well out of uneven trade agreements enforced on other nations, such as the Navigation Acts of the 17th century (Chang 2003: 21), which stipulated that trade to Britain had to take place on British-built ships, and the Corn Laws of the 19th century that protected British grain producers from cheaper imports.[5]

The UK's rapid economic growth can be attributed to a fortunate combination of powerful overseas and domestic drivers. Colonial power allowed the early capture of important international markets and provided extremely cheap access to raw materials and labour (such as the introduction of rubber plantations into Malaya in the late 19th century), while dramatic industrial innovations at home utilized an ever-wider segment of domestic labour power, especially women and girls who were rapidly drawn into factory work. Textile mills existed across many northern and central English towns. Mills in the Midlands were typically water-driven, such as Richard Arkwright's Cromford and Masson Mills outside the Derbyshire town of Matlock, built in 1771 and 1783, respectively. Most of Arkwright's mills ran two 12-hour shifts, representing mass production about 150 years before Ford.

Another important innovator of the factory system was Josiah Wedgewood (1730–1795). His pottery works in Stoke-on-Trent produced extremely high-quality and innovative pieces of ceramics that were sold all over the world, including specialist orders for Catherine the Great of Russia, and US President Theodore Roosevelt. His Etruria factory, completed in 1772 and situated next to the new Trent and Mersey canal (the building of which Wedgewood himself partially financed) was one of the most modern plants in the world. It featured what was possibly the world's first ever 'clocking-in' system using individual tickets, a precursor of the 'punch-clock' – the very symbol of industrial working time. Etruria was also a site of some of the earliest examples of major industrial unrest. Workers staged demonstrations about what they perceived to be unjust treatment by management, which were said to have greatly bemused and upset Wedgewood who regarded himself as an enlightened employer (Koehn 1997: 47).

[5] Interestingly, tariffs began to return in the late 1800s (Chang 2003: 21) and were widely restored in 1931 at the onset of the Great Depression. The received wisdom today is that tariffs were largely responsible for prolonging the depression, but it is important to note that the UK's reputation as a free-trade champion is not fully supported by historical evidence.

The UK has long been at the forefront of economic globalization. Just as Wedgewood's ceramics adorned the houses of the world's rich, British textile mills were supplied with cotton from southern US slave plantations (Chandler 1977: 20). Regions controlled by the British Empire (such as Kenya, India, Malaysia and Hong Kong) conferred significant trade benefits, often based on brutal exploitation and suppression of colonial unrest.[6] The empire opened up the markets of the East into a long-term relationship with London banking, which survives today. For example the name of the London-based banking giant HSBC (established 1865) stands for Hong Kong & Shanghai Banking Corporation. In the first half of 2011, this London-based bank made profits of US$6.7 billion from Hong Kong and the Asia-Pacific, compared to US$2.1 billion from Europe.[7]

The UK is today the world leader in international marine and aviation insurance, with 19% and 31% of international markets, respectively (Golding 2003: 11). It is also dominant in foreign exchange dealing (31% of world markets), over-the-counter derivatives trading (36%) and the secondary market in international bonds (70%, all figures from Golding [2003: 11]). Lloyds of London is unique in the world as by far the largest market for high- and low-risk insurance and re-insurance (Coggan 2002: 120–124). Now housed in a remarkable postmodern building at 1 Lime Street, London, it was originally a coffee house opened by a certain Edward Lloyd in 1687, which provided a quiet place for rich gentleman to conduct their business (Coggan 2002: 120). In later times, 'the City Gent' with suit, umbrella, briefcase and bowler hat was an enduring image of London's historically massive financial power and its very tight, elitist socio-economic networks. Although internationally focused, the City was a closed and self-serving environment until it was radically reformed in the 1980s (see below, and Augar 2000). Scotland also has a large and early developed financial services sector. Edinburgh is the birthplace of many of Britain's insurance firms and investment trusts. Many of the entrepreneurs of the First Industrial Revolution had surplus funds to invest and so clubbed together with their professional advisers (lawyers, accountants), to pool their investments into larger 'mutual' funds (Coggan 2002: 74). British private capital was, from an early stage, massively invested overseas (Davis and Huttenbuck 1986: 46), to a far greater extent than any of the other industrialization nations, arguably contributing to Britain's comparatively limited investment in its own domestic economy. See Table 4.1 opposite.

[6] 'Mau Mau Torture Ruling May Open Way for Thousands of Claims Against Government', *Guardian*, 6 October 2012.

[7] Figures from HSBC's interim report 2011, as quoted in 'HSBC Chief Warns Banking Reforms Will Put More Jobs at Risk', *Guardian*, 2 August 2011.

Table 4.1 Total Investment of Private Capital (as a % of GDP)

	UK	Germany	USA	Japan
1950–59	14.6	20.7	17.4	23.3
1980–87	16.9	20.5	17.9	29.0

Source: adapted from Crafts and Woodward (1991: 10). By permission of Oxford University Press.

According to Turner (1971: 6), in the period 1870–1913 British investments overseas totalled around £4 billion, approximating to 40% of all British investment, whereas in Germany for the years 1901–5 and 1911–13, only 5.7% of total German investment went to overseas destinations. Between 1865–1914 just under 32% of all Britain's private capital was invested into the UK itself, whereas over 22% of it went to North America, and over 13% to South America and the Caribbean (Davis and Huttenbuck 1986: 46). The historical upshot of this is that Britain today 'is a country with an exceptionally large and well-developed "financial tail" that frequently wags an underweight "industrial dog". ... in no other nation is the financial centre so powerful relative to the rest of the economy' (Golding 2003: xvii). Many have argued that the historically and currently very high level of internationalization of British finance meant that UK bank support for its own industry is lacking, especially when compared to the close industry-bank relationships in Germany and Japan. Although British industry has suffered terribly since the second half of the 20th century, the financial and international arms of the UK remain comparatively strong. The financial wealth of the UK is still in part derived from its early development and early internationalization (which was heavily dependent on its colonial history). Great Britain was a dominant economic force during the age of the First Industrial Revolution, but it seemed unable to translate this success into continuing dominance during the Second Industrial Revolution, especially when it came to the need for mass production of complex manufactured products. Its foreign policy position also dramatically declined during and after the Second World War.

The UK's powerful overseas influence had certain important drawbacks which apply both during the Second Industrial Revolution and today. Chandler (1990) and Elbaum and Lazonick (1984) argue that the UK never fully developed the modern corporate form and Fordist mass production. Botticelli (1997: 73) notes that the leading British companies were never as large as their US counterparts, noting that US Steel employed 'over five times as many workers as did Britain's largest firm, Fine Cotton Spinners and Doublers', which employed approximately 30,000 at the time.

While the 1851 Great Exhibition is much trumpeted in British history, other advanced nations had caught up and overtaken the UK a little more than 25 years later. According to Barnett, such was the level of sophistication of the technology on show at the Paris Exhibition of 1878 the UK's Royal Commission on Technical Instruction reported that Britain had been 'overtaken in terms of industrial science and the quality of industrial management and workpeople' (1987: 675). Barnett argues that the UK was unable to translate its huge spurt in innovation and development into lasting, sustainable growth over many decades. This represents a great example of 'the penalties of going first' – an idea that harks back to Gerschenkron and path-dependency theory (see Chapter 2). The UK's early success in the First Industrial Revolution was largely based on individual and local innovators with little or no formal education or training. Their ventures were backed by family wealth, rather than by the state or state-influenced bank lending. This has had the perverse effect of locking in the 'myth of the practical man' (Barnett 1987: 671), or the 'cult of the amateur' (Wilson 1995: 116–7) – the idea that industrial and management developments tend to spring from the hard graft and inspiration of practical and able persons, and that there is no real need for widespread training programmes or state intervention. Barnett quotes from the Royal Commission on Secondary Education of 1895, which found that state education:

> has not been either continuous or coherent; i.e. it does not represent a series of logical or even connected sequences. Each one of the agencies was called into being, not merely independently of the others, but with little or no regard to their existence. Each has remained in its working isolated and unconnected with the rest. (1987: 675)

This absence of strategic planning and coordination in the education, training and research sectors still sounds extraordinarily relevant to the problems of UK training and education today (Wilson 1992: 1–17).

A state-led version of the Fordist mass-production model did eventually arrive in the UK 'under the banners of collectivism, planning and welfare' (Gamble 1994a: 29), but this was after the war and probably too late to provide an established basis for ongoing industrial competitiveness. Perversely, once new export-driven competitors re-emerged in the form of Japan and Germany, UK industry appears to have been put at a disadvantage by its early industrialization and early internationalization, a disadvantage that it never fully recovered from. Compared to the French system of state-administered banking, the UK financial system was never strongly enough coordinated to deliver the kind of centralized Fordist mass corporate structure that the advanced nations were developing. What emerged was a halfway house of underpowered government institutions, such as the Import Duties Advisory Committee, formed in 1932. In the words of Elbaum and Lazonick:

> Lacking the requisite authority to shape industrial development, the committee found itself overseeing a process of industrial quasi-cartelization that ensured profits for weak and strong firms alike ... [leaving] British industry with the worst aspects of both competitive and monopolistic worlds. (1984: 579)

As we shall see in the next section, this 'barely visible hand', was feeble in comparison to the vertically integrated firms in USA (Chandler 1977) or the bureaucratic coordination of the state in Japan (Johnson 1982), and was unable to push UK industry especially far in the race towards integrated mass production. '[T]he Second Industrial Revolution produced only a handful of British firms on anything like the scale typical of companies in the United States, Germany, and later Japan' (Botticelli 1997: 76). UK industry remained comparatively underdeveloped and overspecialized in niche and craft industries. Its unions successfully resisted Taylorization (Botticelli 1997: 82–83; Elbaum and Lazonick 1984). Education levels of managers remained low in comparison to European competitors France and Germany (Lane 1992; Wilson 1992, 1995). As the next section indicates, having dominated world economic affairs since the First Industrial Revolution, the UK faced a very uncertain future after the Second World War.

Labour's welfare state and the establishment of national managerial capitalism

The UK suffered around 500,000 deaths in the Second World War (Sixsmith 2011: 359) amid widespread destruction of domestic industries. It also lost many of its colonies. In keeping with the experience of most of the countries examined in this book, there was widespread acknowledgement that a significant degree of economic coordination would be needed in order to rebuild the nation following the war. What emerged was the British 'post-war settlement', a form of 'organized capitalism' (Lash and Urry 1987) comprising a wide and complex set of formal and informal agreements or bargains struck between various stakeholders in the British political economy. The government would develop Keynesian economic policies designed to provide full employment. Unions would be asked by government to restrain their wage demands in order to curb inflation. Companies and individuals would pay a range of taxes and pensions contributions. An advanced and extensive welfare state would be built to provide a safety net for those who fall out of employment or require care of various kinds. This post-war settlement formed the basis of the so-called 'age of consent' in UK politics, or the post-war 'golden age' of economic growth from 1950 until the crises of the mid-1970s. During this era, Britain's economy developed what could be called a form of 'national managerial capitalism', whereby the country developed some features of the CME model, but never fully became one. Each of the Western European powers (and Japan) developed their own versions of this settlement, as they developed their own versions of organized capitalism or the 'second spirit of capitalism' (Boltanski and Chiapello 2005; Hall 2008; Lash and Urry 1987). Perhaps because of the USA's far more dominant economic position post-war, it never really needed to develop one, although the New Deal from the 1930s was similar in many ways, which laid the basis for America's period of managerial capitalism (see Chapter 3).

The UK's socio-economic system underwent substantial change under national managerial capitalism. In a dramatic electoral turnaround, the Conservative government of Winston Churchill lost the 1945 general election to a massive 11% swing to Labour. The new government under Clement Atlee began building a modern welfare state that still exists (in highly modified form) today. A large segment of the Labour Party was comprised of socialists whose intellectual direction was largely derived from a group known as the Fabian Society. During the war the Fabians drew up plans for a socialist market economy for the UK (not unlike the one developed in postcolonial India (see Chapter 9). For a flavour of this kind of development, see Exhibit 4.1 opposite, taken from their 1943 text *Plan for Britain* (Cole et al 1943).

Although poverty-stricken after the devastation of war, the country committed itself to a plan of recovery, involving a massive public housing building programme, a drive for full employment, a welfare system and the establishment of universal healthcare coverage in the form of the NHS. It is interesting to note the contrast from that era to what is considered possible today. Following the Second World War the UK economy was ruined, yet the government of the time believed that the time was right for the building of a new infrastructure owned and run by the state, similar in many ways to FDR's New Deal following the Wall Street Crash of 1929. Today however, in the aftermath of the 2007–9 subprime mortgage crash, such options are said to no longer exist (McCann 2013a).

Back in the post-war era, state coordination of the economy, centralized welfare provision, and a technocratic industrial policy were regarded as essential for rebuilding the economy. Along with the rapid growth of public employment in the welfare state, industry was widely

Exhibit 4.1 The Fabian Society's vision of a socialist planned economy for 'the key industries' in post-war Britain

'We want a planned economy by the nation for the nation. How are we to accomplish that job? How are we to plan the key industries of the nation after the war? [...] if we are to have a national plan at all, planned by the State for the whole of the nation, there are certain key controls which must be possessed by the nation. Unless they are in the hands of the nation, no national plan can possibly succeed. [...]'

'The work done by the industries of the country during the war has revealed some of such a plan if adopted. The war has shown that there exists among our people the organizing capacity, the technical ability, and the skilled craftsmanship necessary to rebuild industry as a public service.'

'What we have to do is to weld this organising genius, the technical ability, and this craftsmanship into a team that can develop a common will inspired by a common purpose. Free industry from the restrictive control of the financiers. Remove the dead hand of privilege. Sweep away the industrial nepotism that puts the wrong men in charge of operations. Give to all the men engaged in industry the feeling that they are working for the benefit of the whole nation. This will create a social purpose that will generate the social will that will make success certain. Thus we can lay the foundation of a reconstructed industrial organisation that will provide for the new, and better, Britain of to-morrow.'

Griffiths, J., (1943: 54–5, 65)

nationalized in the 1950s; firms were often grouped together into large state-run organizations, such as British Steel, British Rail and later British Leyland (a group of automotive companies). The economy had been on a war footing, and the widespread introduction of Fordist mass production to meet war demands (Botticelli 1997) gave UK planners a base to build on. However, as this section will show, the attempt to build something of a CME in the UK was to fail. Later sections will tell the story of how the LME model re-asserted itself, pushing the UK model closer to that of the USA.

The post-war settlement did lay the foundation for a major growth phase in UK, as in the other European nations, USA and Japan (Eichengreen 2007). Conservatives and Labour roughly agreed on the basics of full employment, Keynesian demand management and a welfare state; hence 'the age of consent'. The Conservatives were re-elected in 1951 under Harold Macmillan. He was more of a believer in free markets than Atlee, but he continued with corporatist policies, a mixed economy and welfare state. He oversaw a particularly rapid growth period in the 1950s, noting in a speech in 1957 that 'most of our people have never had it so good.'

Interestingly, however, many authors also trace the beginnings of the long-term sickness of the UK to around this point. The UK's post-war golden age was considerably less shiny than other major nations. Economic growth rates were moderate relative to other powers, and the profitability of industrial firms particularly poor in relation to European competitors, showing a trend of terminal decline through 1960–78 (Williams et al. 1983: 63). One major problem was the relatively low levels of skills at workplace level. One often thinks of British universities as powerful or 'world class' in contemporary parlance, but many authors, such as Barnett (1987), suggest that academic knowledge was poorly harnessed by the rest of society, especially when compared, for example, with the skills generation demonstrated by Germany. There seems to be a problem with a lack of widespread industrial capacity in Britain, something that seems to have haunted the country for decades.

One of the main reasons was industrial firms' difficulties in gaining access to capital. Williams et al. (1983) describe two main forms of banking lending; the 'going-concern approach', whereby the lender takes account of possible future income streams, and the 'liquidation approach', where the lender considers the borrower's fixed assets as potential securities to be sold off to repay the loan. They write:

> it is clear that German, French and American banks adopt a going-concern approach, while only British banks adopt a liquidation approach ... If Soichiro Honda had turned up with his accounts at a Barclays branch in West Bromwich in the 1950s, the manager would have interpreted the progress of Honda Motor Company as a cautionary tale of over-trading and would have suggested, not a bank loan, but the appointment of a receiver. (Williams et al. 1983: 69–70, 73)

Symptoms of a 'British disease' afflicting manufacturing were emerging rapidaly. These are widely described as 'poor management, overmanning, restrictive practices, low investment and low productivity' (Gamble 1994a: xvii).[8] Trade unions retained powerful control of the shop floor, which managers resented (Elbaum and Lazonick 1984: 582). National Wage Boards set national pay bands for specific jobs, industries and sectors. The Keynesian demand management policy involved the state owning and running large parts of the 'commanding heights' of the economy, with the economy geared at a high rate of demand, making it vulnerable to inflationary pressures, especially since the 1970s (Sentance 1998). The period saw some considerable improvements for working people, and standards of living grew. Economic policies of the Labour Party governments contained significant degrees of wealth redistribution and social protection for those who most needed it. This orientation is similar to what is often found in the

[8] 'Restrictive practices' refers to trade union control of the shop floor.

'social market model' of Western Europe (see Chapters 5 and 6) and in stark comparison to the rather basic forms of protection available in the USA (see Chapter 3).

However, the economic system in the UK seemed to lack mechanisms for holding the different power groups in check, particularly since crisis tendencies appeared after the 1970s oil price rises; demand management policies tended to inflate consumer prices, thereby sending up employees' and unions' wage demands. Employers' associations and unions were often at loggerheads over pay, with industrial action frequent. Unions were rarely consulted about major changes in companies and a low-trust industrial relations climate persisted. For their part trade unions often failed to change and modernize, and would often refuse to cooperate with management on a range of issues. Their confrontational style could be destructive to all parties. Huw Beynon's classic study (1984) of carworkers at the Ford plant in Halewood, Liverpool, vividly illustrates the atrocious morale and deeply ingrained conflict pervasive across British industry. According to one of 'the lads' interviewed:

> Nobody trusts anybody in this place. What they're afraid of is the lads saying 'sod you' and either going home or doing bad jobs. It happens, you know. When there's trouble like this you often get lads going down the lines with pennies or knives, scraping the paint off the cars. (Beynon 1984: 166)

Levels of workplace democracy were low and this low-trust climate meant that unions were often frozen out of company decision making (Cressey et al. 1985; Hutton 1995). Workplace 'Joint Consultative Committees' never had much power and their influence declined further from the 1980s (Marchington et al. 2011: 51). National incomes policy was somewhat ad hoc and inconsistent, nowhere near as detailed or comprehensive as its counterparts in CMEs, such as West Germany or Sweden (see Chapters 6 and 7).

Although the UK's partially centralized and state-led version of managerial capitalism did contribute to significant rebuilding of the wrecked post-war economy, British growth rates were sluggish in comparison to those of France, Germany, Japan and USA (Eichengreen 2007: 19). The overall direction of political and economic policy was unclear, and businesses and investors had little idea of how to plan effectively for changes in policy direction. The UK's post-war trajectory, after some stability in the 'age of consent' of 1950s and 1960s, became hazy and growth rates slowed. The Labour governments of Wilson and then Callaghan did not survive for long, ousted by an 8% swing to the Conservatives of Margaret Thatcher in 1979 (see below).

A useful overview of the period described the regular changeover of governments:

> the trend of relative failure continued inexorably, regardless of the complexion of government. In terms of conventionally measured gross domestic product per head – a crude approximation for standard of living – Germany and France had surpassed [Britain] in the 1960s, Japan in the 1980s and Italy by 1990. (Chandler 1998: 12)

Politically, the climate seemed to shift from unhelpful swings between irrational faith in government (Labour) and irrational faith in 'free' markets (Conservative). It was hard for firms or the civil service to plan for longer-term horizons when the political climate was so volatile. A good example of a victim of this turbulence is the ill-fated National Economic Development Council, or NEDC. Modelled on the French *Commissariat gênérale du Plan* (see Chapter 5) it was introduced in 1962 (Chandler 1998: 12) yet was never imbued with the powers it needed to make a real difference to the UK economic scene. Andrew Shonfield (1965: 88), a supporter of national planning, notes that the British approach to planning was short-term and splintered, with no overall strategy. Essentially, the state was not given the authority to establish a French-style grand plan. British government planning seemed to mirror the disaggregated, individualized, competitive, low-trust, and conflict-ridden model of British industry:

> Coordination was *ad hoc*; the longer-term policies of each department and agency of government were largely left to look after themselves. ... there was no compulsion, for example, on the Coal, Electricity, and Gas Boards to evolve a national fuel policy in unison with one another. They each went their separate ways, unless there was an exceptional assertion of authority by the Minister of Power. (Shonfield 1965: 91)

NEDC was often jokingly referred to as 'Neddy'. It was sidelined throughout the Thatcher years and abolished in 1992.

In a similar development to that in the USA (see Chapter 3), a great many academic, journalistic and political writers heaped criticism onto the failings of the UK economy. Books appeared with titles such as *Why Are The British Bad At Manufacturing?* (Williams et al. 1983), and writings on the UK have largely continued with the tone of pessimism and dismay ever since (Ackroyd and Procter 1998).

This is not to say that somehow the UK has no manufacturing skills or technical expertise. There have always been pockets of advanced engineering that have continued to survive since the UK's industrial heyday. But overall, there seems to be little capacity for the kind of in-depth national-level coordination required to make systems work together. For example, the state-owned British Rail Engineering Ltd designed and built the Advanced Passenger Train in the late 1970s and early 1980s, an ambitious project for a high-speed electric train that can run safely at 155 mph, featuring a tilt mechanism to allow high-speed cornering, and hydrokinetic brakes to allow it to slow in time for signals. This new train was highly rated by drivers and engineers but was let down by an absence of coordination elsewhere in the system; it could not run at the high speeds it was designed for given existing railway infrastructure limitations, and its power-drawing, tilting and braking mechanisms all suffered problems (Williams 1985: 100). Typically, the railway drivers union ASLEF was not involved in its development, and reacted furiously by 'blacking' the train when presented with prototypes with only one driver's seat, regarding this as a unilateral move towards a new management policy of single-crewing of trains! The project had to be abandoned, chalked up as another example of a state-run 'white elephant'. Similarly the UK and French governments collaborated on the design and construction of the Concorde supersonic airliner - a fantastic engineering feat but widely considered an extremely costly enterprise for the manufacturers. Both of these projects seem to be ruined by an absence of coordination between parties involved, and confusion about future economic viability of the whole enterprise. Even today, the UK government, business and public opinion struggle to come to a decision whether or not to build the HS2 (high speed 2) line between London and Birmingham, which would be only the second electrified high-speed train line in the country. Compared with the train systems of CME nations such as France, Korea or Japan, where governments took the decision to radically upgrade its infrastructure, the situation in the UK is somewhat embarrassing - a reversal of its dominance in the railways sector in the 19th century. The UK's post-war policymakers, while attracted to planning, never seemed to develop the capacity or willingness to fully move the country towards a CME-type economy.

Attempts were made, however, by the Labour government elected in 1964 under Harold Wilson, which embarked on a project of nationalization of industry. This was another controversial shift in policy involving conflicts and compromises. An attempt was made to modernize the UK car industry through clubbing automotive firms together into a nationalized British Leyland, again with little success. British Leyland's models were not popular with overseas customers and they increasingly lost out at home to European, US and latterly Japanese competitors (Williams et al. 1983). The electronics and computing firm ICL received large proportions of its custom from government orders, such as contracts for integrated computer systems for the Post Office, Inland Revenue and the Ministry of Defence. ICL was effectively a

French-style national champion, but it received rather limited amounts of genuinely commercial business, especially from overseas. In the words of Gamble '[o]nce again the attempt to break out of the constraints which for so long had governed British economic management had failed, and the economy was left in an extremely weak position' (1994a: 126).

The British economy entered a major period of uncontrolled boom and steep recession following the 1970s oil shock (Donaldson and Farquhar 1988: 123–124). Keynesian demand management helped to run the UK economy at a persistently high level of demand, which kept unemployment low at the cost of high inflation (Sentance 1998: 42–43). A chart of GDP growth for the post-war era up until the mid-1990s (Figure 4.1) shows a dramatically corrugated picture, with three major recessions, including a massive boom–bust cycle in 1973–5.

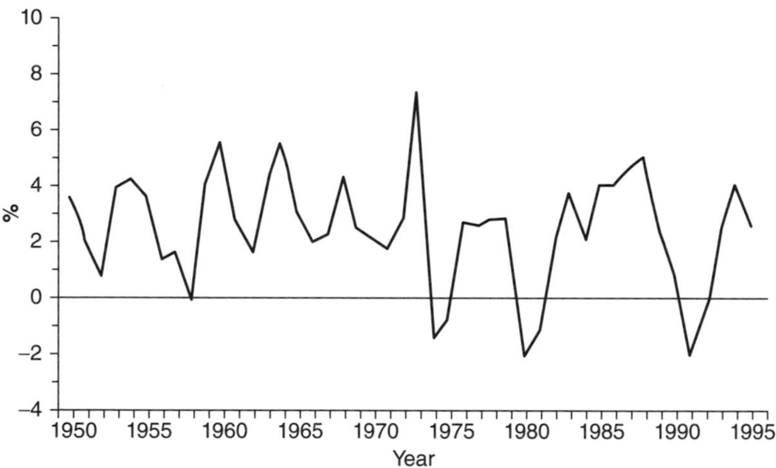

Figure 4.1 Boom-Bust Cycles in UK GDP Growth, 1950–1995

Source: Sentance (1998: 43)

Inflation eventually ran out of control, triggering a currency crisis and an application for an emergency IMF loan in 1976, the first time a major European power had to apply for one. The final crunch-point for the Labour's attempt at a state-managed economy was the so-called 'Winter of Discontent' of 1978–9. The government attempted to freeze public sector pay rises in order to control inflation, but several public sector unions went on strike in response. The crisis seemed to reflect government weakness in the face of union power, and confidence in the government fell. It led to a massive general election defeat of Labour and the election of a Conservative government under Margaret

Thatcher in 1979.[9] Thatcher immediately abandoned the rather rudimentary incomes policy and embraced 'free' markets (Donaldson and Farquhar 1988: 125), including removing currency exchange controls (Coggan 2002: 73).

Mainstream economic analysis tended to claim that Thatcher's approach was necessary and that there was no real alternative to radical neoliberal reforms. According to this view the UK suffered from too few producers, and that commercial investment and development were being 'crowded out' by an overbearing state with excessive levels of public employment and high taxation (Bacon and Eltis 1978). The new Conservative government set about dismantling what was left of the planning apparatus. Economic policy of the Conservative government was strongly influenced by radical neoliberal theories (such as those espoused by Milton Friedman and Friedrich von Hayek (Johnson 1991: 220; Klein 2007; Steger and Roy 2010). Alongside similar changes enacted by Reagan in the USA, the UK experienced its own neoliberal revolution, involving the widespread application of neoliberal monetarist policies. Limiting the power of the state and curtailing the influence of trade unions were two central planks of this radical policy shift. As we shall see in the following sections, Thatcherism became as important to the UK and the rest of the world as Reaganism was to the USA, as a new era of investor capitalism came to the fore.

The 1980s: Thatcherism, neoliberal reform and the collapse of UK industry

As the UK entered the 1980s, its economic outlook was universally described as poor, in decline or in crisis. The opening page of a major economic textbook on the UK edited by Derek Morris contains a rundown of the symptoms of the 'British disease': rates of inflation had been rising since the late 1960s, living standards were growing more slowly since the mid-1970s, balance of payments were in deficit, the value of the pound had fallen calamitously in the 1970s then risen to uncompetitive levels in the 1980s. And, 'most damaging of all, unemployment rose to over 3 million, or almost 1 in 8 of the workforce, over 1 million of whom had been unemployed for at least a year' (Morris 1987: 1).

[9] Andrew Gamble described this crisis 'with its images of closed hospitals, rubbish piling up in the streets and dead bodies rotting unburied in graveyards' as a 'masterpiece of selective news management in the Conservative interest', surpassing even the 1976 IMF crisis (1994b: 103).

The new Conservative government wrestled with all of these problems, and there is a huge debate around the appropriateness of its policy measures. A widely held view is that the Thatcher revolution represented a kind of shock therapy or harsh medicine that was unpopular but necessary, dragging the British economy away from its dependence on high taxes and widespread public employment, removing its vulnerability to inflation and laying the foundation for the high-tech, stock market driven services economy that was a major success story for the UK in a new financialized and globalized age. Others regard the Thatcher reforms as unnecessarily draconian, citing a serious rise in unemployment (and, at certain points, rampant inflation), the run-down of social services such as education and health, and a total, unrecoverable collapse of many areas of British industry while the well-connected 'fat cats' of the financial system enriched themselves. The 1984–5 coalminers' strike was, of course, the most famous manifestation of the battle to reform Britain's socio-economic system. The eventual defeat of the National Union of Mineworkers (NUM) had a symbolic effect similar to that of Ronald Reagan's defeat of PATCO in the USA.

The Conservative governments of 1979–97 reformed and removed much of the post-Second World War-managed state apparatus that had been (somewhat haphazardly) assembled by the Labour governments of 1945–51, 1964–70 and 1974–9. It is during the Thatcher period that the UK economy distanced itself from European models and the EU, and started to most closely reflect the Anglo-Saxon or LME model. Just as the USA moved decisively from managerial to investor capitalism or from 'organized' to 'disorganized' capitalism in the 1980s and 1990s, important changes in the UK also served to propel the economy in the same direction (Donaldson and Farquhar 1988: 257).

The British government abandoned its commitment to demand management and industrial policy (Ackroyd 2002: 244) and embarked on a wave of privatizations. A central aim was to tackle inflation, even if it meant rising unemployment and the total eradication of industry in certain areas. An influential report published by the right-wing think-tank the Institute for Economic Affairs in 1979 entitled *The Taming of Government,* argued that the state should be employed only in the tasks that only the state can exclusively do, and that it should have no input in other areas (implying that schools, public services and even the NHS should also be privatized, see Johnson 1991: 79). Donaldson and Farquhar (1988: 291) list a string of public enterprises that were sold off in rapid succession during the early 1980s (British Airways, British Gas, Rolls Royce, British Leyland, British Shipbuilders). Many more have been privatized since, such as British Steel, and British Rail.

Trade union rights were curtailed following the defeat of the miners' and print workers' strikes (Johnson 1991: 220–221). The abandonment of incomes policy led at first to rapid inflation, but by 1983 the inflation had been curbed to 3.7%, remaining around 4–5% for the mid-1980s. Public spending was reined in, and the budget deficit – helped by the discovery of North Sea oil – was eliminated by 1989. Taxes were cut in the four budgets of 1986–9. The basic rate of income tax was cut from 30 to 25%, and top-rate taxpayers had their tax burden slashed from 60 to 40% (Sentance 1998: 52). Income inequality, as measured by the Gini coefficient, rose rapidly (see Figure 4.2). The results of the abandonment of prior attempts to program capitalism into some sort of coordinated or consensual format could hardly be more graphically demonstrated.

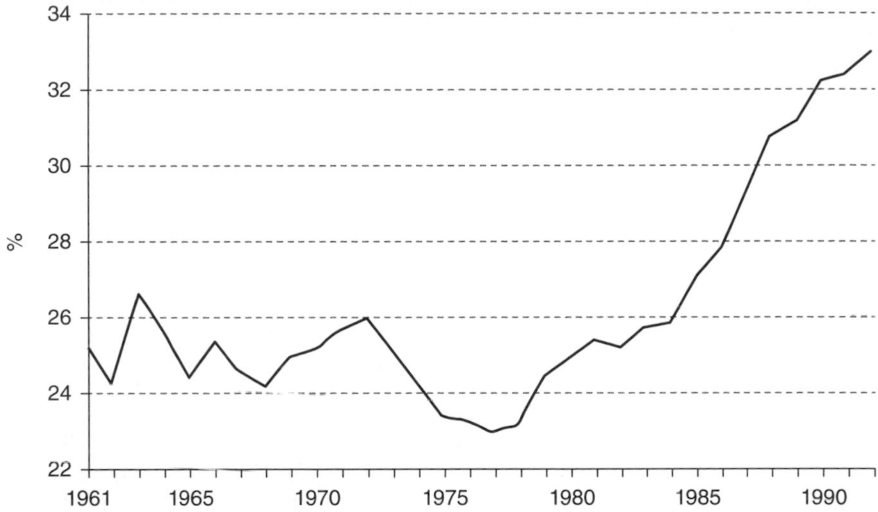

Figure 4.2 Annual Change to UK Gini Coefficient 1961–1992

Source: Chapman amd Temple (1998: 313)

Another result of these new 'monetarist' policies was a significant growth in unemployment. Some of the industrial heartlands of the UK (the shipyards of Scotland and Northeast England, the pottery factories of Stoke-on-Trent, the steelworks of Yorkshire and South Wales), not to mention the coalmines dotted across much of the nation, have never fully recovered from this period. Jobs, skills and industrial capacity have been lost forever. Bearing in mind the top-end tax cuts, it is difficult to disagree with Buxton et al. (1998)'s statement, that: '[p]eople with very high incomes have gained the most and those with the lowest have suffered the worst' (Buxton et al. 1998: 1–2).

The Conservatives also radically reformed the UK's powerful financial sector. Thatcher's 'Big Bang' reforms of 1986 significantly deregulated the City of London, and changed its closed and elitist world forever. It allowed a massive growth of newcomers to the sector, both domestically from outside the traditional elite social grouping of the privately educated 'City Gent', and from overseas, with the investment banking giants of the USA moving into the Square Mile (Augar 2000). In the long term this had the effect of pushing the whole economy further towards acceptance of higher financial risks and the expectation of greater short-term returns, and inflated the size and importance of institutional investors. Institutional investors came to be the new holders of power in the UK economy, holding ever-larger stocks of publicly traded large firms. Their investment decisions came to have huge ramifications for employment across the country to such an extent that '[t]he investment institutions are the new barons of the land' (Coggan 2002: 69). The Big Bang reforms were a fundamental driver in the British economy's shift from managerial to investor capitalism (Coggan 2002; Golding 2003).

Mainstream economic thought essentially finds in favour of Thatcher's policies. Thatcher's most senior economic advisors during this period were strongly influenced by neoliberalism, especially Friedman-influenced monetarism, with its anti-Keynesian and anti-union position. They believed that state employment and trade union power distorted market forces, and that unfettered free markets are the only means to lasting economic growth. The mainstream argument of the neoliberal economists was that state employment was 'crowding out' private sector investment (Bacon and Eltis 1978), and that further deregulation was needed to unleash market forces and stimulate growth. Other analysts offer completely the opposite interpretation. Pointing to the long-term weaknesses of British industry, recent work by Buchanan et al. (2013: 400–1) has suggested that public sector employment has, from the Thatcher government onwards, actually played a crucial role in 'filling in' jobs and investment where markets have failed. This situation still pertains today, and Buchanan et al. suggest the public sector cutbacks in the early 2010s following the subprime crisis are dangerous in that the private sector does not have the capacity to 'rush in' to replace the reduced public sector. The mainstream view, however, that the public sector was bloated and inefficient, and that the UK economy needed an emergency infusion of market forces, was widespread during that period and remains the received wisdom today.

Neoliberal approaches, however, struggle to explain how and why powerful economies in the East (such as Japan and Korea) have had prolonged success with strong, interventionist states (Johnson 1982), as well as the industrial success of Germany (see Chapter 6), which retains strong features of the coordinated economy model. Critical authors, such as the left-of-centre commentator Will Hutton (former editor of *The Observer* and now director of think tank The Work Foundation), argues that aping the neoliberal policies of Reagan in the USA is the wrong policy choice for the UK. He claims that Britain's socio-economic system is closer to a Western European model than to the North American (Hutton 1995). Hutton argues that British neoliberalism has dissolved post-war managed capitalism into a rapacious, Hobbesian form of zero-trust capitalism, whereby any mechanisms for modelling a British version of a Japanese or German 'trust-based' coordinated capitalism no longer exist (Hutton 1995; see also Coates 2000: 51).

He is very critical of what he regards to be an aristocratic, irresponsible and unaccountable City of London, which cannot provide the necessary long-term capital support to industry, and refuses to cooperate with trade unions or other forms of industrial democracy (Hutton 1995: 87–88). *The State We're In* is also critical of unions for their intransigence. He essentially argues that the UK lacks any structures for building consensus, unlike in CME nations in Western and Northern Europe. Interestingly, financial deregulation also limited the Conservative government's power to influence macroeconomic policy (Sentance 1998: 50). The genie was out of the bottle, as the Labour government was to find out when it faced a massive financial crisis of its own in 2008.

However the changes are interpreted, there is little doubt that the Conservative revolution changed the British economic landscape fairly fundamentally. It is also fairly clear that the New Labour governments of Blair (1997–2007) and Brown (2007–10) essentially continued the same neoliberal trends. Although the UK did emulate some aspects of the mainland European social market economy (there was a major increase in public spending and employment, a national minimum wage was introduced and European Commission-driven changes reformed employment law in employees' favour), this did not really change the fundaments of the finance-driven UK economy. New Labour occupied 'the centre ground' of politics and was just as keen to nurture finance and the City as their Conservative counterparts before and since. Income inequality continued to rise leading to the highest level since comparable data was first gathered in 1961. The Gini coefficient for the UK hit 0.35 by the mid-2000s (Brewer et al 2008: 2–3).

Amid all the change, the struggle of UK industry remained constant. Given the long-run constraints facing British manufacturing it was naïve to assume that if the non-market impediments were removed, UK industry would somehow naturally recover. For example Swann (1998: 122), cites a 1981 National Economic Development Office study on reasons why British farmers decide to buy British or foreign farming equipment. Of the farmers surveyed 55% gave the high performance of foreign technology as a reason for buying foreign, whereas only 17% mentioned they bought British because of high performance. Conversely, 29% suggested they would buy British on price, but only 9% suggested they would buy foreign on price. British-made products (in this and many other sectors) were perennially the cheap but unreliable option. All of the above hints at a lack of capacity for high-end, high-skill and high-wage manufacturing work in the UK, and a weak export sector.

The focus on short-term returns engendered by the investor capitalism mentality meant that:

> [m]ost British firms do not see themselves as producers but as asset managers; issues such as developing new products and technologies to enhance Britain's long-term competitiveness are treated very much as second- or third- order importance to ensuring a decent return on capital, even if this means divesting all direct manufacturing activities. (Rubery 1994: 343)

The Conservatives promised to revitalize the British economy once the 'dead hand' of the state and the unions had been eradicated. But there appeared to be little unrealized potential that the unions were holding back (Elbaum and Lazonick 1984: 582). The economy did not really grow once unions were reduced in power:

> When Margaret Thatcher left office in 1990 trade unions had been weakened by a decade of high unemployment and anti-union legislation. The Government claimed the change in the climate of industrial relations as one of their greatest successes. Management had regained the power to manage. But the symptoms of the British disease appeared little affected. (Gamble 1994a: xvi)

What were the effects of this neoliberal model at workplace level? The UK's banking system has traditionally favoured an arms-length and short-term focus, but the LME model that developed after Thatcher accelerated this trend, as companies increasingly focused on 'shareholder value' and banks and investors looked overseas for new opportunities. This meant that UK firms often lacked capital to invest in longer-term projects and in human capital. As investors increasingly demanded short-term returns, cost control started to become paramount (Hassard et al. 2009: 124–126). Funding for staff training and augmenting the skills capacity of employees can be very hard to come by (Finegold and Soskice 1988).

Many authors have – since at least the early 1980s – advocated the UK copying a German-style Vocational Education and Training (VET) system (see Chapter 6). The UK was said to be 'becoming notorious with the European Union as the one country not to endorse the high-skill, high-value-added model for the future of an integrated Europe' (Rubery 1994: 335). There was a rapid expansion in what is often called 'precarious employment' in the UK (McGovern et al. 2004);

low-paid, low-skilled, temporary and insecure. This is highlighted year after year in studies based on the annual Workplace Employment Relations Surveys, or WERS (for the latest, see Brown et al. 2009). Collective bargaining coverage has declined from around 70% of the workforce to around 27% (Marchington et al. 2011: 50). Trade union density in the private sector has fallen from 21.4% in 1995 to just 14.1% in 2011, and over the same period in the public sector from 61.3% to 56.5% (ONS 2011: 26). Life on poverty-level wages in the UK is comparable to that in the USA. Three famous studies of everyday life on low wages by journalists Toynbee and Abrams (in the UK), and Ehrenreich (in the USA) contain much similar ground; insecure, non-unionized jobs with zero-hours contracts, poor working conditions, minimal training, low pay and questionable deductions from wages (such as essential uniform and cleaning materials costs!). Low and unreliable income meant poor quality housing, high levels of personal debt, and frequent moves of address (Abrams 2002; Ehrenreich 2002; Toynbee 2003). If parents are enduring this kind of employment (or none at all), then this might provide some explanation for the very low ranking of British child well-being on the UNICEF index (Wilkinson and Pickett 2009: 24), and the shocking stories of neglect, crime and abuse reported in Davies (1998).[10]

Thatcher left office in 1990, leaving the Conservative Party in political decline. There was an upswing in the economy in the mid-1990s, but by that stage the political momentum was all with the reinvented Labour Party, or 'New Labour', which had dropped its commitment to socialism and government intervention in the economy. Labour had positioned itself closer to the political centre, marketing itself as both pro-public sector and pro-business. Labour won a landslide general election in 1997 under the leadership of Tony Blair. His government came to power halfway through the biggest bull market of all time. With a change of government, this bull market helped to fuel the promised (and much-needed) investments in public services. Huge sums of government money flowed into the education system and the health service. Nevertheless, the gap between rich and poor continued to widen under Labour. Industry continued to decline as the City of London re-asserted its dominance over the British economy with ultimately disastrous results.

---

[10] Immigrant workers feature strongly in all of these books because they tend to be clustered in the worst forms of employment. They can be especially vulnerable to exploitation, such as a group of Hungarian workers at a Domino's Pizza franchise in Derby who took home virtually no pay for four months in 2007 because of illegal wage deductions. 'Pizza Franchise Staff Exploited', *BBC News,* 26 July 2007.

From boom to bust in the New Labour decade

New Labour's economic policies embraced notions of a post-industrial society or postmodern economy, consisting of financial engineering, publishing, architecture, design, advertising and consulting. Industry was in decline, to be replaced by a weightless ideas economy, a knowledge economy or cultural economy. Those with advanced degrees and/or business acumen were able to profit from the expansion of such 'new economy' jobs. Alongside this focus on services and knowledge economy, the New Labour government also invested heavily in the public sector, such as education, health and social care, creating thousands of new jobs paid for by increased taxation and increased borrowing on international capital markets (where, for the time being, loans were cheap and easy to come by). Labour seemed to have squared an impossible circle - low unemployment was combined with low inflation, and a Labour government's handling of economic affairs was finally credible. This, at last, made the party re-electable - Blair won another easy general election victory in 2001 and a narrower one in 2005.

Shareholder value logic became increasingly dominant in the 1990–2000s, but as the UK developed a US-style version of investor-capitalism, problems in labour markets and industrial performance became more evident. Shareholder value logic puts pressure on staff costs, often meaning widespread redundancies and increases in work intensity for those who remain employed (Hassard et al. 2009: 124–174). Quality of working life in UK is often described as bad at both ends of the labour market. Salaried managers and professionals work very long hours in order to stay on top of growing workloads and responsibilities. Those in low-paid, hourly paid employment work equally long hours as they attempt to make ends meet. While thousands of new jobs were created in the New Labour decade, one of the reasons inflation stayed low was because they were low-paid jobs. Jobs are increasingly insecure (McGovern et al. 2004) even for white-collar workers (Hassard et al. 2009).

Skills development, despite lots of New Labour promises, continued to be a problem. British employers' records of developing 'high-performance work systems' tend to be weak in comparison to European and US competitors (Keep and Mayhew 1999; Lloyd and Payne 2006). Workplaces indicate low levels of skill utilization; British organizations tend to favour strong levels of managerial control and limited staff autonomy. This situation also pertains in services work (which is, of course, now far more prevalent than manufacturing work). Grugulis et al. (2010), in a study of retail jobs in the UK, report that branch managers and line supervisors are given such little trust and control by the systems and protocols from head office, that they are forced to secretly break guidelines in order to exercise discretion and initiative. The UK still seems to lack the institutions required for high-value operations. There seems to be strong path-dependence effects in terms of where wealth and investment in the UK goes - into financial re-engineering, speculation and overseas investments, thereby unbalancing the economy towards finance and away from industry or skills development. According to Coggan 'in 1979, the proportion of pension fund portfolios held in the form of overseas equities was 6 per cent; by 2000, it was 23 per cent' (2002: 73). Coupled with the UK's deep embrace of the ideologies of globalization and free markets, this also opens up UK industry and services to radical reform and frequent sales to new owners, such as private equity partnerships and overseas investors. Shortly before the subprime crash, a string of UK companies was sold into overseas ownership (see Exhibit 4.2).

Exhibit 4.2 The mid-2000s international sell-off of British companies

- British Airports Authority (BAA) sold to Ferrovial of Spain in 2006 for £10bn
- Pilkington sold to NSG of Japan for 2bn in 2006
- Thames Water sold to German utility RWE for 5bn in 2006
- British Energy majority stake sold to EDF of France for 12bn in 2009
- ICI sold to Dutch group Akzo Nobel for £8bn in 2008
- Scottish and Newcastle sold for £8bn to Carlsberg and Heineken in 2008
- P&O sold to Dubai Ports World for £3.3bn in 2005

Source: 'Mandelson admits UK industry could be disadvantaged by foreign ownership', *Guardian*, 26 September 2009

Under the New Labour governments of 1997–2010, manufacturing jobs declined from 4.1 million to 2.6 million, and the share of GDP constituted by industry declined from 18 to 13%.[11] Once-famous brands and factories have been relocated, shut down or drastically reduced in size. London Taxis International, based in Coventry, was one of the few remaining British carmakers of any scale, and even this was eventually sold into Chinese ownership.[12] All of the British car brands (Rolls-Royce, Bentley, Jaguar, Land Rover, Aston Martin) have been purchased by international car groups, such as Ford, Volkswagen and GM. The MG Rover group, bought from insolvency for a nominal price of £10 by four businessmen known as the 'Phoenix Four', was unable to recover and fell into receivership in 2005. Its brands and parts of its

[11] 'Filling the Vacuum', *Guardian*, 24 July 2010.

[12] 'Coventry Taxi Maker LTI Sold to Chinese Firm Geely for £11.4m', *BBC News*, 1 February 2013.

technology were sold to China's Nanjing Automobile. After a seven-year legal battle, 6,500 redundant MG Rovers employers were given a cash settlement of just £3 each, a development that caused understandable outrage.[13]

Earlier in the chapter I mentioned the world-renowned Wedgewood ceramics company. Employee numbers at this enterprise have collapsed from 5,500 workers in 1997 to 1,900 employees in 2009 (with only around 600 employed in manufacturing in Stoke-on-Trent). The company was put into administration in 2009 and was eventually rescued by the US private equity firm KPS Capital. KPS plans to invest but also to shift yet further jobs to Indonesia.[14] Mass production in the UK remains mostly in low-grade industries, such as food or paint production, or in rather basic items, such as the 'Henry' brand of vacuum cleaner. (4,500 of these heavy-duty yet very basic units are manufactured every day at the Numatic plant in Somerset).[15] Lack of funding amid a market-based and fragmented approach to the management and direction of utilities and telecoms companies has meant that the UK – like the USA – has internationally poor standards of broadband network provision.[16]

The UK economy, however, still retains some powerful firms in manufacturing industries, especially in higher-grade, higher value-added goods, such as in the fields of construction, pharmaceuticals, medicine, aerospace and arms. Rolls-Royce continues to manufacture about one-third of the world's aircraft engines, and retained its long heritage as one most highly respected engineering firms in the world.[17] Engineering jobs at Rolls-Royce are highly paid and highly sought-after.

But even at the cutting-edge of UK industry, in its 'world-class' high-tech arms and aerospace industry, there are considerable strains. British Aerospace Engineering, one of the world's largest aerospace and defence contractors, was recently investigated on allegations of false accounting and bribery. It was fined by the US Department of Justice (US$400 million), and the UK's Serious Fraud Office (£30 million).[18] Moreover, as the crisis in public funding after the subprime crash takes hold, the UK Ministry of Defence is having to cut back on its orders of

[13] 'MG Workers to Get £3 Each in Trust Fund Compensation', *BBC News*, 3 May 2012.

[14] 'Wedgewood Goes into Administration', *BBC News*, 5 January 2009.

[15] 'Filling the Vacuum', *Guardian*, 24 July 2010.

[16] See OECD Broadband portal, http://www.oecd.org/sti/ict/broadband.

[17] 'Filling the Vacuum', *Guardian*, 24 July 2010.

[18] 'BAE Admits Guilt Over Corrupt Deals', *Guardian,* 6 February 2010.

new and replacement weapons systems, meaning reduced business for defence contractors, such as BAE.

The subprime crisis revealed that the British economy was massively dependent on debt and public sector employment, both of which had grown significantly since New Labour's election in May 1997. Labour invested heavily in public services, but did this on top of a debt-fuelled economic model and a failed industrial sector. When the financial system started to crack, the contradictions of New Labour's finance-driven version of the social market economy were disastrously revealed. Tony Blair resigned as Prime Minister in 2007, succeeded by Gordon Brown. Almost immediately, Brown found himself embroiled in the panic of the subprime meltdown. Northern Rock, a British bank whose business model was largely based around US-style subprime lending went bankrupt, forcing the UK Treasury to nationalize it. Further UK banks failed in the months of turmoil that followed, and the British public was outraged at news stories of excessive risk-taking and a top-management bonuses culture. As of 2011, 83% of RBS shares were owned by the taxpayer, 41% of Lloyds Banking Group, 100% of Northern Rock and all of Bradford & Bingley's highly risky mortgages arm were also state-owned (its deposits arm was broken off and sold to the Spanish banking group Santander). (Other major banks Barclays and HSBC needed no government capital injections.[19]) The ownership stakes of the rescued banks were controlled by a newly established government entity known as UK Financial Investments (UKFI). A total of around £850 billion was paid in government funds for emergency loans to bailout the failed banks.[20] Abbey National, Bradford & Bingley (deposits and branch operations) and Alliance & Leicester were all purchased by the Spanish multinational bank Santander. The rush to bailout UK banks flew in the face of neoliberal theories of marketization, but such radical measures were needed to prevent a total seizure of the system, as banks claimed they were within days of failing to meet their covenants - literally running out of cash to supply their customers' accounts. Classic analyses of crises by the Marxist theorist Ernest Mandel seemed to remain accurate:

> The deeper and more generalized recessions become, the greater is the injection of credit and the expansion of bank money supply necessary to prevent these recessions deteriorating into full-scale depressions – and therewith the more acute grows the danger that inflation will escape the control of the bourgeois State in a runaway rush towards a bank panic and collapse of the whole financial system. (1975: 468)

---

[19] http://www.ukfi.co.uk/about-us/market-investments/.

[20] '£850bn: The Official Cost of the Bank Bailout', *The Independent*, 4 December 2009.

While Brown received some credit internationally for coordinating with world leaders to restore confidence in global financial markets, domestically the New Labour project seemed exhausted by this stage. Brown's government stumbled into seemingly inevitable electoral defeat in 2010. Industry continued to contract dramatically during the 1990s and 2000s. The deregulated banking system - with large numbers of households attempting to service high levels of personal debt - was horribly exposed by the subprime mortgages collapse of 2007–8. Yet the nation was unwilling (or unable) to move away from its LME model. Such is the dominance of the City of London that following this crash it was the UK government and businesses that most strongly lobbied against re-regulation of hedge funds or bankers' pay when compared to other EU nations. In December 2011, with the EU in deep crisis and looking for solidarity among its members, Prime Minister David Cameron dramatically vetoed a proposed new treaty designed to more strictly enforce budgetary discipline across the 27 EU members. With the voting 26–1 in favour, the UK was the only country to vote against. His reasoning was that he wanted to secure adequate safeguards of the City of London from EU regulation, and for that he believed it was worth relegating the UK to the sidelines of the European Union project.[21]

The Conservative–Liberal Democrat coalition immediately made major cuts to public spending. An emergency June 2010 budget slashed the budgets of almost all government departments by 25%. The Comprehensive Spending Review of October 2010 contained more bad news for public sector workers and the poor. The total package of cuts amounted to £83 billion over five years, involving an estimated half a million public sector job cuts. The plans were designed to ensure that Britain's economy remains 'credible' to international money markets, that it is not too heavily indebted, that it can borrow from money markets at reasonable interest rates, and that the currency is not compromised. They rested on the risky assumption that the private sector can rush into the gaps left by public sector cuts, thereby driving economic growth. Left-of-centre newspaper the *Guardian* claimed that the Chancellor 'drove his axe deep into the heart of the British state', and that the cuts 'were beyond the dreams of Margaret Thatcher'; 'a neo-liberal cutting machine ... drawn from a Chicago School blueprint'.[22] Policymakers remained committed to an LME model even after the disastrous crash.

However, outside of the public sector, the economy remained moribund and the bailed-out banks, low on confidence, still refused to lend

[21] 'UK Alone as EU Agrees Fiscal Deal', *BBC News*, 9 December 2011.

[22] 'Axe Falls on the Poor', *Guardian*, 21 October 2010.

on a sufficient scale to sustain the kinds of output and consumption that prior growth was built on. Much like the USA, a new age of austerity has come to UK after about 13 years of economic success (roughly the period 1994–2007). By January 2010, the UK government faced a budget deficit of £178 billion. The coalition government repeatedly argued that this deficit had to be dealt with by significant public services cuts or the interest payments on this debt would become totally unmanageable, and its AAA credit rating would be downgraded by rating agencies.[23] Pay freezes for public and private sector workers have been predicted to last until 2020, with journalists suggesting a Japanese-style 'lost decade' for middle-income families.[24] The outlook for the UK economic model seemed poor at the beginning of the 2010s. From where will the growth come from now that the financial-driven model seems exhausted? Cuts to the UK's large public sector will also mean the end of the 'filling-in' role it played very strongly under Labour (Buchanan et al. 2013), and job cuts in schools, local government, universities, hospitals, police and the armed forces will contribute to further unemployment and suppressed demand. At the beginning of 2012, unemployment rose to nearly 2.7 million - 8.4% of the workforce.[25] Data at the time suggested that private sector job creation was so far failing to fill in for lost public sector jobs.[26]

For such a rich country, the UK does appear to have a serious problem with poverty, crime and deprivation, which can make for a pliant workforce for the illegal economy. Journalistic accounts such as that by Davies (1998) make the UK sound as bad as the USA for inner-city violence and drug-related crime. British news media in recent years has increasingly reported on the rise of fringe lenders such as pawnbrokers, loan-sharks, cash-till-payday outlets and 'weekly payment' shops, which charge huge interest rates but get plenty of business from families that feel they have no other option in order to make ends meet.[27] The loss of basic industry has had profoundly difficult results for the UK's large low-skill workforce (Williams at el 1990). Where are they expected to work? The effects of de-industrialization are:

> repeated across the advanced economies; in Detroit, in Glasgow, in Stoke-on-Trent. Despite the best efforts of crisis management teams or local

[23] 'David Cameron: Conservatives Will Not Make Swingeing Cuts', *Daily Telegraph*, 31 January 2010.

[24] 'Pay Freeze to Last Until 2020 for Millions', *Guardian*, 23 January 2012.

[25] 'Rocky Time Ahead as Joblessness Nears 2.7m', *Financial Times*, 19 January 2012.

[26] 'Private Sector Labours to Fill Gap', *Financial Times*, 19 January 2012.

[27] 'A Nation in Hock to Pawnbrokers', *Metro*, 6 September 2010.

> redevelopment agencies, training programmes and adult education drop in centres, many former unskilled factory workers are not equipped with the social and cultural capital to become website designers or tanning salon entrepreneurs. (Granter 2009: 171)

Political discussions of 'broken Britain' and a culture of 'extreme worklessness'[28] among disadvantaged communities are common. There are pockets of poverty in the UK that suggest not so much a particular socio-economic 'model' but a society and economy undergoing long-term breakdown.

So what is the UK variety of capitalism? How successful is it as model or system? The final section of the chapter will review these questions. Once a dominant industrial power, the economic status of the UK has slipped alarmingly. With industry in long-term decay, it is a country with a still relatively large public sector, a huge services industry especially in retail and banking (which are closely linked),[29] some cultural industry (fashion, films, video games, advertising), and a strong knowledge industry (universities, consulting). Many of its professional services firms (such as its law and architecture firms) are internationally powerful, trading perhaps on Britain's traditional reputation for high standards of professionalism (see, for example, the recent trend of super-rich Russian clients seeking representation by British lawyers, such as the trial between 'oligarchs' Boris Berezovsky and Roman Abramovich in 2011–12 at London's Commercial Court[30]). Britain's banking system is also highly internationalized, and remains globally powerful even after the subprime disaster. The UK also has one of the world's largest and most effective universal health services. The UK's substantial public sector spends large sums on those with no or little income, but many regard this to be in perennial crisis, perhaps reaching a tipping-point where such provision might no longer be available.

Manufacturing has been uncompetitive and shrinking since at least the 1960s, yet there is some scope for high-end niche products (especially in defence contracting such as aerospace). Shipbuilding is now all but gone except for some major Royal Navy contracts. The UK car industry is practically all Japanese-, German-, US, or Indian-owned. Train-building has all-but collapsed, with contracts for new

[28] 'David Cameron's Solution for Broken Britain: Tough Love and Tougher Policing', *Guardian*, 16 August 2011.

[29] Banking work today strongly resembles retail sales work, and a large portion of retail depends on personal loans and credit cards.

[30] 'Abramovich v Berezovsky: When Oligarchs Attack', *Daily Telegraph*, 9 October 2011.

trains usually given to overseas constructors, such as Siemens, revealing the UK's inability to think and act long-term (Froud et al. 2011). In contrast, the UK possesses some powerful firms that operate in less visible but nonetheless important sectors, and whose brand names are less recognizable. These include some influential companies involved in complex subcontracting chains such as the general services outsourcing firm Serco, and the construction and civil engineering giants Balfour Beatty and WS Atkins. The business models of such companies are increasingly moving towards selling knowledge, rather than building products, and some would argue that this is a highly lucrative strategy when competition is increasingly playing in terms of high-end 'knowledge work' rather than low-end construction work. (For example WS Atkins designed and built the retractable roof on Cardiff's Millennium Stadium, and the company is now in a position to license their technology and designs for sports stadia all over the world, leaving the actual construction to less skilled contractors.) One of the services firm Serco's thousands of projects around the world involves providing electronic tagging systems for offenders who can then be released from overcrowded prisons and watched more closely in the community. It is winning many contracts for these systems in East European nations such as Russia and Poland where these kinds of complex outsourcing and expert knowledge systems are rudimentary. The UK is clearly a shadow of the industrial power it used to be, but it is far from finished yet. While it has clearly lost out in world-class volume manufacturing, it remains a force to be reckoned with in financial services and in the so-called knowledge economy. Certain companies, such as the above, have carved out important niches in sophisticated, low-visibility business strategies.

In the wake of the subprime crisis - which hit the UK's finance- and investor-driven model of capitalism so hard - debate has rumbled on about reforming the economy, with Prime Minister David Cameron discussing 'fair and worthwhile capitalism', and Labour leader Ed Miliband suggesting tightening corporate governance rules to prevent hostile takeovers, introducing caps on excessive bonus pay in the City, and new policies to tackle the 'growing inequality that scars our society'.[31] However, taking a long-term view - as this chapter has - it is difficult to see whether the UK socio-economic system really has the capacity to genuinely change and regulate its own highly liberal version of capitalism.

[31] 'David Cameron Says UK Must Build "a Better Economy"', *BBC News*, 19 January 2012; 'Our Toxic Blend of Capitalism and Short-termism', *Financial Times*, 19 January 2012.

Conclusion: an unstable, unresolved model

The UK's journey from the world's first great industrial power to Europe's most globalized and financialized economy represents the changes of globalization in perhaps its sharpest form. To some extent all developed nations have followed this trajectory, but none have done so with such speed and intensity as the UK. The UK was the first major industrializer, boasting a string of impressive industrial innovations. But it was unable to transform this burst of development into sustainable growth, and was eventually overtaken by other major powers in Europe, USA and Japan. Industry, in general, has performed poorly since the Second World War as favourable socio-economic institutions are not in place to support it. The increasing reliance on imported goods therefore means that the UK has a colossal balance of payments deficit (one of the world's largest, at around 15.2 billion in the third quarter of 2011, the highest ever on record).[32]

One of the main reasons for the UK's failing manufacturing sector is the lack of sufficient capital to replace, develop and drive industry forward. The dominant role of the City of London means that few strategies are given the time and investment to work out. Throughout the 1960s and 1970s, continual shifts of policy and an unclear overall strategy of how to compete was reflected at government and at firm level. By the 1980s, governments increasingly turned to US-style neoliberalism and globalization, which further cemented the dominance of shareholder value logic, the onward march of finance and services, and the retreat of manufacturing.

Despite arguably being at the forefront of the knowledge economy, the UK still receives criticism for its skills development system being underdeveloped by European or East Asian standards. The country seems to lack a coordinated and coherent system for developing and sustaining the practical and technical skills of its workforce. A high percentage of jobs created in Britain are low-paid, low-skilled and insecure. Conversely, the higher education sector of Britain has for some time punched above its weight, and the UK's professional services sector is advanced. This system is now possibly unbalanced towards higher education, with apprenticeships and technical skills training traditionally underfunded and under supported.

Those of low economic status and prospects are protected to some degree by the UK's health and social care system. Public spending

[32] 'Balance of Payments – 3rd Quarter 2011', Office of National Statistics, www.ons.gov.uk/ons/rel/bop/balance-of-payments/3rd-quarter-2011/stb-bop-3rd-quarter-2011.html.

in the UK has for some years equated to around 40% of GDP (Crawford et al. 2009: 5). Much of this spending goes to the huge and generally effective NHS. The British health system was ranked 18th in overall performance in the world, and between 2nd and 11th in terms of fairness, according to the World Health Organization (WHO 2000: 155). The Conservative–Liberal coalition elected in 2010 is currently in the process of reforming many aspects of the social security system, initiating substantial cuts in public spending. Quite what impacts this will have on the truly disadvantaged segments of the UK remains to be seen, but comparisons with the more cut-throat US system seem inevitable. In the words of Elbaum and Lazonick 'The British economy, once the workshop of the world, seems to have fallen victim to some century-long affliction' (1984: 567). It remains an open question whether a viable new 'model' for a revived British economy can be found.

Further reading

Williams, K., Williams, J., and Thomas, D., (1983) *Why Are the British Bad at Manufacturing?*, London: Routledge and Kegan Paul.

This book is somewhat dated, but it contains some very important arguments and data. The authors take an institutional approach to studying UK industry which works well for those interested in VoC theory. What is really useful about this book is that the institutional theory is backed up with detailed case studies on classic cases of industrial decline, namely British Leyland, the shipbuilding industry, and General Electric Company. They show that the institutions of British capitalism have long been unable to adequately support an internationally competitive industrial sector.

Brown, W., Bryson, A., Forth, J., and Whitfield, K. eds, (2009) *The Evolution of the Modern Workplace*, Oxford: Oxford University Press.

This is a set of high-quality chapters that provide a detailed overview and interpretation of the latest statistical information available on British workplaces. It is based on Workplace Employment Relations Survey data, which is one of the best large-scale national

(Continued)

(Continued)

surveys of this kind available in the world. The volume contains masses of data on such issues as workplace representation, working hours, and the quality of working life in the UK, and is indispensable as a guide to the latest state of play in the UK's workplaces, labour markets, and trade unions.

Hassard, J., McCann, L., and Morris, J., (2009) *Managing in the Modern Corporation: The Intensification of Managerial Work in the USA*, Cambridge: Cambridge University Press.

The fourth chapter of this book explores UK capitalism by interviewing middle managers in large UK employers about their careers and working conditions. The analysis is pessimistic about Britain's economic prospects and is highly critical of the short-termist focus of UK companies, arguing that this approach is reflected in a low quality of working life for white-collar employees, involving long hours, work intensification, low morale and isolation from top-level decision making.

Mokyr, J., (2009) *The Enlightened Economy: Britain and the Industrial Revolution, 1700–1850,* London: Penguin

The current chapter is somewhat downbeat about the UK and tells a sad story of long-term decline. If the reader is looking for something more positive about the UK, then Mokyr's brilliant book about the UK's industrial and scientific history is well worth looking at. It argues that the UK was an early adopter of scientific and technical innovations, and it is interesting to see how early it manages to do this in relation to later industrializers. His work implies a powerful message about the importance of education and science as a potential way out of economic decline.

FIVE France: Powerful Traditions Turning to Radical Change

Chapter objectives

- To provide an introduction to the traditional French approach to economy and society: essentially one in which the state is a grand orchestrator of economic action
- To explore French political culture: a culture which has tended to hold and sustain a far greater appetite for socialist or left-of-centre politics than the rest of the OECD
- To describe how the French economy recovered from the disaster of the Second World War
- To evaluate the effectiveness (or otherwise) of heavy French governmental regulation, planning and the policy of promoting 'national champions'
- To discuss how the traditions of French *dirigisme* may be disappearing amid a neoliberal resurgence
- To evaluate the moral and economic legacy of the French variety of capitalism

Introduction

At just 34 kilometres apart at their closest points, one might think that France and the UK would share many socio-economic features. But this is not the really the case. In some ways France is more similar to Japan than it is to the UK. For decades the French economy has been heavily state controlled and state regulated. Part of the reason for this is

France's defeat, occupation and resistance in the Second World War and the necessity of major economic rebuilding after widespread devastation. Successive French governments have favoured Keynesian demand management policies and ambitious public works programmes. French trains are among the best in the world. France's lack of oil and gas resources makes it dependent on imports and has encouraged the government to invest heavily in nuclear energy. Boardrooms of large French firms have traditionally been dominated by insiders, many of whom are lifetime 'company men'. Traditionally, France has a reputation for being a rather elitist, exclusive society, suspicious of outsider influences. It has a healthy disrespect for Anglo-Saxon ways and for globalization in general. All of the above are features quite similar to Japan (see Chapter 11).

But this is probably where the similarities with Japan end. French company life, although paternalistic, is almost the mirror image of Japanese. Compared to the devotion that Japanese employees usually give to their firms, French employee–firm relationships tend to be much more casual and instrumental (Johnson 1996: 53–60). Demands made on workers in France are considerably less severe. French workers have a tradition of almost wilful independence from – even disregard for – management fiat. French employees traditionally refuse to submit life and soul to their companies in ways that Japanese (and probably American) workers would find disrespectful.

France possesses many features that make it a fascinating country to study. Politically, it is poles apart from the USA, UK (and Japan). It has a much greater appetite for socialist politics than the rest of the OECD. Just as the Anglo-Saxon countries were embarking on their neoliberal transformations in the 1980s, France was developing ambitious socialist policies. Margaret Thatcher was elected Prime Minister of UK in 1979 and Ronald Reagan was inaugurated president of the USA in 1981; but in France 1981 saw the election of a socialist president, François Mitterrand. France bucked the trend towards liberalization and privatization just as the rest of the OECD was embracing it. Even today, France retains some powerful forms of 'social market economy' regulation, including a law prohibiting most employees from working more than 35 hours per week, a law that exists nowhere else in the world.

France's perversity in matters like these provides a fascinating insight into the 'globalization versus national divergence' debate. For how long can France maintain such arguably luxurious and possibly excessive employee-friendly systems? Many have suggested that they are on the way out for good. With the 1973 oil crisis, and the failure of the major attempted leftward shift of the Mitterrand government, suddenly an opportunity for a neoliberal attack on traditional France opened up. But neoliberalism is very controversial in France, and has been the subject of intense debate by French scholars and from observers around the globe. For example, French sociologists Luc Boltanski and Eve Chiapello (2005), describe in great detail how the 'second spirit' of capitalism (which amounts to a highly regulated form of managerial or 'organized' capitalism) has been replaced by a rapacious, ruthless, soulless 'third spirit' that is redolent of US investor or 'disorganized' capitalism (see also Lash and Urry 1987). Others (notably but not exclusively from outside France), fail to see much change at all, and regard France as a reluctant and sluggish reformer, that counterproductively persists with an 'outdated' and 'inflexible' socialism (Johnson 1996).

For all this, France is a powerful economy and a rich, civilized and technologically advanced society. It has developed highly influential traditions in arts, sciences, literature and philosophy. Obviously it has social and economic troubles (some of which are profound), but in general its recovery from war has been a huge success, and it possesses a well-educated workforce, especially in fields such as medicine, engineering and mathematics. It is a society with a powerful 'quality of life' movement, where neoliberal ideas about economic 'progress' are often shunned in favour of a more simple, contemplative, socially aware existence. It also possesses powerful armed forces, including a nuclear arsenal of around 300 warheads that is entirely independent from US control. This fact instantly places it in the top rank of powerful nations, including a permanent seat on the UN Security Council.

This chapter proceeds in the following four sections. First, it describes how France rebuilt itself following the horrors of the Second World War. Essentially this was done though a model that became known as *dirigiste* capitalism, whereby (much like Japan and Korea) the state is the driver and manager of economic action at many levels. The chapter will explore the period of strong post-war economic growth, often known as *Les trente glorieuses* (The Thirty Glorious Years). During this period *dirigisme* matured into a form of state-led organized capitalism (Lash and Urry 1987) which involved an interesting combination of bureaucratic central planning and Fordist mass consumption. Second, the chapter explores how this growth had a darker edge; how social protests erupted in 1968 which prefigured certain changes to this centralized, bureaucratic and elitist model. Third, the chapter will discuss the extent to which this state-led model has been eroded in the face of globalization and financialization. It asks whether the traditional French *dirigiste* model has a viable future, or whether it will be consigned to the ash-pile of history. In the conclusion, the chapter considers the legacy of France, especially its long-standing philosophy that markets, finance and economy should be our servants rather than our masters. It argues that this is an attractive idea that differs fundamentally from the discipline and regimentation of Japan or Korea, or the 'market fundamentalism' of the USA.

Les trente glorieuses: the high tide of the French model of state-led organized capitalism

In comparison to the 'early industrializing' UK, France was a somewhat slower industrializer (Amatori and Colli 2011). It was comparatively less technologically developed than the UK in the mid-18th century (Chang 2003: 36), and remained overwhelming an agrarian society as late as 1911.[1] In that year, 66% of the French population lived in the countryside, and there were only 15 cities with populations of over 100,000, compared with 49 in Britain and 45 in Germany (Dormois 2004: 10). French industry was dominated by small- and medium-sized firms (mostly family-owned) which had been 'insulated from foreign competition for decades' (Zysman 1983: 100). In keeping with world trends, there was a post-Second World War baby boom, and the French population eventually grew to 52 million by 1971. But France's population today (at 62.3 million) remains relatively small for its geographic size and relatively un-urbanized (77.4% urbanized) for its economic size.[2]

Although it industrialized at a slower rate and in less dramatic fashion than in the UK (Mokyr 2009: 99), the French industrial revolution produced a wide number of innovations adopted elsewhere. These included Pasteur's method of protecting food from microbial contamination and Jacquard's semi-automated textile loom (Mokyr 1990: 88, 102). Industrial-scale production was eventually established at the steel works of Le Creusot, and eventually in the petrol, rubber, publishing, glass, cement and electricity industries (Amatori and Colli 2011: 94).

Before the world wars, France possessed numerous colonies including Algeria, Tunisia, Morocco, West Africa, Equatorial Africa, Madagascar, Indochina and parts of India.[3] By 1931, the French empire consisted of 12.4 million square kilometres and 64.3 million persons outside of France (Adams 1989: 146). The colonies provided cheap imports of raw

[1] One reason for the relative slowness in French industrialization may be a developmental time-lag resulting from 26 years of political and economic chaos during the Revolutionary period from 1789 onwards (Botticelli 1997: 66).

[2] Population and urbanization figures from www.worldbank.org.

[3] A French East India Company was in existence between 1664–1794, set up by Minister of Finance Jean-Baptiste Colbert as a competitor to the Dutch and British East India Companies.

materials and captive export markets for French industrial output but appeared to play a lesser role in French economic expansion than the British Empire did for the UK (Beaud 2001: 192–193). Since the Second World War French colonial influence, much like that of the other European powers, has been in terminal decline, pretty much disappearing by 1962 (Adams 1989: 148).

Politically, France is widely said to be proud of its revolutionary history (1789–1815) and its values of 'liberty, equality and fraternity' which contributed to the destruction of absolutist monarchy, to be replaced by the Enlightenment ideals of citizenship and inalienable rights. These revolutionary values are often combined with a strong sense of national uniqueness, arguably reinforcing a value system based on national, rather than global, values. This is most important where the role of the state in everyday life is understood. According to Dormois, French economic and civic life is inward-looking:

> The republican *État* or state (one of the few French words to take a capital) is not perceived as a mere administrative apparatus providing a number of services to the voting and taxpaying public: it is the highest expression of the nation's collective will and rationality. ... While individual politicians can be corrupt and/or incompetent, the state never ceases to guide the nation's destiny and take responsibility for its prosperity and power: it is the bulwark of the French way of life. (Dormois 2004: 44)

This is almost the reverse of the situation in America; politically the countries are both 'model' democratic republics with presidential systems, but their citizens tend to hold opposing views of the role that government should play. Simplifying greatly, for French citizens, the state is a central aspect of social and economic life. For Americans, government is often regarded with suspicion and distrust. When related to economic concerns, many in France therefore argue that markets should be restrained, regulated and managed by a higher set of powers. The French state is also heavily centralized with Paris dominating the machineries of government.

Between the wars the French economy was dominated by small- and medium-sized firms. French entrepreneurs had made some major innovations (particularly in the automotivie industry; the world's first corporation dedicated solely to motor car manufacturing was Panhard et Levassor in 1889, see Allen 2011: 46), but these early industrialists seemed unable to emulate large-scale Fordist production on the scale of the USA (Amatori and Colli 2011: 94). According to Cohen (1991: 755) French manufacturers Renault, Citröen and Peugeot produced only 50,000–70,000 vehicles per year between 1938–9, 'far from the millions produced by the principle American manufacturers'. Pioneers of the French automobile industry Louis

Renault and Andre Citröen visited America in 1911 and 1912 and attempted to bring back the secrets of Fordist mass production and (less so) Sloanist corporate organization. Over time, French firms successfully developed systems of mass production, importing and adapting certain US ideas as well as developing their own. The influence of the highly centralized managerial approach of Henri Fayol for example (see below), possibly inhibited the take-up of GM-style divisionalization (Cohen 1991: 760).

In common with many other nations featured in this book, French economy and society were shattered by the Second World War. A total of around 810,000 French civilian and military lives were lost in the conflict (Bullock 1991: 1086–7). About a million homes were destroyed (Dormois 2004: 17). Even before the war, France was not in strong shape. It had been hit hard by the Wall Street Crash of 1929 (Shonfield 1965: 125), and it had suffered horribly in the First World War. France actually suffered twice the number of war casualties it sustained in the Second World War, with 1.4 million killed in the First (Dormois 2004: 2). This, along with a long-standing social trend (encouraged by the civil tax code) for families to have just one child, had the effect of limiting France's population size.

Although the need to rebuild from the wreckage of the two World Wars was obviously a major factor in explaining the powerful role of government in French economic life, such an approach has been used in France throughout many eras. It has clearly influenced the development of the French variety of capitalism at various points in time. An alternative word for *dirigisme* is 'Colbertism', a term whose roots can be traced back to the 17th-century monarchy. Jean-Baptiste Colbert (1619–83) was Minister of Finance under Louis XIV who believed in the state's moral and practical superiority to the somewhat sullied world of markets and commerce. He advocated strong regulation, infant industry protection and 'national champions', although this approach did not hold in all historical periods (Chang 2003: 36).

Although unpopular in mainstream Anglo-Saxon economic circles, the state-led approach has known success. The period 1945–73 is often known as *Les trente glorieuses*. The post-war boom stimulated huge changes in the structure of French life. Standards of living rose quickly, and, in France at least, levels of inequality in wealth stayed reasonably flat, even narrowing in the 1980s. According to Dormois (2004: 7), the salary range after tax narrowed from 1 to 4.1 in 1967, to 1 to 3 in 1984. Leisure time grew as the range of leisure services to be traded also widened. Working hours shrunk from above 2,600 hours per year at the turn of the century to under 2,000 in the 1950s and 1,500 in the present day (Dormois 2004: 8–9).

Large-scale economic growth in France's period of organized capitalism was also stimulated by active state planning policies.[4] This included regular currency devaluations to drive export growth and a major role for long-range planning. The first French Five Year Plan focused on heavy industries (much like in the Soviet, Chinese and Indian experiences (see Chapters 8–10), such as steel, transportation, fuel and power generation. The aim was to get the fundaments correct from which further industrial development might flow. French economists such as Caron (1979) tend to argue that this state-led model was a great success which fully justified state intervention. Others, such as Adams, in a book published by the US-based Brookings Institution (Adams 1989), suggest that the success of France's growth phase is hard to attribute to government policy.

The state-led, post-war organized capitalism model 'depended on the selective allocation of credit make possible by the credit-based, price-administered financial system' (Zysman 1983: 99).[5] The Ministry of Finance had to approve bank loans to industry of anything above the value of 1 million francs (Shonfield 1965), giving the Ministry very significant powers of economic coordination. In keeping with CME norms, the French financial system was bank-based, with bank loans often making up nearly half the total stock of corporate finance (Bertero 1994: 70). *Dirigisme* was encapsulated in the creation of the Plan Commission immediately after the war in January 1946. The *Commissariat générale du Plan* attempted to harness the latest developments in administrative science to coordinate and control the French economy in the name of national rebuilding and modernization. Its first Plan of Modernization was announced by Jean Monnet in 1946 (Shonfield 1965: 125). France took planning seriously. The Commission was staffed by civil servants, unlike its British counterpart (the National Economic Development Council) which was 'placed firmly outside the ordinary machinery of government' (Shonfield 1965: 122–123). The commanding heights of the French economy were 'staffed at the top by a set of bureaucrats recruited from special schools', using 'considerable discretion' which 'made it possible for the bureaucracy to pursue its objectives by discriminating in favour of some groups and against others' (Zysman 1983: 103).

[4] Marhall Plan aid from the USA was also hugely important to post-war rebuilding, just as it was in much of Western Europe (Djelic 1998).

[5] Zysman's (1983) *Governments, Markets and Growth* is a seminal text that has strongly influenced the development of VoC theory, especially as regards the idea of 'financial systems'. The language of 'credit-based' or 'capital market-based' financial systems relates closely to Zysman's work.

Zysman describes how 'French governments walked a tightrope to modernization: the financial system was their balancing rod for that crossing' (1983: 100). He suggests that the state-dominated financial system of France made planning and bureaucratic coordination possible (1983: 168–169). It also gave large firms in France a prod towards developing into vertically integrated, 'modern corporations', which were modelled on the US giant firms of the 'managerial capitalism' era. With state encouragement, France thereby attempted to move beyond its insular focus on small and medium-sized businesses, and this allowed much greater involvement of French firms in overseas operations and trade.

France was destined to stay with state-administered managerial capitalism well beyond the time when it fell out of favour in the USA and the UK. A stabilized and inward-looking French economy could tolerate the existence of a small Paris elite which managed economic policy behind closed doors, not necessarily in the public world of government. Technocrats could pull the levels of power while 'their tactics remained hidden in the shadowy world of finance' (Zysman 1983: 169). Although such an approach today appears outdated, in the middle of the 20th century these were perfectly acceptable and feasible policy options. Andrew Shonfield, writing in 1965, claims that '[e]conomic planning is the most characteristic expression of the new capitalism. It reflects the determination to take charge, rather than be driven by economic events' (1965: 121). At this time the USSR and China were still broadly in growth phases, and planning as an economic concept had not been discredited. Keynesian demand management policies were widespread across Europe, Japan and South Korea, and New Deal systems were still powerful in the USA. Many believed that 'the violence of the market ha[d] been tamed' (Shonfield 1965: 66) and that the large firm had evolved into a 'purely neutral technocracy' (Hassard et al. 2009: 56). The explosion of competition and internationalization, which rocked managerial capitalism to its core, was to come rather later, particularly after the crises of the 1970s.

Another major way in which the French government attempted to stimulate economic growth was to establish a system of promoting 'national champions'. These are firms selected by the state to receive government protection. Strongly related to the points above about the French state's selective allocation of capital, national champions were typically very large firms, usually headquartered in Paris, and usually with the state owning significant or controlling equity stakes, and providing subsidies and cheap loans. Its managers (or *cadres* to use the term more often in use in France) would almost exclusively be drawn from *les grandes écoles* – highly academic and highly exclusive universities. Many of the most senior directors would have had long backgrounds in the French civil service before entering the world of business administration relatively late in life (Hancké 2002: 16–17).

Many of the largest firms - in true CME style - would hold mutually reinforcing blocks of each others' shares (Clift 2007). For example the glass manufacturer Saint-Gobain and the banking giant Paribas towards the end of the era of French 'managed' capitalism had as much as 40% of their entire market capitalization tied up in friendly blockholdings (Hancké 2002: 33).

Firm leadership, therefore, would be loyal to France, and would, in theory, have the French economy's needs fully in mind even when operating in overseas markets. The development of multinational 'national champions' represents a peculiarly French approach to globalization. Good examples of national champions are the technology firms Groupe Bull and Thomson, insurers such as Axa, the automotive giant Renault and, of course, utility and transport monopolies such as Gas de France and SNCF. In 1962 state-owned enterprises 'contributed 100 percent of the crude natural gas, virtually 100 percent of the tobacco products and matches, 65 percent of the miscellaneous minerals, 62 percent of the military products, 47 percent of the aircraft, and 37 percent of the health services provided in France' (Adams 1989: 62).

The socialist government of the early 1980s pushed ahead with further nationalizations, taking all of France's major banks under government ownership in 1982. The French government has regularly reshuffled firm ownership and control around when it sees fit, such as forcing Thomson to take a 21.6% share in the struggling bank Crédit Lyonnaise (Johnson 1996: 70). Such policies reinforced the focus of the French economy towards a national and strongly regulated form of organized capitalism. While the degree of protection that state assistance brings is obviously welcomed by large firms, state control can be problematic. It was sometimes hard to disentangle management authority from governmental authority. Johnson describes how these complications could brew into conflict, for example, at Groupe Bull, where '[t]he minister was saying "I run Bull". The chairman was saying "No, I run Bull"' (1996: 18).

This raises the interesting issue of where government assistance blurs into interference. Today the policy of national champions is pretty much ridiculed by neoliberals. The state, so conventional neoliberal wisdom goes, is poor at 'picking winners' and is likely to waste money by 'throwing good money after bad'. This disrupts the free working of markets and distorts price signals. It gives certain firms unfair advantages. What's worse, subsidizing firms in this way is actually self-defeating in that it is likely to postpone their much-needed reform, leading to firm stagnation rather than innovation. Arguably, this could lead firms into a dangerous blind alley, in that they appear to become 'too big to fail' and generating 'moral hazard'. Recently in the UK, for example, the pro-business newspaper the *Financial Times* carried an editorial that was highly critical of what it saw as a revival of a 'French policy' of national champions when the UK government gave a £80 million development loan to the specialist steels firm Sheffield Forgemasters in 2010.[6]

However, in an interesting twist of fate the fallout from the economic crash of 2007–8, has witnessed a (minor) swing back to the policy of national champions, even in neoliberal UK. Arguably, and especially in times of crisis, some degree of state intervention is unavoidable in certain sectors that *actually are* 'too big to fail' – literally – such as US and European banks that have been bailed out with vast amounts of taxpayers' money. Moreover, it is likely that the state might be right to attempt to 'pick winners', possibly in firms that have unique capacities shared by no other competitors. This could be in the fields of advanced technologies (possibly new green technologies), where short-term risk-averse capital would typically not choose to invest. It is also possible to argue that there are certain investments that a sensible government will enter for the wider good of society, such as high-speed electric train lines, where there may be no obvious financial pay-off. Protecting and sustaining a welfare state of such significance as France's is also at least as much a moral issue – about what is a 'good society' – rather than a narrow issue of economic utility.

The French system, especially during 'the thirty glorious years', represented a clear case of a Fordist model, with large firms locked into bureaucratic organizational forms, technocratic and detached senior management and a low-skilled, highly controlled blue-collar labour force, conflictual labour relations, and the state providing the Keynesian high-growth macroeconomic backdrop. Henri Fayol's theories of general management (see Exhibit 5.1 opposite) reflected the ways in which French firms were a mixture of paternalism and authoritarianism (Gallie 1978), which is pretty much exactly what one associates with Fordism or US managerial capitalism (Hancké 2002: 9, 16). French firms tended to provide minimal training and autonomy to workers, emphasizing narrow skills and a strict, Taylorian division of labour (Maurice et al. 1986). This necessitated relatively large numbers of managers and tight control of workers, meaning that in later years it was difficult for French firms to develop 'high-performance work systems', devolve authority downwards, enter into partnership agreements with unions, and upskill blue-collar workers in the ways (supposedly) managed by cutting edge, 'best practice' firms such as Toyota or Southwest Airlines.

[6] 'A French Policy', *Financial Times*, 18 March 2010. Interestingly, the new Conservative–Liberal coalition government elected in May 2010 cancelled this loan, allegedly under lobbying pressure from a Conservative Party election campaign donor. 'Secret Files Reveal Lobbying Behind Axeing of Sheffield Forgemasters Loan', *Guardian*, 22 July 2010.

Exhibit 5.1 Henri Fayol (1841–1925)

Fayol enjoyed a long career as an industrial engineer and manager. Later in life he published some significant pieces of work about industrial administration which have had a wide impact on France and Europe. Many have suggested that he was a French (or European) version of Frederick Taylor. His writings are very similar to Taylor's; his whole approach is to develop a 'scientific' approach to administration that could be applied generally, to any form of organization. His main contribution *General and Industrial Management*, (1949 / first published in French in 1916) is perhaps a little more academic and detached than Taylor's *Principles of Scientific Management* and, arguably, it focuses rather more on top-down management principles. It contains many references to organizational charts and the appropriate levels of training and competence of the different levels of hierarchy, demonstrating very clear parallels with US managerial capitalism. Interestingly, just as with Taylor's observations at Bethlehem Steel, Fayol's work is based on his years of experience in the metallurgy industry. Throughout, the focus is on a 'scientific' approach to the 'elements of management', that is, planning, organizing, commanding, and co-ordinating (Fayol 1949: 43–110).

Throughout the text Fayol argues that most organizations fail because they are irrationally organized, and that all readers should urgently attempt to implement his theories in their organizations. He advocates the growth of rational, planned, establishments with clear rules, tall hierarchies, and small spans of control (about 6 subordinates being the upper limit). More so than Taylor, he puts great emphasis on the importance of installing 'unity of command' (1949: 66–70). He also stresses the importance of managers leading by example (1949: 100), focusing on improving morale or 'esprit de corps' (1949: 40–41), and suggests that staff should be 'treated with kindliness' (1949: 38). On the other hand, he also mentions the importance of removing 'incompetent' members of staff (1949: 99) although here he shows a degree of humility which might be considered quaint in today's era of intense downsizing and restructuring. He does acknowledge the importance of managers' attempts to act ethically and to maintain morale. 'The entire body corporate feels the effect of the amputation of one of its members, [...] and the sense of security of each of the other employees will be disturbed and his confidence in the future, and consequently his keenness will be lessened unless there was the conviction that it was a just and necessary action.' He even suggests that the 'able and kindly manager' in charge of pursuing redundancies can provide a laid-off worker with 'non-financial rewards or light duties' in order to find 'the means of salving wounds', reflecting the traditions of French paternalism.

Fayol was also a big believer in state planning. He argued that the French government should adopt his general scientific approach; many would suggest that it did ultimately do this. The traditional French approach of long-range planning and elitist bureaucratic organizational forms does appear to reflect many of Fayol's ideas. Compared to Taylor he appears as a minor figure in history (which probably says a lot about the influence of US hegemony over business school teaching). However his ideas do seem to have had wide appeal in France. Lyndall Urwick (himself a major figure in the early years of management theory), in his foreword to the British edition of *General and Industrial Management,* describes him as 'the greatest of the European pioneers of management' (Fayol 1949: vi).

Although the era of organized capitalism provided stability, it did so at the cost of being controlling, micromanaging and undemocratic. This bureaucratic element of France's post-war trajectory was similar to Japan's, in that it was secretive and dominated by elite insiders. The Japanese word *amakudarai* (literally descent from heaven) neatly captures the privileged and undemocratic way in which top managers can be 'found a job' in industry using political ties. In France, the word *pantouflage* (derived from the French word for slippers) describes much the same system. Dormois calls this 'cosy' and 'crony capitalism' (2004: 80, fn22). He even draws parallels with the Soviet *nomenklatura* or Communist Party bosses (see Chapter 8).

This all seems a long way from equality, liberty and fraternity. By the end of the 30 glorious years many French citizens were asking stern questions about what all this growth really meant. Who was really benefitting from the post-war boom? The next section explores the dramatic events of May 1968 and how it prefigured a turn to the left in the 1980s that is fairly unique among the countries studied in this book.

May 1968 and the shift towards socialism

The May 1968 uprisings in Paris were a major event with global repercussions. They reflected the growing appreciation and resentment of the stultifying and unfair nature of entrenched elite privilege in French economy and society. Originated by students, the protests were joined by many thousands of other discontents. According to Boltanski and Chiapello:

> Students (and young wage-earners recently graduated from universities or ***grand écoles***), had seen their numbers increase significantly, during the previous decade ... but had simultaneously seen their conditions deteriorate and their expectations of obtaining autonomous, creative jobs diminish, ... [The movement] developed a critique of ***alienation***. It adopted the main themes of the artistic critique (already pervasive in the United States in the hippie movement): on the one hand, the disenchantment, the inauthenticity, the 'poverty of everyday life', the dehumanization of the world under the sway of technicization and technocratization; on the other hand the loss of autonomy, the absence of creativity, and the different forms of oppression in the modern world. ... In the sphere of work and production ... the dominant themes were denunciation of 'hierarchical power', paternalism, authoritarianism, compulsory work schedules, prescribed tasks, the Taylorist separation between design and execution, and, more generally, the division of labour. (2005: 170)

People took to the streets in huge numbers. Demonstrations and marches were widespread, a wave of strikes hit key employers, sit-ins and teach-ins took place, running battles with police ensued. The uprisings were also, to a certain degree, international; they took place alongside a wave of popular revolt in the late 1960s, such as the Prague Spring protests against Soviet power, and the widespread and at times violent protests in US city streets and university campuses against the Vietnam War, and for the women's and civil rights movements.

The 1968 uprisings spoke to certain general complaints felt by many citizens at large. Those who consider themselves *les soixante huitards* (or 68ers) might be expected still to be critical of abusive power relations. This attitude, some argue, persists in France, making organizational change difficult (Johnson 1996). Others argue that the main points of the protestors were adopted by French companies (and not always to the benefit of staff, see Boltanski and Chiapello 2005; Sennett 2007), and that 1968 prefigured the dramatic shift to the left in French politics in 1981 with the election of the Socialist President Mitterrand.

While the Left did achieve some of its radical agenda, much of it was quickly withdrawn, or not implemented at all (Ambler 1985: 193). The timing was not favourable. Tax-and-spend policies often tend to work best during growth phases, when people are tending to earn more and economic confidence is high. But when economies enter a downturn - as France did in the 1980s - citizens tend to be more likely to criticize high taxes and social welfare spending.

The model of France that emerged after the shift to the Left in the early 1981s looked like an adapted, more humanized version of state-led capitalism. The socialist government enacted several important pro-employee reforms and a wave of nationalizations took place in 1982. The socialists were influenced by the growth of a quality of life movement in France, which has made a lasting impression on French society, such as the generous welfare, holiday and maternity entitlements passed by the socialists, most notably the 39-hour working week (introduced by Mitterrand), and then the 35-hour week passed by the centre-left Jospin government in 2000. Lionel Jospin (interestingly when speaking to Tony Blair in London) summed up his vision of socialism as 'yes to market economy but no to market society'.[7] It is a view that is widely popular and enduring in France, but seems to have disappeared from the political map in

[7] 'Blair Practices Football Diplomacy with France', *BBC News*, 24 July 1998.

the UK, perhaps partly due to the huge influence of the City of London (see Chapter 4).

In contrast, French right-wingers (and Anglo-Saxons) have attacked what they regard as an overbearing state and French citizens' apparently casual approach to work. Former president Nicolas Sarkozy declared 'the France that I love is that France that works ... the France that does not count its hours or its efforts, the France that gets up early' (as quoted in Granter 2009: 142). Although the French work comparatively few hours per week and year, they are among the most productive in the world during those hours (Dormois 2004: 89).

The history of the leftward shift in France is one of the reasons neoliberals (such as Johnson 1996) regard France as overly conservative, and stuck in a now-unworkable 'socialist' past. See for example, the criticisms he makes in his book *French Resistance*.

Exhibit 5.2 An English view of France in the global economy

Michael Johnson's book on France is an excellent example of an expatriate business memoir. While sympathetic to some elements of the French system, mostly he is deeply critical of its insularity and its socialist leanings. In the following extract, he outlines early on in his book the central difference of France from what he believes to be 'world trends'. Just like Exhibit 2.1 in Chapter 2, the construction of a table of two columns represents another 'us and them'-type argument. Johnson writes:

'What makes the French worker tick is a unique set of values that contrast with those emerging in most of the industrialized world. Each contrasting quality represents a barrier to the acceptance of imported techniques.'

FRANCE	WORLD TRENDS
1 Job security is my right	Job security is dead
2 I will not leave Paris to find work	Mobility makes life interesting
3 Work is incidental to my real life	My work defines me, give my life meaning
4 If I advance, I want guarantees	The more responsible the job, the less secure it will be
5 Responsibility co-opts my soul	Adding responsibility is self-realization
6 The team threatens my identity	Our team will get the best results
7 Job descriptions protect me	Job descriptions are starting points, not boundaries
8 Beware of new ideas	Anything is worth a try once
9 Management cannot be trusted	Management has a job to do
10 Profits enrich shareholders	If the company does well, I do well'

(Johnson 1996: 16)

Like much of his book, this table is enjoyable to read and makes some powerful points. But Johnson clearly exaggerates 'world trends'. Johnson is probably deluding himself if he thinks most workers across the world are so compliant with the values of companies and the values of neoliberal capitalism. Johnson's book at times veers into crass cultural stereotyping, although he also uses a lot of knowing irony, and his arguments should perhaps not be taken too seriously. He also demonstrates a profound attraction to French society and business, despite his exasperation, even defending elements of the French approach. He seems to be in favour of the French idea that the firm should try to act in the interests of a wide range of stakeholders, rather than slavishly devoting every effort towards shareholder value (1996: 17).

Although elements of French industry enjoyed government protection, the socialist government struggled with continued industrial decline. Like the UK, French industry has suffered more than in other nations, such as Germany and Japan. Although endowed with thousands of highly skilled and well-educated engineers and designers, French firms have arguably relied too long on Fayolist, low-skilled and highly controlled labour on the shop floor. Movement towards high-performance work systems has been hamstrung by an insular managerial elite and belligerent unions. Major auto groups such as Renault and Peugeot-Citröen have long suffered poor reputations for quality, and today often do not exactly excel in customer satisfaction surveys.[8]

Under the socialists, the French state continued to act as a major economic actor. One interesting example of this was the Minitel system. The state-owned firm France Télécom pioneered Minitel, bringing it to market in 1984. This was a terminal-based information system which allowed households to connect to state and private companies offering commercial services such as banking or travel information. Minitel was (almost) a forerunner to the internet, especially when private messaging services were introduced. It was very popular in France, used in over 1 in 4 households at its peak, and it generated huge revenues for France Télécom. The technology was interesting, but doomed to failure by its in-built limitations (Castells 2000: 372–5). Minitel demonstrated the double-edged sword of state-led development; it enables

[8] According to a 2010 UK survey, the Citröen C1 is the only 'French' car to make it into the top 10 most reliable cars available in the UK. It came 8th, after several models from Honda (1st, 2nd, 6th, 7th), Daihatsu, (3rd), Hyundai (4th) and Ford (5th). 'Honda Tops Reliability Survey', *Daily Telegraph*, 25 May 2010. I use the inverted commas because the C1 is a joint venture with Toyota, built in Czech Republic.

very quick distribution and adoption of new technologies, but if the 'wrong horse' is backed, the system slumps into disuse just as quickly. Minitel was intended as a centralized, statist solution for the challenges of the IT age (and it has survived today in some form),[9] but surely the future in IT seemed to lie with Silicon Valley, and venture capital start-ups, hence the almost total dominance of US software and hardware firms since the 1980s, and the terminal decline of French (and British) alternatives.

Generally speaking French workers did well out of the post-war period, with successive reductions in working hours and increasing pay. Laws were passed to limit working hours, improve workplace safety and labour representation by unions. The official retirement age was lowered to 60 in 1981 (Dormois 2004: 8). Works councils' laws were passed in 1946, meaning that any workplace with more than 500 employees must have a works council, or in French, a *comité d'enterprise.* This reflects the social market philosophy of French capitalism, and is not dissimilar from systems of employee voice used in Germany (see Chapter 6).

However, few can disagree that French workers have faced major challenges driven by globalization as firms rationalized their employment systems and exported jobs to cheaper regions. Even Dormois admits that labour 'bore the brunt of the global shake-up in the production system' (2004: 93). Unemployment went back up to 10.1% of the total workforce in 1986.[10] Youth unemployment was particularly severe: 20.4% of men under 25, and 25.7% of women under 25 were unemployed at the end of the 1990s (Dormois 2004: 99). Job loss also affected cadres; 4.6% of them were unemployed by 1999. Unemployment would have been much higher without massive government spending to undergird the economy. According to Dormois, 'Between 1973 and 2000, government expenditure to prop up employment went from F1.6 billion (or 0.9% of GDP) to F58 billion (or 4% of GDP). In a typical boom year, such as 1999, with a buoyant labour market, the government still subsidized around 120,000 jobs' (2004: 99–100). The growth of temporary and insecure employment – and

[9] Although in decline, as late as 2003, 4.8 million original Minitel terminals were still in use, and 32% of the population still had access to it. One of its advantages was that it was a closed system running on France Télécom phone lines, making it very quick and simple to use. It's first 3 minutes' use were free, so it was mostly used for quickly finding standardized information such as checking stock prices or train timetables. Mintel emulators were developed which ran on PCs, but this only prolonged its seemingly inevitable decline. 'France's Minitel: 20 Years Young', *BBC News*, 14 May 2003.

[10] According to official figures, that is. The real numbers of those out of work would have been considerably higher.

of government-sponsored training schemes – massively outpaced the growth of stable, salaried jobs (Appay 1998).

The shift towards socialism could be regarded as fairly successful as regards social change; in a dramatic contrast to most other advanced and developing nations, income inequality actually fell during this period (Dormois 2004: 7). But economically the socialist period was less successful. The persistence of the state-led economy in France (especially the policy of nationalizations) seemed to run counter to broader economic trends towards globalization and integration. The socialist government's election coincided with a dramatic economic crisis and radical change to the French model of capitalism started to become a possibility. As the next section shows, France's state-led model of organized capitalism (Lash and Urry 1987) or its 'second spirit' of capitalism (Boltanski and Chiapello 2005) is under increasing strain.

The 'second spirit' evaporates? France faces up to a neoliberal reform

In keeping with all of the countries examined in this book, changes to traditional business systems have been afoot in France for at least the last 20 years. Some will say these changes are driven by the inexorable logic of globalization or internationalizing capitalism. Others will argue that little of substance has changed, and that the fundaments of *dirigisme* remain in place. Still others will suggest that a mixture of both positions is correct (Clift 2012). While France has a reputation for being resistant to globalization and social change, there is no doubt that change has come to France in certain distinct ways, and many would argue that this change has arrived quickly and with force (Appay 1998; Hancké 2002).

Discussions of France, therefore, have important ramifications for VoC theory. If France has changed so fast – from socialism and *dirigisme* to neoliberal globalism – then what are we to make of the concepts of embeddedness, path-dependency and complementarities? Are these effects weaker than VoC theorists usually claim? This section of the chapter reviews recent literature on France, showing significant changes, and takes issue with the stereotype of France as a proud, stubbornly resistant, nation stuck in a time-warp.

While French authors seem most likely to sense change, Anglo-Saxon authors appear more likely to see (and bemoan) its absence. There may be a hint of envy and resentment in the mainstream Anglo-Saxon view. A subtext to neoliberal interpreters of France goes something like this: 'we've embraced harsh changes since the onset of neoliberalism, but why don't you, too?'. Anglo-Saxon authors often regard France's left-wing critics of globalization as stuck in the past, and that French workers (especially *les fonctionnaires* employed in the public sector) still enjoy artificially protected and cosseted working lives, and therefore have little to complain about. For example, while Johnson (1996) believes that France has only barely, reluctantly changed, Dormois, insists that '[i]n the past fifty years the supposedly traditional French way of life has all but disappeared and the circumstances of most French people have converged onto a Western standard' (2004: 9). An article in the *Wall Street Journal Europe* in 2009 noted that the traditional long French lunch break has become a thing of the past, with working lunches shrinking from an average 90 minutes in 1975 to 30 minutes in 2008.[11]

One of the most interesting and widely discussed French books about capitalism in recent years is Boltanski and Chiapello's (2005) *The New Spirit of Capitalism*. It argues that capitalism has evolved in distinct phases, and that in each phase it develops an appropriate justificatory and explanatory 'spirit', which serves to generate wide public support. They argue that there has been a profound shift from the 'second spirit of capitalism' (which is basically organized capitalism or managerial capitalism predicated on lifetime employment, Taylorist mass production and strong blue-collar unions), to the 'third spirit of capitalism' (which conforms to a much more open, globalized, disorganized and ephemeral form of investor capitalism). They argue that this shift has been dramatic and painful in France. In a chapter entitled 'Dismantling the World of Work', they provide a compelling story of change and its deleterious results. The most obvious problems generated for French citizens in recent years are job insecurity, lack of labour representation and lack of legal clarity about employment status. Their discussion of how entitlements have been removed, real pay has stagnated, jobs made less secure, work made more intense and opportunities reduced, is very convincing, and familiar to many OECD nations (see also Bourdieu 1999). These are especially acute problems for younger French workers. This issue came to a head in France with the widespread protests around, and eventual retraction of, Chirac's proposed new First Employment Contract in 2006, which would have severely curtailed employment rights for staff aged under 26.[12] Exhibit 5.3 is an extract from *The New Spirit of Capitalism* which provides a strong indication of its content:

[11] '"Restauration rapide" Nation.' *Wall Street Journal Europe*, 20 November 2009.

[12] 'France to Replace Youth Job Law', *BBC News*, 10 April 2006.

Exhibit 5.3 The collapse of stable work in the third spirit of capitalism

French sociologists Luc Boltanksi and Eve Chiapello, in their massive study *The New Spirit Capitalism* provide a rich critique of contemporary management philosophies, typically those emanating from the USA. Their view is essentially a Marxist one. As such it is a good example of a defensive French position that argues that the state should be doing more to protect its citizens from the ravages of contemporary economic globalization, especially the growth of fragile employment and 'McJobs'.

'The process of social discrimination compounds that of job discrimination, and encloses these workers ever more tightly in their 'poverty trap'. Without going so far as to regard such extreme conditions as representative of all instances of job insecurity, we cannot fail to register the accumulation of handicaps by those who arrive on the labour market already in possession of the fewest qualifications. Unqualified blue-collar workers are thus most affected by unemployment and job insecurity. When they do eventually find a stable job, it is invariably at the end of several years of casual jobs, involving temping, skills contracts, or fixed-term contracts. The situation is scarcely better for other blue- and white-collar workers. How could such a difficult, harrowing existence not affect their physical and psychological health, and erode their productive capacity? How could it give them the opportunity to develop their skills [...]? How could it permit them to create a family that will be a source of support, when their prospects are utterly uncertain and, even when they have a stable job, their firms do not allow them to be with their family, or do not care about their future? More generally, how could it enable them to have long-term projects in a society where they can make only short-term plans?'

Boltanski & Chiapello (2005: 231–2). By permission of Verso Books.

The above text may resonate with the experiences and fears of many young people towards labour markets, whichever country they hail from. The problems are common to all mature OECD nations facing up to slow growth and hyper-competition, especially in the 2010s after the impact of the subprime crisis. But the text also reflects some deep-seated and specifically French issues. Bob Hancké (2002), in an important book on France, argues that long-term planning shackled government and firms together too tightly, bringing both down when change was needed. He demonstrates that, by 1980, French firms were the most heavily indebted in the whole of the OECD (Hancké 2002: 51). Hancké's argument is most interesting as he claims it was the large French firms, as opposed to the state, which really pushed for changes and succeeded in developing new institutional forms for French capital. His book is upbeat about France, claiming that it has gone through an 'astonishing economic turnaround' (2002: 7), yet it still does not resemble a regulated Anglo-Saxon economy; the state remains important, despite being a shadow of its former self. Hancké also clearly describes the U-turn of the socialist government as it faced up to economic crisis. As it came to power in 1981 it was nationalizing industry and finance; by 1984 it was liberalizing and privatizing, including issuing major banking reforms along the lines of a British or Japanese 'big bang' deregulation. Schmidt argues a similar line on France's liberalization, arguing that French firms have basically freed themselves from state control, allowing them to 'go to the financial markets for further capital infusions', and that 'by the late 1990s French business had grown tremendously in size, scope, competitiveness, and profitability, while public sector ownership went from a peak of 10 per cent of the economy in 1985 down to its pre-war level of 5 per cent by the late 1990s' (Schmidt 2002: 188, 189).

French firms have 'modernized, slimmed-down and streamlined their operations' (Schmidt 2002: 189). French unions have been marginalized and 'neutralized' (Hancké 2002: 190) and flexible, team-based, high-performance work practices have been introduced. Today French unions have (at least on paper) among the weakest positions in the OECD (Hancké 2002: 20). Union density in France – at 8% – is actually lower than that of the US level of 12% (although collective bargaining coverage remains far higher, at around 97.7% compared to the US's level of 13.3%).[13] According to Dormois 'unlike in the German cooperative institutional arrangements, [French] unions now appear increasingly marginalized, as just another galaxy of self-interested pressure groups' (2004: 79–80).

While these might be regarded as encouraging developments for capital, they pose clear threats to labour. Employment is widely considered to have become increasingly precarious in France. One of the reasons for this is because of the perversities of French labour protection. Firms make wide use of temporary, non-standard, and agency labour precisely because hiring new staff on standard employment contracts ties them in to long-term, open-ended employment, and makes it difficult to dismiss troublesome staff or make cuts in lean times. French employers often skirt around pro-employee legislation by using temporary and contract labour. Recruitment agencies such as Adecco and the US multinational firm Manpower have a major presence in French labour markets. (France is Manpower's number one market, with 840 branches nationwide.[14]) This is a very important point, and is worth bearing in mind for those who describe the French model as 'employee favouring' – in theory employees are well-protected in France, but in practice firms can be very effective in finding ways to avoid this regulation.

[13] Figures from International Labour Organization, International Statistical Inquiry, 2008–9: htpp://www.ilo.org.

[14] France provides 29% of Manpower's total revenue, more than the UK (12%) and USA (10%). Details from Manpower company website: http://www.manpower.com/about/about.cfm.

Perhaps France's most grievous difficulty is persistent unemployment, and a poor record of job creation. Unemployment was remarkably low during the post-war boom. Official figures put unemployment at below 2% of the working population from 1950–65. But in the latter half of the 1970s unemployment started to rise, and has remained a problem ever since. By 1977 unemployment had grown to 4% of the workforce, and the steep upward rise continued to 6% in 1980, 8% in 1982 and 10% by 1987. There was a reduction to 8.5% by 1990, but this was a brief respite as unemployment climbed again – to the very serious level of 12% by 1998 (Dormois 2004: 25). The French workforce in general is very well-educated, but the country struggles to create adequate jobs for them all (a similar situation to that in Germany in recent years, see Chapter 6). Youth unemployment is a particular headache. Government policies aimed at tackling these problems have included raising the age of school leaving and expanding higher education provision. In the year 2000, barely 26% of men and women in the age cohort 15–24 were in employment, 'compared with 45 per cent in Britain and 46 per cent in Germany' (Dormois 2004: 8).

Public employment retains a major role in the French economy, despite the frequent calls in the 1990s for the state to be 'rolled back' and, in particular, bureaucratic 'red tape' to be cut. It employs about one-quarter of the whole workforce. Public sector employment grew from 785,000 staff in 1914 (3.9% of the entire workforce), to 5.6 million staff in 2000 (24.7% of the workforce) (Dormois 2004: 45). President Sarkozy (2007–2012) frequently spoke of his desire to reduce the size of the state. Upon his election he promised '100 steps' to streamline public administration, which will cut the burden of red tape by 'by 25%', supposedly generating savings to companies of €15 billion per year. France in 2007 spent approximately €1 billion per year on public administration, and this was predicted to fall to €850 million (roughly into proportion with Germany). This would also entail reducing the number of public officials by 100,000 over five years.[15]

Enacting those reforms proved to be extraordinarily difficult. There have been numerous strikes and demonstrations by public sector unions who protest vigorously if government threatens to erode their job security or downgrade their pension provisions. Members of the general public often join in these demonstrations in order to show solidarity with the public servants whose jobs and conditions are being threatened. It is not easy to imagine this situation in the UK, where the general public is often today fairly hostile to striking union members, and where the media tends to reinforce this hostility. In France, perhaps

[15] 'Sarkozy's 100 Steps to Slimmer Government', *Financial Times*, 13 December 2007.

harking back to its revolutionary past, public protest and resistance is seen not just as a right, but almost a civic duty. Mainstream critics suggest that these protests are becoming 'increasingly perfunctory' (Dormois 2004: 79). This might be premature. Three million protestors took to the streets in March 2009 in protests about the government's economic policies during the recession.[16] President Sarkozy unexpectedly lost the 2012 Presidential election to the socialist candidate François Hollande, who promised an end to austerity measures, much heavier taxation of top earners and tougher regulation of the banks. However, attempting to do this while retaining France's 'credibility' to capital markets has proven difficult. France lost is AAA credit rating in January 2013 and at the time of writing unemployment is staying stubbornly high at around 3 million.[17]

The difficulites of reforming French government are mirrored by the ambivalent status of corporate reform in France. The mounting pressures of international financial capitalism do not automatically mean that French businesses have changed their behaviour (Clift 2007). Shareholder value logic is a loose term with several interpretations (Froud et al. 2006). French ownership of overseas firms could be equally as important as foreign ownership of French firm equity. In recent years large French multinationals have controlled 19,000 subsidiaries worldwide, employing some 3.5 million people (Dormois 2004: 42). Johal and Leaver (2007) suggest that at least two-thirds of the employees of companies in the CAC 40 (the index of top French stock market listed companies) work in locations outside of France. Vivendi is probably the best (worst?) example. It embarked on a highly ambitious spree of acquisitions as it attempted to emulate the model of US multimedia empires such as AOL Time Warner. But Vivendi radically overstretched itself, leading to massive losses and the dismissal of its flamboyant CEO Jean-Marie Messier (nicknamed 'J2M'). There any many other examples of French firms expanding overseas. The then nationalized Thomson electronics bought USA's RCA and the consumer electronics division of General Electric in 1987. In 2000 France Télécom purchased the UK cellphone company Orange. UK insurer Sun Life was purchased by Axa in the same year. 35% of the CAC 40 was foreign-owned by 1997 (Morin 2000: 42). Thomson has since sold off its consumer electronics lines of business to TCL of China. In keeping with the post-industrial trends of France, Thomson now concentrates on media, broadcasting and IT-related services and in 2010 rebranded itself as Technicolor.

---

[16] Police estimates put the number at 1.2 million. 'French Unions Claim 3m on the Streets', *BBC News*, 19 March 2009.

[17] 'Hollande Tours Provinces as French President's Popularity Hits Record Lows', *Guardian*, 11 March 2013.

The *Commissariat du plan* was finally wound up by centre-right Prime Minister de Villepin in 2006. Traditional members of the French planning elite were being replaced since the 1970s by economists trained in econometrics which was 'dominated by Anglo-American academics' (Boltanski and Chiapello 2005: 198). The complexity, unpredictability and internationalization of the world economy made long-range planning appear redundant and self-defeating. This marked the official end of French state planning, 14 years after it was formally abandoned in the UK.

Globalization appears to be opening France up to inward and outward investment. Some believe this is having profound convergence effects. Dormois (2004: 1), for example, begins his book by suggesting that '[t]his process of convergence and standardization, often referred to as "Americanisation", in many aspects of social life, economic and otherwise, has affected France, as it has its European neighbours, with increasing vigour in the second half of the century.' Interestingly for an author who is otherwise fairly pro-business he argues that:

> in this very 'postmodern' country, professional activity (or gainful employment) seems to have receded to a shorter proportion of people's lifetimes and to be interspersed with longer waiting periods (of training, retraining, unemployment, and eventually early retirement): a person's working life appears much shorter but perhaps more intense at the same time. While working time has dwindled, employment has become an obsession; work demands less physical energy but far more mental energy, concentration, focus. People increasingly organize their personal life around their career and even temporary unemployment causes most people affected by it grave psychological and material disruptions. (Dormois 2004: 9)

This is precisely what Genda (2006) argues about Japan (see Chapter 11), and it could be a 'postmodern' condition found in all OECD nations. People are questioning the value of contemporary working life in France, just as they are in all of the advanced nations discussed in this book. Economic change has 'fuelled stress, a growing sense of insecurity, and an "existentialist" quest for a new identity among the French who have become the world's largest consumers of tranquilisers' (Dormois 2004: 10).

Economic uncertainty bred by the global economic downturn of 2008 onwards has triggered widespread strikes and stoppages, mostly in the public sector, but not exclusively. In 2009–10 there were strikes at SeaFrance, at French ports, in the French postal service and the state railway company SNCF. Probably the most tragic and frightening events seemingly tied to the neoliberalization of France have been the suicides of staff at workplaces that have been heavily affected by change. In a shocking development, 23 staff at France Télécom took their own lives over 18 months in 2007–9. They were so dismayed by the organizational changes and a bullying work culture that their indignation and anxiety took them to the ultimate extreme.[18] It was perhaps telling that this was a very conservative French firm, a former monopoly provider that in prior eras would have been almost immune from global change. Maybe the incoming management believed that only a form of 'shock therapy' would be able to effect change in such a stable environment?

Another recent development of concern has been the spate of 'bossnappings'. In several high-profile cases, French staff barricaded their senior managers into their offices, effectively holding them hostage on the premises. This has included senior managers of the US firm 3M and the HR manager of Japanese firm Sony. In 2009, as the recession took hold, these events became more frequent, perhaps fuelled by the resentment created by the huge executive pay deals that were struck in recent years.[19] Much as Johnson (1996) argues, heaven help incoming executives who try to act 'macho' in France, as the unions can be relied on to respond in kind.

Amid all of the signs of crisis and restructuring, it is important to bear in mind the enduring size and success of the French economy. There are several sectors in which it retains huge influence. For example, France boasts a powerful group of arms contractors. The French defence industry is the third largest in the world, employing around 400,000 staff in the mid-1990s when it was almost completely state-owned (Gordon 1996: 30). Today these firms include EADS (formerly Aerospatiale) and the Dassault Group, manufacturer of the advanced Mirage and Raffale fighter-jets. The Mirage has been a highly successful export to many nations, including Argentina, Greece, Taiwan, India, China and Australia.

France also has some major multinationals in the retail field. While USA's retail giant Wal-Mart is the third largest company by revenue in the world, France's Carrefour is a very respectable 25th, having pioneered the hard discounting, 'everything under one roof' hypermarché model that Wal-Mart in many ways emulated. France is by some distance the world's most popular tourist destination. In 2009 it received 74.2 million tourists, compared to 54.9 million visiting the USA and

[18] 'France Télécom Bosses Hold Crisis Talks Over Staff Suicides', *Guardian*, 15 September 2009.

[19] '"Boss-napped" Manager Set Free After Climbdown', *The Times*, 26 March 2009.

52.2 million Spain.[20] It has a huge presence in the food, wine, fashion and cosmetics industries (Gordon 1996: 31–32). A major example is the giant firm L'Oréal, a multinational of over 67,000 employees and revenues of around 23 billion Euros.[21]

Recent years have also seen rising inequalities. The salary range moved up from 1 to 3 in 1984, to 1 to 6 in 1996 (Dormois 2004: 7). French firms have also made widespread use of performance-related pay (Marsden and Belfield 2010). In a real sign of the extent of French 'enmeshment' into international capital flows (Clift 2007: 567), parts of the economy have been drawn into crises and scandals more reminiscent of free market financialized capitalism. An estimated $7 billion loss was incurred by 'rogue trading' at the major French bank Société Générale (France's fourth largest firm by revenue), which was blamed on the workings of one employee amid an allegedly much wider culture that encouraged high risk, reckless lending.[22] A French *grande école* graduate was also revealed to have been at the heart of a scandal at US investment bank Goldman Sachs, whereby the bank was alleged to have been secretly betting that some of the bank's own clients' subprime investments would collapse in value.[23] Clearly at some level the changes and behaviours associated with financialized, global capitalism are taking place in France, and it is wrong to assume that France is somehow totally resistant to 'external' threats of globalization. There are obvious pressures from within. INSEAD, based at Fontainebleau outside Paris, is one of Europe's most prestigious (and market-focused) business schools. One of its most famous academics is the Dutch leadership 'guru' Manfred Kets de Vries, whose writings and teachings are steeped in just the kind of American-style 'third spirit of capitalism' language of which Boltanski and Chiapello write. Lionizing Anglo-Saxon top leaders such as Richard Branson and Jack Welch, he claims:

---

[20] UN World Tourism Barometer, Interim Update, April 2010, www.unwto.org/facts/eng/pdf/barometer/UNWTO_Barom10_update_april_en_excerpt.pdf.

[21] http://money.cnn.com/magazines/fortune/global500/2009/countries/France.html.

[22] 'Société Générale Scandal: A Suspicion That This Was Inevitable', *New York Times,* 5 February 2008.

[23] Trader Fabrice Tourre, boasted in an email to a friend that 'the whole building is about to collapse anytime now ... only potential survivor the fabulous Fab ... standing in the middle of all these complex, highly leveraged, exotic trades he created without necessarily understanding the implications of all these monstrosities!!!'.'Wall Street Regulator Charges Goldman Sachs with $1bn Fraud Against Sub-Prime Investors', *Guardian,* 17 April 2010.

> Vision is important in that it provides a road map for the future, generates excitement, creates order out of chaos ... [top leaders] exude enthusiasm and radiate self-confidence when talking about what they are trying to do, and where they want to go, and this makes their vision contagious. (Kets de Vries 1996: 492)

Such ideas are inimical to traditional French modes of 'organized capitalism' yet they are being taught to new generations of French (and international) MBA students.

French theorists, more accustomed to continuity than change, tend to see change as more radical than Anglo-Saxon observers, who usually regard France as a slow reformer. Marxist French authors, such as Morin (2000), argue that the socialism-infused traditional model of France has now completely collapsed under the pressures of neoliberal, Anglo-Saxon capitalism. Shareholder value logic dominates the thinking of French firms, and the long-termism and employee-favouring elements of French corporate life have evaporated. Overseas ownership of the CAC 40 has grown, and friendly blockholdings between French firms have unravelled. Anglo-Saxon notions of 'flexibility' replace traditional focus on hierarchy and stability. *Grande école* cadres are fading away as business school-educated MBA general managers start to take control. It is not only French authors who see it this way. Mary O'Sullivan (2003) argues that shareholder value logic has moved into France in a big way, and – just as in the USA (Lazonick and O'Sullivan 2000) – large French firms are moving from a 'retain and reinvest' to a 'downsize and distribute' strategy. Again, the focus is on the force of international pressure changing the nature of French capital.

There is also the distinct possibility that the French variety of capitalism can be destroyed from within. There are many French individuals and groups who want to see greater individualization, privatization and liberalization. These might be private businesspersons or they could be French academics schooled in neoliberalism, such as Guy Sorman (2009). They could be lobby groups working on behalf of large firms or institutional investors. They could be celebrity CEOs, such as Jean-Marie Messier the former CEO of Vivendi Universal who declared the end of *'l'exception française'* (Dormois 2004: 1). Interestingly, with the failure of Vivendi, this company's story became almost a French Enron, with Messier playing the role of hate figure for much of France (Johnson and Orange 2003). In a conservative business system when a 'norm entrepreneur' fails, the media often turns on them as they defend the righteousness of the old ways of economic life.

Conclusion: the ideal of French socialism – an unattainable dream?

As we have seen, interpretations of the future of French capitalism vary widely, from those who believe the last vestiges of *dirigisme* and socialism have been swept away, to those who argue that the French economy remains dysfunctionally wedded to strong state control and regulation. Evaluations of the strengths and weaknesses of this system also differ; some are optimistic (Hancké 2002), others downbeat (Dormois 2004). Analysts more in tune with the critiques of *les soixante huitards* (Boltanski and Chiapello 2005) use strongly morally-infused arguments to heavily criticize France's move towards an unethical and ruthless neoliberalism. This brief concluding section will offer some final comments on where the French economy might be headed, and what this might mean for our understanding of VoC.

Throughout the 1980s and beyond, broader economic and political forces impacting on France had profound effects. A good example is European Union integration, which is bound to mean closer cross-national trade, attempts to harmonize economic policy with that of the other member states, and a diminution of the French state's abilities to attempt to control its national economy. The introduction of the European currency in 1999 means that the European Central Bank now sets interest rates for all 16 of the nations in the Eurozone, bringing to an end the *dirigiste* tactic of devaluation of the franc to boost exports.

Since the 1990s, French policymakers and intellectuals have also increasingly discussed problematic *social* issues, such as chronic poverty, long-term unemployment and the isolation of disadvantaged persons from mainstream society – a concept often labelled 'social exclusion'. The high rise public housing on the outskirts of Paris were the setting for the famous film *La Haine* ('Hate'; director Mathieu Kassovitz, 1995) that vividly depicted the lives of socially-excluded French ethnic minorities. Research reports pointed to dysfunctional and underfunded social policy and schooling, with parts of inner-city France described to be as comparably bad as the UK or USA for drugs, burglary and violent crime as young people become excluded from the labour market and cut off from sources of support such as friends and family (Martin 1996). Statistics for certain forms of violent crime rose steadily in the 1990s, with strong correlations to rises in youth unemployment. Effects were particularly severe in certain depressed regions (Fougère et al. 2009). Although the French socio-economic model clearly differs from Anglo-Saxon neoliberalism and is widely defended by liberals and socialists on ethical grounds, France is far from immune to serious social problems. As of 2012, the French economy, in keeping with most of the advanced, mature economies such as the UK, USA and Japan, is struggling with low growth, low confidence, high unemployment and severe public sector debt. State spending is reported to be as high as 54% of GDP, and predicted to rise.[24] Even when faced with such difficulties, the French economy has traditionally been deeply imbued with the social market philosophy, and seems unwilling to fully reform in Anglo-Saxon directions. In the words of Johnson:

> The mistrust of Anglo-Saxons is acute. Anglo-Saxons have an ideological attachment to open market policies, self-reliance and profit. The French can accept some of these qualities, but only if a prior company condition is met: a commitment to social responsibility. (1996: 16)

This, again, is much the same as the prevailing view about firm behaviour in Japan – that Japanese firms are not, and should never become, simply tools for delivering shareholder value. Firms are profoundly social organisms, embedded in wider society, contributing to it, and being constrained by its moral and institutional norms. Despite the wide changes in French economy towards more openness and towards an (arguable) increase in shareholder value mentality (Morin 2000; O'Sullivan 2003), it seems unlikely that France will ever abandon the viewpoint that capital and finance should be our servants, rather than our masters. Jospin's 'yes to market economy, no to market society' is a powerful and enduring statement. Notions of socialism and social justice, while clearly in long-term decline, retain an important presence in French society. For example, while on paper French unions are a shadow of their former selves, in practice they still wield considerable power. Even if employees have chosen not to join, it is likely that, when conflict erupts, many of them will join their unionized colleagues out on the picket lines or in mass demonstrations. The French approach to capitalism – where the state and society take primacy over markets – is a morally attractive position for millions of people. For this reason, it is doubtful that French capitalism will ever fully resemble the more socially detached and more ethically dubious Anglo-Saxon version. France is a powerful player in world politics. It has a formidable military and is a major player in arms exports. Its independence from the USA is notable (there have been times when France has pulled out of NATO). Even centre-right politicians such as de Villepin spoke out at the UN against the US-led invasion of Iraq in 2003.

---

[24] 'If the Left Wins in France, a Critical Battle of Ideologies Must Surely Follow', *The Observer*, 29 January 2012.

There is a lot of rhetoric around the future of the French model and the advance of globalization or 'Americanization'. After the subprime collapse, Sarkozy spoke of the need to introduce a 'more moral' form of capitalism.[25] The European Parliament in 2010 debated legislation designed to better regulate hedge funds and private equity.[26] The trajectory of France seems undeniable - away from organized capitalism and *dirigisme* and towards globalization and financialization, and in a fairly short timeframe. Yet there will always be tensions and resistances to this trend (Clift 2007; Schmidt 2002). Parts of the distinctly French system, and its underlying economic and social philosophy, are likely to survive.

Many analysts have probably exaggerated the differences between liberal capitalism and French state-led capitalism, especially when making comparisons with Soviet practice (Dormois 2004: 80), or describing it as crony capitalism, or 'frozen in time' (Johnson 1996: 12). I would argue that no country is frozen in time, and that traditional practice tends to go hand in hand with significant changes. France, while clearly facing some serious difficulties, is a successful nation, with numerous powerful multinational firms, an advanced welfare state and a good quality of life for millions of its citizens. The sceptical and detached approach of French workers towards management and work could be read as healthy rather than outdated. Income inequality is less severe in France than it is in Anglo-Saxon nations. The share of total French wealth owned by the richest 10% in France came down from 37% in 1967 to 30% in 1982, before stabilizing at around 33% in the 1990s, with progressive taxation the probable reason (Piketty 2003: 1010). After taxes and transfers, the Gini coefficient in France stood at around 30 in the 1970s, dropping just below 30 in the 2000s. It now seems to have crept slowly upwards to 32.7.[27] According to Wilkinson and Pickett's (2009: 20–21) calculations of income inequality and the prevalence of health and social problems, France is situated around the middle of the scale - less egalitarian than Japan and the Nordic societies, but considerably more egalitarian than the free market Anglo-Saxon countries. The French welfare state, while perennially threatened by budget cuts (Dormois 2004: 62), almost certainly plays an important role in sustaining this more egalitarian society, where in many cases people are put before profits. The French public health service (in

[25] 'Davos 2010: Sarkozy Calls for Revamp of Capitalism', *BBC News*, 27 January 2010.

[26] 'EU Prepares Vote on New Hedge Fund Rules', *BBC News*, 17 May 2010.

[27] OECD figures on income distribution, http://stats.oecd.org/Index.aspx?QueryId=26067andLang=en; 'In Praise of Inequality', *Forbes*, 17 March 2003.

which the state pays for around 77% of all treatments) is rated by the World Health Organization as the best in the world (WHO 2000: 153). The 35 hour work week has its critics, but it provides an attractive alternative to the overwork culture so prevalent in nations such as Japan, Korea, the USA and the UK. The transport and business infrastructure of most of France is also excellent. French capitalism has of course changed, but we should not dismiss its legacy and its enduring achievements.

Further reading

Johnson, M., (1996) *French Resistance: Individuals Versus the Company in French Corporate Life*, London: Cassell.

This is a short, highly readable book about working life in large French firms, written by an Anglo-Saxon businessman who worked in France for many years. Johnson writes eloquently - often amusingly - about the specifics of Gallic corporate culture, especially the stubborn and wilful ways in which French workers often refuse to submit to managerial power. In his harsher moments he borders on xenophobia and cultural essentialism, but he also understands France well and he is clearly attracted to many parts of the society. He was sympathetic enough to be able to survive as an expat manager in France for far longer than most. Mostly, however, he characterizes the traditions of French business as futile remnants of a bygone era. This makes his book very useful as a document on how the captains of Anglo-Saxon globalization believe they are right and how they expect non-conformists to gradually disappear.

Dormois, J.-P., (2004) *The French Economy in the Twentieth Century*, Cambridge: Cambridge University Press.

This is another short but highly useful book on France. Interestingly in comparison to Johnson, as a Frenchman, Dormois sees things differently, arguing that France already has pretty much converged on the Americanized version of capitalism. His viewpoint is essentially a neoliberal one, and he is very critical of some of France's *dirigiste* traditions.

Shonfield, A., (1965) *Modern Capitalism: The Changing Balance of Public and Private Power*, Oxford: Oxford University Press.

Although not exclusively about France, this is a hugely useful book which has a great deal to say about the French system of *dirigiste* capitalism. It is very much a product of its time, in that the author believed that the high performance of the French system post-war would continue indefinitely. He therefore gives France model status, and argues that other nations, especially a struggling UK, should adopt this model. It is a huge and influential text that makes several important arguments which look dated today, but do indicate the power of state-led economic systems during the 1960s.

Hancké, B., (2002) *Large Firms and Institutional Change: Industrial Renewal and Economic Restructuring in France*, Oxford: Oxford University Press.

Hancké makes several important points in this very detailed book on the French economy. Using in-depth case studies of Renault, EDF, and Moulinex, he argues that large French firms have managed to break away from the managing institutions of the French state. He notes that institutions themselves can change and adapt, which amounts to an important criticism of VoC theory. The book is also useful for containing some discussions of how the German economy has also adapted in recent years. Indeed, Hancké argues that Germany has been more of the model for France's reforms than the Anglo-Saxon countries.

Boltanski, L., and Chiapello, E., (2005) *The New Spirit of Capitalism*, London: Verso.

This is a major tract of social theory by two French sociologists. It is on a much broader topic than French capitalism and convergence, and it is challenging to read, but provides a fascinating and very useful overview of how French capital has changed over the last 20 years. Like Dormois, they believe that French traditional economic ways have basically been all-but destroyed by the irreversible march of Anglo-Saxon financialized capitalism, but unlike him, they are highly critical of these developments.

SIX Germany: Europe's 'Production Machine'

Chapter objectives

- To describe how Germany became a major economic power formed out of dozens of small independent states and principalities
- To show how the relatively late unification of Germany retarded its economic development but also formed the basis for the German Empire's rapid growth based on 'late industrialization' strategies
- The chapter will note the strong path-dependent effects of many of these historical features of Germany: many survive today to some degree
- To explain how defeat and rancorous peace terms in the First World War foreshadowed the disastrous collapse of Germany's first democratic state and the slide into totalitarianism and the Second World War
- To explore West Germany's enormously successful recovery from the Second World War, and the establishment of a popular and enduring 'social market economy'
- To discuss the extent to which the social market economy may be in terminal decline following the economic challenges of globalization and the severe difficulties in reunifying West and East Germany

Introduction

The rise of industrialism in the late 19th century saw Germany emerge as a major economic player. After initially making slower progress than the UK it eventually became the dominant industrial power in Europe. Germany's GDP today is around US$3.6 trillion, and its population around 81 million.[1] It has become famous at least during the last 50 years for its export-led, high-quality manufacturing industries, with the products of its leading-edge multinationals, such as Siemens, Bosch, Volkswagen (VW), and Mercedes-Benz, recognized the world over for reliability, safety, attractive design and build quality. There are also many powerful German firms in the services sector, including major banks and insurers, such as Dresdner Bank and Allianz, software developers such as SAP, and European-wide telecommunications companies such as Deutsche Telekom. It is also a major force in the global pharmaceuticals and chemicals industries. Germany is noted for its extremely well-educated population and well-trained workforce, most famously in the fields of science, technology and engineering.

The majority of its large- and medium-sized companies feature advanced and popular systems of employee involvement and worker voice, very high levels of training and staff development, and forms of workplace democracy that try - where possible - to minimize internal conflict among the various stakeholders that constitute the corporation. German firms are typically understood to operate on a cautious and conservative basis, led by loyal and dedicated senior managers who have tended to work their way slowly up the corporate hierarchy and have not hopped jobs (Smyser 1993: 70). Parallels are often drawn to Japanese-style understandings of what a corporation is and to whom its most important responsibilities lie; Germany, along with Japan, is a strong example of a CME. Firms are traditionally closely supported by long-term, trusted relationships with banks and insurers which provide 'patient' capital. Corporations are embedded into defensive group company networks that insulate firms and management from hostile takeovers. Corporate governance laws and customs reinforce this stability. The longer-term approach of the German system means that German corporations typically have no need to endlessly restructure themselves in frantic efforts to appeal to the short-term demands of stock markets and rating agencies as companies are so likely to do in LMEs. This also makes it logical for core staff to pursue long-term careers with one employer, meaning that the top management of German companies are traditionally promoted through the ranks.

Although the German model has its critics, many have noted that Germany seems to have outperformed a number of other advanced economies in the aftermath of the subprime collapse of 2007–8, typically citing Germany's more 'balanced' economic model as the reason. Germany's very powerful export-driven industrial sector has helped the nation to weather the crisis. In contrast, the more finance- and

[1] Figures from World Bank (2011).

services-driven economies, such as those of the UK and the USA, have endured prolonged macroeconomic struggles as the subprime crash exposed the vulnerabilities of their highly leveraged and financialized model, in which so much of their manufacturing industry has been allowed to wither away. In certain niche yet important product markets (such as the manufacturing of tunnel-boring machines) German firms are practically the only 'world-class' suppliers.[2]

German economic strength has been claimed as a moral victory of sorts for those who believe in trade unions, social democracy, extensive social welfare systems and workplace democracy, as it suggests that taking a 'high road' towards long-term investments in people, skills, careers and training can pay off economically. Given the above, it is no mystery why many observers have Germany down as their 'favourite' socio-economic model.

Germany's prolonged success is remarkable given its traumatic and turbulent history. The nation was first unified as a modern state at a rather late stage – in 1871, far later than other major powers such as France, the UK and Russia. Before that point there existed hundreds of independent states and principalities, and Germany in its various guises has experienced imperialism, democracy, fascism, wartime devastation and division into two nations (West and East Germany during the Cold War) before reunification in 1990. Since the end of the Second World War Germany has been a major force (along with France) in the development of the European Union, and a key believer of the 'social market' approach to capitalism that has traditionally been popular in continental Europe (such as in France, Austria, and the Nordic countries).

But, in common with all nations featured in this book, Germany also faces many troubles of its own: some new, others long-standing. In some ways the country is well-placed to benefit from globalization, especially as regards its high-quality manufacturing sector, its favourable geographic location for trade in the EU, and its well-placed financial centre in Frankfurt. Yet in other ways Germany looks upon globalization with anxiety, as international change and integration appears to erode and threaten many traditional German ways of life and work (such as its high-trust industrial relations system). It has also had to contend with huge challenges thrown up by reunification, in which West Germany

[2] The global leader in this industry is Herrenknecht AG, which has been extremely successful in recent decades as existing highly developed cities often need to upgrade their transport infrastructures (especially before hosting mega-events such as global sporting events), and developing countries require new industrial pipelines. Family-owned, it employs 3,800 staff and is involved in projects around the globe, with sales income of over €1 billion in 2011. Figures from http://www.herrenknecht.com.

absorbed an economically weak and politically troubled former communist German Democratic Republic (or East Germany).

At present, the nature of and prospects for the German 'model' are somewhat ambiguous – it seems to receive praise and criticism in equal doses. While the US economy boomed in 1992–9 and from 2002–7, Germany looked moribund in comparison, and was castigated in the American business press for its conservatism, inflexibility and its excessively employee-friendly system.[3] But with the discrediting of Anglo-Saxon models after subprime the German model seemed to grow in stature once more. This chapter will explore the various historical phases of the German socio-economic model and will demonstrate that many of its fundaments appear reasonably secure. While it has certainly abandoned many features of its pre- and post-war 'organized' model of capital and taken clear steps towards 'disorganized' or investor capitalism since the 1990s (Lash and Urry 1987), its post-war approach to business and management is economically successful and socially progressive.

The historical roots of Germany's 'cooperative managerial capitalism' (1815–1918)

Germany's emergence as Europe's top industrial power had relatively humble beginnings. Several historical examples of pioneering work in science and industry can be found (most notably Johann Gutenberg's printing press of 1439 which played a pivotal role in the spread of the Renaissance and in paving the way for the later Enlightenment and scientific-technical revolutions). But in the early modern era there was no unified German nation as we recognize today and the political fragmentation of the region seems to have retarded its economic growth. Up until the mid-19th century the region now known as Germany consisted of a vast array of independent regions. In the words of the economic historian Jeff Fear: '[t]here were ecclesiastical and lay territories, estates of the Holy Roman Empire, Imperial cities, free cities, and noble lands filled with myriad counts, knights, and princes' (1997: 135–136). Prussia and Austria were the largest states, but this largely uncoordinated group of political bodies was overrun by Napoleon's invasion of 1806.

Napoleon forcibly united much of the region into the Confederation of the Rhine, at one point clustering together as many as 39 states. Prussia, the largest state outside of the Confederation, engaged in a major modernization drive in response, involving the beginnings of a

[3] 'Germany's Dismal Future', *Forbes*, 31 January 2005.

more recognisably 'German' form of nationalism. Prussia grew economically and militarily strong under the leadership of Otto von Bismarck, culminating in victory in a war against the Confederation and the Austrian Empire in 1886. Germany was to eventually unify as the German Empire (*Reich*) in January 1871 following victory in the Franco-Prussian War of 1870–1. From then on Germany went on to become the powerful state and economy it has been throughout the 20th century.

Prussia's modernization under Bismarck involved many crucial developments. Much of the roots of the German model of capitalism (and of models of modern state bureaucracies more broadly) emerge from Prussia (Beck 1992). These include the establishment of universal primary education in the 18th century (which became almost universal across all of unified Germany by the 19th century [Allen 2011: 42]), the emergence of a civil service, and the fundamentally modern concept of abstract formal systems and government 'offices' with their professional careers (Beck 1992). The German sociologist Max Weber famously wrote of the importance of such formal institutions for stimulating widespread economic growth, buttressed by more cultural and ideational social features such as 'the Protestant ethic', which imbues workers and citizens with the 'spirit of capitalism': the drive to work, to act rationally, to harness science and technology, to think and behave within established and accepted rules (Weber 1905/1962). Weber notes the crucial socio-cultural ingredient needed for industrial modernization and the basis of capitalism, and these insights remain highly relevant for institutional theory and its various offshoots (such as VoC theory).

United Germany built on and continued these Prussian developments (Beck 1992), and the new German Reich emerged as a federal political structure headed by a Kaiser (emperor), and a Federal Council (*Bundesrat*) made of federal princes or state representatives, and parliamentary parties and headed by an elected chancellor. The high degree of historical fragmentation was a major reason why industrialization took place rather later in Germany than it did in the UK. Some use the phrase 'late industrialization' in relation to Germany (Vitols 2001), and have used Gerschenkronian arguments about the need for the state to step in to guide or force development in such a scenario. An idea widely present in the literature is that German would-be industrialists lacked access to risk capital due to the limitations of the regionally scattered and relatively small banking and insurance companies (although this is disputed [Borchardt 1991: 16–29]). There may also have been a lack of *demand* for borrowing, in that traditional Protestant norms around self-reliance and stoicism could imply that it was wrong, almost immoral, to be a debtor (Borchardt 1991: 22).

Germany's colonial economy was very small by the standard of other major European powers and could not play a significant role in economic growth. In 1876, the UK's colonies covered an area of 22.5 million square kilometres and an enormous population of 251.9 million, whereas Germany had no colonies during this time. In 1914, the British Empire had expanded to 33.5 million square kilometres and 393.5 million people. Germany's had grown to just 2.9 million square kilometres and 12.3 million population (Beaud 2001:160).

Given these constraints, something of a 'late-industrializer' state-driven modernization programme emerged in Germany. Indeed, it was the German economist Friedrich List and his 1841 treatise *The National System of Political Economy* which made one of the most major statements of the argument for systems of state coordination and infant industry protection in modernization, and these views seemed to have some traction in Germany (as well as being clearly influential in the USA, France and Russia, see Chapters 3, 5, 8). Listian ideas were adopted, such as developing a unified internal trading area, integrating national transportation and communication infrastructures, putting up import tariffs to protect infant industries and a deep commitment to national education (Allen 2011: 41–42).

Although initiated somewhat later than in comparator nations, the scale of German industrialization became very broad and deep. In 1900, the UK possessed around 10.4% of world GDP, the USA 21.5% and Germany 5.1% (Hikino and Amsden 1994: 286). On the eve of the First World War (1914–18) German industrial firms had caught up with the UK in scale. Whereas in 1870 Germany had around 13% of world industrial output, the UK 32% and the USA 23%, by 1913 Germany had 16%, the UK 14% and the USA 36% (Chandler 1990: 4). German firms, however, typically remained significantly smaller than their American counterparts, and their incorporation into joint-stock companies did not mean the transfer of organizational control from traditional owners (entrepreneurs and/or their families) to professional, salaried middle managers in the way documented by Chandler in the USA (Djelic 1998: 52–53). Peculiarities in German legal and institutional norms meant that the incorporation of a company into a joint-stock corporation or *Aktsiongesselschaft* (AG) did not necessarily mean the division of ownership from control. Ownership structure of German firms was 'much more concrete and much less disembodied in Germany than in the USA' (Djelic 1998: 53). The legal designation GmBH (*Gesellschaft mit Beschraenkter Haftung*) was adopted by most small-and medium-sized corporations, which was a hybrid ownership form that allowed share capital to be issued but placed restrictions on their transferability, meaning that founders and family owners remained in control (Djelic 1998: 54).

Bismarck famously set in motion the beginnings of Germany's highly advanced system of social insurance and welfare, including the pioneering of industrial accident insurance, health insurance, pensions and unemployment insurance. Many of these were the first of their kind in the world and the way in which the German state legislated to encourage the spread of these practices remained some way ahead of other industrializing nations (see Table 6.1). German society has a long tradition of 'connecting the health of the individual with 'the health of the people' or wider community (*Volksgesundheit*)' (Fulbrook 2005: 90). Some have noted a *Sonderweg*, or 'special path' taken by Germany that emphasized the state's role in improving social conditions even if democracy was absent.

Table 6.1 International Comparisons of the Introduction of Key Social Welfare Institutions

Introduction of social welfare institutions in the Now-Developed Countries				
	Industrial accident	**Health**	**Pension**	**Unemployment**
Germany	1871	1883	1889	1927
Switzerland	1881	1911	1946	1924
Austria	1887	1888	1927	1920
Norway	1894	1909	1936	1906
Finland	1895	1963	1937	1917
UK	1897	1911	1908	1911
Ireland	1897	1911	1908	1911
Italy	1898	1886	1898	1919
Denmark	1898	1892	1891	1907
France	1898	1898	1895	1905
New Zealand	1900	1948	1898	1938
Spain	1900	1942	1919	n.a.
Sweden	1901	1891	1913	1934
Netherlands	1901	1929	1913	1916
Australia	1902	1945	1909	1945
Belgium	1903	1894	1900	1920
Canada	1930	1971	1927	1940
USA	1930	No	1935	1935
Portugal	1962	1984	1984	1984

Source: (Chang 2003: 104). By permission of Anthem Press.

Welfare and insurance systems were central political concepts endorsed by the Social Democratic party, the presence of which is yet another long-standing element of Germany's socio-economic system that survives today. Education and training institutions continued to grow and spread from the 19th century onwards, as powerful research-driven universities grew in stature and scientific research was applied to industrial innovation in the economy. A system of polytechnic colleges was established for training, defending and improving upon craft skills. Scientific and administrative theories were practically applied. The Berlin Institute provided courses in factory management in the 1830s, well ahead of European competitors (Fear 1997: 140).

The *Zollverein* or customs union was established among the German states, to provide an internal free-trade area. Common systems of weights and measures were eventually established, and commercial codes across the states were brought into closer alignment. Import tariffs were placed on strategic products such as iron and steel to protect German infant industry. Unification also stimulated booms in industrial manufacturing and railway construction. In 1853, just five years after the opening of the historic Liverpool–Manchester railway, a line from Nuremburg to Fürth was running. Around 63,000 kilometres of railway line were open by the eve of the First World War (Allen 2011: 42). A national rail network emerged and was taken into state ownership in 1879 (Fear 1997: 138).

The rise of the archetypal German form of universal banking is closely associated with this railroad boom. Universal banks such as Deutsche Bank were large, national-scale combinations of commercial bank, investment bank and investment trust. Before unification capital markets were highly fragmented along regional lines, and these new major banks provided the kind of consolidation needed for large-scale capital investments such as railroads or steelmaking. With long-term timescales for collecting a return on such investments necessarily the norm in such industries, banks and industrial firms formed tight allegiances. Some suggest that German banks 'played a determining role in national economic growth' (Amatori and Colli 2011: 88). Arguably, the close connection between banking and industry in Germany that many see as a defining feature of German capitalism can be traced to this period (Fear 1997; Moss 1997); although others such as Vitols (2001) and Feldenkirchen (1991) are more sceptical of this interpretation. Table 6.2 overleaf reveals the strong degree to which major German banks owned and controlled German industry before the wars.

No longer was capital short in supply or demand. Railways, ports and telegraph systems were rapidly built, forming indispensable parts of the emerging national communications and transport networks, that 'made possible a flow of goods and information large enough to exploit the economics of scale and scope' (Chandler 1990: 397). The basis was laid for industrialization on a large scale. Germany developed its distinctive form of 'organized capitalism' (Kocka 1978) or

Table 6.2 Representation of the 'Big Banks' on the supervisory boards of German joint-stock companies by sector: number of seats (chairmen/vice-chairmen) circa 1910

	Number of seats on Supervisory Boards	Mining	Stoneworks	Metalworking
Bank fuer Handel und Industrie	101 (19/16)	10 (1/1)	4 (1/2)	2 (–/1)
Berliner Handels-gesellschaft	101 (11/18)	18 (3/3)	1 (–/–)	8 (–/2)
Commerz- und Disconto-Bank	35 (4/3)	1 (–/–)	2 (–/1)	2 (–/–)
Deutsche Bank	134 (25/20)	13 (1/3)	1 (–/1)	3 (1/1)
Disconto-Gesellschaft	125 (12/8)	21(3/–)	2 (–/–)	2 (–/–)
Dresdner Bank	102 (19/14)	13 (1/1)	2 (–/–)	3 (–/1)
Nationalbank fuer Deutschland	102 (3/3)	13 (1/–)	4 (–/1)	3 (–/–)
Schaffhausen scher Bankverein	113 (26/16)	26 (6/–)	2 (–/1)	4 (1/2)
Total	813 (119/98)	115 (16/8)	18 (1/6)	27 (2/6)
	Engineering	**Chemical Industry**	**Textile Industry**	**Foodstuffs Industry**
Bank fuer Handel und Industrie	16 (2/2)	3 (1/1)	5 (1/2)	7 (2/1)
Berliner Handels-gesellschaft	10 (3/3)	7 (–/3)	–	3 (–/2)
Commerz- und Disconto-Bank	8 (1/1)	1 (–/–)	1 (–/–)	3 (–/–)
Deutsche Bank	27 (5/3)	1 (–/–)	6 (–/2)	3 (–/–)
Disconto-Gesellschaft	10 (–/2)	7 (1/1)	–	1 (–/–)
Dresdner Bank	14 (2/2)	1 (1/–)	2 (–/1)	2 (–/–)
Nationalbank fuer Deutschland	18 (–/–)	3 (1/–)	–	7 (–/1)
Schaffhausen scher Bankverein	16 (3/1)	2 (–/1)	5 (2/1)	1 (–/–)
Total	119 (16/14)	25 (4/6)	19 (3/5)	27 (2/4)

Source: Feldenkirchen (1991: 145–6)

'Cooperative Managerial Capitalism' (Chandler 1990), consisting of large corporations seeking to exploit economies of scale and scope, but operating in a less competitive and more collaborative manner than in the USA, supported by patient capital from banks as long-term investors or 'Hausbanken' and protected by an intricate system of corporate cross-shareholdings (Smyser 1993: 86).

Enormous growth took place in the iron and steel industries as well as machine tools manufacturing, especially in the Ruhr valley, with firms such as Thyssen and Krupp establishing themselves as major international producers (Fear 1997: 139). Electrical engineering giants such as Siemens and AEG emerged and had great success in domestic and international markets. These powerful corporations were built on strong craft traditions; unlike in the USA, Taylorism never had as much of a grasp. A high degree of training and dedication to craft expertise meant less need for managerial supervision (Fear 1997: 139), and this tradition of devolved authority remains strong in today's German employers (Doellgast 2012; Randlesome 1994; Smyser 1993: 71).

Educational investment was put to good use as chemists and physicists were appointed into industrial firms. Many automotive innovations flowed from the German states. The first gasoline engine-powered vehicle was built in Austria by Seigreid Marcus in 1870, and he went on to pioneer ignition systems and carburettors. Karl Benz built perhaps the first workable automobile in 1885, closely followed by the versions developed by Gottlieb Daimler and Wilhelm Maybach (Allen 2011: 46). German entrepreneurs visited the USA 'in search of ideas, training and technologies' (Djelic 1998: 57), including Carl Duisberg of the German chemicals firm Bayer, and the farm machinery manufacturer Heinrich Lanz. Many were interested in adopting the new US innovations in corporate organization (such as nationally federated structures and distribution chains), but these ideas found little favour back in Germany where the founders and owners of firms typically wished to retain traditional forms of organization and control (Djelic 1998: 57), including cartels in which large firms tended to club together rather than to engage in takeovers and mergers into one large, US-style corporate giant.

Germany developed systems of large-scale industrialism faster than UK and France, and achieved this without sacrificing its traditional competences in craft practices (Chandler 1990). Rather than merging, German corporations tended to cluster themselves into cartels and profit-pooling organizations known as *Interessengemeinschaften* or IGs (Djelic 1998: 55). Powerful German business associations shielded firms from the intrusion of Taylorian managerial innovations designed to break work down into simple standardized procedures, and they instead promoted the coordination and spread of professional and craft concepts by influencing the education and training curricula used in polytechnics.

German customs and laws have long tolerated and encouraged forms of inter-firm collaboration that would be illegal under American anti-trust legislation (Vitols 2004a: 333). Today's characterization of Germany as a paradigmatic CME has strong historical roots. Trade, craft, industry and professional associations, as well as regional chambers of commerce have a far more powerful and legally inscribed role in the German economy than their comparator organizations in the UK or USA, and company management also traditionally paid more attention to these associations and trade unions. This reinforced trends for stability, order and compromise rather than endless corporate reinvention (Chandler 1990: 395).

Much of the literature emphasizes the emergence of an 'organized capitalism' (Berghahn 1986: 14; Höpner and Krempel 2004: 340; Kocka 1978; Lash and Urry 1987: 3), or 'political or economic order', known as *Ordnungspolitik* or *Wirtschaftordnung* (Fear 1997: 135), in which associations and compromise, rather than markets and competition, are the dominant forces. Although political unification came late to Germany its economy arguably developed as a CME from an early stage. German economic development (with the exception of the interwar years) exhibits very strong path-dependent effects: almost from the beginning an observer can detect many of the features that characterize contemporary German capitalism: an interventionist state, cartelization among large corporations, a bank-based financial system, no market for corporate control, patient capital, powerful industry associations and trade unions, and well-educated and technically highly competent workforces.

By the turn of the 20th century, the German Reich was among the world's foremost economic powers, matching or beating competitors such as the UK and the USA. According to Allen: 'In 1850–4 Britain smelted about 3 million tons of pig iron versus 245,000 in Germany and about 500,000 in the USA. By 1910–1913, Britain was producing 10 million tons, while Germany smelted 15 million, and the USA 24 million' (2011: 45). Tragically, the trade rivalry between the UK and Germany 'stoked international tensions in the approach to the First World War' (Allen 2011: 45).

Competition for arms, iron, steel and raw materials contributed to the disastrous First World War. This was essentially an imperialist contest between the growing powers of the UK, France, Russia, and Germany and Austria-Hungary, with the USA reluctantly entering in April 1917 on the side of the UK, France and Russia. Much of the fighting took place outside Germany on the Western and Eastern Front. German defeat in 1918 came, therefore, as a nasty surprise to many, especially to its aristocratic leaders, for whom 'their world had collapsed' (Burleigh 2001: 33).

The Versailles Treaty imposed vindictive terms on Germany, making it lose 'roughly 80 per cent of its iron ore supplies, 44 per cent of pig iron capacity, 36 per cent of steel capacity, and 32 per cent of rolled steel product capacity' (Fear 1997: 155). Germany was compelled to hand over millions of tons of coal and one-quarter of its pharmaceutical and dye production to France, Belgium and Italy until 1925. Overseas assets of German corporations were expropriated, Germany was barred from establishing its own industrial tariffs, and tariffs were raised across Europe against German products (Fear 1997: 156). Worst of all, the infamous 'war guilt' clauses of the treaty forced Germany to admit sole responsibility for the war's outbreak. To many it felt as if Germany had not legitimately lost the war, but had instead bargained its seemingly strong military position away not only to one of total defeat but also sole responsibility for the destruction. The infamous 'stab in the back' and 'November Criminals' explanation for Germany's defeat fed on this feeling. As we shall see in the next section, the totally unsatisfactory conclusion to the First World War lead to far-reaching and utterly disastrous consequences for Germany and Europe.

Inter-war chaos and the descent into Fascism and war (1919–45)

The royal family quickly abdicated after the war and the 1920s were a decade of mostly deep crisis for the newly democratic German republic. Such was the turbulence that its capital city had to move from Berlin to Weimar because of political unrest. Its first President Friedrich Ebert was swamped in problems. Somehow Germany had to find the money for war reparation payments totalling around 132 billion gold marks or roughly US$30 billion dollars (Burleigh 2001: 54). In 1920–1, industrial production fell by 20%, 2.1 million jobs were lost and unemployment rose to around 12% (Holtferich 1991: 267). The French military occupied the Ruhr to seize reparation materials (Fear 1997: 156) and the Reichsmark was destroyed by hyperinflation. The exchange rate in June 1918 was around 8 marks to 1 US dollar. In December 1921 it was 192 marks. By the end of 1922 it was 7,600, and a year later it was 4.2 trillion marks to the dollar. By December 1923 wholesale prices were 656 billion times higher than in 1918 (Moss 1997: 242).

In time there was some settling of economic affairs, assisted by widespread borrowing from American banks (loans were often used to pay the reparations). Large industrial trusts were formed such as Hoescht, IG Farben and Daimler-Benz, and German industrial groups and trade associations developed new standards and systems of certification that are still widely in use today (Fear 1997: 158). Powerful banks such as Deutsche underwrote some of these defensive corporate mergers (such as the creation of Lufthansa in 1926 [Moss 1997: 245]). The state of Prussia formed a government-run mining and power conglomerate VEBA (now owned by today's E.ON).

This all contributed to a degree of industrial recovery in the mid-to late 1920s (Holtferich 1991). The US-led Dawes plan of 1924 cancelled some of the reparations, and further US loans to German industry arrived, in many cases made conditional on reforming German corporations in US directions (Djelic 1998: 58). However, in a sign of path-dependence which was to repeat itself after the Second World War, German business owners wanted to retain control and were resistant to US forms of restructuring (Djelic 1998: 59). The Weimar government introduced some important social policies in an effort to give some ground to workers' demands and to pre-empt the spread of communism. The Works Council Act of 1920 (Berghahn 1986: 18) established some important forms of workplace democracy, including a legal guarantee of employee representation.

But the 1920s were marred by severe political and economic turbulence. The Wall Street Crash of 1929 was especially devastating to Germany as its fragile recovery was widely dependent on US loans, many of which were suddenly called in. The result was again runaway inflation and widespread economic misery for workers and middle-class Germans. The political turmoil that had characterized the decade re-emerged strongly as extremist right- and left-wing parties gained ground, and frequent violence broke out between fascists and communists.

One of these extremist groups was Adolf Hitler's National Socialist (Nazi) Party, an organization openly opposed to democracy, espousing fascism, racist extremism and military adventurism. Hitler was imprisoned in 1923 following a failed attempt at a seizure of power, and few at this stage saw him as anything more than an extremist oddity. Germany's brief economic recovery in the second half of the 1920s looked to have caught hold, and there was optimism that growth would undergird Germany's newly democratic republic. But the second severe economic contraction after the Wall Street Crash ushered in a new period of uncertainty. Unemployment rose to the staggering height of 33% in 1932–3 (Fear 1997: 160). There was great concern among many circles of Germany (industrial leaders, middle class business-owners, the civil service, the military and the aristocratic 'residual right') that Bolshevik-style revolution – 'a German October' (Burleigh 2001: 58) – could break out in the homeland of Marx. Unrest was undermining the already very weak authority of the Weimar regime, which had increasingly resorted to rule by emergency decree. There was some grassroots support in the early years for the Nazi party (Fulbrook 2005: 291), and significant segments of Germany's political, military and business elites eventually abandoned democracy and endorsed fascism. Senior political figures of the so-called 'residual right' such as Chancellors Franz von Papen and Kurt von Schleicher - who welcomed a return to German empire and rearmament - pressed for the appointment of Hitler as Chancellor in a coalition government in January 1933, convincing themselves that this was a temporary measure, that his extremism could be worked around, and that Hitler was a naïve political operator who could be controlled by forces around him.

This turned out to be one of gravest mistakes in European history. Hitler and his Nazi inner circle set about expanding and consolidating their hold on power in totalitarian fashion, removing any real or potential opponents such as intellectuals or army officers who might oppose him. Hitler's manoeuvrings culminated in the establishment of outright power, and by March 1933 Hitler had emerged with dictatorial powers. Other political parties were swiftly outlawed and the Third Reich became a fascist, militaristic, one-party state. The Nazis demonized social and ethnic groups deemed to be 'enemies' of the regime especially Jews, Gypsies, people with disabilities or mental illness, trade unionists and leftists. With Stalin's rise in the USSR and Hitler's in Germany, this was the 20th century's darkest chapter.

The Nazi regime, for all its horrors, did provide many of its citizens something to believe in. Full employment was achieved and an ambitious programme of public works was established, buttressed by cultural and political control that emphasized military-style devotion to duty on the part of all citizens (Beaud 2001: 199–207). The economic model of Third Reich essentially gambled everything on putting military expansion first. It believed that if its war machine could be built faster than that of other powers (the USA, UK, USSR and France) it could quickly defeat them and then live off the plunders of war. The Third Reich attempted to mobilize the entire society for war and imperialism. The ominous sounding policy of 'synchronization' or *Gleichschaltung* was a prominent theme, an Orwellian nightmare, with which the Nazi Party attempted to force out and replace all other possible forms of organization (trade unions, professional associations, the church). German traditions of social solidarity and collective support to provide for health and security were twisted and corrupted by racialized Nazi ideology (Fulbrook 2005: 90–91), such as the 'strength through joy' programme, which harnessed Nazi propaganda to attempt to improve citizen and worker fitness and hence productivity, while excluding 'inferior races' (Fulbrook 2005: 91).

Part of 'synchronization' involved developing a command economy. Although this was conducted on nothing like the scale of the Soviet or

Chinese models, the Nazi government developed a system of state planning and strict regulation and control of the economy. Industrial groups such as IG Farben (a giant chemicals group later broken up into the major firms BASF, Bayer and Hoechst) were increasingly subjected to political control as the Nazi economic policy built on and intensified the long-standing trend for cartelization; politicizing this process and pushing it in the direction of autarkic development for war (Carr 1972; Djelic 1998: 57). The state enforced capital controls, engaged in currency manipulation, and controlled wages and prices. Import agreements were struck with nations outside Europe (which Germany often broke) (Weitz 1997:190). Domestic wages were set at a very low level and works councils abolished. Trade unions were crushed and replaced with the 'official' German Labour Front.

Job creation schemes found some base of support among the unemployed workers who had suffered for so long under the Weimar years. Workers became officially rebranded as 'followers' (Fear 1997: 163). Civil liberties were curbed, and certain social groups ruthlessly and violently oppressed. The VW plant at Wolfsburg was intended to create a 'people's car' along Fordist mass production lines, and was a 'stunning exception to the traditional manner of German shopfloor organization' (Fear 1997a: 163). This turned out to be largely a scam typical of totalitarian regimes, not unlike many of the Soviet 'show-piece' projects which never came to fruition (see Chapter 8). Few cars eventually reached those who had put money aside to order them. Instead Wolfsburg was largely put to use manufacturing military vehicles, such as the Kübelwagen jeep. Six hundred thousand jobs were supposed to be created constructing the autobahns, but the real number was probably closer to 120,000. Workers were employed in very dangerous conditions with extremely low pay (Burleigh 2001: 241).

A Four Year Plan to gear the economy and industry for war was established under the supervision of Hermann Göering, and a state-owned steelworks the 'Reichswerke Hermann Göering' was built. Large corporations were often opposed to the moves towards increased state control, but were typically threatened with arrest and violence when voicing any concerns. Hitler was said to have referred to business executives as 'gullible fools' (Fear 1997: 164). Big business was thus drawn ever more closely into the crimes of the regime. Many *Mittelstand* (small- and medium-sized) industrial firms also gained from military rearmament contracts. 'This form of weak resistance and eventual involvement sent business executives ever deeper into active accommodation with the Third Reich, and placed them on a slippery slope that ran all the way to Auschwitz' (Fear 1997: 164). This phrase by Fear is reminiscent of historical and sociological writings on how 'ordinary people' and advanced technologies and 'rational' management and planning became complicit in the appalling crimes of the Nazi regime (Bauman 1991, Browning 2001, Sereny 1996). The 'Aryanization' Laws of 1938 effectively barred Jews from public life. Jews and other demonized groups had their homes and businesses taken from them, and were increasingly moved into ghettos, labour camps and concentration camps. Slave labour was widely employed in the rearmament and war economy (Burleigh 2001: 774–775; Fear 1997: 168).

Many have wondered how such tyranny and brutality could possibly have occurred. Historical and psychological research has suggested that those living under totalitarian regimes can be frighteningly easy to manipulate and coerce (especially when threatened with violence) and can be surprisingly indifferent to the suffering of others (Browning 2001). Other nations have, of course, also been responsible for horrific crimes (see for example the systems of forced labour in the USSR and China, British treatment of its colonies, the treatment of slaves and indigenous peoples in the USA, and Imperial Japan's colonial and wartime atrocities). The Nazi regime became more murderous as the Second World War progressed and as the Holocaust took hold. Ultimately the Nazi regime appears to be directly responsible for the loss of around 12 million lives.[4] The wider Second World War cost around 50 million lives in Europe (Burleigh 2001: 1).

After dramatic early success for the German military in the early parts of the war – especially the rapid defeat and occupation of France – the Axis powers (Germany, Italy and Japan) overextended themselves, especially following the invasion of the USSR, which commenced in June 1941 (see Chapter 8). Defeat on the Eastern front was the beginning of the end for the Third Reich, and with the entry of the USA into the Second World War, total defeat of the Axis powers came in the spring of 1945. German population, cities and industry were devastated through US and UK aerial bombardments including the use of hugely controversial 'area bombing' tactics and 'firestorm'-inducing incendiary weapons that ultimately killed perhaps 600,000 civilians.[5] In the end, Hitler's 'thousand year Reich' lasted twelve and a half years. Germany faced an extremely difficult prospect of rebuilding and recovery, but this time as part of Europe, and set

[4] 'Hitler vs. Stalin: Who Killed More?', *New York Review of Books*, 10 March 2011.

[5] 'Germany's Forgotten Victims', *Guardian*, 22 October 2003.

against the tensions of the Cold War. The USA thus took upon itself a much more active role in attempting to provide its own blueprint for the rebuilding of German (and indeed European) capitalism.

The *Wirtschaftwunder*: the ascendance of the German post-war socio-economic model (1955–1990)

At the Second World War's end, Germany was divided into four occupational 'zones' under the influence of the UK, France, USA and the USSR. Each of these occupiers had their own plans for Germany but ultimately the end results were most keenly reflected by the influence of the two dominant powers of the Cold War era - the USA and the USSR. The USA aimed to help reconstruct West Germany in its own image (Halberstam 1992: 334) while East Germany became a client state of the USSR.

The Democratic Republic of Germany (GDR) became a 'model' Soviet-type economy (see Chapter 8), and became the most advanced example of its type in Eastern Europe (Fulbrook 2005).[6] The Sozialistishce Einheitspartei Deutschlands (SED) instigated a Soviet-style revolution from above, imposed on the shattered and demoralized post-Nazi East Germany. This included the establishment of a command economy, collectivization of agriculture, Five Year Plans (which placed economic primacy on developing heavy industry) and the insertion of price and wage controls (Randlesome 1994: 10). State ownership and control over the economy grew from around 58.2% of the economy in 1953 to 81.4% in 1960 and to 92.4 % by 1972 (Fulbrook 2005: 34). In common with Soviet-type systems the command economy went hand-in-hand with a one-party state and strict forms of social and political control. While Western historiography often depicts East Germany as a totalitarian, secretive and sometimes violent dystopia, more nuanced appraisals show that it was possible to lead 'perfectly ordinary lives' under 'really existing socialism'. Many elements of the system were morally defensible - it provided full employment, cheap housing, and free health and education (Fulbrook 2005: ix). Nevertheless, wages

[6] Most analyses of the German economy focus almost exclusively on West Germany and skate over the experience of those in the East. Unfortunately this text will do much the same for reasons of space and clarity. For a detailed treatment of economy and society in the GDR, see Fulbrook (2005).

were low, living conditions hard and political controls extensive. The planned economy ran into chronic difficulties in the 1980s and was later to collapse, with far-reaching consequences for Germany and indeed the world (see below).

In the Western occupational zone, the USA was initially keen to stimulate reforms to post-Nazi Germany that would rebuild the economy and society in distinctly US directions. A key element of US influence over Germany and Western Europe was the Marshall Plan (more correctly the European Recovery Program), which provided around US$13 billion in reconstruction loans, aid and expertise to the nations of Western Europe, and encouraged the removal of tariff barriers and the 'modernization' of industry. It was a kind of Global New Deal in which the American benefactors encouraged German firms to adopt America's 'mass manufacturing miracle' (Djelic 1998: 65).

US influence over Germany extended to the very highest levels of US diplomacy. A letter from Secretary of State Dean Acheson to the British Foreign Secretary Ernest Bevin in 1950 reads:

> We all recognize that one of the most important aspects of the occupation is in its educating the Germans in economic and political democracy. This can best be done, as I am sure you recognize, by example and not mere precept, and the decartelization program furnishes a most valuable and important area for such action. (as quoted in Djelic 1998: 162).

The Americans had to make German capitalism work, otherwise its failure or slow progress would play into the hands of Soviet claims about the ills of capitalism (unemployment, alienation, poverty) the 'inevitability' of its collapse and the 'superiority' of socialism (Ellwood 2012: 340–341).

Many of the US loans came with the condition that European industry adopts the 'scientific' efficiency of statistically driven quality control techniques or the latest forms of marketing research. Some expected and hoped that convergence on the (assumedly superior) US model would be a relatively straightforward and uncomplicated affair (Halberstam 1992: 326–327). But as we shall see, convergence was only ever partial. Exhibit 6.1 is an excellent example of attempted US-driven convergence and globalization, through the highly influential international journal *Foreign Affairs*.[7]

---

[7] Passages from this article are cited in Ellwood (2012: 381) and I am indebted to this source for this fascinating document.

Exhibit 6.1 Visions of Post-war Germany in the American century

The Marshall Plan was a hugely important project designed to rebuild post-war Europe with the vision of American Fordism in mind. As part of the 'American Century', Richard M. Bissell, an archetypal Cold Warrior, once a member of the CIA and the Ford Foundation, writes in the journal *Foreign Affairs* of the need to 'win hearts and minds' in Germany towards US-style capitalism, to get rid of traditional German forms of 'restrictionism'. The writing carries a patronising tone, which is not dissimilar to 1990s/2000s rhetoric of some business elites urging European nations to modernize and converge on Anglo-Saxon 'norms', supposedly for their own good, and the good of the world economy.

'[T]he United States must exploit to the full the example of its own accomplishments and their powerful appeal to Europeans (and others) [...] Coca-cola and Hollywood movies may be regarded as two products of a shallow and crude civilization. But American machinery, American labor relations, and American management and engineering are everywhere respected. The hope is that a few European unions and entrepreneurs can be induced to try out the philosophy of higher productivity, higher wages, and higher profits from the lower prices of lower unit cost. If they do, if restrictionism can be overcome at merely a few places, the pattern may spread. The forces making for such changes are so powerful that, with outside help and encouragement, they may become decisive. It will not require enormous sums of money [...]. But it will require a profound shift in social attitudes, attuning them to the mid-twentieth century.'

(Bissell 1951: 404–405)

With the UK and France relatively weaker, the USA came to dominate the Western occupational zones (Djelic 1998: 80). The US occupation attempted to decartelize industry and banking and introduce US-style antitrust legislation. A policy of 'de-Nazification' removed from positions of power civil servants and businesspeople deemed to have been corrupted by the Nazi regime. Britain's Labour government was keen on a nationalization of Ruhr coal, steel etc., but this was blocked by US authorities (Djelic 1998: 80). Germany's major banks were split up (Moss 1997: 255). Restrictions were placed on the scale and scope of German banking in an attempt to model it on the traditionally very decentralized and regionalized US banking model (Moss 1997: 256; see also Chapter 3).

However, these changes were largely resisted by German bankers who strongly believed in their historical version of 'universal' banking and were adopted only in the most grudging way. After full sovereignty was restored to West Germany in 1955, universal banking quickly reasserted itself. By this stage, the USA was content to let West Germany develop along its own pathways. Efforts to force it to conform to US economic norms were dropped as it became expedient just to ensure that it was economically and politically strong. What mattered was that

West Germany was capitalist and strong – its actual variety of capitalism mattered less.

Interestingly, the re-establishment of Works Councils into the Ruhr iron and steel industry was influenced by the British occupational forces (Marsh 2000: 73), with the support of the British Labour government of the time (see Chapter 4). It was designed to pre-empt the demands of the more radical communist unions. The Americans were not keen on the idea, but it turned out to be a major success and laid some of the basis for today's system of codetermination or *Mitbestimmung* in which workers were given a strong voice in company decision making.

Post-war economic recovery saw the revival of trade associations and employer groups crippled or destroyed under the Nazi regime (such as the umbrella organization for the employers' associations, the BDA [*Bundesvereinigung der Deutschen Arbeitgeberverbände]*) (Fear 1997a: 174). The West German workforce became around 40% unionized in the post-war years, slowly falling to around 37% in 1980 (Streeck 1997: 244).[8] Just over 80% of workplaces were covered by collective bargaining agreements, a situation that persisted until 1990 (Streeck 1997: 244), before falling to around 60% today (Keller and Kirsch 2011: 211). Major unions affiliated to the DGB trade union confederation (especially the giant metalworking union IG Metall) negotiated successfully with employers for the reduction of working hours, improved safety standards, and increased holiday and pension entitlements (Fear 1997: 176). In return, the employers often gained 'no strike' agreements.

Codetermination Acts restored Germany's traditional 'dual' system of management executive committee (*Vorstand*) and supervisory board (*Aufsichstrat*) and the Works Councils Acts 1952 – modelled on early Weimar legislation – re-introduced the powerful and enduring institutions of works councils. Workers' representatives in the iron and steel industries (and later in other sectors) were given half the total number of seats on the supervisory board, and enjoy veto powers when it comes to appointments of the labour relations director to the executive committee. In 1996, around 400,000 German employees are covered by such arrangements (Dore 2000: 183).

Works councils have important, respected and deep-seated roles in German companies. By law they are bound to operate in 'a spirit of mutual trust' for the 'good of the employees and the establishment' (Dore 2000: 184). While in many ways they represent a brake on executives 'right to manage', senior managers in Germany are typically also

---

[8] This rate, however, fell to historic lows of just 20% in the 2000s (Keller and Kirsch 2011: 201).

favourable towards the mediating role they play in 'disarming' industrial relations conflict, and allowing parties to resolve their differences on the basis of communication, contemplation and trust, rather than strikes, 'management by showdown' and conflicts. Most industrial relations experts regard German codetermination as a model for the stimulation of harmonious and productive work practices, yet the very concept is alien to Anglo-Saxon capitalism where 'managerial prerogative' reigns supreme.

Laws passed in 1976 further cemented the role of codetermination and spread it to workplaces in other industrial and services sectors. Firms with more than 2,000 employees must form work councils and dual boards for the purposes of codetermination. Codetermination laws also cover firms with between 500–2,000 staff, although workers' representatives are entitled to only one-third of the seats on the supervisory board. West German workplace democracy has long been among the most sophisticated in the world (Jackson et al. 2005; Keller and Kirsch 2011) and, in stark contrast to 'employment at will' traditions in the USA, German legislation in this field represents a serious effort to take into account fundamental issues of democracy and human dignity at work. See, for example, the quotation below from Eurofound, an EU foundation dedicated to 'the improvement of living and working conditions':

> The Federal Parliament's Standing Committee on Co-Determination (*Mitbestimmungskommission*) has ... expressed the opinion that, with due regard to the protection of human dignity and the right of individuals to develop their personality freely as enshrined in the Basic Law, the subordination of the employee to other people's managerial and organizational authority is acceptable only if the guarantees of freedom afforded by the Constitution are reflected in the opportunity to have a voice in the shaping of the work process. The Act of 1972 consequently contains minimum participation rights which can in principle be extended.[9]

Such institutions and norms are crucial ingredients of Germany's social market economy.

More generally, West Germany became a high tax regime supporting very well-developed forms of social welfare to protect the weaker in society and to subsidize industry and agriculture (Randlesome 1994: 4). Rival political parties, the Christian Democrats and Social Democrats, have traditionally both endorsed the fundamental concepts of the social market economy. In the 1960s and 1970s, few saw the need to reform or attack this system.

---

[9] http://www.eurofound.europa.eu/emire/GERMANY/WORKSCONSTITUTION-DE.htm.

West German economic growth, like that of Japan, was described as a 'miracle', or the *Wirchtschaftwunder*. Annual GDP growth, beginning under the era of Konrad Adenauer (1949–63), was around 5% between 1950–73 (Eichengreen 2007: 17). Extremely high rates of investment were posted (nearly 25% of GDP), and German exports rose from 9% of national income in 1950 to 19% by 1960 (Eichengreen 2007: 93–94). Exported products became renowned for their durability, build quality and reliability. German manufacturers increasingly sought to incrementally improve their consumer products year on year to retain brand value and market share (Streeck 1997). Migrants were attracted by German labour markets, but migration was closely controlled by multilaterial agreements between the government of Germany and nations such as Italy, Turkey, Morocco, Tunisia and Yugoslavia to provide low-wage workers as part of *gastarbeiter* 'guest worker' schemes for employment in jobs requiring few qualifications. The West German economic boom was, to a large extent, therefore, a *nationally controlled* regime of organized capitalism (Lash and Urry 1987) that depended on distinct national institutions, laws and norms, involving the close cooperation of German banks, and the employers' associations and trade unions.

Germany's post-war growth phase was the most successful in Europe, and Germany eventually gained economic superiority in relation to the UK and France (see Chapters 4 and 5). Politically, Western Europe became gradually more integrated. Franco-German relations improved markedly from the 1950s onwards, and the basis for a peaceful and more united Europe was laid. Germany's distinct social market philosophy or 'ordoliberalism' (Bonefeld 2012) differed considerably from the more liberal American economic model which was the supposed 'model' for all capitalist systems. This divergence became even more acute as American capitalism itself moved further away from its own 1940s–70s model of managerial capitalism from the 1980s onward (Dore 2008, Useem 1999, also Chapter 3).

Ordoliberalism as a philosophy endorses the idea of a liberal, capitalist economy driven by market forces, but also places strong emphasis on the need for coordination, for political order, for public welfare and state steering. 'In order to preserve a free market, it is necessary to have a strong state' (Vatiero 2010: 707).[10] This was the fundamental basis of the West German system of organized capitalism – a system which maintains a significant scepticism and distance towards Anglo-Saxon neoliberalism.

Keynesian demand-management programmes were the predominant macroeconomic policy option of the West German governments of the

[10] Eichengreen (2007: 94) disputes this, claiming a different interpretation of ordoliberalism that appears much closer to the Anglo-Saxon interpretation of liberal markets and minimal state involvement.

1960s and 1970s, overseen by the politically independent Bundesbank that developed an awesome reputation for overseeing currency stability (Smyser 1993: 47–48). Growth was steady throughout the period, before dropping back sharply to around 1.6% from 1973–2000. In keeping with crisis tendencies throughout the capitalist nations, unemployment became an issue following the oil shocks of the 1970s, with the number of unemployed climbing to around six million by the early 2000s (Marsh 2000: 78). Chancellor Helmut Kohl faced a three-year recession in the early 1980s and adopted something of a shift to the political right in the 1980s (known as *Die Wende* or 'the turn'), but not on a scale approaching that of Thatcher or Reagan (Smyser 1993: 24). Several state-run corporations were completely or partially privatized, such as VW, Lufthansa and the rail freight operator Schenker (Randlesome 1994: 3, 7). But these changes could hardly be described as revolutionary. Many long-established German companies have survived the tumultuous 20th century and continue to prosper today.

Moreover, it is important to remember that large firms (while often dominating the media and academic coverage) are not necessarily the most important part of an economy. Small- and medium-sized companies - many still family-owned - contribute enormously to Germany's industrial strength. Below Fear outlines the meaning of Mittelstand:

> Being Mittelstand was perhaps more an attitude than a statistical category. Sales representatives could roll up their sleeves and fix machines. Many had engineering degrees. Customer service, tight product focus, and high-quality engineering and design were the hallmarks of these firms. They tended to compete on quality instead of price. Many remained deeply committed to the culture and well-being of their local communities. (1997a: 180–181)

In short, Modell Deutschland did not fully replicate the American socio-economic model (much like Japan after its own period of post-war American occupation). Over time, it appeared as if many of the American influences did not transfer over to Germany without resistance, or their change and 'translation', to better fit national institutional regimes (Djelic 1998: 272). American anti-trust laws were a particular failure (see Table 6.3). Ownership of the largest publicly listed firms in Germany remains much more concentrated than in the US, with large blockholdings that make it extremely hard to develop a US-style market for corporate control. Hostile takeovers are 'almost impossible to execute' (Fear 1997: 143), partly also as a result of the unusual legal framework of German corporate governance which provides powerful proxy rights to shareholders. The 'voice' in German corporate government is louder internally, through codetermination,

Table 6.3 Comparative shareholding in thirty largest publicly-listed US and German firms

	Largest shareholding		
Company	**% of shares**	**Shareholder**	**Type**
Adidas-Salomon	<5		
Allianz	18.1	Münchener Rückversicherung	Insurance
Altana	50.1	Quandt Family	Founder/family
BASF	9.4	Allianz AG	Insurance
Bayer	5.9	Allianz AG	Insurance
Bayerische Hypo- und Vereinsbank	18.4	Münchener Rückversicherung	Insurance
BMW	48	Quandt Family	Founder/family
Commerzbank	10	Assicurazioni Generali S.p.A.	Insurance
Continental	5.5	Barclays Global Investors	Institutional investor
DaimlerChrysler	12.5	Deutsche Bank	Bank
Deutsche Bank	<5		
Deutsche Börse	5.1	The Capital Group	Institutional investor
Deutsche Post	68.8	Bundesrepublik	State
Deutsche Telekom	42.8	Bundesrepublik	State
E.ON	<5		
Fresenius Medical Care	50.8	Fresenius AG	Company
Henkel KGaA	57.8	Henkel Family	Founder/family
Infineon Technologies	12.5	Siemens AG	Company
Linde	12.6	Allianz AG	Insurance
Lufthansa	10.5	Allianz AG	Insurance
MAN	36.6	Allianz AG	Insurance
Metro	55.7	Beshaim/Haniel	Founder/family
Müncher Rückversicherung	10.0	Bayerische H +V	Bank
RWE	7.6	Allianz AG	Insurance
SAP	43.0	Tschira/Hasso/ Hopp/Plattner	Family/Founder
Schering	10.6	Allianz AG	Insurance
Siemens	<5		
ThyssenKrupp	16.9	Krupp Stiftung	Founder/ family
TUI (formerly Preussag)	31.4	Westdeutsche Landesbank	State
Volkswagen	18.2	Land Niedersachsen	State
Median	12.6		

Source: Bundesanstalt für Finanzdienstleistungsaufsicht database as appears in vitols (2004b: 366).

rather than through external forms of shareholder activism or shareholder 'exit' through selling shares.

Moreover, Germany's traditionally strong industrial, craft and business groupings (such as chambers of commerce) remain powerful institutional coalitions against radical reorganization plans (Berghahn 1986: 182). The size and scale of these organizations is impressive (Lash and Urry 1987: 17–28).

Indeed as the German economy recovered and prospered, its traditional features not only re-asserted themselves, but also appeared to many as strengths to appreciate rather than non-market anomalies to reform away. These institutions allowed German capitalism to move beyond the Fordist/Taylorist model of managerial capitalist America; indeed to surpass it in important ways, much like Japan during its own post-war miracle (see Chapter 11). The result was Germany's industrial system of 'flexible specialization' and craft production (see Piore and Sabel 1984: 229–234) that became recognized and praised in the 1980s as the weaknesses of the American industrial model began to manifest themselves (see Chapter 3).

Foremost among these growth-reinforcing German institutions was the banking regime that the occupying powers once tried to reformat. Patient capital allows for the development of 'diversified quality production' (Streeck 1997), and the institutionalization of processes of continual incremental improvement, of long-term careers and training and skills certification, and the promotion of a 'productivist' culture in which staff and managers at all levels of the firm share deep knowledge of the company's products and services. Universal banks such as Deutsche continued to exert huge influence over many parts of the German economy. By the mid-1990s it had over US$350 billion in assets under management, and underwrote securities issuance for many vital companies. It held equity stakes of between 6–35% in 7 of Germany's top 50 companies, holding voting blocks of 15% or greater in 8 of the 20 biggest German companies. Its representatives occupied 110 seats of company advisory boards (Moss 1997: 230).

The values and goals of German corporations often appear more 'authentic' to employees than the corporate behaviour in the UK and USA, in which too often the imperatives are shareholder value, financial engineering and marketing, to the detriment of genuine care for people and products. German workers thus tend to exhibit a greater working pride in the process and the product than their counterparts under Anglo-Saxon regimes. The power of the German manufacturing 'craft' culture exposes the deep limitations of Fordism (see Chapter 3), in regimes such as the USA, the UK, France and even the USSR, where mass production was all too often associated with breakdowns, low quality production, poor worker morale, strong managerial impetus to control the shop floor, and little or no worker voice. Patient capital undergirded a progressive working culture of German firms, characterized by management/labour trust and formalized rights and responsibilities on the shop floor or in the office, removing the need for micromanagement and strict standard operating procedures. Staff were well-trained, were trusted to be professional and were given wide discretion in handling their workloads (at least in theory [Doellgast 2012]).

In a well-cited paper, Wolfgang Streeck (1997) argued that German firms were forced by institutional features to listen to workers' problems and to protect employment. Rather than indulging in downsizing or casualization to save costs they instead 'stuck with' the workforce that they were obliged to keep because of powerful political and legal reasons (some of which are even enshrined in the West German Constitution). Top management thus tried to utilize their workforces to the best of their abilities. This led to high levels of training, relatively short working weeks, and high levels of workplace trust and communication. This sophisticated German production system was supported by strong governmental policies such as schooling and education, and strong forms of training and certification overseen by the state, firms, unions, and professional/trade associations. The German state spent about 7% of GDP on education and training, including spending on schools, apprenticeships and vocational training (Randlesome 1994: 144–155). Firms generally competed on quality, rather than on price, pursuing incremental improvements in product and process to maintain market share in high-value domestic and export markets, partly because of Germany's relatively modest stock of raw materials. This trust-based system contained none of the 'macho' style restructuring so common in USA, in that the system of rules was widely respected and did not need enforcing by supervisors and line managers.

German post-war reconstruction and growth, and its return to democracy in a peaceful Europe have been a huge success. But as Germany entered the 1990s, problems facing its social market model were looming ever larger (Siebert 2005). Reunification was a joyous event, but tempered by fear of the difficult prospects of uniting a weak East European economy and society with a West Germany economy that had been increasingly facing up to problems of its own (Streeck 1997).

The 1990s and beyond: restructuring *Deutschland AG?*

The collapse of the GDR was perhaps the centrepiece of the tumultuous year of 1989, when state socialist systems in Eastern Europe, the USSR and even China faced deep crisis. The demise of the Berlin Wall was the beginning of the end for state socialism in Eastern Europe and the USSR; East Germany was rapidly incorporated into a reunified Germany. But

West Germany's strong economic performance was running into difficulties associated with globalization that affect all of the European economies (Grahl and Teague 1997), and Japan (Dore 2000) and the timing of this new development was far from ideal.

As Germany's problems mounted, the 'model' status that Germany enjoyed in the 1980s as shown in texts such as Piore and Sabel (1984: 229–234) rapidly ebbed away in the mid-1990s and early 2000s. In early 2005, *Forbes* magazine published a damning article entitled 'Germany's Dismal Future', in which unemployment, inflexible labour markets, overly powerful trade unions, and slow corporate decision making were argued to be likely to lead to continual stagnation unless Germany rapidly adopts Anglo-Saxon systems and norms.[11]

According to Streeck (1997), the issues threatening Germany were threefold: the increasing exhaustion of the high-wage, quality-competitive model; the shock of reunification and the pressures of globalization, notably a 'deregulatory bias' (Streeck 1997: 256) that favours neoliberal political economies such as those of the USA and UK. Persistently high unemployment has marred the model since the 1980s (Streeck 1997: 247), with critics arguing (as in France) that the protections employers must extend by law to workers are excessive, meaning that companies are reluctant to hire staff in the knowledge that it is costly and politically difficult to make cutbacks. Streeck suggests also that product innovation in Germany started to become insufficient to keep the high wage-paying German firms profitable. Many feared that success in product markets was becoming more likely to result from faster product turnover rather than long-term incremental improvements to existing outputs (Siebert 2005: 338; Smyser 1993: 298), and that Germany's slow, consensual and complex model of capitalism was weak at the kind of discontinuous innovations that seemed to flow regularly from USA (and even from Japan). Germany's strong dedication to the EU project placed it among the forerunners of monetary union. In doing so, however, like France, it gave up one of its main macroeconomic levers – the ability to set its own interest rates or devalue the currency to boost exports.

As for reunification, the West German approach was to attempt to transport practically all of the institutional features of the West over to the East as quickly as possible. This involved transferring wholesale the advanced (and costly) 'social market' into a much weaker economic environment. This was done in order to preserve the core institutions of West Germany and to prevent East Germany becoming a low-wage zone that may threaten the powerful yet potentially vulnerable high-wage, high-skill economy built up with such care and involving so

[11] 'Germany's Dismal Future', *Forbes*, 31 January 2005.

much consensus and integration of various parties since the war. According to *Die Spiegel*, the Federal government subsidizes the new Eastern Länder by around €70–80 billion per year (or US$100 billion [Streeck 1997: 251]). This huge transfer of wealth triggered the ballooning of Federal public debt (Siebert 2005: 289–290) particularly as German welfare state policies were also transferred wholesale over to the East, where some regions suffer from severe problems of unemployment as the command economy of the GDR fell apart and state-owned enterprises closed (Streeck 1997: 251). While probably the right thing to do morally, it was extraordinarily ambitious and costly. Broader processes of globalization have also threatened the German economy, such as the influx of low-wage migration from Eastern European nations which has thrown the highly controlled and regulated former West German labour market into confusion.

Many now argue that senior management of major German corporations are increasingly leaning towards Anglo-Saxon norms and values (Beyer and Höpner 2003), and many authors (Siebert 2005) advocate German moves from organized capitalism to disorganized or investor capitalism. According to Marsh 'the wave of restructuring to make German companies more global, more cost-efficient, more open to shareholder interests and less reliant on their domestic production base adds up to the most drastic period of corporate reshaping since the Second World War' (2000: 79). These restructurings are similar to those pursued in Japan (Dore 2000, and Chapter 11), including changes to corporate governance law to allow for greater protection of shareholders and to stimulate a market for corporate control. German universal banks were becoming increasingly interested in emulating the riskier, more globalized forms of US-style investment banking. For example Deutsche Bank acquired the London-based investment bank Morgan, Grenfell & Co in 1990 as it tried to move into riskier, more globalized, more Americanized forms of financial trading.

The takeover of the industrial and telecoms firm Mannesmann by the UK–US telecoms giant Vodafone Airtouch in 2000 was highly emblematic of changed times (Höpner and Jackson 2001). According to Höpner and Jackson, a significant segment of *Deutschland AG* is now subject to markets for corporate control. There is substantial, ever-growing pressure on senior management to demonstrate and stimulate increased stock market value of firms under their stewardship. Not only Mannesmann, but other blue-chip German corporations, such as Krupp, Hoescht and Continental, have been embroiled in hostile takeover battles (Höpner and Jackson 2001: 5). While few would say that Germany has now converged on Anglo-Saxon systems, the 'direction of travel' seems obvious (Dore 2000).

A group of researchers has increasingly argued that German corporate governance is changing significantly (Beyer and Höpner 2003; Höpner and Krempel 2004). They observe 'rapid changes towards market orientation in the 1990s' (Höpner and Krempel 2004: 179), such as the system of defensive and mutually reinforcing corporate shareholdings apparently dissolving, banks withdrawing their seats on supervisory boards, chief executives (such as Schrempp of Daimlez-Benz, Dormann of Hoescht and Cromme of Krupp steel) increasingly proclaiming the need for 'shareholder value' and radical restructuring (and receiving an ever-greater share of their remuneration in stock options). The pace of privatization was accelerated, and legal reforms (known as *KonTrag*) designed to abolish uneven voting rights and legalize share buybacks came into force in 1998. Capital gains tax placed on the sale of block shareholdings were lifted. All of the above is driven by the ideological and financial imperatives of a much more aggressive and investor-driven capitalism that has clearly penetrated the mindset of top German executives and politicians.

With cross-shareholdings being unwound at the meso-level, at the micro-level (inside companies) change is also afoot. Codetermination appears to be weakening. According to Dore: '[i]n many firms the powers of the supervisory board have *de facto* become attenuated, and in some firms a dominant shareholder group deals directly with the management board, overruling the employee representatives as a matter of course whenever necessary' (2000: 184). Union density and collective bargaining coverage have been falling steadily since the 1980s. Many authors (Culpepper 1999; Doellgast and Greer 2007; Hassel 1999) are pessimistic about the prospects for survival of the German model of industrial relations, describing an employer 'offensive' against traditional forms of workplace representation. Hassel (1999) shows that intense pressures for corporate competitiveness and the decentralization of industrial relations throughout the 1990s has meant that by 1999 only 15% of the German workforce was covered by both an effective collective agreement and a works council. Thus the 'core features' of 'the German model' emphasized so strongly in VoC theory applies to an ever-smaller part of the workforce, thus severely impeding the ability of actors such as unions, employer associations and government to 'fine tune' the economy in time-honoured fashion (Culpepper 1999).

Ronald Dore (2000: 222–224) suggests that is Germany less likely to resist pressures for Anglo-Saxonization than Japan because of a number of reasons, especially the much higher degree of embeddedness of Germany into European and global norms than the traditionally more isolationist Japan. In an interesting and provocative article, Kinderman (2005) argues that the emerging fissures and breakages in the German post-war consensus are already deep and serious. He argues that German employers are subverting the system from within in which formal structures remain in place at the meso-level, but are becoming increasingly irrelevant as managerial practices within firms change radially towards LME norms. Membership of industry associations is in decline (Keller and Kirsch 2011: 198) and a wave of union mergers took place in the mid-1990s (just as we have seen in the USA and UK) as unions attempted to reverse the trend for falling membership (Waddington and Hoffmann 2000).

Germany does not have minimum wage legislation, because it was traditionally believed to be unnecessary due to extensive collective bargain coverage. But some would argue today that there is a need to introduce it because of the rise of the 'working poor' in Germany; those who earn wages of such low levels that they struggle to make ends meet (Keller and Kirsch 2011: 215). 'Non-standard' employment, such as part-time, temporary and other forms of casualized employment is on the rise (Keller and Kirsch 2011: 219) and the opening of Eastern Europe has seen huge migration of manufacturing jobs to cheaper regions on Germany's doorstep, such as Poland, the Czech Republic and Hungary. Job security has become a much more pressing issue, just as it has in France and in the Anglo-Saxon world. In a powerful example, in 2005 Siemens workers at two plants agreed to work an extra five hours per week for free to avoid losing jobs to Hungary.[12] Given such pressures it is easy to appreciate why some authors argue that the institutions of codetermination are in 'deeper and more serious difficulties than ever before' (Keller and Kirsch 2011: 221).

Like the Mannesmann takeover, other high-profile examples of radical change have come to German corporate life. One was the merger between Daimler-Benz AG and Chrysler Corporation in 1998. This was supposed to help both parties, but it became a famous failure. It seemed impossible to merge companies with such differences in 'national business system' characteristics. At no stage did the new firm seem able (or willing) to properly merge and integrate product lines to make the promised efficiency gains. The German CEO of the merged company, Jürgen Schrempp, was persistently portrayed negatively by the US business press for his apparent high-handedness towards the US part of the business. So bad was the financial performance that DaimlerChrysler was sued by activist investors, and in 2007 a controlling stake in Chrysler was bought by the distressed companies specialist Cerberus Capital Management for US$7.4 billion.[13] The companies went their separate ways once more. Chrysler was left to an uncertain fate, resorting in the end to requesting bailout

[12] For full details, see the story posted on EU foundation Eurofound's webpages: www.eurofound.europa.eu/eiro/2004/07/feature/de0407106f.htm.

[13] 'Cerberus Buys Chrysler Majority', *BBC News*, 3 August 2007.

monies from US Congress in 2009 (see Chapter 3) before its eventual sale to Fiat of Italy.

Elsewhere German firms have had more success as they have internationalized. VW purchased the elite luxury brands Bentley and Rolls-Royce from the British company Vickers in 1998, and the Rolls-Royce badge was then licensed to BMW in 2002. Throughout the 2000s Porsche was one of the world's most financially viable car companies (in stark contrast to the parlous state of US and UK manufacturers), and it eventually purchased a controlling stake in VW. German carmakers VW, BMW and Mercedes-Benz are still by some distance Europe's most advanced and successful car manufacturers, with export success all over the world. Although the top-level corporate governance and the public exhortations of German executives have certainly adapted to reflect changed times, the core goals and orientations of German firms often reflect deep-seated commitment to 'world class' manufacturing. Although the conglomerate Siemens has undergone substantial change, its extremely diverse portfolio of products is well respected around the world, especially in very high-value items such as trains, heavy electrical machinery and medical systems, such as MRI machines. In certain industries German manufacturers enjoy as much as 80% of global market share.[14]

However, structural unemployment continues to be an issue for the less fortunate not employed by such world class firms. Unemployment reached around 10% in 2000s. In an effort to combat the slowdown, Chancellor Gerhard Schröeder announced his 'Agenda 2010' plans in March 2003. This consisted of a 25% cut in the basic rate of income tax, and cutbacks to pensions and unemployment benefit. The Hartz reforms enacted throughout the early to mid-2000s, were redolent of neoliberal reforms pursued in the UK and USA in the 1980s, and similar attempts in France, to make labour markets more flexible by reducing wages and employers' legal burdens to their workforces thereby encouraging them to hire (often on part-time or other non-standard forms of employment). As of the early 2010s, German unemployment stood at around 7% but concerns remain about the low quality of jobs being created, and prevalence of non-standard employment.

Some argue that significant parts of the German employers are keen on unravelling the traditionally consensus-built nature of the German system. Kinderman (2005) suggests that the much-vaunted complementarities in the German system no longer really exist, noting intense conflict over the future of the model and an 'employer offensive' that 'shouldn't be happening' (Kinderman 2005: 433) if these complementarities were really as powerful as the VoC paradigm asserts. He describes an active and committed campaign by employers to dismantle

[14] 'Germany's New Boom: Making Money by Making Stuff', *Guardian,* 14 March 2011.

and subvert Germany's post-war industrial relations and corporate governance systems, with the public face of this campaign centred on the employers-association funded 'New Social Market Initiative', which provides relentless lobbying and media campaigns to push for the development of Anglo-Saxon structures. Much of this change is done in ways that are invisible if we focus too tightly on the continuity of existing structures such as works councils.

Privatizations have proceeded at a faster pace than before, with Deutsche Post, Deutsche Telekom, several airports, the government printing office and even the railways Deutsche Bahn slated for sale (Höpner and Krempel 2004: 188). These changes in Western Germany were given political impetus by the rapid sale (at low prices) of East German former state-owned enterprises. Vertical disintegration in product markets also affects German unions (Doellgast and Greer 2007). Concession-bargaining becomes more common as German workplaces are threatened by closure and the transfer of jobs to East European regions with much lower labour costs. Roughly 6 million union members were lost between 1991 to 2003 (Doellgast and Greer 2007: 57). Non-standard work is on the increase amid the reduction of working hours, and the transfer of workers into subcontractors - different employers who may or may not be covered by collective bargaining agreements.

While threatened from within, traditional forms of German corporate governance and employment relations have also been heavily criticized from outside. Some ugly scandals emerged at major corporations, such as Siemens and VW, in the mid-2000s. A bribery scandal erupted at Siemens, in which it was disclosed that several senior directors had paid bribes for the awarding of contracts to Siemens in Russia, Venezuela, Iraq and Israel. Siemens paid a fine of €1 billion to German and US authorities.[15] A gigantic scandal involving bribery, sexual misconduct, political corruption and financial irregularities emerged in VW, which tarnished the reputations of dozens of executives, politicians and works councillors, leading to two prison sentences.[16] Scandals such as these were seized on by critics of the German model, as proponents of the more 'dynamic', 'flexible' and 'investor-friendly' Anglo-Saxon system argued that they are symptomatic of a sclerotic and cronyist system in which unions and insiders have too much power and investors enjoy no transparency.

Less dramatically, German firms have been criticized for spending too much energy on 'over-engineering' their products to such high specifications that they may no longer be practical or suitable for customers' needs. (The Mercedes S-class has been described as 'a cathedral on

---

[15] 'Siemens Directors to Pay Damages', *BBC News*, 2 December 2009.

[16] 'VW Sex and Bribery Scandal: Sentences Handed Down in Corruption Affair', *Spiegel Online*, 22 February 2008.

wheels' [Randlesome 1994: xiii].) Top management in Germany has traditionally been dominated by doctorates in engineering, quite a contrast to the finance, legal and marketing-dominated MBAs that run US companies, meaning that German corporations are not market-focused enough. (Similar criticisms are often made of Japanese manufacturers).

Even the much-admired German education system has come in for criticism, with many arguing that university degrees take too long to complete (Siebert 2005: 250) and are too theoretical in nature. A student can be aged 28 by the time he or she has received their first degree (the diploma). Statistically, they would also be 'well advised' to take a doctorate if they want to reach the upper reaches of management (Randlesome 1994: 152–153). Recent years have seen a concerted move towards more 'global', more generalist and more 'transferable', management education for businesspeople, such as American-style MBAs. Certainly the public announcements of high-profile German CEOs (Beyer and Höpner 2003: 181) would support the view that a finance-driven, pro-restructuring mentality has emerged among German corporations.

The situation today is an odd hybrid. As Allen's (2006: 93) meticulous research into German firms reminds us it is important to bear in mind widespread within-country divergence; there are many firms that do not conform to the high-skills, high-wage, high-quality, employee-democracy stereotype of Germany. One excellent example is provided by Wortmann (2004) who describes the emergence (and success) of 'hard discounting' stores Aldi and Lidl, who compete on cost rather than quality.

The solidity of *Modell Deutschland* is more uncertain than ever (Siebert 2005). Yet it retains many supporters, especially among those of a left-of-centre persuasion. Harding and Paterson (2000) are more optimistic in their support and advocacy of the high-trust, high-quality model. Labour remains a relatively powerful actor in Germany, with rights and privileges still relatively strongly protected by law, especially when compared to Anglo-Saxon countries in which formal workplace democracy has all-but disappeared or where its existence rests entirely on management goodwill (Doellgast 2012).

Even taking into account national legal changes or takeover battles affecting major German corporations, anthropologically, German companies still feel and behave in familiar ways – Fear's assessment of the Mittelstand remains accurate, as does Smyser's (1993: 68–71) description of the lean managerial structure, strong customer focus and powerful 'engineering culture' of German firms. The social market economy remains a fairly powerful concept among political elites and is often publicly defended, such as when Social Democrat Franz Münteferung famously described private equity firms as 'locusts' (Yorozu et al. 2013: 204).

An interesting development which hints at the incompatibility of Anglo-Saxon concepts and systems in the German institutional environment was the failure of the Neuer Markt, a stock market modelled on

America's Nasdaq. Launched in 1997 this was supposed to provide a capital market for 'mid-cap', or smaller to medium-sized and high-tech companies. After an initial boom in Initial Public Offerings in the early 2000s, this experiment did not continue to capture the imagination of investors, and the Neuer Markt was closed in 2003 (Vitols 2005: 391–392). One interpretation of this story might be that German firms, investors and bankers are sceptical of New Economy fads and are happier with the country's more traditional areas of strength. Between 1997–2010, industry's share of German GDP moved from 20 to 21%, while the figures for the UK went from 18 to 13%.[17] The German economy seems to be much more comfortable with industrial engineering rather than financial engineering, and many of its business leaders were confident that its success in industrial manufacturing and export will continue in the years after the subprime crisis.[18] There are clearly some enduring features of the German system that are powerful and vital to defend; features that competing economies (notably the UK) have lost in their embrace of US-style investor capitalism.

Conclusion

Despite its struggles (notably in the eastern Länder), Germany remains a very powerful economy and a highly successful society. Its most recent ranking on international indices such as the human development index (ninth in the world),[19] and the World Economic Form's index of international competitiveness (sixth in the world)[20] is impressive. Like Japan and the Nordic nations it has a relatively low Gini (just 0.25 in 2000, compared to 0.368 in the USA and 0.345 in the UK according to figures cited by Vitols [2005: 393]), a large middle class, and relatively low levels of social problems (Wilkinson and Pickett 2009:17). Hardly a 'dismal' future, then. In an important sign of the continuity of German forms of workplace negotiation, Siemens struck a deal with the metalworkers' union IG Metall to provide indefinite job security to its 128,000-strong workforce in September 2010.[21]

But the national institutions of Germany (such as codetermination) are by their nature very locally embedded and parochial and are

[17] 'Filling the Vacuum', *Guardian*, 24 July 2010.

[18] 'Germany's New Boom: Making Money by Making Stuff', *Guardian,* 14 March 2011.

[19] UN Human Development Index, 2011.

[20] World Economic Form *Global Competitiveness Report* 2012–13.

[21] 'Siemens Promises Workers Jobs for Life', *Financial Times*, 22 September 2010.

unlikely, therefore, to be spread outwards to other nations. Rather, they are increasingly threatened by more mobile and more 'footloose' Anglo-Saxon norms and actors, especially international finance which increasingly aims to detach itself from national institutions and norms (Streeck 1997: 254). Germany on some levels has clearly moved from its model of organized capitalism towards a form of disorganized capitalism.

Much of the contemporary writing on Germany is therefore pessimistic about the survival of the model as a distinct variety of capitalism (Beyer and Höpner 2003; Kinderman 2005; Siebert 2005). This includes writings by supporters of the model (such as Doellgast and Greer 2007; Dore 2000; Streeck 1997), who reluctantly suggest that there are few prospects for the survival of this distinct and ethically attractive model; a rare model that takes employee democracy seriously. Some are more sceptical about the extent of change, pointing as much to continuity, such as the development of 'negotiated shareholder value' (Vitols 2004b) in which the adoption of a more shareholder-oriented viewpoint among banks and top management does not drive out traditional German constructs, but takes its place alongside more traditional forms of bank-based, stakeholder and insider governance (see also Frick and Lehmann 2005). Jackson et al. (2005: 118) also suggest rather slower change and important forms of accommodation in German institutions, which are, after all, set up to deal with negotiation and compromise between various stakeholders.

Analysts will debate the meaning of these changes back and forth. For example Becht and Böhmer (2001) report the persistence of strong blockholdings in the early 2000s, showing highly concentrated ownership, with more than half of all DAX-listed companies controlled by a single majority block, and where 'only 17.4% are without a blockholder with at least a veto minority (25%)' (Becht and Böhmer 2001: 142). This is a problem if you believe – as neoliberal critics such as Siebert (2005) do – that blockholdings are a restraint on trade that severely limit the openness of the stock market to potential participants. The total amount of stock market capitalization available to market participants amounts to just 14% of GDP, as compared to 48% in the USA and 81% in the UK (Siebert 2005: 238), which results in an artificially closed economy that is hemmed in by inefficient non-market restrictions. Conversely, Höpner and Krempel (2004: 340) make the very important point that although blockholdings and inter-company linkages on supervisory boards still exist, they may be changing in their usage. It should not be assumed that large blockholders such as banks are using these traditional connections to sustain stable relationships. They may now use them to stimulate change, such as when Deutsche Bank used its seat on the Thyssen supervisory board to support Krupp's hostile takeover rather than to block it.

Many, including some German authors such as Siebert (2005), do not regard the slow reform or abandonment of German institutions as something to bemoan, but as evidence of the inevitable movement of the German system towards global integration and 'world best practice' as the globalization of world markets continues apace. Siebert claimed that Germany is reforming too slowly and cautiously, that it has 'gone astray in its economic governance'.

> It has expanded its social security systems to such an extent that they are now weakening the country's economic foundations and negatively affecting its economic performance. ... Unlike other countries, it has not succeeded in modernizing its institutional setup according to the changing international conditions. (Siebert 2005: 377)

It remains quite possible, however, to be sceptical about the supposedly 'inevitable' march of neoliberal globalization (especially as the weaknesses of that model were so strongly revealed in 2007–8). Harding and Paterson (2000: 11) for example, argue that the complex, highly networked structure of corporate Germany will have the flexibility and sophistication to respond and adapt to the seemingly endless new challenges that globalization creates. Once again, the German case reveals the indeterminacy of these debates around models, convergence and globalization. These revolve, to a very large extent, around authors' own subjective interpretations of what is going on, what will happen next, and whether or not country models are well adapted to these changes, both from the perspective of economic outcomes, and of more moral judgments about the prospects for the emergence and survival of elusive notions of the 'good society'.

Further reading

Chandler, A.D., (1990) *Scale and Scope: The Dynamics of Industrial Capitalism*, Cambridge, MA: Harvard University Press.

This famous volume includes an enormous amount of historical detail on the growth and establishment of German 'cooperative capitalism', usefully comparing it to developments in the USA and the UK. In short this is a masterwork and a major classic of business history. It is great for those needing a broad historical overview, but its rather detached and technical approach does not describe much about the realities of working life in such corporations.

(Continued)

(Continued)

Yamamura, K. and Streeck, W. (eds) (2003) *The End of Diversity? Prospects for German and Japanese Capitalism*, Ithaca, Cornell University Press.

This is a very useful collection & detailed chapters on contemporary charges to the CME models of Germany and Japan. The chapters range over issues of banking and finance, industrial relations, innovation systems, institutional change and political economy, and student of VoC are likely to find the volume very helpful.

Doellgast, V., (2012) *Disintegrating Democracy at Work: Labor Unions and the Future of Good Jobs in the Service Industry*, Ithaca, NY: Cornell University Press.

This very detailed and up-to-date book provides a clear and useful picture of the changing nature of German and American work regimes. Its focuses on services workplaces rather than on industry, which is helpful as the latter tends to dominate discussions of Germany. Services jobs are often associated with low-pay, low discretion, no union representation and no career opportunities. Her research shows, however, that German workplaces in the telecoms industry are typically much less 'low road' than their US counterparts, with German institutions of codetermination and union representation providing much more decent work for German services employees. Even so, change is certainly afoot, and German services employees are facing up to an erosion of 'good' jobs (although not to the extent shown in the USA).

Kinderman, D., (2005) 'Pressure from Without: Subversion from Within: The Two-Pronged German Employer Offensive', *Comparative European Politics*, 3, 4: 432–463.

Daniel Kinderman argues that the well-known institutions that structure the German socio-economic model are now in disarray due to the pressures of globalization, financialization, the liberalization of markets and the ascendency of neoliberalism. The paper is not only very informative on the German situation but is also an excellent critique of the VoC approach. It advocates a much more detailed understanding of the dynamic power plays within German economy and society, rather than resting on the assumptions that path-dependency and complementarity of institutions will continue to reproduce stability and 'system-ness' in Germany (which Kinderman regards as always exaggerated). A strongly argued and engaging article.

SEVEN Nordic Economies: The Employee Dignity Agenda

Chapter objectives

- To explore the fundamental features of the socio-economic models of Sweden, Denmark, Norway and Finland – the Nordic societies – and to show why they are widely regarded as both economically competitive and ethically sound
- To show why and how these economies (especially Sweden, the largest) developed such egalitarian models from the 1930s onwards after deades of severe industrial relations conflict
- To describe the main macro-level features of Nordic business systems, namely their very well-developed forms of social welfare, large public sectors and high taxes, powerful unions and employers associations, and very flat income distribution
- To describe Nordic capitalism at workplace level, drawing attention to the attempts to foster enhanced levels of employee dignity at work, such as powerful forms of industrial democracy, work redesign which aims towards worker involvement and discretion, work–life balance policies, and improved levels of gender equality
- To discuss the extent to which these societies have been affected by, or have embraced, the worldwide drives towards neoliberalism and globalization, exploring the prospects for change and continuity in these powerful and distinct models

Introduction

Another region of the world widely discussed in the VoC and NBS literature is Scandinavia[1] or the Nordic nations of Sweden, Norway, Denmark and Finland.[2] These are nations with relatively small populations and located at the northern periphery of Europe. But the Nordic variety of capitalism is widely discussed as not only a distinct model but also a highly successful one. The term 'social democracy' is used to refer to the political agenda that has traditionally existed in these nations, in which a cross-party consensus supports high taxation rates, a large public sector and a powerful social welfare system. Notions of 'wage solidarity' and 'social partnership' are prominent and serve to compress differentials in income. Social democracy is broadly a far less conflictual political system than that seen in Anglo-Saxon environments, and a system that has provided a strong degree of stability to Nordic politics in the post-war era. The nations have tended to be high tax environments, and have sustained very high public spending as a proportion of GDP (often above 50%).

The Nordic nations are typically understood to correspond broadly to the CME model, featuring extensive and often universal public welfare systems, bank-based financial systems, highly skilled workforces with well-developed forms of worker voice, and 'active' labour market policies (such as state-run schemes to upskill or re-skill workers during times of economic transition [Campbell and Pedersen 2007]). The Danish model of 'flexicurity' (flexible labour markets combined with strong public protection and government policies for retraining) has gained wide prominence in comparative economic, social and political debates (Zhou 2007). Employers in the region are often praised for pursuing sophisticated and enlightened practices, such as 'work redesign' and a focus on human relations that extends high degrees of discretion and autonomy to workers (Blackler and Brown 1978; Dobbin and Boychuk 1999). In the 1980s and early 1990s, for example, the Kalmar and Uddevalla plants at the Swedish automotive manufacturer Volvo were nearly as famous examples as NUMMI or the GM Saturn plant (Adler 1992), as enlightened (and no

---

[1] The word 'Scandinavia' is rarely used in these countries, and is in much more common usage outside of the region (Hildebrand 1978: 590). An alternative term is to refer this group of countries as 'Nordic Europe'.

[2] Technically Scandinavia does not include Finland (as the Finnish language has a different origin to Danish, Norwegian and Swedish). Some include Iceland, Greenland and the Faroe Islands in the category of Nordic nations, but these rarely feature in the economic literature due to their very small populations.

less efficient) alternatives to Japan's lean manufacturing (Berggren 1992; Sandberg 1995; Wallace 2008).

The Nordic approach to management education has also traditionally emphasized human dignity, quality of working life, and teamwork and collaborative approaches between management and unions, as opposed to the typically conflictual, finance-driven and 'profit before people' approach often associated with the North American MBA-style approach to management. Nordic society features low levels of income inequality and the majority of the population identifies as 'middle class'. Despite their small populations, these countries have strong reputations in science and academia, and many of the multinationals originating from the region produce well-known and high-quality products for international markets, such as Finland's Nokia, Sweden's SKF (steel products), SAAB (automotive and aerospace) and Tetra-Pak (packaging) and Denmark's iconic and highly globalized consumer products firms such as the toy company Lego, and Bang & Olufson in electronics.

Nordic 'models' are often popular with left-of-centre analysts due to their traditional support of worker dignity, work–life balance, gender equality, socialized ownership of significant parts of the economy, flexible working and labour democracy. But the countries have also combined a social conscience with business success. Sweden, Denmark, Finland and Norway typically appear around or at the very top of international ranking lists of 'economic freedoms' and 'ease of doing business'; perched atop the ranks alongside much less labour-friendly economies such as Singapore and the USA. Nordic countries score low on Gini (Sweden's figure was 0.252 in the mid-2000s) and sixth in the world on UN's human development index (both figures from Steinmo 2010: 31). To their supporters, the Nordic countries show that the tax-and-spend 'high road' can be economically successful as well as more morally acceptable than Anglo-Saxon neoliberalism.

Not everyone would agree. To begin with, the nations possess certain features (notably very small populations) that make comparisons with larger nations difficult to sustain. Lash and Urry (1987: 10), for example, remind us that the sum total of those living under America's non- corporatist 'disorganized capitalism' is 'more than *three times* larger than the combined population of Austria, Switzerland, Denmark, New Zealand, Holland, Belgium, Finland, Norway and Australia.' Moreover the USA has at least 34.6 million people living in poverty (entitled to at least some form of welfare support) plus another 50 million in 'near-poverty' (outside of welfare entitlement yet still struggling to make ends meet) (Perrucci and Perrucci 2009: 113–116). The combined figure of around 85 million is about four times the size of the total populations of all four Nordic nations combined. The Nordic experience is therefore probably not realistically transferable as a 'model' to other nations.

Moreover, some severe problems have emerged in recent decades that have threatened the effectiveness and even the survivability of the Nordic model. Just like other CMEs (Japan, Germany, France) many describe these 'high-road' models as exhausted or eroded by globalization. Confidence in the Nordic economies (especially Sweden and Finland) was shaken by a severe banking crisis in the early 1990s that necessitated widespread government bailouts and subsequent cutbacks in welfare spending (Drees and Pazarbasioglu 1998; Fulcher 2004: 58–64; Pontusson 1992). Scandinavian multinationals have outgrown their national homes and many have been acquired by overseas investors and restructured for 'best practice' and 'shareholder value'. Volvo's car division, for example, was purchased by Ford in 1999 and subsequently sold to Geely of China in 2010. In a potent symbol, the much-trumpeted Uddevalla plant was closed in the early 1990s (Sandberg 1995: 83). Swedish-owned Volvo Trucks has since abandoned most of its experiments with work redesign and humanizing work conditions in its cab plants (Wallace 2008). Does social democracy and the human-focused Nordic model have a future?

This chapter will explore the Scandinavian models, mostly focusing on Sweden (for the simple fact that it has the widest coverage in the literature). While it is clearly wrong to discuss 'the Scandinavian model' or 'Nordic capitalism' as if it is a unified whole rather than four (or more) countries, some form of shorthand is applied in this chapter for the sake of clarity and space. This chapter will also be somewhat shorter than the others because properly exploring the historic roots of the nations would require separate chapters on all four countries. Regretfully, therefore, the chapter will sometimes skate over Norway, Denmark and Finland and will be more reliant on Sweden. Sweden has the largest economy and easily the largest population of the region. Current populations and GDPs are displayed in Table 7.1.

Table 7.1 GDP and population figures for the four main Nordic societies.

	Sweden	Denmark	Finland	Norway
Population (million)	9.43	5.57	5.38	4.98
GDP (billion USD)	539.7	333.6	263.0	485.8

Source: World Bank figures, correct as of March 2013

Sweden, Denmark and Finland are members of the EU, but only Finland has so far adopted the euro as its currency. Norway's population has twice voted against joining the EU. Despite having the smallest population among the four major Nordic societies, it is the second richest after Sweden, largely due to its status as the world's fifth-largest oil exporter. Although not an EU member, it is part of the European Economic Area and is a major trading partner of EU nation states.[3]

In what follows, the chapter provides a broad overview of the Nordic approach to capitalism. The next three sections follow Lash and Urry's (1987) taxonomy of 'liberal, organized, and disorganized capitalism', as the chapter charts the development, entrenchment and possible decline/reform of the Scandinavian models of social democracy and welfare capitalism. Conclusions then follow, in which it is argued that an identifiable Nordic social democratic model still exists, but has adapted itself in order to accommodate to – and indeed contribute to – the ascendancy of neoliberal globalization.

Late industrialization and capital–labour compromise: the historical bases of the Nordic models

The impact of Nordic history and culture has been significant worldwide. Norse epic poems or sagas – many of which were composed in the 1200s – record the founding of Viking settlements and conquests in Iceland, Greenland, Britain and Northern France (Normandy) between the 8th, 9th and 10th centuries. Some expeditions reached as far as the northeastern extremes of what is now the USA in the 10th century (about 500 years before Columbus!), while others sailed eastwards and into Russian waterways. In the modern era, Scandinavian nations are typically described as economically peripheral to Europe and relatively late industrializers. Their populations were small; the four countries combined added up to just 4.1 million in 1800, rising to 14.6 million by 1950 (Hildebrand 1978: 590). Politically they were reasonably well-integrated into Europe, with 'efficient systems of government and a well-organized administration, comparatively honest for the time' (Hildebrand 1978: 590). But economically they were predominantly agrarian societies, historically most active in raw materials export, especially iron and copper, as well as timber, cereals, butter and fish. Denmark benefitted from trade passing through the Baltic, and Norway was a major seafaring nation (Hildebrand 1978: 591). Finland's prospects for development were hindered by its lack of independence from the Russian Empire (1805–1917). The small size of the economy has meant that emigration from Scandinavia has historically been commonplace as the population looks elsewhere for economic opportunities (Swenson 2002: 77).

[3] 'Non-EU Norway "Almost as Integrated in Union as UK"', *BBC News*, 17 January 2012.

With small populations providing limited domestic market size, all of the Nordic nations expended great efforts on export earnings to stimulate growth. Mining and metalworking provided a major part of Sweden's export economy. Stora Kopparberg is a great example – this mining, electricity-generating and steelmaking company emerged out of the beginnings of the excavation of Kopparberg mountain in 1288 and the subsequent granting of a Royal Charter in 1347. It is probably the oldest company in the world still operating today (Sjögren 2008: 24).

Industry in Sweden, according to Hildebrand (1978: 594), rapidly moved 'from timber to pulp, from iron to engineering, for less-processed to more highly processed industrial products.' Norway saw a rapid development of electrical industries, such as hydroelectric power stations. Railways grew rapidly in the mid 19th century and modern factory systems were established in the textiles industry, and in brewing and distilling (Hildebrand 1978: 592). The major industrial leap forward for the region came towards the mid-late 19th century and up until the First World War. The Swedish economy rapidly liberalized during that period, removing traditional restraints on trade such as the guild system in 1846. The Company Act of 1848 permitted joint-stock companies and limited liability companies. Tariffs and duties were progressively scaled back in the 1860–70s as the economy increasingly traded with Europe (Sjögren 2008: 26). Schooling and education developed and literacy rates soared. Lars Magnus Ericsson began to produce telephones in 1878 marking the origin of the now-global Ericsson telecoms and electronics corporation. Much of the initial industrial expansion was funded by retained profits (Hildebrand 1978: 610), but by the 1900s Scandinavian banks had grown rapidly to provide investment funding for corporate expansion. To a degree, Sweden, Denmark and Norway modelled themselves on Germany's late industrialization strategy. Bank finance was therefore typically 'of the German type' (Hildebrand 1978: 612), that is, providing industrial capital in the form of long-term loans based on the bank's own capital (see Chapter 6).

Sweden today enjoys a well-earned reputation for workplace democracy and peaceful industrial relations. However, the path it took to get to this position was long and very acrimonious. Labour relations in the early 20th century were extremely troublesome. The employers' federation (SAF) was well-organized and took extremely draconian measures to reduce labour costs (Swenson 2002: 77). Multi-industry lockouts were the preferred strategy of SAF as it attempted to drive down wages and run unions dry of their strike funds. In many cases not only unionized but also non-unionized workers were unilaterally locked out of their workplaces (Swenson

2002: 71–82). This was about as far as one can imagine from the progressive traditions now associated with Swedish employers. In Sweden's era of liberal capitalism, such 'managerial absolutism' (Swenson 2002: 84) created considerable counter-pressures as trade union membership grew rapidly and unions responded with strikes and protests, such as the 1909 general strike that lasted five months (Fulcher 2004: 59). With powerful unions and powerful employer associations, labour peace was won only after decades of intense class conflict. Historical 'compromises' between capital and labour were eventually found, such as the Soltsjöbaden Agreement between the Union Confederation LO and SAF in 1938, which established the highly centralized wage bargaining system that was to follow (Wilks 1996: 447). In Denmark, modifications of the negotiation rules and the Conciliation Act in 1934 and 1936 'locked in' similar forms of corporatist and mutually very well-organized wage bargaining between the Danish Trade Union Confederation (LO) and the Confederation of Danish Employers (DA) (Madsen et al. 2010: 229). Again, this was after decades of intense labour strife, involving lock-outs and strikes (Madsen et al. 2010: 227).

Being 'peripheral' to Europe had some advantages. All of the Scandinavian countries stayed out of First World War. Blockades, however, did hamper their economies, which were further weakened by economic depression in the early 1920s. Social Democratic parties with close links to trade unions became the dominant electoral force across the Nordic countries since the 1930s. The Swedish Social Democrats (SAP) held uninterrupted power between 1932–76. Sweden was an early adopter of Keynesian policies and 'high and progressive taxation', which helped pull Sweden out of the early 1920s economic downturn (Fulcher 2004: 60). Recovery from then on was swift, with each of the Nordic nations showing rapid urbanization, high levels of industrial investment and the building of modern transport and communications infrastructures (Hildebrand 1978: 595–596).

In the Second World War, Sweden remained neutral, but was nevertheless forced to develop rationing, price and investment controls (Meidner 1993: 212), developing a 'war economy' of a kind. Norway and Denmark were occupied and Finland established state control over the economy during its conflict with the USSR (Fellman 2008: 168). Following the end of the war - much as we saw in the UK–Nordic socialists argued that the immense collective effort of the wartime struggle could be channelled into peacetime economies, and that state ownership and administration could be harnessed to oversee the development of a more structured, logical, planned and fair form of capitalism. It was at this stage that the basis for the social democratic model of Nordic Europe was truly laid.

Living in 'the people's home': the post-war heyday of the Nordic model

In keeping with many of the nations in the post-war expansionary phase of capitalism, Scandinavian economies pursued full employment policies and developed especially powerful forms of government welfare, which extend into most areas of health and into higher education, along with highly subsidized childcare, paid parental leave and child support payments, and subsidies to industrial firms (Gramlich 1987: 250). Not unlike post-war France, the Nordic models were particularly good examples of 'organized capitalism' (Lash and Urry 1987), or the 'second spirit of capitalism' (Boltanski and Chiapello 2005) in that their economies were 'managed' to a very considerable degree by government authority and other institutions such as labour unions and employers' associations. It is during this period that the famous (and much envied) features of the Scandinavian models fully assert themselves. At the macro level these are an economic policy focus aimed at macroeconomic stability, full employment, political consensus, high taxation, a universal welfare state and advanced public services provision. At the micro-level, some firms focused their efforts on improving employee dignity by engaging in radical forms of work redesign and by developing powerful forms of worker voice and codetermination, meaningful work–life balance policies, and major steps towards encouraging gender equality at work. It is this 'golden age' that is so highly respected by left-of-centre political analysts in other nations. Swedish social democracy was famously described as 'the people's home' or *folkhemmet* by Prime Minister P.A. Hansson in 1928 (Meidner 1993: 211–212).

In many ways the Scandinavian models resemble the West German economy (see Chapter 6). Nordic corporate governance is historically similar in some ways to German practice (although it lacks the German two-tier corporate board). Works councils were introduced in Sweden in 1946 (Wedderburn 1977: ix), and into Denmark as 'cooperation committees' in 1947 (Madsen et al. 2010: 249).[4] Defensive cross-shareholdings constituted a kind of 'group company system' in Sweden, whereby 'corporate groups, ownership spheres and dynastic families' controlled major sections of corporate Sweden (Sjögren 2008: 51). Ownership was thus strongly concentrated in a fashion not dissimilar to that of West Germany (see Chapter 6), including widespread family ownership. In 2000, the typical publicly listed firm on the Stockholm Stock Exchange (SSE) had a clearly identifiable majority owner, and 82.2% of listed firms

[4] Works councils seem to be less influential in Scandinavia than in Germany, and they certainly enjoy a much lower profile than in the literature on Germany.

had a clear owner with more than 25% of the votes. The largest shareholder on average owned around 37.7% of the companies' shares (Agnblad et al. 2001: 234). These forms of ownership reinforced the trends towards stability and consensus, and meant very limited markets for corporate control. The system of 'wage solidarity' involving bargaining between highly organized unions and highly organized employers severely compressed wage differentials, and income inequality decreased dramatically in the 1960s and 1970s (Flanagan 1987). When coupled with extensive welfare states the Scandinavian countries emerge as among the most egalitarian of the advanced economies.

Many regarded this system as economically unsustainable, especially since such a flat wage structure seems likely to encourage lazier workers to 'free ride' at the expense of the more committed. Where is the incentive to work hard if everyone is paid much the same? (Flanagan 1987). Yet the Nordic countries generally demonstrate relatively high levels of productivity, at least before the problems of the 1970s and 1980s set in (Hibbs and Locking 1995). This is likely to be, at least to some extent, a product of higher levels of job satisfaction that is typically associated with the enlightened employment policies associated with Nordic organizations (Kristensen 2011b: 222). Certainly there are examples of 'free riders' and of others not being financially rewarded for the extra efforts they put in. But the latter are likely to be motivated by professional pride rather than cash incentives. National pay scales are very common for public sector jobs in many nations, especially for professionals such as teachers, police and medical staff, so there is no necessary reason why this approach cannot work for industrial and service workers, assuming that job evaluation is carried out in a way that professional employees regard as fair and accurate.

Even the introduction of new technology - in most nations typically a matter reserved only for top management and justified solely on the basis of projected efficiency savings - is handled sensitively by many Scandinavian companies, as matters of human dignity are (sometimes) put ahead of profit-making and speed to market. In fact, in the Nordic tradition of Socio-Technical Systems dignity of work is indistinguishable from organizational harmony/dignity. It is not considered possible to have effective organizational performance if human dignity is ignored, or thought about as somehow separate from the technical structure (Bjorn-Andersen and Hedberg 1977). Many have argued that this deep-seated approach to organizational upgrading can be far more effective and less prone to dysfunction than the rushed and hasty implementations so often seen in Anglo-Saxon contexts, where disruption, conflict, and obstruction are so common. Sadly, in practice, however, those implementing changes often put the needs of the technology first and the needs of people last (Bjorn-Andersen and Hedberg 1977).

Women have gained a much larger involvement in Nordic labour markets than in most other societies (Steinmo 2010: 57). Work-life balance policies (inadequate though they often are) were developed much earlier and more seriously in Nordic countries than elsewhere. Interestingly, however, although working life under social democracy was perhaps 'as good as it gets' in international terms, much of the literature on the Swedish economy describes major problems with low worker morale, high rates of absenteeism and widespread 'alienation'. To some extent this may have reflected the way much industrial work required very high levels of strength and endurance and were 'designed' with men in mind (indeed particularly physically strong men). Many women found these jobs to be particularly unpleasant, and women would typically also bear responsibility for childcare and housework, meaning they would be more likely than men to be forced to take time off work to handle household emergencies (Berggren 1992; Meidner 1993).

High levels of absenteeism and labour difficulties in the 1980s were some of the most pressing reasons behind Volvo's attempt to humanize work (in some, but by no means all, of its plants) (Berggren 1992: vii). Perhaps the high degree of complaint was itself a product of the egalitarian and enlightened management style typical of Swedish employers. Granting workers involvement and job security can encourage them to complain more as they are not so fearful of unfair treatment, victimization or redundancy if they speak out (Berggren 1992: 17).

There were widespread demands for greater work autonomy, with the outbreak of wildcat strikes in the 1960s outside of the official bargaining agenda (Ryner 2002: 126–128). This emergence of a 'submerged labour radicalism' (Fulcher 2004: 62) born out of growing alienation and disaffection was common to a number of industrial economies (Beynon 1984: 15–16; Granter 2009) and its manifestation in Sweden is captured in detail in Göran Palm's *The Flight From Work*, see Exhibit 7.1.

It is peculiar that what is often regarded as a model of worker participation and employee democracy - and looked upon enviously by workers outside the Nordic business system - is regarded by many of those actually living and working under it as oppressive and alienating. As we shall see in the next section, the rise of worker alienation described by writers such as Palm was to foreshadow a major crisis in the social democratic model. This broke out in the 1990s (rather later than the 1980s, which was the watershed for managerial or organized capitalism in the Anglo-Saxon nations).

Although parties of the right enjoyed some electoral success between 1976–82, there was no dramatic Thatcher or Reagan 'moment' during this period. However, 'solidaristic' wage bargaining was became increasingly problematic as the bargaining machinery became more complex, especially with increasing numbers of white-collar unions

Exhibit 7.1 A 'flight from work' in Sweden? Disaffection and alienation at Ericsson in the 1970s

Work dissatisfaction became a widespread phenomenon across the advanced societies since at least the 1960s. Although the piece below by Göran Palm was written in Sweden in the 1970s, it could just as easily describe almost any contemporary workplace in the advanced economies, suggesting that the Swedish model was not as employee-friendly as you might think, and that issues of work overload and work dissatisfaction go back a long way. Here Palm reports the viewpoints of Roland, an experienced metalworker at Ericsson:

'There's a poorer spirit of solidarity. Definitely poorer. Everyone is rushing off to look after his own interests. Formerly union meetings were fairly well-frequented, most people lived near their work places. If a boat excursion was arranged for union members in the summer, you could count on six or seven hundred participants. That sort of thing is impossible today.. [...]'

'Prices and rents and taxes have run far ahead of the agreement wages. As a result, there have been real wage reductions. The workers are forced to find solutions of their own and that means increased pressure in piece-work jobs without regard for consequences. [...] At the same time, the work takes all his energy so that he simply can't manage union activities during his leisure time. Formerly there were plenty of fine jobs which could engage one's interest because of their versatility and if your interest is engaged, you have energy for other things as well. But many of those jobs have been broken down into small piece-rate jobs nowadays. Pull a lever, fasten some screws, it makes for a deadly monotony. If you add this to the piece-work stress, you have the explanation why many workers can't stand the strain purely physically. And when that happens, there's no energy left for solidarity.'

[...]

'Only if today's industries are compared with the poverty, dirt and boss rule of the pre-war period can one claim that the workers' conditions are better today. If instead, one compares conditions with the 1940s and the early 1950s one cannot possibly claim that the workers have essentially better conditions. Today's industrial workers have to stand worse knocks than they did 20 or 30 years ago, that is the bleak truth of the matter.'

(Palm 1977: 61-2, 74)

and professional associations being drawn into the system (Fulcher 2004: 61; Pontusson 1992). A major problem with solidaristic bargaining was that it had the potential to restrain and frustrate both capital and labour. Corporate management was forced to negotiate with unions and to accept national rates of pay for specific posts based on job evaluation, a situation that limited their options to engage in competition to drive down wages or to incentivize employees with the promise of higher pay. For their part, unions were frustrated by the way solidaristic bargaining forced them to restrain their demands for wage increases in order to hold down inflation. Weaker companies went into bankruptcy if they could not pay the centrally negotiated wage rates. More profitable companies generated 'excess' profits that they could not pay to workers – this seems to 'punish' the workers of profitable firms. Swedish trade unions proposed a plan whereby these 'forfeited' extra wages could be transferred from the owners of capital into union-controlled 'wage earner funds' which were collectively owned by workers. This was known as the Meidner Plan, which was justified as follows:

> Experience has taught us that the free market forces guarantee neither full employment nor equality. To give the highest priority to these goals means challenging the principles of the capitalist system which is based on the profitability of privately owned capital. (Meidner 1993: 218)

This radical and progressive plan was very unpopular with the business community and wage-earner funds were established in very limited, mostly symbolic, form in 1983 and were abolished in 1992 (Swenson 2002: 315). Changes became more profound in the 1990s.

Challenges to Scandinavian social democracy in the 1990s: towards disorganized capitalism?

In the 1990s the Nordic countries broke significantly (but far from fully) from their 'organized' models, developing versions of Anglo-Saxon style 'disorganized capitalism' (Lash and Urry 1987) or the 'third spirit of capitalism' (Boltanski and Chiapello 2005). These changes were complex and multidimensional, with many reforms taking place simultaneously.

Foremost among the changes was a broad employer counterattack in which firms demanded reforms of what they regarded as restrictive and counterproductive employment laws and overly powerful unions (Fulcher 2004: 62). Government spending and borrowing to fund the welfare state were becoming unmanageable, with some estimates putting it at around two-thirds of GDP at its peak point in the early 1980s (Gramlich 1987: 252).[5] This represented rapid growth from around 30% of GDP in 1961. Much of the growth in size of the public sector was constituted by 'nonprofitable investments', such as unemployment insurance and expansions of public sector jobs in healthcare and

---

[5] Neoliberal authors tend to give much higher estimates of the size of public sector spending relative to GDP (around 66%) than supporters of the Swedish model such as Meidner, who puts it at around 55% at its peak in the mid-1980s (1993: 219).

municipal government services (Gramlich 1987: 253–4; Swenson 2002: 306). Even within the constraints of solidaristic bargaining, union wage demands were widely given as the cause of inflation that was eroding national competitiveness (Meidner 1993; Pontusson 1992).

The wage-setting system became progressively harder to administer as white-collar unions belonging to the Swedish Confederation for Professional Employees (TCO) were not officially committed to the explicit wage-flattening goal of solidaristic bargaining, and the growing number of services jobs were harder to evaluate due to their less tangible nature. Many local conflicts broke out about what is a fair, comparable, or reasonable wage as the Nordic economies matured and became post-industrial (Meidner 1993; Palm 1977). National wage settlements eventually collapsed completely (although there remains very significant wage bargaining between employers and union groupings at sub-national levels).

The ideological consensus gradually evaporated through the 1980s and Nordic social democrats, like other parties of the moderate left (New Labour under Tony Blair in the UK, the Democrats under Clinton in the USA), moved to 'occupy the centre ground'. Sweden's SAP effectively began to embrace neoliberalism as it turned to a so-called 'third road' after winning re-election in 1982. This 'Third Road' stood for 'first growth, then redistribution' signalling a clear move towards greater marketization while reforming and scaling back on social welfare but also maintaining it where possible (Pontusson 1992: 314). The 'third road' later became part of the inspiration for the later 'third way' adopted by centre-left parties across Europe and the USA that involved the embrace of markets and the general abandonment of socialistic national policies to control and manage the economy (Callinicos 2001; Giddens 1998). SAP's new policies initially were pursued 'by stealth' (Ryner 2002: 148) as politicians originally committed to solidaristic wage bargaining, strong welfare states and government macroeconomic management increasingly turned towards market forces, no doubt influenced to some extent by 'business-sponsored think tanks' such as SNS (Ryner 2002: 175–6). Language, argument and ideology had made subtle but significant shifts towards neoliberalism and LME models, as the 'problems' of Nordic economies were 'framed' (McCann 2013a; Vogel 2012) in terms of excessive dependence on non-market 'distortions' that restricted growth, just as business groups and employers' associations had long argued, such as in the Federation of Swedish Industries' *The Welfare State in Crisis* (Meyerson 1982). Reforms to solidaristic wage bargaining were already underway under SAP in the 1980s and processes of change were accelerated when Carl Bildt was elected Prime Minister in 1991. His Liberal Party stood for privatization, further welfare state reform and the preparation of Sweden for EU entry (Ryner 2002: 126).

Nordic governments were thus increasingly attracted to neoliberal policy measures that promised to restore economic growth by embracing deregulation and globalization. Financial controls were progressively lifted, and international capital controls abolished. The financial sectors of Scandinavian nations grew substantially, and suddenly there was much more speculative activity and liquidity. These changes were praised by those with the Anglo-Saxon model in mind, in which open markets for corporate control exist and in which capital markets are extensive (for example, Agnblad et al. 2001).

Yet as these economies gave up control by deregulating and opened up to embrace international financial capitalism, they also found themselves embroiled in destructive crises. Major financial crises erupted in all of the Nordic countries in the early 1990s. Similar to Japan's 'bubble economy' (see Chapter 11), deregulation of financial markets had taken place during an upturn in a boom–bust cycle and the sudden availability of credit created an unsustainable real-estate bubble that suddenly collapsed in value in 1991 (Drees and Pazarbasioglu 1998; Ryner 2002: 152). The responses of the Nordic governments to the bank failures differed, with Norway taking the most drastic actions by completely nationalizing two of the four largest banks, thereby wiping out shareholders. In Sweden all savings were guaranteed, but shareholders again lost out when the government completely purchased Nordbanken and set up two state-run 'bad banks' (Securum and Retriva) which were to take on the assets of other failed banks, separate the performing from the non-performing loans, and write off the latter. Swedish GDP fell 5% in the period 1991–3, and unemployment grew to around 10% (Fulcher 2004: 64). The Finnish economy contracted for three straight years and unemployment reached 20% in 1994.[6] But in the longer-run, the painful yet decisive actions of the Nordic governments are now looked upon as correct, rather than the halting and confused response of so many governments to the subprime disaster of 2007–8. The state's policy of recovery was arguably much more decisive and effective that those of Anglo-Saxon nations to subprime (Chapters 3 and 4) or Japan's to the bubble collapse (see Chapter 11). This is further evidence of the potential economic value of the organizing and directive capacity of government in the Nordic models. The British response, for example, has been multifaceted and fragmented, perhaps because its neoliberal institutional structure makes it unaccustomed to, and afraid of, decisive government intervention at the expense of shareholders. UK and US governments are wary of 'looking too "socialist"'.[7]

---

[6] 'UK Turned to Nordic Bail-out', *Daily Telegraph*, 13 October 2008.

[7] 'Insight: US Is Ready for Swedish Lesson on Banks', *Financial Times*, 12 March 2009.

Even if the recovery has proved impressive, the Nordic financial crisis intensified the pessimism surrounding the Nordic models which were mired in confusion even before the crash (Meidner 1993; Pontusson 1992). In common with crisis conditions elsewhere, the crash created the space for formerly radical or fringe proposals to become acceptable, even 'essential' (Klein 2007; McCann 2013a). The crash triggered cutbacks in public spending, and Anglo-Saxon style 'new public management' reforms were broadly adopted, involving privatization and partial marketization of areas of welfare provision that were until that point exclusively state monopolies. In Denmark, quite deliberate steps have been taken to remove labour market regulation and embrace 'flexible' labour markets as part of a neoliberal agenda (Madsen et al. 2010) (although so-called 'flexicurity' combines deregulation with powerful forms of government welfare and retraining to cushion the blows of redundancy and unemployment) (Campbell and Pedersen 2007; Zhou 2007).

Such fine-tuned, delicately negotiated, and above all nationally focused Scandinavian models are proving vulnerable to turbulence as globalization continues apace. The financial crash provided an impetus for Sweden to join the EU, which represented another major move away from national-level economic governance. The EU rather awkwardly combines elements of neoliberalism with Continental European 'social market' approaches to social policy (such as support for trade unions and workplace representation). An excellent example of these contradictions is the Vaxholm/Laval dispute of 2004–7. When a Latvian construction firm Laval un Partneri won a contract to refurbish school buildings on the Swedish island of Vaxholm, it attempted to undercut the Swedish negotiated wage structure by paying 14 Latvian workers wages around 40% below lower than those paid to their Swedish counterparts. Swedish unions and many politicians regarded this as 'social dumping' and condemned the company, before eight unions boycotted the site in November 2004, stopping work from progressing. Laval sought legal redress and a long-running dispute eventually found its way to the European Court of Justice (ECJ). Laval's argument was that the union blockade contravened EU laws on the free movement of labour. In December 2007 the ECJ handed down a somewhat ambiguous ruling that upheld the right to take industrial action against 'wage dumping' but only within strict parameters. Unions cannot engage in industrial action with the aim of asking for better conditions from overseas companies than the minimum set down by legislation. Since so much of the Swedish industrial relations climate is negotiated by employers and unions rather than legally established by legislation, this is quite a problem, and implies that Sweden will need to draw up minimum wage legislation if unions are to defend wage rates from international 'dumping' (Gennard 2008: 476–477). Sweden's entry to the EU represents another step towards the internationalization of its economy and the (at least partial) abandonment of distinctive Nordic measures of national economic control and wage negotiation.

In corporate life, many firms have experienced major changes in tone towards the Anglo-Saxon norms of 'investor capitalism' and shareholder value logic, changes that have led in some cases to dramatic and often troubling reforms cascading down from top management. This entails a shift away from the traditionally more egalitarian and consultative management styles of Denmark, Sweden, Norway and Finland, and towards new norms of corporate life that are at once more 'global', less 'national' and oddly less tangible. Clear elements of a 'third spirit of capitalism' (Boltanski and Chiapello 2005) are visible in a number of major Nordic firms, especially the many that are export-focused and increasingly 'global' in orientation.

In aviation, for example, SAS (Scandinavian Air Systems) embarked on a major culture change programme brought in by CEO Jan Carlzon in the 1980s. Carlzon's book, published in English as *Moments of Truth* (1989) is a classic example of the 'business turnaround in changed times' genre. Attacking bureaucracies' tendencies towards inertia, he advocates 'tearing the pyramids down' and claims, much like many authors of Anglo-Saxon business memoirs, to have reversed the decline of the company. More recent years have seen the emergence of several famous Nordic business 'gurus', such as Kjell Nordström and Jonas Ridderstråle, the Swedish authors of pop management texts such as *Funky Business Forever* (2007) and *Karaoke Capitalism* (2004). These are paradigmatic examples of Tom Peters-style 'change is good, change is necessary' ideology (with a self-consciously 'weird', 'different' and 'Scandinavian' twist) that urges readers to become effervesced by the excitement and turbulence of capitalism and radical new forms of management. This literature is about as far removed from the traditional Nordic concepts of solidaristic bargaining and universal welfare state provision as one could imagine. These gurus are called upon at great expense to provide 'turnaround' consultancy services to struggling organizations around the globe.

Meanwhile in Denmark Anders Knutsen, the new CEO of the luxury electronics corporation Bang & Olufson, brought in a dramatic change/turnaround process known as 'Breakpoint 93'. This was very redolent of the symbolic 'all or nothing' approach to 'culture change' that is common to high-profile 'celebrity' CEOs since the 1990s. In Exhibit 7.2 reproduced opposite, Krause-Jensen (2006) brilliantly describes the very Anglo-Saxon style reforms enacted at this firm based on in-depth ethnographic research conducted inside the company.

Exhibit 7.2 A new spirit of capitalism at Bang & Olufsen

In this exhibit, Jakob Krause-Jensen explores the emergence of new forms of corporate rhetoric in the Danish consumer products firm Bang & Olufsen. This marks a profound shift into very US-style territory of celebrity CEOs, corporate 'turnarounds' and culture management, that top management claim is essential but often receives a frosty reception from staff. In many ways Bang & Olufsen's new vision was actually ahead of US practice, in that the company had abandoned its earlier, stricter forms of corporate control and gone for a more amorphous vision of 'Synthesis, Poetry, and Excellence' (2011: 268). Below he quotes from an HR manager who was cynical about the new forms of corporate management that now circulated his organization.

'Many of the words used in this world are so inflated, hyped up and hysterical (*gummiagtige, forskruede, og overpumped*) that often you don't know what you are talking about. You find that here as well. It's often a load of bullshit that some smartass in the United States invented to earn a lot of money. It really does sound pretty smart: 'it's the learning organization' and all that, but when you go deeper [...] it's all pretty banal. Organizations are sometimes very self-centred, and there are periods when it has been too much: Bang & Olufsen don't believe that there is anything in the world but the vision, and everybody should know that. But the truth is that Mrs Hansen in Humlum [small hamlet near Struer] doesn't give a damn what Bang & Olufsen's vision is.'

(Krause-Jensen 2011: 282)

It is easy to get carried away here. These high-profile stories are fascinating and eye-catching in their resemblance to Anglo-Saxon practice; both in managements' attempts to effect a dramatic change to the status quo partly by harnessing faddish concepts and texts and of employees' often cynical reaction (McCann 2013b). It is crucial to remember, however, that significant parts of the Scandinavian business systems remain institutionally and culturally distinct from 'best practice' in the USA or UK. Trade union density has remained extremely high across these nations - around 81% in Sweden (Fulcher 2004: 63), and 69% in Denmark (Madsen et al. 2010: 236) and, even though there have been some defensive mergers of unions in the face of membership decline - such as that between Sweden's IF and Metall in 2006 - this decline is nowhere on the scale seen in most other nations (including in other CMEs). Danish and Swedish economic models remain both highly advanced and more egalitarian on many indices than major competitors such as Germany and the USA. The Gini index in 2000 for Denmark and Sweden was 0.247 and 0.252 respectively, while for Germany and the USA it was 0.252 and 0.368. Illiteracy rates (percentage of 16–65 year olds without functional literacy) in the late 1990s were 9.6% and 7.5% in Denmark and Sweden, and 14.4% and 20.7% in Germany and the USA (Campbell and Pedersen 2008: 314). The Scandinavian versions of 'disorganized capitalism' thus remain significantly more 'organized' than those of the USA or UK.

Conclusion

Given the scale of the transformations associated with globalizing markets, Nordic capitalism has had to find some sort of accommodation to neoliberalism, at least *to some degree* (Fulcher 2004: 64). But these relatively small, materially well-endowed and export-focused economies possess some remarkable strengths that mean their distinctive features are likely to enjoy powerful forms of persistence and support. Scandinavian economies remain enduringly popular as 'models'. Cultural exports have proven to be increasingly valuable as economies mature and change. At the time of writing (these trends tend to date and change extraordinarily quickly!) Scandinavian literature, music, film and television are growing in popularity and visibility, such as the so-called 'Nordic Noir' novels that have become runaway international bestsellers and transformed into Hollywood movies.[8]

Much more significantly, the Norwegian policy of enforced gender quotas of 40% of management boardrooms being constituted by women has also gained wide publicity, with many observers suggesting that this kind of radical and very controversial policy is a workable option for other nations if they are genuinely interested in gender equality.[9] Denmark's 'flexicurity' concept has also been highly influential among policymakers and employers across many nations, as are Scandinavian work–life balance policies such as the extension of more substantial and more flexible forms of paid maternity and paternity leave. Like Germany, Nordic Europe is also considerably advanced when it comes to environmental protection and green innovations, and firms and local and federal government bodies have judiciously linked these changes to related markets such as 'ethical' tourism to attract more interest, investment and visitors to their regions. Research still shows that Nordic employees report comparatively high levels of employee involvement and job satisfaction (Kristensen 2011b: 222), with Kristensen (2011a) arguing that Nordic models have engaged in largely successful forms of 'experimentalist' change and adaptation. Amid significant change and the partial abandonment of social democracy, the Nordic 'models' continue to reinvent themselves and remain at the competitive cutting edge of European business.

[8] 'Inspector Norse: Why Are Nordic Detective Novels so Successful?' *The Economist*, 11 March 2011.

[9] 'Ignore the Doubters. Norway's Quota on Women in the Boardroom is Working', *Guardian*, 18 July 2011.

Further reading

Fellman, S., Iversen, M.J., Sjögren, H., and Thue, L., eds, (2008) *Creating Nordic Capitalism: The Business History of a Competitive Periphery*, Basingstoke: Palgrave Macmillan.

This is an indispensable guide to the Nordic socio-economic 'model' (in all of its forms). It is essentially a textbook that combines historical, country-based narrative and in-depth company case studies. It that sense it is similar to McCraw's (1997) *Creating Modern Capitalism* and it is just as readable and useful. A highly recommended introduction to the Nordic varieties of capitalism.

Berggren, C., (1992) *The Volvo Experience: Alternatives to Lean Production in the Swedish Auto Industry*, Basingstoke: Macmillan.

This is a very detailed and interesting discussion of the radical forms of work redesign brought in at Volvo as the company tried to deal with labour problems by providing front-line operators with enhanced forms of control and discretion. Although now rather dated, it remains a powerful and thought-provoking book, encouraging the reader to consider what is actually meant by the 'success' or 'failure' of humanistic experiments such as those conducted at Volvo. Is it really possible for firms to be financially successful while also being more human-focused? Berggren believes so, and his work is well worth exploring.

Jonung, L., Kiander, J., and Vartia, P., eds, (2009) *The Great Financial Crash in Finland and Sweden: The Nordic Experience of Financial Liberalization*, Cheltenham: Edward Elgar.

This volume contains 10 very informative chapters on the Nordic financial collapse of the early 1990s. It provides valuable details into the ways in which the governments of Sweden and Finland acted to stabilize their financial sectors, and on how Denmark largely avoided the crash. The final chapter on 'lessons' for liberalizing financial sectors is especially valuable given that rising powers such as India, Russia and China are currently experimenting with liberalizating their own financial sectors.

(Continued)

(Continued)

Swenson, P.A., (2002) *Capitalists Against Markets: The Making of Labor Markets and Welfare States in the United States and Sweden*, Oxford: Oxford University Press.

This is a stunning work of comparative industrial relations. In-depth and highly authoritative, it explores the ways in which Swedish and American systems of industrial relations formed and changed through several historical eras. This is a very advanced text that goes into massive detail, and its scale and scope may be off-putting for some. But for those who want to explore to an advanced level how and why Swedish and American systems of employment developed and changed, then this book is strongly recommended.

EIGHT Russia and the Former Soviet Union: The Radical Adoption, Creation and Abandonment of Models

Chapter objectives

- To explore the complexity of Russian and Soviet history, moving through stages in the country's development from Tsarism to the USSR, and to the post-Soviet development of capitalism
- This will include in-depth discussion of the Soviet 'model' of society and economy, one dominated by a centralized state that had near-complete powers over economic matters
- It will also explore how and why this system collapsed, noting the importance of this collapse for the rise of globalization theory and the VoC school of thought
- The post-Soviet era is then discussed, starting with the chaotic era under President Boris Yeltsin followed by the move towards partial recentralization under Vladimir Putin
- To discuss which 'variety of capitalism' is emerging in Russia, and suggest what this might mean for the world economy in general

Chapters 1 and 2 mentioned that the collapse of the USSR is often the point of origin for discussions of VoC. Why is this? The USSR was, for about seven decades, a major alternative 'model' to that of market-driven capitalism. Similar state socialist planned economies were adopted in China, India and in a number of Central and South American, Asian and African states. The USSR and its near neighbours had developed modern, industrialized economies based on state socialist economic and political systems. Although many regarded these systems as essentially despotic and authoritarian, for some time the socialist system seemed to be working fairly effectively, particularly when viewed in the historical contexts of severe economic crises that afflicted Western nations recurrently since the 1970s. Unemployment in the USSR was almost non-existent. Crime, poverty and income inequality rates were low. Reasonable quality housing, and very advanced levels of education and healthcare were all available free of charge or extremely cheaply from state providers. Yet the system ran into long-term stagnation in the 1980s and ultimately collapsed throughout the region in the years 1989–91. Suddenly the grand ideological battle between capitalism and communism that was the backdrop to the Cold War was settled in capitalism's favour. Developing countries now faced a new choice, no longer one between capitalism and communism, but between rival models of capitalism (Albert 1993; Thurow 1992). Clearly the history of the Soviet system – how it grew, why it collapsed – is hugely important to an understanding of political economy and the study of national business systems.

Moreover, Russia itself after the collapse of the USSR is an important nation to explore (the country is now technically known as the Russian Federation). It has a large population (around 143 million at the time of writing), vast natural resources wealth, and its economy has mostly been growing strongly since around 2000. It has always had the potential to be a major world economic player and now, in the guise of a market economy of sorts, Russia looks like it might finally become one.

Such is the complexity and fluidity of the Russian scene, it is difficult at this point to accurately pin down quite what kind of capitalism now exists, what it might develop into, and what this might mean (Lane 2000). Many point to the legacy of authoritarian rule hanging over it, potentially retarding or corrupting its development. Russia has been through wrenching change in the last hundred years, yet many traditional historical Russian forms seem to persist, even today.

The theme of movement from traditional business systems to something new runs through all of the countries studied in this book. But the changes undergone in Russia are probably unparalleled across these nations. Indeed, the whole makeup of the country has itself changed fundamentally several times since the 19th century, involving wars, revolutions, the rise of state socialism, the unexpected fall of the Soviet empire, the headlong rush into an anarchic, chaotic, and highly unequal form of capitalism, and then a significant movement back towards forms of authoritarian state control since the 2000s. All of this took place in the space of 140 years, dated from the abolition of serfdom (agrarian slavery) in 1861. Other societies have experienced major conflicts and changes during this time, but few have experienced turbulence on such a scale. As other nations were heading out on the rocky road to industrialization, democratization and growth, Russia was seized with radical convulsions and revolutions. On the eve of revolution in 1917 Russia was struggling to develop and sustain a very uneven and incomplete form of industrial modernity, and was then thrown into a revolutionary experiment with communism.

Russia has a dark, fascinating, often violent history. Many have remarked that the Russian nation is personified in the form of characters from a Dostoyevsky novel, such as Dmitri of *The Brothers Karamazov*. He is intelligent, but wild and capricious, with no sense of the consequences of his actions. The reader is sympathetic to him yet also revolted by his behaviour; his chaotic and selfish nature, his rowdiness, unruliness and a destructive streak that threatens himself, his friends, family and enemies. Dostoyevsky's writings, like those of other Russian literary giants, such as Tolstoy and Gogol, were at the forefront of what is now described as 'one of the great chapters of European intellectual history' (Kahan 1989: 1). Their novels, while of course fictional, were highly instructive in the way they documented an imperial Russia on the verge of collapse, struggling to hold together as it lurches uncomfortably into capitalism and industrial modernity. Russia's literary tradition has long been a source of fascination around the world.

Russia has also attracted huge academic interest from political scientists, economists and sociologists because it is the nation where the most advanced and successful model of state socialism emerged, and from where it was exported to many other nations during the Cold War of the second half of the 20th century. During this period the USSR was one of only two world superpowers, facing the USA as a direct rival and competitor. Around 300 million people lived in the USSR and the mature Soviet model seemed broadly capable of sustaining itself. Its collapse in 1991 was unexpected to many observers, who had become accustomed to its existence and power. Following the collapse, Russia was thrown into turmoil once again as it was suddenly forced to adapt from state-run communism to capitalism and global markets. After a decade of intense struggle in the 1990s, the Russian economy is now talked about as a major driving force of world economic growth.

This chapter will explore the economy of Russia through the pre-revolutionary, Soviet and post-Soviet eras. It will demonstrate that the

Russian economy, despite certain powerful features, has never lived up to its potential, and has always had a very awkward relationship with markets. Russian growth has often had to rely heavily on the state as the driver of economic action. Today Russia seems finally to have some sort of a working market economy that is partially integrated into the global economy. But Russian business and society remains bedevilled by problems of severe inequality, poverty, abuses of political power, and widespread informality and corruption. We begin our discussion by exploring Russia's pre-revolutionary history.

An archaic system lurches into modernity: the Pre-revolutionary era (1812–1917)

As we have seen elsewhere in this book, many traditional societies across Europe made tremendous economic progress in the 19th century. But Russian society during this time was mostly isolated from these changes. Its political system was an absolutist autocracy, an imperial system whereby the Tsar ruled over a large empire via a centralized bureaucratic apparatus, with no democratic powers extended to the wider population. While geographically huge, extending in the East to ports on the Sea of Japan and in the West to the borders of major European powers (including sovereignty over nations such as Poland and Finland), it was an economically underdeveloped empire and, in hindsight, terribly vulnerable to collapse. Its economic system was feudal. In 1858, around 94% of the Russian population lived in small, rural village communities, mostly carving out a hand-to-mouth existence. A large percentage of them were effectively slaves, bonded to the land by serfdom.[1] 'The "modern" revolution, which was already transforming the societies and economies of Western Europe, had barely touched the Russia of Pushkin and Gogol' (Christian 1997: 42). Life expectancy was around 27, skewed by an appallingly high infant mortality rate. It was estimated that a Russian child born in this era would have a 45% chance of living to the age of five (Christian 1997: 46). Estimates based on an official census data suggest that over half the population between 1812 and 1816 were serfs. (Christian 1997: 39-40).

Even as certain parts of the Russian economy were modernizing, the country's class structure remained closer to a medieval than a modern society. The Tsarist system concentrated enormous wealth and power for

[1] A small percentage of what are usually labelled 'peasants' were industrial workers, often moving away seasonally from villages to work in factories (Gatrell 1986: 29–30).

the nobility (around 1.1% of the population) while abject poverty persisted for peasants and the small but growing class of industrial workers (a combined total of around 87% of the population). According to Blackwell 'Serfdom pushed its masters into indolence; and in the eighteenth century, intensifying Western influences prompted the nobility to dissipate their wealth unproductively in the attempt to imitate European modes of luxury and pomp' (1974: xxi). This resulted in some absurd developments, such as the famous 'Potemkin villages' - fake façades of towns and buildings supposedly built to impress important visitors.[2] It also meant that economic development was radically uneven, and often 'pushed' 'from above' by an interventionist state. Peter the Great, Tsar of Russia in the years 1682–1725, was one of world history's most famous modernizing figures. He massively increased the scale of the Russian navy, adopted a Western calendar and, most famously, built the new capital city of St Petersburg. This was constructed in the northwest, closer to Europe and its architecture modelled on a classical Western European style rather than a traditionally Muscovite style. Marshall Berman (1982), in his famous text *All That is Solid Melts into Air*, highlights the tragedy of the desperate rush to imitate Western European modernity before the country was ready; serfs worked in shocking conditions to build the city, with perhaps hundreds of thousands killed by drowning, disease, or construction accidents.[3]

In an attempt to demonstrate technological parity with advanced European nations, the Russian elite held a huge exhibition for the tercentenary of the Romanov dynasty, involving a grand display of electric illuminations. In a way, it was Russia's own version of Britain's Great Exhibition of 1851 (Figes 1997: 3). Such were the inequalities and contradictions of the Tsarist system that it was content to provide a sheen of capitalist modernity atop an archaic agrarian system while doing little to close the gap on these contradictions.

Many have argued that Russia's inability or unwillingness to modernize was partly a result of deep-seated cultural norms (Blackwell 1974: xxii; Gerschenkron 1962). Figes, in his epic history of the Russian revolutions, describes 'the idea of a mystical union between the Tsar and the Orthodox people, who loved and obeyed him as a father and a god. It was a fantasy of paternal rule, of a golden age of

[2] It is unclear how historically accurate this story is - it may be something of an enduring myth, but it is typical of the kind of 'black humour' frequently used by Russians to describe the many tragicomic elements of their nation's economic and political system.

[3] Such scenarios were later to repeat themselves in the Soviet system, such as the construction of the Kolyma Highway, a Siberian road built using prison camp labour that is informally known as 'the road of bones'.

popular autocracy, free from the complications of a modern state' (Figes 1997: 7). The growth of a state bureaucracy (often seen as a key stage in the development of a modern, capitalist and eventually democratic nation) was regarded with suspicion by the elites (perhaps also by the peasantry), as it would obstruct the Tsar's ancient 'bond with his people'. Many modernizing forces, therefore, were kept to an absolute minimum. Tsar Alexander III was notoriously anti-reform. As late as 1881, he pronounced 'The Tsar's Manifesto on Unshakeable Autocracy' shortly after ascending the throne following the murder of his father by a revolutionary group. It stated that 'the voice of God orders Us to take up the task of ruling, with total strength and righteousness of Our autocratic power. We are summoned to reaffirm that power and to preserve it for the benefit of the people from any encroachment upon it.' (as quoted in Sixsmith 2011: 149). In personal correspondence he wrote that 'The very idea of electoral government is something I can never accept!' (as quoted in Sixsmith 2011: 149).

Autocracy was also reinforced by religious ideology. The Orthodox Church was opposed to scientific-rational forms of education (Blackwell 1974: xii) and the rural peasant community or *mir* acted as a centuries-old system of governance that reinforced stability and opposed change. These socio-cultural forms of conservatism stood in stark contrast to the rapidly-developing nations such as the UK where the new traditions of science and technology inspired by the European Enlightenment were given space to flourish (Mokyr 2009). Literacy rates across Russia, even in the more technologically advanced European regions, were relatively low. As late as 1897, 72% of Russians aged 10 or over were illiterate, compared to just 17% in France in 1900 (Gatrell 1986: 34). The Russo-Japanese war of 1904–5 exposed Russia's weakness and complacency – a supposed great power decisively lost a war to a rapidly growing Asian nation whose strength had been totally underestimated by an out of touch Russian aristocracy.

Russian industrial power grew during the years 1885–1910 (Gatrell 1986; Kahan 1989) but remained hampered by weaknesses in the transport, education and banking sectors. The Russian economy did not reach a 'critical mass' quickly enough to experience the kinds of explosive, self-sustaining growth seen in, for example, the UK (Chapter 4) or post-war Japan (Chapter 11). The Russian émigré economist Aleksandr Gerschenkron (1962) famously argued that, in the absence of enabling institutions such as powerful banks and a robust legal infrastructure, a country is unable to escape from 'economic backwardness' by markets alone. Instead growth would have to be 'pushed' by some sort of centralized plan overseen by the state. Alexander III appointed Count Sergei Witte as Minister of Finance in 1892, a role with very broad powers. Witte had in mind a Listian growth model that was not far from US Treasury Secretary Alexander Hamilton's 'American System' of the 18th century (see Chapter 3) or French *dirigiste* policies (see Chapter 5). Witte has therefore been described as a 'Russian Colbert' (Harcave 2004: 3). Witte once wrote:

> International competition does not wait. If we do not take energetic and decisive measures ... then the rapidly growing foreign industries ... will establish themselves in our fatherland. ... Our economic backwardness may lead to political and cultural backwardness as well. (as quoted in von Laue 1974: 206)

Witte placed Russia on the Gold Standard, which allowed the nation to borrow more cheaply on international financial markets, and encouraged widespread inward foreign investment. Advanced foreign industrial technology was imported on a huge scale (about 37% of annual Russian technical equipment purchased was imported [von Laue 1974: 214]), and Russia built up significant international debts. Keeping the rouble pegged to gold was a challenge for the Russian state, which had to keep up protectionist tariffs on industry and increase grain exports, and place heavy taxation that was 'especially burdensome to the peasantry' (Harcave 2004: 69). Inward investment and high taxation fuelled a railway building boom, which increased the demand for steel and coal, and linked together some of Russia's far-flung regions. Work began on the Trans-Siberian Railway, which was eventually to connect Moscow with the Far East. Eleven thousand miles of track were laid during this period (Harcave 2004: 69). Steps were finally taken to educate the population in the requisite skills for an industrial economy, with over 140 new commercial schools opened along with trade schools for the growing industrial working class. Business newspapers and journals started to appear (Harcave 2004: 71).

But even as cities, technologies and international trade were developing, the Russian agrarian economy remained extremely large and extremely weak (Harcave 2004: 73). A critical issue is whether the 'backwardnesss' of Russian economy and society inevitably led to revolution and then Soviet socialism, or whether the whole historical 'tangent' or 'experiment' of the USSR could have been avoided entirely if the economy and society had developed more successfully. The creaking structure of Russian society was destined not to contain the forces of change being unleashed:

> 'The Witte System' aimed to attract foreign investment, enterprise, and loans through fiscal stability achieved by high levels of grain export which produced favourable trade balances. ... But it impoverished the peasantry and exposed state finances to the danger of collapse under war and famine. It was a house of cards mined with social dynamite. (Blackwell 1974: 197)

Revolutionary forces had been building in Russia for some time. The first revolution took place in 1905, when Tsar Nicholas II finally conceded the need for a representative government in the wake of the deaths of 200 protestors on 'Bloody Sunday' when police fired upon a crowd of 60,000 demonstrators. But urban and agricultural unrest continued. The real tipping point was the Russian military's disastrous performance on the Eastern Front (1914–17) in the First World War where Russia lost around 1.8 million men (Gatrell 1986: 60). Radical writings on socialism and communism were spreading around Russia, both Western European (such as Marx and Engels) and domestic in origin. Marx once said that in Russia his *Capital* 'was read and valued more than anywhere', with Figes noting that Marxism 'spread like a wild craze' across the empire (Figes 1997: 139).

The Russian revolutionary leader V.I. Lenin (1870–1924) adapted the arguments of Marx and Engels to argue that a working-class revolution will take place not in the most economically advanced nations such as the USA, UK and Germany, but in 'the weakest link in the imperialist chain' – that is, Russia. The intense struggles Russia was experiencing at this time made his viewpoint appear logical. The nation was unable to maintain pace with the other great European powers, and its weaknesses were horribly exposed by the First World War. After a period of intense protest and desperate attempts at economic and agricultural reform, the Tsarist system finally ended with the abdication of Nicholas II in March 1917, and his government was replaced by a Provisional Government. Russia was in chaos, with its countryside in turmoil and its factories occupied by the nascent urbanized proletarian workforce demanding 'peace, land and bread'. It seemed as if Marx's predictions of the capitalist class creating 'its own gravediggers' was turning out to be true, not in the economically advanced UK or Germany, but in semi-industrial, 'economically backward' Russia. By October 1917 the Provisional Government had also collapsed, and the Bolshevik party, headed by Lenin, seized power in a revolutionary coup, claiming a new stage in Russian history – that of socialism – of an economy and polity owned and run by the people, for the people, with capitalists and rich landowners 'liquidated as a class'.

The Bolshevik Revolution was one of the most dramatic events of 20th-century world history, and the economic and political system that developed out of it would eventually become defining for around one-third of the world's population, as nations such as Poland, Hungary, Czech Republic, as well as China, Vietnam and several African nations adopted (or were forced to adopt) versions of state socialism.

'A modernized autocracy of great power': the Soviet system (1921–1991)

Lenin's seizure of power led to a long and extremely brutal civil war in Russia between 1917–21 (Figes 1997: 522). Nicholas II, his wife and five children, their doctor and three of their servants were brutally murdered on Lenin's orders in a basement in Yekaterinburg in 1918. Russia immediately pulled out of the First World War (which was widely regarded as an imperialist adventure), angering its former allies. Fourteen nations, including the UK, France, the USA, Canada, Japan and China sent a total of more than 100,000 troops in an attempt to support Russian White (counter-revolutionary) forces. So important did resisting the rise of communism appear to Western powers, that these interventions took place even before the end of the First World War. Despite this, Lenin and the Bolshevik Red Army emerged victorious from the civil war and set up a new government in Moscow. But it soon became clear that the mode of government would be a one-party state (Figes 1997: 808), and the USSR became 'a modernized autocracy of great power' (Christian 1997: 320).

Lenin was succeeded by Josef Stalin (1878–1953) who set in motion what turned out to be a spectacular economic growth phase, but the violence and paranoia of the era were hugely destructive, causing profound and lasting damage to the society as a whole. Completely intolerant of any views he perceived to be contrary to his interpretation of Marxism-Leninism, he built an impregnable party machine that froze out all opposition and treated opponents (real and imaginary) with brutality. He intensified the levels of political and cultural repression in the USSR, sending millions of Soviet citizens to incarceration in prisons, labour camps or to their deaths by execution or exhaustion. Robert Conquest, the conservative British historian, placed the total number of deaths attributable to the terror, executions, death in labour camps or famine at 20 million. More recent estimates have suggested 9 million[4] or 12–20 million (Applebaum 2003: 521).

Stalin's 'model' for the modernization of the USSR was radical and extreme. A programme of collectivization of agriculture banned most forms of commercial farming and took all agricultural production into giant 'collective farms' (*kolkhozi*) or state-run farms (*sovkhozi*). Peasant farmers often resisted these reforms, and collectivization was accompanied by violence and repression. Famine broke out in Ukraine in 1930–3. This terrible event is now often known as the *Holodomor*,

[4] Hitler vs. Stalin: Who Killed More?', *New York Review of Books*, 10 March 2011.

'Killing by Starving' – a word redolent of the Nazi Holocaust, as around five million perished in what appears to be deliberately engineered (and at least partially ethnically motivated) disaster intended to exercise total control over the countryside.

Accompanying this agricultural 'modernization', Stalin in 1928 set the USSR on a dramatic programme of 'crash' industrialization. The Soviet leadership was becoming concerned that the predicted socialist revolutions were not spreading into Western Europe. This meant that the USSR was surrounded by hostile nations, and the revolution would not survive unless it built up its industrial and military strength without delay. The journalist Brian Moynahan describes Stalin's vision to build 'The Second America', an economy as powerful as that of the USA, only it was to be done with centralized government planning, not with market forces and entrepreneurs (Moynahan 1997: 123–135). Using such slogans as 'There are no fortresses the Bolsheviks cannot storm!', and 'When one cuts down the forest, the chips will fly', the Stalinist system demanded total loyalty and self-sacrifice. Any viewpoints perceived as deviant, any attitudes perceived as indolent, ran the risk of punishment by political and social ostracism, or imprisonment, execution or forced labour. Memoirs of those involved in the industrialization drive are fascinating in their description of widespread disruption and struggle but also dramatic successes. Viktor Kravchenko's (1947/1988) *I Chose Freedom*, or John Scott's (1941/1989) *Behind the Urals* describe Stalin's industrialization drive as a chaotic and disruptive era of wrenching socio-economic change conducted at high speed.

The Stalinist bureaucracy constructed a planning apparatus based around Five Year Plans for the modernization of the economy. These included detailed targets for the output of 'Category A' industrial products, such as steel, coal, minerals, electricity production and railway lines, following a 'big push industrialization' strategy not unknown elsewhere in the world. But Stalin's was clearly the most dramatic and most driven by top-down government control (Allen 2011: 132–135). Indeed, the Five Year Plans industrialization drive was described by Stalin as a 'revolution from above', led by the vanguard of the revolutionary Communist Party – dragging the nation into a modernized, urban future.

Firms (socialist ideology preferred the word 'enterprises') of the Stalinist economy were practically all state-owned, and run by party-appointed directors. Capitalism and its exploitative class relations were thus supposedly 'abolished'; the means of production were owned and run by the people (that is, by the Communist Party of the USSR as the representative of the people.) The ideology of Marxism-Leninism was used to defend this authoritarian model, and the ideas were mobilized

Exhibit 8.1 'The art of socialist accounting'

The economic planning apparatus put in place under Stalin essentially locked the Soviet economy into a bureaucratic straightjacket for the remainder of the socialist period. Below some wonderfully detailed descriptions are provided from the memoirs of Gennady Andreev-Khomiakov. He was a young writer who, upon his release from a labour camp as a former 'enemy of the people', managed to rebuild his life, working up into an accounting position in a timber enterprise. He explains the absurdities of economic planning – and the endemic corruption, labour and resource hoarding, and bureaucratic machinations it entailed – as 'the art of socialist accounting':

'At the end of the first day of each month, we had to send Moscow the initial data on the previous month's production. The second day, we had to send follow-up data, and the third day, we had to send a complete statistical report consisting of dozens of complicated tables. On those three days we worked until midnight or one o'clock in the morning.'

'Delaying or neglecting to send this information was out of the question. Our head office [*glavnoe upravlenie]*, which received data from dozens of factories, had to quickly compose a summary report and present it to the people's commissariat within a prescribed period. The people's commissariat had to give a summary report on all its branch industries to the Central Statistical Board and Gosplan, also strictly on schedule. The Central Statistical Board had to present a summary about the enterprises of the entire country to the Council of People's Commisars, the Politburo, and Stalin himself, also to a specific deadline.'

'All of the links in this chain are tightly intertwined, forming an essential, carefully structured ornament of the socialist façade. If some information or other is not available, then it has to be invented somehow out of thin air; God help you if it is omitted. The entire chain can be broken because of a single inadequate piece of information, and the thunder and lightning of orders, reproofs, and even arrests for "disruption of the accounting process" might shower down from on high. To avoid this, we even had to keep three full-time employees who were bored to death from lack of work during the rest of the month. [...]'

'On the basis of these figures as well as obligatory norms, prices, and regulations approved by the government, we composed work plans for each shop and a general plan for the factory for the coming year, all calculated down to the smallest detail. Every item was projected, right up to when, where, and how much we could spend on rags for wiping up the machines, or when and where we might need to hammer in a hundred grams of nails. You can understand, then, why we tried in any event to maintain reserves in the plan, to give ourselves more leeway to manoeuvre.'

(Andreev-Khomiakov 1997: 82–3).

to encourage workers to accept that they were contributing to their own bright future of communism where exploitation and even money relations would be things of the past. With the abolition of class war, workers were theoretically supposed to have nothing to complain about. But in order to achieve this goal, workers and citizens were forced to endure incredible hardships.

Enterprises were set output targets by the state economic planning ministry Gosplan. Soviet industrial enterprises were not firms or corporations in the capitalist sense of those words, existing in order to make profits and return investment value to shareholders. Instead, they were more akin to civil service bureaucracies, ordered to hit performance targets with set amounts of inputs of labour, capital, raw materials and energy. There were ministries for all areas of the industrial economy such as a Ministry of Coal Industry, Ministry of Metallurgy or Ministry of General Machine Building, and these bureaucracies essentially commanded the industrial enterprises under their authority to realize the plan. According to Blackwell:

> These plans were not so much strategic projections for economic growth as they were statistical expressions of a totally bureaucratized economy ... the results of negotiation with industrial management at all levels ... in one sprawling administrative apparatus. ... the amount produced, measured in various ways, determined the rewards (or punishments) of the producers, be they factory managers, workers, peasants, or forced labourers. (1974: xxxi)

But in 1939 in some sectors as much as 35–30% of industrial output was estimated to be defective in numerous ways (Kotkin 1997: 422). Such was the reality of the Soviet planned economy, or 'command economy'.

To plug skills and technological gaps, enterprises hired thousands of foreign expert engineers as contractors during the construction of new Soviet industrial facilities. 'Help from Ford enabled the Russians to build 140,000 cars in 1932; in 1929, at a time when there were already 26 million automobiles in the US, the Soviet Union had just 30,000' (Moynahan 1997: 131). Senior figures in the planning and management of the Soviet economy were widely known to have been influenced by the writings of Frederick Taylor on mass production. The historian Schultz (1990) describes 'building the Soviet Detroit', that is, the Soviet car industry at the VAZ plant in Nizhnii Novgorod in the years 1927–32. Stephen Kotkin's (1997) study of the development of the giant steel plant at Magnitogorsk describes how Western engineers were often horrified by the conditions they saw. Such was the mania to grow at any cost that sections of industrial plants were unready while others surged ahead. Finished metal products were allowed to rust in the rain and snow as storage facilities were non-existent. Cities and housing were equally a low priority – workers often had no choice but to sleep in tents near their factories as they waited for housing blocks to be built. 'Storming' took place in order to meet plan targets in a rush, which often led to machinery breaking under the strain and lying idle for subsequent weeks.

Many Soviet citizens were enthused by the prospect of modernizing their economy, and some Westerners shared the belief that this great experiment of building modernity without capitalism would actually work. A major reason that foreign specialists were lured to 1930s USSR was because of the intensity of the Great Depression in 1930s Europe and USA (Blackwell 1974: xxxiii). With Western economies in the doldrums Keynesian economic principles - that markets contain fundamental weaknesses that the state must counteract - were widely believed (see, for example, the New Deal in the USA [Chapter 3], or planning in India [Chapter 9]). This added some credence to the view that the great Soviet economic experiment may be successful, and that it could even prove more economically resilient than market-driven capitalism.

Under Stalin industrial output increased dramatically (Blackwell 1974: xxxiii). The USSR achieved one of the most rapid industrializations in world history - a fourfold increase in gross industrial output between 1928–50 (Jasny 1974: 300), with the USSR eventually becoming the second largest industrial power in the world. But at what human cost? Real wages were the lowest in Europe, actually falling in 1952 to three-quarters of their level in 1928 (Jasny 1974: 305). The USSR managed to grow so fast because the state grasped all resources and capital available and posted huge rates of industrial investment. It did this by keeping wages low, taxes high and enforcing extremely tough forms of bureaucratic labour discipline. Its political isolation from the capitalist West meant that it was unable (at this point in history) to secure loans from foreign banks, making the growth rates even more spectacular. The figures are disputed, but annual growth in the region of 12% between 1928–37 seems reasonable (Christian 1997: 279). Soviet society rapidly urbanized, and the basis for a modern, industrial, organized society of a certain kind were laid. Diseases such as cholera were largely eliminated. Mass education was made available to all children and students. Women were given the same employment rights as men, and moved into the labour force in large numbers. Soviet industrialization also allowed the nation to build a formidable military capacity, which came to underpin the USSR as a major geopolitical power by the end of the Second World War.

Personal incomes, however, increased by only one-third from 1928–1952, an extraordinarily low figure for a period which involved mass industrialization and the trebling of the urban population. In comparison, funds under state investment grew by a factor of nine, with the proportion of these funds spent on the Soviet armed forces going up 26 times (Jasny 1974: 302). About a quarter of GNP was invested in industrial development; the UK in the 19th century could only manage to invest around one-eighth (Cohn 1968: 43). The state grew powerful while its citizens were repeatedly asked to go without. The average urban living space for a Soviet citizen was around 5.8 square metres on the eve of Stalin's revolution from above. It fell to 4.6 in 1937, before rising to 6.4 in 1964 (Cohn 1968: 44). In many cases families had little alternative but to live in communal apartments, which tended to be hugely unpopular. Educational provision in the USSR improved dramatically with school enrolments up 70% on pre-war levels (Cohn 1968: 28). Teaching curricula of most subjects, however, were subjected to stiff political controls.

Tragically, the 1930s were also, of course, characterized by a vicious regime of political control that became known as 'the Great Terror.' Thousands of Soviet citizens were denounced as political enemies, and purged, imprisoned, sent to labour camps or executed, usually on fabricated evidence.[5] This fierce authoritarianism laid the basis for the chronic lack of trust in political and judicial processes that persists in Russia today. Historical accounts of the terror are often shocking and bizarre - an Orwellian nightmare of fear, lies, mistrust and abuse of power in which no-one is safe from arbitrary accusations, arrests and imprisonments. Gripped by 'a psychosis of fear and suspicion' (Swainiewicz 1974: 282) the Soviet leadership believed it was encircled by enemies from outside and threatened by traitors from within - intent on 'wrecking' the industrial, scientific and ideological achievements of the revolution and the Five Year Plans. Moynahan writes that: 'Scientific-theoretical wrecking' was said to operate all over the USSR, such that '[h]istorians were accused of belonging to "historiographical counter-revolutionary wrecking centres" and were deported to Siberia' (1997: 132).

Memoirs of those who lived through the terror and the labour camps, such as Ginzberg, Solzhenitsyn and Shalamov, while of course banned under the USSR, have survived to become modern classics of literature. A charity known as 'Memorial' continues to work in Russia today to try to remember and explain what happened to the millions who were incarcerated and/or killed by the regime. The Terror led to a massive expansion of a truly dreadful system of forced labour camps and 'indescribable human suffering' (Swianiewicz 1974: 280). Millions of Soviet citizens, perhaps as many as 29 million (Applebaum 2003: 518), were

[5] Based on evidence from recently declassified Soviet archives, it appears that around a million Soviet citizens were killed in the Great Terror, 'Hitler vs. Stalin: Who Killed More?', *New York Review of Books*, 10 March 2011.

at one stage '*zeks*', or Gulag labour camp inmates.[6] The internal affairs machinery known as the NKVD oversaw the camps and effectively ran its own mini-economy within the economy, such as the Dalstroi camp complex at Kolyma in the extremely remote Soviet Far East (Applebaum 2003). Construction of canals, mines and roads, for example, were often carried out with convict labour.

Such operations were necessary in the eyes of the Party. The defeat of Hitler's invading forces in the Second World War served to validate the Stalinist regime. The centralized Soviet economy turned out to be adept at changing over to a war footing, and by the latter parts of the Second World War was producing tanks, aircraft and munitions in massive numbers. The defeat of the Third Reich gave the USSR major influence over Eastern Europe, eventually establishing state socialist political and economic systems across the region and in East Germany. The Soviet army also defeated Japanese forces in occupied Manchuria, gaining control over south Sakhalin, and establishing major influence over North Korea.

Stalin died in 1953. His successor Nikita Khrushchev promised a change of direction away from the terror and repression, and allowed a degree of cultural freedom. (This included allowing the publication of Solzhenitsyn's short novel *One Day in the Life of Ivan Denisovich*, a depiction of life as a Gulag inmate.) However, the USSR was still largely isolated from the Western world, as the Cold War standoff with the USA and NATO powers continued until the 1990s. But eventually the USSR (within its own limitations) became a mature economic and political system.

Industrialization and militarization had been achieved, but the USSR seemed unable to understand what had to come next. It was still poorly integrated into the emerging global economy, and its citizens had low standards of living relative to the other industrial powers in the West. The Soviet economy was still heavily balanced towards so-called 'Category A' heavy industry, and had an extremely limited consumer products sector known as 'Category B'. Levels of domestic savings were low as the state continued to expropriate funding from its citizens through very high levels of tax on individual earnings. The Soviet state was the dominant economic force, and citizens were essentially forced to trust it to invest this capital in projects that would benefit citizens.

---

[6] The word *zek* comes from the Russian word *zaklyuchennyi*, meaning 'prisoner'. The word is derived from the abbreviation 'z/k' that would appear on a convicted person's identification papers, marking them for life as an outsider – a member of an underclass of undesirables upon release (Applebaum 2003: 592). It appears as if around 2–3 million died in the Gulag during the Stalin era, see 'Hitler vs. Stalin: Who Killed More?' *New York Review of Books*, 10 March 2011.

To some extent it did, with cheap housing, schooling, health services and university education, provided free or extremely cheaply. Soviet state-owned enterprises typically operated paternalistically, with a very flat wage structure, providing a job for life and a wide range of vital fringe benefits to their workers, such as kindergarten facilities and pioneer camp (holiday care for children), holiday houses, and free health care and pensions contributions (Krueger 2004: 105). Such benefits were known as *sotskultbyt* - social, cultural and 'everyday life' provisions (Schwartz 2004: 73). Soviet enterprises were not solely workplaces; they were supposed to be also microcosms of socialist society, the places where workers would 'experience' socialism. This notion of socialism at work was reflected in the workforce being referred to as 'the labour collective' and becoming the official manifestation of Soviet ideology about the end to divisive capitalist class relations (Schwartz 2004: 73–74).

The USSR spent vast sums on its military, and invested heavily in science and engineering research that could be utilized in the space race and arms race with the USA. Cutting-edge science and technology was skewed towards military and space applications, with Soviet design bureaux producing extremely advanced weapons systems such as jet fighters, submarines and nuclear warheads, as well as cheap but robust mass products such as the phenomenally successful AK-47 assault rifle. This weapon has (sadly) been produced in its tens of millions, and used worldwide in countless conflicts. The Soviet space exploration programme was also a huge source of pride. Present-day Russia is now endowed with a well-educated population and a strong tradition of higher education, especially in the 'hard' sciences, medicine, mathematics and engineering. However, dramatic 'showpiece' investments continued to be made throughout the Soviet era in the construction of factories and hydroelectric facilities, many of dubious economic value. There are many stories of bridges and power plants that existed in official facts and figures but had not actually been built. One famous example of the madness of Soviet planning was Stalin's proposed tunnel from the Russian mainland to Sakhalin island, a project that began in 1952 under NKVD stewardship and was never completed.

Problems of huge wastage and falsification of statistics continued throughout the Soviet era, and bottlenecks and shortages in the system often grew more and more problematic. A large 'shadow economy' grew, of informal, illegal trading in scarce goods and an 'economy of favours' developed, which always existed in the USSR but became increasingly important as the formal economy began to stagnate in the 1970s onwards (Ledeneva 1998). Nevertheless, despite its lack of flexibility and inability to develop into a more modern consumer-based or 'informational' economy, the economic system put in place by Stalin and modified by his successors was powerful and seemed to be durable. In 1928, the GNP of the USSR was approximately equal to that of individual major Western European economies such as the UK or France, and about one-fifth the size of the USA. In GNP per capita, the USSR was seventh among the world's major powers, at about one-seventh of the level of the USA and one-fourth that of the major West European nations. By the early 1970s, the USSR was the world's second largest economy, half the size of the USA, and equal to the combined GNP of West Germany, France and Italy. It was fifth in the world in per capita terms; at around two-fifths of the US and two-thirds of Western European levels of GDP per capita (Cohn 1968: 29).

However, by the mid-1970s, long-term economic stagnation had set in; a fact that the Communist Party tried to hide from the West and from its own citizens. The system stagnated as it matured, and seemed incapable of making the shift from labour intensive to capital intensive production, and from industry to services. It could not develop income streams from an export-driven consumer goods model, such as those developed so successful by Germany and Japan. With hindsight, total economic collapse seemed unavoidable. The next section explores why.

Stagnation and collapse: why did the USSR fail?

Leonid Brezhnev became the new General Secretary of the Communist Party of the Soviet Union in 1964. A less 'colourful' character than Khrushchev, he oversaw the long-term bureaucratic stagnation of the economy. 'Eventually, like the Tsarist government before it, the Soviet government would find it harder and harder to compete economically and militarily with capitalist societies that enjoyed higher rates of innovation and higher levels of productivity' (Christian 1997: 6). Officially, Brezhnev's time was labelled the 'Period of Developed Socialism' which the Soviet leadership claimed was 'for the best in the best of all possible socialist worlds' (Sixsmith 2011: 435). The oil crises of the 1970s helped USSR oil exports, but this burst of export value covered up cracks elsewhere in the system. By the time of the Ninth Five Year Plan (1971–5) a remarkably critical article appeared in the newspaper *Pravda* in 1979, written by Eduard Shevardnadze, later to become President of Georgia. He wrote: 'For the first four years of the Five Year Plan, an average of just 91 apartments were built for every 10,000 people across the Soviet Union. ... For every rouble we invest in agriculture, we get back a total of 39 kopeks' (Shevardnadze, as quoted in Sixsmith 2011: 435). The dissident physicist Andrei Sakharov estimated that the purchasing power of an average Soviet worker was one-tenth that of an American worker (Sixsmith 2011: 435). Not only that, given production bottlenecks and the low priority afforded to consumer production, it was often difficult for citizens to find goods to buy. Shops would sometimes be empty of stock with long queues forming for basic goods. Long waiting lists developed for expensive consumer durables in short supply, such as cars and refrigerators. Russian 'black humour' about the era of stagnation is well-known.

By 1985, the USSR was the third largest economy in the world, but was ranked 43rd per capita (Sakwa 2008: 240). The Soviet economy started to rely on foreign loans (Sixsmith 2011: 440). Finance for further investment and growth seemed to have dried up. Where were the 'gales of creative destruction', the financial and industrial innovation, the next surges of growth? Without competition, there was little incentive for enterprises to improve their processes and outputs, nor to invest in research and development. The Stalinist 'extensive' industrial expansion model was exhausted and it was never clear what or who would provide the incentive for the next developmental model. The industrial Soviet model was terminally weak in new technological developments at the forefront of globalization, such as finance and IT developments. The system lurched into major international crises, such as the Chernobyl nuclear disaster in 1986 and the militarily disastrous invasion of Afghanistan in 1979. The system was in dire need of reform but seemed politically incapable of change. Brezhnev's long tenure as General Secretary ended with his death in 1982. He was succeeded by two very ineffective general secretaries. Each had health problems and both had died by 1985.

An American economist Stanley H. Cohn here provides a very prescient statement about the problems facing the USSR, originally published in 1968:

> Though the Stalinist solution yielded very rapid growth and ultimately proved itself by successfully providing economic support in time of war, it did so at the cost of inefficient use of resources and by means of postponing essential consumer and infrastructure investments. As long as growth could be sustained by massive infusion of manpower and capital, [...] this atypical path of development could be followed, and the economic institutions directing the effort could remain unaltered. However, toward the mid-fifties, as the pool of resources no longer appeared to be inexhaustible, the effect of their inefficient utilization on the growth process became more acute. [...] the pattern of Soviet development has had to veer toward more traditional market economy paths and suggests that it is likely to do so to a greater degree in future years.
>
> (Cohn 1968: 24–5)

With the appointment of Mikhail Gorbachev as General Secretary in 1985 finally there was a younger person at the helm who was prepared to make extensive changes, accelerating the processes noted above by Cohn. His aim was to reform the system to preserve it, but the forces of change he helped set in motion ultimately led to the USSR's destruction (Nove 1992: 394–419). He initiated dramatic reforms of *perestroika* (restructuring) and *glasnost* (openness), but he proved unable to contain the forces of change he help set in motion. He introduced the Law on Cooperatives, allowing citizens to develop their own small businesses along free market lines while the largest enterprises would remain under state control. Entrepreneurs such as Vladimir Gusinsky, later to become one of Russia's richest men, started out selling copper bracelets which cost three kopecks to make and were sold for five roubles each (Hoffman 2002: 151). Gorbachev gave state-run enterprise managers more freedom from centralized control, allowing them flexibility over their operations once plans had been fulfilled. This was 'an attempt at a halfway house between market and plan, but it was fundamentally inconsistent with either system' (Krueger 2004: 27). Gorbachev's personal position reflected this contradictory situation and he became vulnerable. He was caught in the middle as reformers wanted change towards markets and democracy to progress at a faster rate, whereas communist 'hardliners' wanted a return to greater centralization and Party control (Nove 1992: 410). In thc end, the hardliners moved against Gorbachev in a military coup, a move that backfired as the Russian public rallied around the reformist Russian President Boris Yeltsin. The coup collapsed after three days, marking the point of no return for state socialism. It appeared that markets and democracy were the only option, and the USSR was finally disbanded in December 1991 with its fifteen nations recast as independent democratic countries. The rest of this chapter will explore how Russia fared in this brave new world of capitalism, speculation, rapid change and globalization.

Rushing headlong into a neoliberal future – chaos and reform under Yeltsin (1991–1999)

The USSR's collapse came at a time when neoliberal ideas were in the ascendancy in the West. Many reformers in Russia, as well as Western observers and policy advisors, tended to see the collapse as a narrow window of opportunity in which to act. The approach was to press ahead as soon as possible with radical neoliberal reforms so that turning the clock back to communism became impossible. If the dead hand of the Soviet state could be dismantled quickly and the power of markets immediately unleashed, then free market capitalism would soon build a middle class and a rich elite that would want to defend the new system of capitalism (Klein 2007: 218–245; Yergin and Stanislaw 2002: 280–308). What emerged in the 1990s was an economic reversal on a gigantic scale, amid widespread organized crime, official corruption, industrial collapse and the shrinking of government capacity. Reformers ignored the historical role that states can play after economic collapses, such as Roosevelt's New Deal America (see Chapter 3) or the role of MITI in the post-war growth boom in Japan (see Chapter 11). Furthermore, the Soviet state itself had no authority and was in collapse during this time, so the prospects for the state to coordinate an economic recovery were low. But the reforms of the 1990s now appear mismanaged, and the economic and social collapse of Russia was probably harsher than it needed to be. Amid the collapse, it is important to note also the birth of a garish, 'wild' 'no holds barred' form of capitalism in Russia, of which many have drawn parallels with the 'robber baron' phase of USA (see Chapter 3). New business empires began to emerge, and the boundaries between economic, political and criminal power effectively broke down.

In a fine overview of Russia's wild 1990s Gustafson (1999: 20) describes how one of the chief architects of the transition to the market economy, Yegor Gaidar, was greatly impressed by right-wing neoliberal writers such as von Hayek. Reformers refused to acknowledge that nations such as Japan, France, Germany (and even the USA) had benefitted from policies of state intervention. This was probably helped by ordinary Russians, Ukrainians and other former USSR nationals resenting and mistrusting state power, having experienced nearly 70 years of an overbearing and in many ways incompetent state control over their economies. However, in hindsight it looks as if far too much trust was placed in the miracle-working powers of market forces. Many observers writing in the late 1990s and early 2000s (such as Reddaway and Glinski [2001] and Gustafson [1999]) have been highly critical of the crash reform or 'shock therapy' approach that was taken. Goldman (2003) describes the 'piratization' of Russia, in which the rushed and ill-thought-out reform process was captured by criminal and otherwise illegitimate interests. After chaotic reforms Russia has ended up with a 'deformed', 'mutant' or 'oligarchic' capitalism, with a tiny super-rich elite, a relatively weak middle class, and widespread and very severe poverty for the majority. In a strange irony, post-Soviet Russia (especially in the 1990s before matters improved) was like a ghastly caricature of capitalism, as unfair and exploitative as the 19th-century version described by Marx and Engels (Freeland 2000: 9–22).

The scale of the economic collapse in Russia following the demise of the Soviet model is hard to comprehend. By the end of the 1990s, Russian GDP was half the size it was in 1990 (Krueger 2004: 36). By 1998 Russian GDP per capita was ranked at 135th in the world, around the same level as Costa Rica (Sakwa 2008: 241). Having lost its biggest customer (the state Plan), Russian industry simply stopped producing, leading to the biggest loss of industrial capacity ever seen in any country during peacetime. As enterprise income dried up employees' wages went unpaid, often for months and even years. The predicted explosion of unemployment never fully materialized as state-owned enterprises continued to keep staff 'employed' even if they were not always paid. Workers, for their part, saw continued reasons to remain attached to their enterprises owing to the informal bargaining over fringe benefits that access to these companies can provide (Southworth 2004). There was an extremely low wage floor (McCann and Schwartz 2006: 1344), and wages collapsed, contributing to widespread poverty and a steep decline in average life expectancy. In 1998, average monthly income was 3,868 roubles (about US$110) (Sakwa 2008: 241). The enterprise training system inherited from Soviet days was woefully outdated, as it was designed to provide workers for specific industries which no longer functioned (Walker 2011). Mass unemployment looked likely for generations of Russian youth.

Russia's once-proud space programme ran into the sand. One of the Vostok space vehicles which now resides in the UK's National Space Centre museum was apparently found abandoned in an outdoor parking area. The space shuttle 'Buran' was destroyed in 2002 when its hangar roof in the Baikonur cosmodrome collapsed onto it, killing eight workers. A vainglorious attempt to emulate NASA's reusable space vehicle programme, Buran had only flown once, unmanned. Such neglect and abandonment was repeated across the country, such as a fire that destroyed the engine plant of the KamAZ heavy truck manufacturer. Country wide there was a lack of care and attention, and poor levels of safety. Whole areas were abandoned without any thought as to how or why; they just decayed and collapsed over time as funding, goodwill and human energy dried up.

Registered crimes doubled in Russia in the years 1985–98 (Varese 2001: 19), with homicide rates in the mid-1990s climbing to three times higher than that in the USA, and higher than Mexico and Brazil (Varese 2001: 20). Law enforcement officials (such as police, tax inspectors and customs officers) were woefully underpaid and susceptible to bribery. Drug trafficking, murder and prostitution became widespread and organized crime networks insinuated themselves into many corners of Russian economy, society and government (Varese 2001). In order to become economically or politically powerful, businesspersons needed to ensure they had a *krysha* – literally a roof – over them, to offer protection from sources of arbitrary force that may seek to impinge on that power. This *krysha* would typically be a well-connected individual who would act as a fixer and ensure that potential sources of threat were bought off and kept at bay by various deals. Sources of threat could consist of business competitors, criminal networks or various sections of the state.

Laws were not effectively enforced and widespread tax evasion led to reduced government revenues. Informal deals, political connections and willingness to pay bribes became essential for the functioning of the economy in a dysfunctional institutional environment. Corporate law, such as property rights and shareholder rights were often unclear, unfit for purpose, or simply ignored by economic actors. This view is emphasized by institutional theorists such as Stark (1995), Elster et al. (1998) and North (1991). They argue that the 'laws of the game' – in Russian *pravila igri* – were wide open, allowing all kinds of sharp practice that the powerful used to exploit the weak or gullible. The metaphor of the 'Wild East' was widely used as informality and violence, rather than the legal system, were used to settle differences (Adachi 2010: 1).

Gaidar abandoned price-fixing in January 1992 which initially led to runaway inflation of around 250% (Krueger 2004: 30). Citizens lost their savings as inflation eroded the value of their rouble-denominated accounts. However, the opening of the Russian economy to international trade and investment meant a sudden arrival of consumer products of great variety, such as European food products and Japanese electronics. The problem was now not so much that there was nothing to buy, but that most citizens had insufficient funds to do so.

Yet amid the chaos, some growth took place in the 1990s. Small- and medium-sized firms started to develop, often in the consumer and services sector, which was woefully inadequate under state socialism and was an obvious potential area for expansion. Small-scale privately run shops, kiosks and later cafes, hotels and restaurants emerged all over Russia, although these businesses were saddled with large taxes (which they often evaded) and faced constant pressure from organized crime such as protection rackets. 'Seventy to eighty per cent of all Russian private enterprise and commercial banks, according to a presidential report, pay protection money to criminal rackets, amounting to between 10 and 20% of their turnover' (Gustafson 1999: 137). The informal, untaxed or 'shadow' economy has been estimated at around 40% of the formal economy (Sakwa 2008: 327). Setting up small businesses was hard, as Russian banks were undercapitalized and unwilling to lend. Processes for registering a business were long, opaque and deeply infected by corruption and bribery.

In terms of the large-scale state-owned economy, privatization of state-run enterprises began on a massive scale, almost immediately after the collapse. In 1992–5, so-called 'voucher privatization' took place under the supervision of the neoliberal-oriented reformer Anatoly

Chubais. This process transferred economic assets from state to private hands very quickly. Between 1992–6, the number of state-owned enterprises declined from 205,000 to around 91,000, with perhaps as much as 90% of Russian industrial capacity transferred to private ownership (Gustafson 1999: 36). Around 20% of the total value of state assets were simply given away to workers and managers in the form of vouchers, while core, strategic assets were kept under state ownership for the time being. This crash privatization provided a basis for the establishment of competition and market mechanisms in Russia, but the process was incomplete and flawed. Soviet-era managers were the 'big winners' from this process (Gustafson 1999: 37) because they often purchased the vouchers from cash-strapped workers and citizens, meaning a technical change in ownership but the maintenance of management. These were the 'Red Directors' of the Soviet era, who were widely thought to be incapable of dealing with the changes that capitalism would bring about. Their typical reaction (it is often argued, especially by reformists and mainstream Western observers) is to buy time and put off reforms for as long as possible, currying favour with their political connections to gain subsidies or postpone bankruptcy procedures. Bankruptcy laws at this stage were also extremely lenient. State-owned firms were privatized, but their behaviour did not change, with many morphing into so-called 'zombie enterprises' (Krueger 2004: 32). Russian firms were starved of capital as investors were frightened by huge levels of uncertainty and risk. Banks were undercapitalized and largely refused to lend as they had no way of calculating firms' creditworthiness. Russian privatization is often criticized as 'insider privatization', and it ultimately proved very unpopular with the majority of Russian citizens (Gustafson 1999: 43).

The second stage of the privatization programme in 1995–8 was even more problematic, and certainly more corrupt. In this stage, the government sold the shares in key state-owned enterprises (such as potentially very valuable oil and gas companies) rather than giving them away en masse. Shares in strategic firms such as energy, raw materials and telecommunications firms were sold off to groups of large banks, in return for these banks providing loans to the government. The taint of political corruption was obvious, in that the bank loans were sought in order to help re-elect Boris Yeltsin as Russian President, who was struggling with the unpopularity of his free-market reforms amid growing poverty and socio-economic upheaval. He faced a real threat in the 1996 presidential elections from the Communist Party candidate Gennady Zyuganov who promised to slow the reforms, and the millions of dollars of extra campaign finance from the bank loans seemed to play a significant role in Yeltsin's electoral victory. Even then, shares were sold to the banks at perhaps one-fifth of their true value as the government sought a short-term fix to keep its reformist programme on the road. Most of these new owners of firms (which included highly profitable metals and oil companies such as Norilsk Nickel, Yukos and Sibneft) were to become fabulously rich off the back of these deals. These new owners of wealth in Russia became known as 'the oligarchs' and were to play a massive role in the subsequent economic development of the country.[7] This rather ugly episode is known as the 'loans for shares' saga (Freeland 2000: 161–181).

The sad reality was that the vast majority of Soviet-era enterprises were woefully unprepared for the 'transition' to the market economy. Years of working under the command economy had set them up for delivering to plan targets, rather than for making profits. They were used to delivering to one customer - the state - and therefore had no real capacity for customer service, marketing and distribution. Many enterprises produced a very narrow product assortment - for years they had made the same few items for very specific purposes (Krueger 2004). Working to the plan also typically meant labour hoarding; most Russian firms maintained very large levels of employment, often well in excess of what was needed to manufacture items efficiently. Many analysts expected, therefore, for transition to lead to mass unemployment as firms laid off extraneous employees to curtail costs. Interestingly, this did not happen on anything like the scale that was feared. This appeared to be because the former Soviet industrial plant was so degraded and in need of investment that enterprises actually needed to keep employees because they required extra labour to make up for the inefficiencies caused by continued machinery breakdowns. Wages dropped to such low levels that enterprises could afford to keep labour on, reducing wage levels, postponing payments and making 'payments in kind' such as giving products to staff instead of cash (Schwartz 2003; Southworth 2004). However, faced with continual pressures, many enterprises were eventually forced to run down or sell off their fringe benefits to employees such as holiday homes or sanatoria. Local government, and bodies such as the Russian Union of Industrialists and Entrepreneurs (RUIE), also tried to scrape together whatever they could to insulate firms from collapse, cancelling debts or extending subsidies where possible (Sakwa 2008: 241).

Krueger (2004) provides a very instructive study of how Russian firms in heavy and light industry and the food industry attempted to cope with the transition to a market economy. He shows how heavy industry and light industry suffered particularly badly, with growing

---

[7] Vladimir Gusinksy, mentioned above, was one of the most prominent of the first wave of oligarchs to emerge, owning Most bank and a media empire that included the newspaper *Sevodnya* and the NTV television station.

debts, collapse of output, decline in employment and wages, a growing dependence on barter and non-monetary exchange, and fierce competition from overseas imports. Such was the shortage of demand that companies reduced their output and ran two- or three-day working weeks (Krueger 2004: 35–36).

Employment at the Slava Watch Factory in Moscow plummeted from 11,000 in 1990 to just 2,000 in seven years (Krueger 2004: 107). Heavy industrial firms used to be the vanguard of the Soviet economic system; their technology was the most advanced, their products the most respected, and their workforce the best paid. However in the transition period they went to the bottom of the heap (Krueger 2004: 43). The situation for the food companies was less desperate. On a more positive note, Krueger credits Russian firms and managers with a lot more creativity and inventiveness than is normal in this literature. He is somewhat less pessimistic than most, in that he shows a wide variety of firm reactions to the collapse and transition, and that there is some hope for companies that produce in-demand items, such as the Moscow Tire Factory, which was able to pursue a workable strategy for sales growth and even to improve product quality.

Morrison (2008) explores in great detail a textile factory in the Ivanovo region facing horrendous difficulties. Its mostly female workforce was paid 'abysmally low' wages of an average 1,300 roubles per month – around US$37 (Morrison 2008: 167–168). Ordinary Russians were struggling amid great poverty as the economic system collapsed around them. An interviewee in Ashwin's (1999: 51) excellent study of Russian workers summed up the grim reality of late 1990s Russia: 'We don't live in hope of the future, but in fear of the future. We live from day to day and look at tomorrow with fear ... The worst thing about present day life is that there's no hope.' Notions of 'tragedy' feature readily in the literature on Russia (Reddaway and Glinski 2001).

The story of Russian reforms also contains elements of farce. Among the poverty rose a new class of rich, those who had profited from the reforms, often in circumstances which were legally and morally highly dubious. They are often labelled the 'New Russians', who are invariably described as rich yet ignorant, rude, selfish and base. The Communist Party under Zyuganov was able to make great play of these new inequalities, and harked back to the USSR as a time of stability, equity and moral leadership. However, few people seriously entertained the idea of turning the clock back.

If this was capitalism it appeared to be of an odd sort. Much of the literature on the transition places great emphasis on institutional weaknesses, such as a lack of functioning property rights and rule of law (often basing their arguments on institutional economics such as

North [1991). Such an explanation thus lends itself well to a VoC explanation for the emergence of Russia's 'deformed' capitalism. Authors such as Stark (1995) and Elster et al. (1998) suggested that the neoliberal reforms were always likely to fail because they assumed an institutional blank slate upon which to impose market reforms. However, this institutional vacuum never existed. Path-dependent elements remained before, during and after the collapse. The economy had to redevelop itself while the political structure itself was unclear, complex and declining in authority. A great analogy for this is 'rebuilding the ship at sea' (Elster et al. 1998). Enabling institutions that are required for effective capitalist growth were unclear or absent. What does exist is a complex muddle of Soviet-style and new institutions existing together that are not complementary – the result is 'deformed', or 'mutant' capitalism.

Russia's macroeconomic performance in the 1990s was appalling. There were signs of stabilization in 1997, but they turned out to be illusory as the economy ground to a halt in the August 1998 Russian financial crash. The Russian government defaulted on domestic and international loans and was forced to reduce the value of the rouble by two-thirds. This created bank runs as citizens rushed to withdraw roubles. Banks collapsed and confidence in the Russian economy evaporated. Many of the foreign investors who had risked getting involved in Russia (already a very small number when compared to other Eastern European nations such as Poland or the Czech Republic) cut their losses and fled. Although the panic was very unpleasant at the time, the crash turned out to be a blessing in disguise. Domestic industry recovered, as foreign imports became extremely expensive following the collapse of the rouble's value. As Table 8.1 shows, the calamitous trend in industrial output was reversed. Oil prices also rose and Russian oil and gas exports began generating huge surpluses for the government, which began to spend them on much-needed investments in infrastructure and public sector wages.

Yeltsin resigned as Russian President in December 1999, handing power to Vladimir Putin, the Prime Minister who had been in that post only since August 1999. Until that point, Putin was a little-known bureaucrat with a security services background, and few knew what to expect from him. Putin and his inner circle emerged as 'strongmen' or *siloviki*, who managed to reinforce the power of a Russian state that had slid into decay under Yeltsin. He was to endorse another top-down, state-led strategy to rebuild Russia's economy and international standing. Many observers argue that Russians have historically favoured such a *silnaya ruka* or 'strong hand', and that a dominant state has been a major feature of the country's political and economic system for centuries.

Table 8.1 Macroeconomic trends in Russia 1990–2006

Year	Annual change in GDP	Annual change in gross industrial output
1990	–3.0	–0.1
1991	–5.0	–8.0
1992	–14.8	–18.0
1993	–8.7	–14.1
1994	–12.7	–20.9
1995	–4.0	–3.3
1996	–3.6	–4.5
1997	1.4	2.0
1998	–5.3	–5.2
1999	6.4	11.0
2000	10.0	8.7
2001	5.1	4.9
2002	4.7	3.1
2003	7.4	8.9
2004	7.2	8.0
2005	6.4	5.1
2006	8.2	6.3
2007	8.5	6.3
2008	5.2	2.1
2009	–7.9	–10.8
2010	4.4	n.a.

Source: European Bank for Reconstruction and Development (EBRD) website

http://www.ebrd.com/pages/research/economics/data/macro.shtml#macro

A return to state control? Russia under Putin and the 'strongmen'

The theme of rebuilding and recentralizing after the neoliberal chaos and corruption of the Yeltsin era became a central one for Russia in the 2000s and persists to this day. David Lane (2008), for example, writes of a change 'from chaotic to state-led capitalism'. Puffer and McCarthy (2007) draw on institutional theory to offer a similar verdict in that Russian institutions, so weak, fluid and hazy under Yeltsin, had calcified into something altogether more robust under Putin. The rule of law was strengthened in crucial areas, such as tax enforcement and bankruptcy legislation. This helped to increase confidence in the system and reduce the uncertainty that has held back investment from domestic banks and overseas multinationals. Oil prices remained high during the 2000s furnishing the Putin government with large export revenues, which were reinvested in the dreadfully neglected public sector such as local government, the legal system and law enforcement.

However, there are clear downsides to the *silnaya ruka* approach. Arbitrary use of political power remains a problem and Putin's approach is widely condemned as antidemocratic and secretive. Secret US diplomatic cables which found their way onto the Wikileaks website in 2011 described Russia as 'a virtual mafia state', characterized by a 'corrupt, autocratic kleptocracy' centred around Putin's inner circle. Bribery alone was estimated to total US$300 billion per year, and law enforcement agencies operate 'protection rackets for criminal networks'.[8] Putin's re-assertion of state power is not a return to communist autocratic control, but rather a complex situation in which the state is both weak and strong. It is weak in the sense of continued problems with informality, tax evasion and bribery, but also strong in the form of powerful individuals operating at various levels of a complex pattern of state power who can act arbitrarily by using state authority to reinforce and build their own private positions, and to attack those of others outside the circle.

The Yukos/Khodorkovsky saga is by far the most famous example. Yukos was one of Russia's largest oil companies which was sold to Khodorkovsky's Menatep bank in a 'loans-for-shares' deal in 1996. In 2003, just as it was negotiating a deal to merge with rival oil company Sibneft to make one of the largest oil companies in the world, Yukos senior managers Mikhail Khodorkovsky and Platon Lebedev were charged with tax evasion. A long court case followed in which Khodorkovsky was imprisoned throughout as he was considered a flight risk. Predictably enough, Khodorkovsky was found guilty and given a sentence of nine years imprisonment. He was later also convicted of embezzlement and money laundering, extending his prison sentence to 14 years. Yukos was broken up and its assets transferred to the state-run Rosneft. It is important to note that Yukos was infamous as one of the very worst examples of informal corporate governance practices designed to mislead shareholders and investors (Adachi 2010: 29), and the charges of tax evasion are likely to have some grounding in reality (Goldman 2010). The problem was that the attack on Yukos seemed politically motivated, when other large firms were also widely known to have engaged in similar tax evasion and fraud. It is widely alleged that Putin's strongmen went after Yukos only because Khodorkovsky had publicly questioned Putin's authority and had funded rival political parties that could have put up candidates to challenge Putin for the Russian presidency.

---

[8] 'Wikileaks Cables Condemn Russia as "Mafia State"', *Guardian*, 1 December 2010.

Since this ugly episode, Western analysts have typically poured scorn on Putin for his authoritarian and anti-business environment, with news media often portraying him as an unreconstructed Soviet bureaucrat hostile to the West and hostile to free markets. But many ordinary Russians had little sympathy for Khodorkovsky or the other oligarchs. The economic status of the majority of Russian citizens improved significantly under Putin. Real incomes grew by 11.5% in 2006 alone (Sakwa 2008: 247). Putin's popularity remained high throughout the 2000s, as economic stability at last seemed to have arrived. Putin tried to achieve 'equidistance' from the oligarchs, and he did manage this to some degree. Provided they did not speak out against official policy, oligarchs could expect tougher demands for tax collection than they had become accustomed to in the 1990s, but otherwise were free of overt political interference.

Putin regularly mentioned the importance of rebuilding the Russian state, but also distanced himself from its Soviet legacy, criticizing its inefficiencies and describing it as a 'blind alley' (see Exhibit 8.2 overleaf).

Even with a more robust state, corruption and bribery have remained endemic. Russian society seems to suffer from a dire absence of institutional trust. The power structure has its favourites (such as Oleg Derepaska) and its bitter enemies (such as Boris Berezovsky, effectively exiled in London until his death in 2013), Vladimir Gusinsky (fled to Israel) and Khodorkovsky (serving out a 14-year prison sentence).

Elsewhere in Russia the institutional structure of the Russian economy has changed and solidified in important ways. The late 1990s onwards has seen the dramatic rise of the so-called financial-industrial groups (FIG). These are large business empires that have grown up around an oligarch and his/her closest business and political allies. Typically the FIG is centred around a bank which provides investment funding for other firms inside the group, which will often come from a range of sectors such as light and heavy industry, business services and media. FIGs have grown by taking over Russian firms (often those in distress) and then injecting new capital in order to renovate and restructure them. The largest FIGs often have their own private security firms (Hoffman 2002). The FIGs are similar in some ways to large Japanese business groups, in their use of a main bank which can subsidize other firms in the group. Bankruptcy laws were tightened up significantly in 2002, meaning that many more enterprises were pushed into bankruptcy and were thus easy for cash-rich FIGs to purchase cheaply (McCann and Schwartz 2006: 1344). Adachi (2010) argues that large privatized Russian enterprises were deprived by the legacy of state planning of the infrastructure they needed for survival in a market economy. Russian firms with capital therefore set about assembling

Exhibit 8.2 Putin on Russia

Vladimir Putin's somewhat authoritarian approach to politics and economics, while morally troubling, appears to have put the Russian economy back on its feet. The text below is derived from an article written by Putin that was reproduced in an appendix to Richard Sakwa's textbook on Putin (2008). Below he distances himself from the Soviet legacy but also reveals his defence of Russian nationalism, 'uniqueness', and 'statism'.

'For three-quarters of the twentieth century Russia was dominated by the attempt to implement communist doctrine. It would be a mistake not to recognise, and even more to deny, the unquestionable achievements of those times. But it would be an even bigger mistake not to realise the outrageous price our country and its people had to pay for that social experiment. [...] *Communism and Soviet power did not make Russia a prosperous country with a dynamically developing society and free people*. [...] However bitter it may now be to admit it, for nearly seven decades we were moving along a blind alley, far from the mainstream of civilization.'

[...]

'Russia was and will remain a great power. [...] It will not happen soon, if ever, that Russia will become the second edition of, say, the US or Britain in which liberal values have deep historic roots. Our state and its institutions and structures have always played an exceptionally important role in the life of the country and its people. For Russians a strong state is not an anomaly to be discarded. Quite the contrary, they see it as the source and guarantee of order, and the initiator and the main driving force of change.'

'Contemporary Russian society does not identify a strong and effective state with a totalitarian state. We have come to value the benefits of democracy, a law-based state, and personal and political freedom. At the same time, people are concerned by the obvious weakening of state power. The public wishes to see the appropriate restoration of the guiding and regulating role of the state, proceeding from the traditions and present state of the country.'

(Source: Sakwa 2008: 320, 323)

that infrastructure, enhancing their capacity to operate in such a turbulent environment by trying to vertical integrate their supply chains (Clarke 2004).[9]

The FIGs thus have some clear parallels with US business history of the Chandlerian 'visible hand' (Chandler 1977) or perhaps, given the corrupt and rapacious nature of the FIGs and the oligarchs, to the earlier US 'robber baron' phase and the 'trusts' such as Standard Oil

[9] While this process was most obvious in the FIGs, some strategically important state or partially state-owned Russian firms, (such as the energy giants Gazprom and Rosneft or the weapons manufacturer United Aircraft Corporation) are operating as examples of French-style 'national champions'.

(Chernow 2004). After smaller companies had been taken over by FIGs, employment conditions became more stable, wages rose in value and were paid on time, and efforts were made to invest in updating and improving industrial plant, often by purchasing foreign technology. In many ways, the FIG-owned companies actually re-established Soviet-style paternalistic labour management - Simon Clarke (2004) describes the results as 'a very Soviet form of capitalism'. The aim is to gain control over a complex and uncertain supply chain by establishing vertical integration and autarky, much like Chandler describes for US capitalism in the late 19th century.

Meanwhile, Putin continued to press on with market reforms, including the new Land Code of October 2001, which enabled the commercial sale of farm land. This perhaps symbolized the final end of Soviet ideology. Putin continued to preside over a rapidly recovering Russian economy, with annual GDP growth rates of around 6%. While economic conditions were finally improving for most Russian citizens, he drew substantial criticism for his strong methods of political control. He took an extremely robust approach to the Chechen war, which appears to have met with a degree of 'blowback' (Johnson 2002) as some horrific terrorist attacks hit Moscow and the regions throughout the 2000s. Putin's administration took a relentlessly uncompromising approach to fighting terrorism, often drawing criticism for relying on what could be interpreted as excessive and inappropriate uses of force. Putin eventually hand-picked his successor Dmitry Medvedev, who won the presidential election in 2008 with ease. Putin was constitutionally barred from occupying more than two consecutive terms as president, so he took the post of Prime Minister in 2008–12 and ran again for President in March 2012, winning easily with 63.6% of the vote (officially). Widespread voting irregularities emerged, however, in the Duma elections, leading to major street protests against Putin and Medvedev in late 2011 and early 2012, and there are also signs that the 2012 presidential elections were at least partially tainted by fraud.[10] Many inside and outside of Russia have grown tired of Putin's cronyism and macho posturing. The projection of the Putin 'cult of personality' can appear absurd and has been known to backfire, such as the now infamous publicity stunt where he 'miraculously' found ancient Greek urns while scuba diving.[11]

Economic growth was very solid in the 2000s. Russia is now the world's second-largest arms exporter, securing around US$12 billion

---

[10] 'Thousands Rally as Political Forces Vie for Advantage', *Moscow Times*, 4 February 2012.

[11] 'Vladimir Putin's Chief Spokesman Admits Greek urn Find Was Staged', *Guardian*, 6 October 2011.

of weapons sales globally in 2011[12], and Russia's space technologies have staged a remarkable comeback. The Russian Space Agency has built up huge experience of providing an international service for the safe, reliable and comparably cheap launching of satellites. Foreign direct investment in Russia has typically been a small fraction of the volume that has gone to other eastern European nations (Meardi 2006), but there has been significant overseas investment in the Russian oil and gas industry. Although there have been some severe conflicts over many of these investment deals, especially the BP-TNK joint venture, the extra funding has meant the import of new technologies for the extraction of oil and gas from idle fields. Russia has over 30 years of proven oil reserves and there is a strong likelihood of undiscovered or underexploited fields. Oil and gas exports account for about two-thirds of Russia's export income.[13] Yet the opacity of the Russian business system remains troubling, and outsiders (often including Westerners) are often kept at arms' length. Russian companies are notorious for hiding their assets in complex webs of overseas shell companies (Adachi 2010). The opaque and low-trust socio-economic structure has been constantly off-putting to potential investors in Russian firms who remain fearful that their investments will be unfairly taken from them by unscrupulous and unpredictable business and political elements.

Nevertheless, the Russian economy has grown in size and sophistication. Its cultural and creative industries have been growing, such as cinema, fashion and advertising (Goscilo and Strukov 2010). There is a large customer base and workforce for this industry in Russia's growing middle class of well-educated, globally integrated younger citizens with no direct experience of Soviet isolation. Of course, not everyone can share in this economic growth. Income inequalities in Russia are severe and growing. The Gini coefficient in Russia in 2008 was 42.3, higher than the USA, according to World Bank figures.[14] While poverty has reached, in the words of Putin, 'an awesome scale' (Sakwa 2008: 328) Russia also boasted 17 billionaires in 2003 (Sakwa 2008: 240).

It is interesting to note that Russia's path since the Soviet collapse has not been exclusively neoliberal. In some sense the *siloviki* represent a shift back to higher levels of state control, or at least a move in a more ambivalent direction – towards free markets but within a much

[12] '$6Bln in Weapons Sales a Factor in Syria', *Moscow Times*, 2 February 2012.

[13] 'Will Russia Ever Reduce Dependence on Oil and Gas Exports?', *BBC News*, 29 April 2011.

[14] Gini figure from World Bank website, http://data.worldbank.org/indicator/SI.POV.GINI, accessed 31 November 2012.

stronger state (Sakwa 2008). Putin's economic approach is not uncommon in Russian history, in some ways mirroring the Witte System for example. Putin has also muzzled the media to some extent, wresting control of NTV from Gusinsky via investment through the state gas monopoly Gazprom.[15] Putin has attempted to restore Russian national pride, at times aggressively asserting Russian influence over former Soviet territories (such as the war with Georgia in 2008). State-run television, such as the Russia Today TV channel that is free-to-air in many European nations, offers pro-Putin/Medvedev coverage and is often highly critical of US interests.

Despite making considerable strides in the 2000s, there remain some clear vulnerabilities in the Russian economy, notably the dependence on raw materials exports, a rather primitive, low-cost, low-quality, low-wage industrial economy and a rather limited capacity for a high-tech and informational economy (Goldman 2010) (although rapid improvements are taking place in these latter sectors). Foreign investors are still reluctant to involve themselves in such a complex, uncertain and sometimes threatening environment. The economy was also hit very hard by the subprime crisis as the global price of oil declined. In 2009, the GDP of Russia shrank by 7.9% and industrial output contracted by a worrying 10.8%, showing how vulnerable the economy is to falls in commodity prices (see Table 8.2 on page 227). But Russia is clearly now integrated into the world economy, and seems to have a future, unlike the 'blind alley' of the USSR. While there is often some understandable nostalgia for the stability and equality of the USSR days, few seriously consider the prospect of a return to the stifling centralized control and the shortage economy of Soviet system. Despite its obvious faults, the Russian variety of capitalism has made substantial progress since the early 1990s and seems here to stay.

Conclusion: a powerful but unstable economic model

Like the Soviet system before it, the new Russia in its own way is economically and militarily powerful but morally difficult to defend. While Putin clearly has significant domestic critics who dislike his robust and undemocratic approach (which at times is redolent of a Soviet style of leadership), a market economy now does exist in the country, and it is one that has achieved some impressive growth. What has emerged in Russia is a fairly unique variety of capitalism (Lane

[15] Gusinsky was arrested in 2000 while three minibuses of armed men raided his offices (Hoffman 2002: 477).

2000). It is clearly still evolving and changing, and has already shown considerable development away from the horrendous early years of transition (1992–4), through the chaos and corruption of Yeltsin in the mid–late 1990s and then the long period of dominance by Putin in the 2000s onwards. For large parts of its modern economic history Russia has chosen (or has been forced) to rely strongly on the state as a driver of economic action in the absence of other enabling institutions. This is visible in the policies of leaders as diverse as Witte, Stalin and Putin. Such authoritarianism has at times resulted in some strong economic results but invariably has also had extremely damaging effects on the institutional environment into which the economy is embedded. Authoritarian, top-down development models have in the Russian case tended to reinforce a low-trust model and to generate an arbitrary and highly 'political' economic environment.

On a more positive note, Russia has always been identified as a potentially enormous economy. In 2000, Goldman Sachs identified Russia as one of the so-called 'BRIC's (Brazil, Russia, India China) – the nations from which major world economic growth will come. While growth has been mostly solid since the 1998 financial crash, Russia has had to cope with the truly catastrophic 1990s, which has caused lasting damage to the country's economic prospects. The banking sector remains undercapitalized, and SMEs face major problems in terms of a lack of credit and the risks and costs from racketeering. At a higher level, questionable practices such as 'loans for shares' have perverted Russia's institutional structure. Widespread corruption and a gangster culture appears to have become 'locked-in' to the Russian economic structure. It will probably take generations for this culture to change into something more transparent and trustworthy. In the meantime, there is a danger that Russia's dependence on oil and gas exports make it vulnerable to boom-bust cycles in the prices of raw materials, and the economy needs to diversify.

Until that happens, the role of the oligarchs is likely to remain highly important in Russia's 'mutant' capitalism. The growth of large FIG holding companies represents to some extent a rebuilding of Soviet-type labour management at enterprise level, often with the re-establishment of Soviet style paternalism and fringe benefits. However, managerial control can be strong, with wages remaining relatively low and trade union representation and workplace democracy almost entirely absent. Industries that remain outside of FIG control have typically experienced a long-term collapse of employment and output. Since the 2000s, bankruptcies and the total stagnation of former Soviet industrial enterprises have been widespread, and the country has had to cope with de-industrialization on a massive scale.

Russia's rather wild form of capitalism has generated huge wealth but also huge inequality. While a new middle class has recently developed, the extremes of inequality have reached a scale similar to Latin American nations. Current World Bank estimates suggest that 11.1% of the population lives below the poverty line, while Moscow is now home to 79 billionaires according to *Forbes*.[16] More of this vast wealth will need to 'trickle down' to the large numbers of Russian citizens if they are to become more comfortable with value of free markets and democracy.

Further reading

Kotkin, S., (1997) *Magnetic Mountain: Stalinism as a Civilization*, Berkeley: University of California Press.

Influenced by Foucauldian analysis, this superb analysis of Stalinist industrialization explores how different forms of power were enacted in the Soviet system, exploring how ordinary people got on with their lives amid a totalitarian authority structure. Its use of historical sources (including hundreds of formally classified archival documents) provides an extraordinarily detailed account of the everyday realities involved in building the industrial foundations of the USSR.

Moynahan, B., (1997) *The Russian Century: A History of the Last Hundred Years*, London: Pimlico.

This is a short and highly readable overview of the pre-revolutionary era, the Bolshevik revolution, the USSR, its collapse and the beginnings of capitalism. It is very much an overview, but written in a very attractive style, and provides a good 'crash course' in Russian history. Moynahan writes largely from a conservative political perspective and finds little to commend from the Soviet era (or from the beginnings of post-communism for that matter).

(Continued)

[16] Statistics from World Bank website; 'Moscow Leads the World With Most Billionaires', *Forbes*, 17 May 2011.

(Continued)

Adachi, Y., (2010) *Building Big Business in Russia: The Impact of Informal Corporate Governance Practices*, Abingdon: Routledge.

This is an excellent book on the contemporary realities of giant firms in Russia. It argues that the Soviet command economy never furnished Russian enterprises with sufficient mechanisms for working in a marketized environment. In the transition, enterprise insiders tried to build these mechanisms themselves, using highly opaque, informal and often outright corrupt methods. Featuring case studies on Yukos, SibAL and Norilsk Nickel, it is a very useful book for anyone interested in Russian large firms and the weakness of the institutional environment surrounding them.

Schwartz, G., (2003) 'Employment Restructuring in Russian Industrial Enterprises: Confronting a "Paradox"', *Work, Employment and Society*, 17, 1: 49–72.

This paper is an extremely detailed and well-written account of the realities of Russian firms in the late 1990s. It presents a very clear description of how Russian firms have reacted to the transition, with workers bearing the brunt of changes via falling wages and reduced working hours. It highlights the importance of firm-level studies in order to understand why the predicted collapse of employment never really materialized. In doing so it highlights the terrible vulnerability of Russian workers to the deterioration of their wages and standards of living.

NINE India: A Turbulent Transformation

Chapter objectives

- To explore the economic features and prospects of India – a 'lower-middle income' nation that today is widely described as an increasingly potent new force in global business
- To describe the nature and legacy of India's colonial history
- To explain the modernizing mission of Prime Minister Nehru and the system of planning he helped install
- To account for the unravelling of this state-led, 'organized' development model and to explain the increasingly rapid liberalization of Indian economy
- To explore India's recent economic achievements, especially its increasingly sophisticated insertion into global IT service industry, through off-shoring and outsourcing, and the forms of work and organization that are emerging in this sector
- To conclude by documenting the rapid development of India since the 1990s but also to note the sheer scale of challenges that remain

Introduction

India is a vast and complex nation that is steadily being drawn into globalization and international business after generations of isolation and economic weakness. It is the world's seventh-largest country by physical landmass and its population is both huge (the world's second largest at 1.24 billion) and extremely diverse. In ancient times, such as during the era of the Gupta Empire (320–600), Indian science, civilization and technology were highly advanced, with India the most substantial economy in South Asia. But for most of the modern era, India has faced colossal challenges with severe poverty and underdevelopment, and for long periods has been variously exploited, colonized or oppressed by European powers (France, the Netherlands, Denmark, Portugal and, most extensively of all, the UK). The British and Dutch East India Companies drew India into exploitative and unfair trade relationships in the 17th century, with the British East India Company eventually establishing 'company rule' over much of the nation from 1757. India, despite its huge size and enormous economic and geopolitical potential, has consistently been cast in subordinate economic roles relative to much more powerful North American, European and East Asian nations.

Since gaining independence from the UK in 1947, its attempts to break out of economic backwardness (mostly through state-directed development) have been problematic and only partially successful. India has remained a democracy ever since independence - a remarkable achievement which has confounded many expectations. Ironically, however, India's democracy has not - until the 1990s that is - been accompanied by liberal capitalism. The leadership of India since Independence borrowed heavily from Soviet-style economic development models, and its 'mixed economy' of state-owned enterprises and (heavily regulated and controlled) private capitalism was largely incapable of bringing about self-sustained economic growth. For most of its post-independence history, India has featured much more heavily in literature and debates on development (agriculture, education, population control, sanitation) rather than on global capitalism (investment, industry, technology, multinationals).

This pattern may now be changing. Since the 1990s India has engaged in major reforms, liberalizing its economy, abandoning government controls and central planning, and is becoming increasingly integrated into world flows of trade and investment. Much of the contemporary literature on Indian society and economy is optimistic, with India discussed alongside other 'emerging giants' such as China and Russia (Das 2000; Panagariya 2008; Pota 2010). Political parties promote 'India Shining' and 'Incredible India', encouraging domestic and overseas audiences to imagine a globalized and managerial India - a nation no longer looked on patronizingly in terms of exoticism, mysticism and backwardness, but a nation modernized, internationalized - ready to 'do business' (Ganesh 2008). India's contemporary economy is perhaps most famous for the rapid rise of its international IT service sector, such as software development, customer contact centres and back office business process offshoring. But its industrial and services multinationals are also growing in stature, notably the

Tata conglomerate, the Mittal steel empire and IT companies such as Infosys and Wipro.

India is another of the BRICs; a significant trend in the literature is to compare India directly with China (for example, Bardhan 2010; Khanna 2009). There are several similarities: colonialism and humiliation by other powers which held the country back at the precise time when others were modernizing and industrializing, independence at similar times after the shakeup of the Second World War (India in 1947, China in 1949), and a post-independence and post-war growth strategy based on 'big push industrialization' modelled largely on the USSR with very mixed results. Both countries have since turned decisively away from economic planning and socialism, and their economies and institutions have experienced rapid and often problematic change and liberalization. Political and economic corruption are severe in both societies. These two giant nations have huge populations and enormous regional disparities in development and income. There are also huge differences between India and China - India is the world's largest democracy, exhibiting a 'raucous' and 'vibrant' civil society (Khanna 2009), whereas China's political system is described variously as authoritarian or even 'soft totalitarian' (see Chapter 10). Economically, China's growth has been consistently stronger than India's, and its levels of income inequality have also been much lower (Bardhan 2010: 10–12).

This chapter explores the economy of India by briefly describing India's colonial legacy before exploring in some detail the achievements and failures of India's socialist modernization agenda. It will go on to explain how and why India moved away from planning and state control of the economy and towards liberalization of trade and industry, away from its rather extreme form of 'organized' capitalism and towards a much more 'disorganized' model (Lash and Urry 1987). It will explore the kind of political economy emerging in India, embedding this discussion into broader debates about globalization and the virtues of various socio-economic models. While great strides have certainly been made, recent developments in India are surrounded by hype, as excited observers promote India as the 'next big thing' in global business. This chapter will insert a degree of scepticism, pointing to the persistence of chronic problems of poverty, corruption and economic isolation of large swathes of its population.

The colonial economy of India (1757–1947)

Ancient India was one of the most richly developed regions of Asia. Artefacts derived from Indian civilization can be traced to at least the fourth century BCE, such as the famous treatise on economy and military strategy *The Arthashastra.*[1] In the age of the Mughal Empire (late 16th century) India was wealthy enough to sustain a population of 100 million, developing advanced techniques in agricultural and textile manufacturing (Das 2000: 56). Estimates suggest that India possessed 22.6% of total world GDP at this time (Das 2000: 56). Explorers from Spain and Portugal were attracted to India on the promise of plundering and trading gold, silks and spices. Christopher Columbus, on an expedition funded by the Spanish monarchy, was actually searching for India when he 'discovered' the Bahamas and other Carribbean islands; that region thus took on the misleading name 'the West Indies' and native Americans are often still known as 'Indians' (Das 2000: 54; Zinn 2005: 2).

It was obvious why India was so attractive a target for exploration and trade. Self-sufficient India exported 'products that were much in demand by its foreign customers as luxuries - ivory, fine woods, precious stones, perfumes and spices' (Auboyer 1965: 81). It imported raw silk from China, wove the material into extremely high quality garments and shipped the finished products to Egypt and the Middle East, to southern Asia (especially to Samarkand in today's Uzbekistan). India exported woods to the Persian Gulf and had advanced capacity in weapons manufacture and ironworking (Auboyer 1965: 85), with evidence to suggest that iron was manufactured from as early as the fourth and fifth centuries. India had a highly developed banking system (Das 2000: 56) and insurance markets (Habib 1999: 76) and a substantial state apparatus. The state levied taxes on the population in return for irrigation, administering timber and forestry trades, and running strategic industries such as coins and armaments manufacturing and mining operations (Auboyer 1965: 106–10). 'The economic surplus was used to support the vast and growing Mughal Empire and finance spectacular monuments like the Taj Mahal' (Das 2000: 56), constructed in the mid-17th century.

However, in a similar fashion to China (see Chapter 10), India seemed unable to keep to a continuous pace in economic development and was ultimately incapable of responding effectively to the sudden rise of aggressive European international expansion. Truly society-transforming industrial and scientific revolutions did not occur in India (Das 2000: 57), and by the 18th century, India noticeably lagged behind Western Europe 'in technology, institutions, and

[1] This is a work comparable in scale and importance to world-famous ancient Chinese works of philosophy, politics and economy, such as Confucius and Mencius (fifth and fourth centuries BCE). It is also often compared to European Renaissance or early modern writers such as Machiavelli (16th century) or Hobbes (17th century).

ideas' (Das 2000: 57). The peasantry was heavily taxed which may have inhibited innovations in manufacturing and logistics, and there was no ongoing commitment to improve productive capacity or efficiency. This shortcoming was drastically revealed in the fate of Indian textiles. Indian cotton textiles (or calicoes) were of the highest quality and in high demand in world trade (Chang 2003: 22, 53), to such an extent that Great Britain in 1700 banned imports of Indian cotton and silk products in an effort to protect domestic industry (Mathias 1969: 85). Once the cotton mills of England had reached industrial sophistication in the 19th century, Indian exporters were overwhelmed by the flooding of world markets by British cotton products, the production unit costs of which were vastly reduced by the increased scale, efficiency and standardization of the British factory system. Das laments that '[t]heir Lancashire mills crushed our handloom textile industry and threw millions of weavers out of work in the nineteenth century' (Das 2000: 58).

Worse, the British East India Company imposed itself by force and used its dominant position to monopolize all trade in the region. It was eventually granted governing powers over the region, giving it 'control over tax collection for more than 10 million people' (Robins 2006: 3). Between the years 1765–1857 the Company – in the words of the Indian historian Romesh Chunder Dutt – 'considered India as a vast estate or plantation, the profits of which were to be withdrawn from India and deposited in Europe' (as quoted in Robins 2006: 12). It contracted private armies to ensure control. The First Indian War of Independence of 1857, however, ended this arrangement and the British Crown assumed full control of India as a colony, with Queen Victoria assuming the title 'Empress of India' in 1876.[2]

The British colonizers introduced many of their institutions and systems. The Indian Civil Service was formed as a system of administration and control, and became a popular career waypoint for British university graduates (Guha 2007: xii). The British Raj bequeathed a highly elitist system of professions and boasted the third largest railway system in the world (Das 2000: 29). But overall the colony served to provide a captive market for British-made goods and to retard India's possibilities for self-sustaining growth. The Indian economy became dominated by British-owned businesses operating in the colony.

Domestic manufacturers vied for market share by encouraging Indians to buy homemade or *swadeshi* goods (Khanna 2007: 126–127). Indeed, some Indian entrepreneurs grew in strength during the late 19th century and family-run business such as those of Tata and Birla

[2] The British East India Company was wound up in 1874. For full details on this remarkable story see Robins (2006).

'acquired a status in India akin to the Carnegies or Rockefellers in the United States (Khanna 2007: 127). Jamsetji Tata, founder of the now globalized conglomerate that bears his name, met George Westinghouse to discuss hydroelectric facilities and travelled to international exhibitions to learn the latest technological achievements of Western Europe and America (Lala 2004: 12), and built a working relationship with Kaiser Aluminium of Seattle, USA (Lala 2004: 31).

Tata laid the foundations for its later global success during that era, building, for example, the highly productive Empress textile mill before moving on to steel manufacturing, power generation, education, hotels, even airlines. Like many of the figures of US philanthropic capitalism Tata built a powerful reputation as an enlightened business owner, spending considerable sums on education, housing for workers and communities, and the Tata corporation has since closely tended and promoted this legacy (Witzel 2010). Throughout the era of the Raj Indian entrepreneurs faced continual British scepticism and condescension. Lala (2004: 26–27) quotes the chief commissioner of the Indian Railways, a Sir Frederick Upcott, who claimed that Tata will never be able to make steel to the specifications required for railways. But the Tata Iron and Steel Company (TISCO) produced its first steel rails in 1912, receiving a boost in orders from the outbreak of the First World War (Lala 2004: 25). As Lala explains: 'The mother of heavy industry in India, Tata Steel has spawned many children around herself in Jamshedpur - The Indian Tube Company (now the Tubes Division of Tata Steel), The Indian Cable Company, The Tinplate Company of India, Indian Steel and Wire Products ... and biggest of all, Tata Engineering and Locomotive Company (Telco)' (Lala 2004: 31). With developments such as this at the forefront, Indian manufacturing output grew at an annual rate of 5.6% between 1913–38 (Das 2000: xi).

Domestic industrialists such as Tata and Birla had to find a working accommodation with the British colonial regime, but they also strongly advocated independence. Many industrialists supported the Indian National Congress, an organization devoted to the quest for independence. Birla was said to be a 'close ally and patron' of Mahatma Gandhi (Khanna 2007: 127), the man who emerged as the central figure in India's ultimately successful independence movement.[3] Severe social divisions have beset India for generations, such as those of caste, language, religion and class (Guha 2007: xix).[4] The Congress was an attempt to politically coordinate India's diverse and often fractious

[3] His full name was Mohandas Karamchand Gandhi. Mahatma means 'man with a great soul' (Gandhi 1975: 23).

[4] For an outline of the basics of India's caste system see Das (2000: 140).

regions into a single, modernized, independent Indian nation (Guha 2007: xiii). Gandhi played the key role in turning the party into a mass movement. He espoused a strategy of non-violent civil disobedience motivated by *satyagraha*, or 'truth force', which became the philosophical cornerstone of the independence struggle.[5]

While some historians produce a more favourable account of life under the British Raj, others point to colonial horrors - with the sheer number of Indians killed by avoidable famines and in various acts of repression reaching more than 10 million, comparable in scale to the deaths caused by 20th-century totalitarian regimes (Benton and Chun 2010: 10). Certainly the terms of trade were designed to be set permanently in the UK's favour. Indian labour was often moved to other outposts of the British Empire, to be employed, for example, as overseers in Malay rubber plantations. Indian protests, strikes or rebellions were typically met with brutal repression, and British leadership had an extremely condescending opinion towards Indians. Ramachandra Guha quotes Churchill's claim that without empire 'India will fall back quite rapidly through the centuries into the barbarism and privations of the middle ages' (Guha 2007: xv).

Following decades of struggle, the British Crown finally ceded independence to India in 1947, with the nation becoming one of many that had won independence shortly after the tumult of the Second World War. In common with the other newly independent nations, India had to rapidly work out a strategy for economic development in order to maintain independence and self-reliance. The colonial authorities did leave some elements of modernity to build on, such as an extensive civil service administrative system, advanced railways, and a post and telegraph system. Domestic entrepreneurs had built the beginnings of an industrial society, with the share of the economy constituted by industry having grown from 3.4% to 7.5% of national output by 1947 (Das 2000: xi). Yet India remained overwhelmingly an agricultural society upon independence with, for example, just two steel plants (Guha 2007: 211), and only 2.5 million out of a population of 350 million working in industry (Das 2000: xi). India is geographically vast and climatically diverse, with immediate economic prospects for millions dependent on the whims of the monsoon season (Das and Chatterji 1967: 8–10). Indicators of human development (literacy, life expectancy, sanitation) were low among the majority of its very large population. Newly independent India faced a massive task of modernizing rapidly if it was to survive and prosper.

[5] *Satyagraha* has also been extremely influential in other struggles, such as the Civil Rights movement and the protests against the Vietnam War in the USA (Ellsberg 2002: 213).

The 'slowly paced assent up the Marxist mountain': exploring economic planning in India

Independent India's first Prime Minister was the President of the Congress, Jawaharlal Nehru (1889–1964). He was a modernizer and integrator of India, a staunch critic of what he saw as traditional Indian cultural and religious barriers to development, describing casteism, for example, as a 'monster' (Guha 2007: 140). The goal of India's new political leadership was to build the economy as fast as possible, to unite the nation's diverse peoples, restore the county's pride, to assert independence, and to shake off the colonial and historical shackles that fettered economic progress.

Nehru and his advisors were convinced that state-led industrialization and economic planning was the fastest, fairest and most effective way to modernize the nation. At independence India was an overwhelming agrarian and underdeveloped nation, with around 75% of its workforce employed in agriculture (contributing 60% of GDP), and around 12% employed in industry (contributing 25%) (Guha 2007: 201). Although clearly influenced by the apparent effectiveness of the USSR strategy of the time, India's planners, unlike the communists of China and the USSR, did not wish to eradicate markets altogether. The strategy was a mixed approach, combining state planning and private business. Nevertheless, the ambition was to depend heavily on the mechanics of the state to leap into industrial modernity.

Part of the thinking that motivated India's planners was that capitalism itself was intimately bound up with imperialism and colonialism, and that free markets, the profit motive and speculation had uncomfortably close relationships to exploitation. Hence India's postcolonial growth model tried to emphasize forms of socialism, solidarity and equality that planning and regulation of markets were supposed to bring. Markets were allowed, but their tendencies towards irrationality, monopoly, exploitation and income inequality needed to be curbed by heavy regulation. Official documents from the era consistently reveal this mindset. For example, the Directive Principles in Article 29 of Part IV of the Indian Constitution are designed to ensure:

a) That the citizens, men and women equally, have the right to adequate means of livelihood;

b) That the ownership and control of the material resources of the community are so distributed as best to subserve the common good; and

c) That the operation of the economic system does not result in the concentration of wealth and power and means of production to the common detriment. (as quoted in Edwardes 1971: 260–261)

The moderated Marxian language is not dissimilar to the socialism of the British Fabian Society that Nehru was exposed to in his years as a student at Trinity College, Cambridge (Edwardes 1971: 21).[6] For a further flavour of the thinking of the time, see Exhibit 9.1.

Exhibit 9.1 The aims and philosophy of India's Planning Commission, circa 1961

India's Planning Commission made one of the world's most serious and deep attempts to make long-range economic planning work. The approach taken mixes influence from state socialism and from India's own experience, and the attempt to alleviate India's horrendous levels of poverty. Official documents from the era give impressions of the excitement and optimism surrounding the project, as well as the attempt to humanize planning, couching it in terms of peace and Indian-ness, distinguishing it from the more ideologically driven and authoritarian, and typically anti-Western, language more common among Soviet planners, for example.

'Parliament adopted the "socialist pattern of society" as the objective of social and economic policy. This concept, which embodies the values of socialism and democracy and the approach of planned development, involved no sudden change and had its roots in India's struggle for freedom. [...]'

'Thus, ever since Independence, two main aims have guided India's planned development – to build up by democratic means a rapidly expanding and technologically progressive economy and a social order based on justice and offering equal opportunity to every citizen. To change a traditional society into a dynamic one, in a country with a vast population and rooted in the past, was a tremendous task. To do this through peaceful and democratic means and by the consent of the people, made this task even more difficult. It was inevitable that India should adopt peaceful and democratic means as these had been the very methods it has adopted in its struggle for freedom. [...]'

'the basic criterion for determining lines of advance must not be private profit, but social gain, and that the pattern of development and the structure of socio-economic relations should be so planned that they result not only in appreciable increases in national income and employment but also in great equality in incomes and wealth. [...] The benefits of economic development must accrue more and more to the relatively less privileged classes of society, and there should be progressive reduction of the concentration of incomes, wealth, and economic power. [...]'

'The socialist pattern of society is not to be regarded as some fixed or rigid pattern. It is not rooted in any doctrine or dogma. Each country has to develop according to its own genius and traditions. [...]'

'In the context of the country's planned development the private sector has a large area in which to develop and expand.'

(Government of India Planning Commission 1961: 4, 5, 7)

---

[6] The former Clause Four of the British Labour Party constitution (up until Blair's reform and modernization of the Party before his 1997 election victory) similarly mentioned social ownership of the 'means of production'.

Planning, from the very beginning, was also accompanied by various state-run programmes for poverty alleviation, which were ambitious but often had very mixed results (Gupta 2012; Panagariya 2008: 131). There were other, perhaps less noble, aims. India's Five Year Plans were also motivated by a sense of urgency to industrialize and accrue military strength in order to make the nation genuinely independent and internationally credible, in a similar way to that seen in China and Russia. The turn to Marxism and state planning as the quickest, most militarily strategic and most socially equitable way to rebuild a country after colonialism were familiar arguments of leaders in Asia (Mao in China, Sukarno in Indonesia, Ho in Vietnam). In India, a key motivation behind state planning and a relatively autarkic development plan was *swadeshi*, or self-reliance, a perhaps understandable position after years of colonial oppression.

Strategies of state planning and heavy regulation of markets were fairly dominant even in Western nations. 'Under the influence of Keynesianism, the mainstream theories in development economics at the time held that the market encompasses insurmountable defects and that the government was a powerful supplementary means to accelerate the pace of economic development' (Lin et al. 2003: 62). The opening passages of Hanson's monumental study of India's Five Year Plans suggest 'the idea of economic planning has become generally accepted' and that laissez-faire critics such as Milton Friedman were a small, wrong-headed minority (Hanson 1966: 1, 4–5). Planning was regarded as rational and cutting-edge for its time; 'This is the age of planning,' declare Das and Chatterji in their introductory textbook on the Indian economy (1967: 541).

India's development strategy, like China's, meant implementing a 'highly controlled administrative management system', and 'price-distortion policies' (Lin et al. 2003: 64).

Neoliberal economist Jagdish Baghwati once described Nehru's policies as 'a measured and slowly paced assent up the Marxist mountain' (Huang 2008: 19) implying the chosen path was a blind alley (see also Yergin and Stanislaw 2002: 214). Edwardes describes Nehru's approach to planning as 'almost entirely emotional' (1971: 260). Read today, with the hindsight of the collapse of the USSR and the widespread criticism of the false sense of certainty provided by supposedly scientific 'rational' planning and decision making (Byrne 1993), the prospects for India's Planning Commission seem almost doomed from the outset. However, as we shall see below, this would not be an entirely fair assessment. Today's neoliberal economists argue that India would have been better off utilizing its 'comparative advantage' in low-wage manufacturing to export basic items on world markets, rather than choosing a strategy of planned development and import-substitution (Panagariya 2008).

However, current criticism of planning seems to deliberately downplay its successes. Hanson points to some 'great achievements', stating: '(1) it has effected a break with economic stagnation; (2) it has significantly raised the national income per head; and (3) it has strengthened the infrastructure of the economy and thereby created some of the preconditions for self-sustaining economic takeoff' (1966: 526). Much more recently Bardhan claims it would be 'a travesty to deny the positive legacy of that period' (2010: 8). It is wrong to dismiss the achievements of the Five Year Plans out of hand, and it is, of course, impossible to prove that less or no planning would have led to more growth (Hanson 1966).

The National Planning Commission was established in 1950 (with Nehru himself as chair), and its first Five Year Plan of 1951–6 laid down targets for a major programme of public works and land reform. Successes were had in agriculture and cotton manufacturing, whereas the more difficult industrial targets were widely missed. Good fortune with the monsoon is often given as the reason for the hitting of targets for food grains and oilseed production (achieved at the levels of 142% and 135%, respectively). Mill cloth output was 141%. However, production fell short of target in irrigation and electrical energy (71% and 84%, respectively). In finished steel and aluminium output, the performance was even worse (45% and 44%, respectively: figures from Hanson 1966: 112–3). The second Five Year Plan was more ambitious, more explicitly tied to the goal of achieving 'a socialistic pattern of society', and with the emphasis laid more firmly on Soviet-style rapid and heavy industrialization (Edwardes 1971: 262). The language of the planners was less frantic and less ideological than that of their Soviet or Chinese counterparts. Indian industrial achievements were also less dramatic. The modernization process in India was, however, thankfully not marred by the political violence that destroyed any credibility the Soviet and Chinese industrialization might have had. In the second Five Year Plan agricultural performance lagged behind industrial achievements; industrial production in iron and steel had more than doubled since 1951, and machinery industries grew rapidly (see Table 9.1). Throughout the planning era, however, there was always a sense that, although the bases of an industrialized society were laid, India was waiting endlessly for a Rostovian 'take-off' that never came.

Much of the historical analysis emphasizes the failure of planning, either for being hopelessly unrealistic (Edwardes 1971), technically flawed (Hanson 1966) or even insufficiently ambitious (Swamy 1971: 14). Swamy estimates annual growth rates throughout the first three Five Year Plans (1951–2 to 1965–6) at around 3.5%. He claims that the Indian government was unable to prove economic growth would have been any higher without planning, suggesting that an interregnum

Table 9.1 Index of Industrial Production in India (1950–51 = 100)

Group	1955–56	1960–61
General index	139	194
Cotton textiles	128	133
Iron and steel	122	238
Machinery (all types)	192	503
Chemicals	179	288

Source: Panagariya 2008: 37. By permission of Oxford University Press, USA.

without planning (1966–7) demonstrated 4% growth. Nevertheless '22 years of Congress government have yielded better results than 100 years of British exploitation' (Swamy 1971: 122).

In foreign policy, India committed itself to a delicate balancing act of 'principled neutrality', not fully aligning itself with the USSR or the USA during the Cold War standoff, but trying to take a cautious middle path. Ultimately, however, India's chosen economic pathways became considerably more closely entwined with those of Soviet state socialism than of American big business. Nehru was said to be an admirer of Roosevelt's New Deal, but otherwise took a dim view of the excesses of American capitalism (Guha 2007: 155). India's relationship with the USA was often strained and the USSR was India's arms supplier (Guha 2007: 455).

India's position was similar to that of several Central and South American societies in that, mindful of their recent history of being colonized or semi-colonized by advanced industrialization nations, they were concerned about the possibility of remaining permanently on the 'periphery' of the world economy, of becoming dependent on 'core' rich nations and trapped in 'dependency' (Yergin and Stanislaw 2002: 234–235; see also Lin et al. 2003: 61).[7] The proposed route out of these traps involved casting a new national mission, and a heavy industry-led 'leap forward' strategy was often the preferred course of action.[8] Often the new mission is embodied in the figure of a political 'strongman' or authoritarian leader, and infant industry protection, capital controls and centralized planning are used to greater or lesser degrees, resulting in

[7] Nehru wrote about the humiliating subordination of India by the East India Company and then directly by the UK, while imprisoned by British authorities. 'The corruption, venality, nepotism, violence and greed of money of these early generations of British rule in India is something which passes comprehension' (quoted in Robins 2006: 13).

[8] It has also been seen in certain Middle Eastern nations such as Iran.

various degrees of success and failure (Chang 2006; Wade 2003). One argument in favour of planning is that it provides 'rational' channels for industry to invest in products, services and sectors that are most timely, strategic and appropriate for a developing society, into such sectors as steelmaking, hospital building or coalmining rather than frivolous luxury products (the example of lipstick is given by Yergin and Stanislaw [2002: 213]).[9] It was this thinking that stimulated India's planners to control business through establishing systems of licenses, quotas and permits for industrial products. While the so-called 'Permit Raj' which developed out of this system today seems ludicrous and irrational (see below), when placed in the terms of reference of its day it appears at least understandable.

At the 'commanding heights' of the state-run economy, thousands of Soviet advisors came to work in Indian industrialization projects (Das 2000: 90–91; Guha 2007: 208). In a passage of text infused with socialist language – 'tears of joy', 'building the future' – Guha quotes from memoirs of the era about a state-owned steel mill in Bhilai nicknamed 'the Magnitogorsk of India' finally coming on stream:

> The construction team glowed with pride and satisfaction at the new-born plant they had brought to life, the operation team was anxiously eager to nurture it to its full stature ... Each of us were helping build the future ... the first flush of molten iron came out of the blast furnace in Bhilai. All around there were tears of joy and rejoicing. (2007: 212).

Sadly, the assumptions underpinning Indian planning and regulation turned out to be naïve. Indian planned development turned into 'a lesson in disappointment' and 'Nehru and his colleagues failed in their central mission' (Chibber 2003: ix, 3–4). Crucially it seems, the emphasis of the Permit Raj was on *regulation and control of business* rather than *support for business*, with industry hamstrung by red tape rather than supported by soft loans and governmental oversight and coordination of market activities (as in the Korean or Japanese models of state-driven industrial growth [Yergin and Stanislaw 2002: 221]). This impression is strongly given in more recent, pro-business accounts of Indian growth such as that of Das, who claims to have fervently supported Nehru in his youth but came to realize the false hopes invested in the project (Das 2000: 34). He claims that the system of controls 'killed our industry at birth' and that Fabian socialism did us 'incalculable harm' (2000: ix, 8).

Chibber (2003) suggests that Nehru's developmental state lacked resources and had too many opponents in business for it to have

[9] Nehru is said to have once asked 'Why do we need nineteen brands of toothpaste?' (Das 2000: 153).

succeeded. Moreover, Hanson (1966: 308) writes widely on the problems of corruption, bureaucratic infighting and incompetence in the world of planning administration. He suggests the planners were 'well endowed' with economists, econometricians, and statisticians, but had no sociological insights to draw on – they refused to recognize and failed to understand the distinct, varied and vastly complex socio-cultural make-up of India, ignoring critical issues of caste, region and religion. 'For instance,' he writes 'during the course of reading the 2,000 or so congested pages of the three plan reports, I have never discovered more than a passing mention of India's most important institution, caste' (1966: 528).

The machineries of Indian planning resembled the 'technocracy' of the 1950s–1960s scientific-technical revolution. One of the chief architects of planning, Professor P.C. Mahalanobis visited the USA in 1954 where he collected and stored information in a 'deck of 40,000 Hollerith punch cards' (Guha 2007: 207). Indian planning involved the creation of detailed organizational charts, statistical analysis and the 'machinery of planning' (Hanson 1966: 50–88). Often this resembled the dysfunctional miasma of 'goals gone wild' (Ordonez et al. 2009) in which the political need to deliver paperwork that shows targets had been hit outweighed the need to actually complete the work itself. 'Numbers games' took over. Numbers became fictions. Supposedly 'rational', elitist and technical forms of scientific planning blurred into a madness of irrational guesswork and box-ticking. Planning, as in the USSR and China (or in the management of the US war in Vietnam), became bogged down in 'the thick jungle of Kafka-esque bureaucratic controls' (Das 2000: x). Although capitalism itself was not banned, it was hemmed in by controls and quotas, such as the Industrial Policy Resolution of 1956 that set aside 17 industries solely for public organizations to run (Das 2000: 93).

Setting goals is one thing. Actually implementing policies that will deliver them and contribute to the near-mythical goal of stimulating self-sustaining or 'take-off' growth is quite another. How can we know if planning is realistically workable? Are planning and administration superior to market forces? It is some leap of faith to believe that they are. Yet India persisted with this failed developmental state and it became 'reproduced' throughout the 1960s and 1970s (Chibber 2003: 161–221). Hanson (1966: 308) describes the powerful bureaucratic forces of resistance and reluctance to change that built up throughout the period.[10]

[10] In a turn of phrase that seems reminiscent of Japan's corporate and public sector reform struggles after the 1990 bubble collapse, Hanson claims that India's 'status-oriented society' was particularly hostile to change and that 'government jobs were highly prized' (Hanson 1966: 308).

One target was to raise India's status to that of the G7 industrialized nations' 1967 standards by the year 2000. This assumed that India was around 33 years behind the G7. India's planners would need to contrive a growth rate of around 10% per year to achieve this target, and even then it assumes that G7 nations do not accelerate their own growth rates. But the Fourth Five Year Plan had a stated target of just 5.5% growth. According to Swamy, if India stayed with 5.5% economic growth, then it would take 110 years to reach US levels of national income in 1967 - that is India in the year 2080 will be where USA was in 1967! (Swamy 1971: 17). Actual growth rates were around 4.1% per year between 1951–65 (Panagariya 2008: 6) falling some way short of what was needed to effect a 'take-off'. As we shall see below, things were to get worse before they got better.

Stagnation and corruption: the low point of the Congress era

By the early 1970s the Indian economy had fallen into stagnation. As it became clear that production and development targets were being missed, the ambitions of *swadeshi* fell by the wayside as India came to increasingly depend on Western loans and aid. Nationalist authors are typically highly critical of overseas contributions. Swamy wrote of a

> 'neo-colonialist hold on the intellectual elite' which has been 'further strengthened through foreign aid and the pernicious Anglo-Saxon internationalism ... [t]hese experts were completely unfamiliar with Indian conditions and tended to advance solutions which suited their prejudices. Hence most of the solutions they proposed contained phrases such as "modern", "protestant ethic", "western scientific spirit", etc., and blamed the Indian social structure for not resembling western, European society' (Swamy 1971: 135).

India accumulated 'crushing' debts (Swamy 1971: 28); by the end of 1970 this amounted to Rs 10,000 crore,[11] constituting Rs 410 crore in interest and amortization payments every year, or around 30% of export earnings. The Sino-Indian war of 1962 revealed India's militarily unpreparedness and the sudden quadrupling of its military budget unhinged the economy in the early 1960s (Swamy 1971: 33).

Nehru died in 1964 and the Congress Party continued with much the same policies of planning and the mixed economy. Nehru's successor

[11] The notification 'crore' signifies 10,000,000 Rupees; 'lakh' signifies 100,000.

Lal Bahadur Shastri made some efforts to improve agricultural output, but Indian policymakers throughout the mid-20th century seemed unable to get to grips with agrarian reform. Poverty and illiteracy in the countryside remained widespread. A survey of the Indian economy published in 1967 asserted that '[t]he fundamental economic problem for India is how to raise the income of the people above its absurdly low level', and reported that over 82% of the population lives in rural regions (Das and Chatterji 1967: 3).

Shastri died suddenly in 1966 and was succeeded as Prime Minister by Nehru's daughter Indira Gandhi. Indira signalled a leftward shift in economic policy in her Ten-Point Program of 1967 which included nationalizing banks and general insurance firms, placing ceilings on urban property and incomes, more robust anti-trust laws and channelling of bank funds into 'priority sectors' (Panagariya 2008: 50; Khanna 2007: 128). Her period of government also became more authoritarian. A state of emergency was declared in 1975 as a reaction to a ruling by the High Court of Allahabad that Indira was guilty of electoral fraud in 1971. During the 'Indian Emergency', the constitution was rewritten to restrict the power and independence of the judiciary, and a number of high-profile trade union leaders were imprisoned (on fabricated charges of terrorism in one famous case). This move towards authoritarian control was widely unpopular, and the Congress Party suffered its first electoral defeats in 1977. If Nehru is often regarded by pro-business writers as an unrealistic dreamer who was at least well-intentioned, Indira's place in history is treated with a lot more hostility (Das 2000: 178). Panagariya's major text on Indian economy policy since independence (2008: 5) claims that the period 1951–64 was characterized by reasonably liberal trade policies (and an average annual growth rate of 4.1%), but that the period 1965–81 marked a tightening of the failing system of socialist controls and regulation, with growth slowing to an annual average of 3.2%. In the late 1970s around 50% of the population lived below the poverty line of one dollar per day (Gupta 2012: 4). The agricultural situation remained so erratic that India had to import many food products that it really should have been self-sufficient in (Panagariya 2008: 49).

Yet Indira was returned to power in 1980. Under her government the 'permit-license-quota Raj' (Khanna 2009: 39) fettered the economy in even tighter bureaucratic knots. 'If a businessman wanted to shift from making plastic shovels to making plastic pails, he had to get approval' (Yergin and Stanislaw 2002: 214). The Congress Party planners were neurotic about the inefficiencies and irrationality of allowing markets to allocate investment to such an extent that inefficient investments became a self-fulfilling prophecy. The Permit Raj retarded trade, innovation and investment, made markets cumbersome, and encouraged bribery and corruption as entrepreneurs had to seek favourable relations with state and federal government agencies in order to get anything done. Political and bureaucratic corruption became endemic throughout the 1960s and remains very prevalent to this day (Gupta 2012: 75–138; Guha 2007: 470; Khanna 2007: 54–5). According to Chibber (2003: 249) Indira's political style relied on 'fealty and unquestioning loyalty to her as criteria for selecting political allies, as well as resorting to backroom manoeuvres as a way to settle political disputes'.

Critics of the socialism of the Nehru-Gandhi 'dynasty' claim that central planning and state ownership propped up inefficient companies, shielded them from competition and rewarded failure (Das 2000; Yergin and Stanislaw 2002). Indian Airlines and Air India, for example, had their beginnings as a private company owned by the house of Tata, but were nationalized in 1952 and their performance became 'synonymous with delays, bad customer service, and limited schedules' (Khanna 2007: 128). Notorious examples are common in the literature on India, a favourite being a state-run fertilizer manufacturer whose staff continued to be

Exhibit 9.2 Indian Railways as a microcosm of Indian economic failures

Gurcharan Das is highly critical of the dysfunctional bureaucracy that seems to have seeped its way into every Indian organization. Here his description of the Indian Railways captures the frustration with the failures of the Nehruvian 'mixed economy' model shared by a great many observers of India:

'The state-owned railways are a miniature portrait of contemporary India, reflecting both the good and the bad. They are the people's transport. For one dollar you can travel 200 kilometers in a second-class compartment. They are cheaper than anywhere in the world because extortionate freight prices subsidize the passenger fares. Yet seventy million Indians travel every year without tickets. The railways symbolize democracy's triumph. The poorest Indian has become mobile. They are also inefficient, corrupt, hopelessly overmanned, and politicized. They employ 1.5 million people, seven times more manpower per kilometre than in the developed countries. Their powerful unions resist scaling down or modernization. The fastest train between Delhi and Bombay averages 65 kilometers per hour and is often late. Yet Indians do not seem to mind because they have no other alternative. Private companies would not dream of transporting goods by rail, not only because of high tariffs and constant delays but because they would be stolen. Consequently, even petrol and diesel are inefficiently transported by road. Politicians make investment decisions in the railways and they bear no resemblance to commercial considerations or consumer needs. They are nationalized and there is no prospect of privatization.'

(Das 2000: 36). By permission of Alfred A. Knoff, a division of Random House Inc.

paid for producing no output: 'Everyone just pretended that it was operating' (Yergin and Stanislaw 2002: 214; see also Das 2000: 160).

With many of the state-run enterprises proving unprofitable, savings rates slumped which encouraged further state intervention and rising inflation (Guha 2007: 221–222). The optimism of the Nehru years was evaporating, as the state-led development project degenerated into an inward-looking and corrupt regime. The Congress Party began to face challenges from numerous directions. From the left were Marxist/communist groups that argued that planning was insufficiently ambitious. From the right came attacks from business leaders wanting more economic liberalization, amid the constant challenge posed by religious conflict and breakaway regions. The government famously threw out the US multinationals Coca-Cola and IBM in 1970 (Khanna 2007: 128) and allegations of corruption and nepotism at the highest levels were common. For instance, out of 18 applications for a license to manufacture small cars, India's son Rajiv's Maruti motor company was given the contract 'with undue haste' (Guha 2007: 470). Richer middle-class citizens started to find a political voice in the right-of-centre BJP party.

Rajiv Gandhi's government (1984–9) started to experiment with gradual moves towards liberalizing the economy, including slowly dismantling the license raj (Panagariya 2008: 78–94). Tragically, political violence has overshadowed India's economic development. Indira (October 1984) and Rajiv (May 1991) were both assassinated. With the murder of Rajiv, the Nehru-Gandhi 'dynasty' was over, and P.V. Narasimha Rao became Prime Minister. Despite his low profile and deep enculturation into Congress Party politics, Rao instigated a series of reforms that radically accelerated the changes Rajiv had cautiously started and ultimately changed the shape of India's economy.

As Rao came to power it was clear that the slowness of economic progress, the problems of inflation, the ineffectiveness of public enterprise and welfare, and the chronic lack of agricultural productivity (Bardhan 2010: 43; Frankel 1978: 548) had built to unsustainable levels, and India resorted to IMF and World Bank structural adjustment loans to survive a balance of payments crisis. Neoliberals argued that India had failed at both socialism and capitalism – the system fell between two stools (Guha 2007: 469). Poverty remained very severe in the 1970s, with around 223 million in poverty, just over 40% of the total population of 530 million (Guha 2007: 468). Sadly the results of the Congress Party's education policies were very poor, with around 40% of the population illiterate even today (Das 2000: xviii). Many argue that the socialism of the Nehru and Gandhi governments ultimately failed the poor (Das 2000; Guha 2007; Khanna 2009).

Central planning did lay something of a basis for India's growth and industrialization (Bardhan 2010: 8). It left, for example, high-value engineering, science and technology institutes which went on to play significant roles in India's rapidly growing IT sector (Guha 2007: 216). But since the mid-1980s criticism of the entire enterprise of planning and regulation have become ever more strident, especially as it became clear that the USSR was edging deeper into stagnation. Following the USSR's collapse in 1989, another major shift towards free-markets and an Indian 'variety of capitalism' started to emerge, albeit rather haltingly.

'A forward march by private enterprise': reforms, privatization and liberalization

By the early 1990s the flagging Indian economy had lurched into a balance of payments crisis, with an internal budget deficit of 55% of GDP, and interest payments on overseas debt at 23% of GDP (Yergin and Stanislaw 2002: 221). The new Prime Minister Rao appointed Manmohan Singh, an Oxford University Economics PhD, as Finance Minister and urged him to find drastic solutions. Looking overseas it was clear that other nations (notably South Korea) had dramatically outpaced India. The IMF loans were conditional on India carrying out 'structural adjustment programs' designed to liberalize the economy. Moreover, the collapse of the USSR seemed to have fatally discredited central planning as an option. Some described the strategy as 'Manmohanomics', with similar overtones of the radical 'Reaganomics' used in the 1980s to break the remnants of Keynesianism in the USA (Khanna 2007: 129–130). In a 'shock therapy' fashion commonly used in many of the world's regions (Klein 2007; McCann 2013), the sense of emergency and crisis were described as once in a lifetime opportunities through which changes had to be 'rammed' despite how unpopular they may be.

Singh's reforms encouraged a move to disorganized capitalism (Lash and Urry 1987) and have been described as 'a full scale attack on the state-controlled economy' (Yergin and Stanislaw 2002: 217). An emergency budget was issued in July 1991, in which the rupee was devalued, industrial subsidies were cut and import tariffs and quotas were removed. The license raj was all-but abolished (Panagariya 2008: 104). Foreign direct investment was encouraged and tariff barriers were lowered (Yergin and Stanislaw 2002: 222). Privatization began to happen, but not at the pace one would associate with 'shock therapy'. Khanna's figures (2009: 38) suggest a rather slow progress of privatization, indicating that 31% of all industrial assets belonged to state-owned enterprises (SOEs) in 2007, compared to 34% in 1991. Privatization and marketization were highly controversial, and therefore slow and problematic, processes. Khanna argues that the Indian government, unlike in China, failed to 'compensate the losers', and in a democracy those who lose out in reforms tend to form blocking coalitions against further change. Das describes the changes as 'slow, hesitant, incomplete' (2000: xi), but nevertheless compares them in scale and importance to Deng's Chinese reform programme begun in 1978. Annual GDP growth rates started to edge towards 4.8% in the 1980s, reaching rates of 6% or 7% in the 1990s (Panagariya 2008: 108).

Sensing the changes afoot, India's private firms were increasingly prepared to find ways around the permit raj. Good examples are the petrochemistry and textiles company Reliance and the automotive firm Bajaj Auto, a maker of petrol scooters who regularly exceeded government quotas.[12] Foreign-invested enterprises also began to grow, and some became very successful. One example is Hero Honda, a joint venture between Hero Cycles and the Japanese automotive giant formed in 1983 to produce vast numbers of cheap, fuel-efficient and reliable motorcycles (Khanna 2007: 128–9). The joint venture with Honda was dissolved in 2010 and Hero MotoCorp is now going it alone, perhaps symbolizing the strength and independence of the Indian company.

In the IT world, Texas Instruments first invested in Bangalore in 1985 (Yergin and Stanislaw 2002: 227), and even before this Indian graduates had for some time started to experience Westernized forms of services work. According to Xiang's ethnographic study of the Indian IT world, '[t]he term "body shopping" first surfaced in this context with the establishment in 1974 of Tata Consulting Services (TCS) in Mumbai, India's first export-oriented software-service company' (Xiang 2007: 5). 'Body shopping' refers to the practice whereby often relatively small-scale companies known officially as IT consulting firms but colloquially as 'body shops' recruit IT service workers on a stand-by and contract basis for specific IT jobs, thereby providing a low-cost insertion of Indian workers into global labour markets. Incentives have been provided by Indian states to draw global multinationals into using Indian labour, such as tax breaks and uprated infrastructure. Firms taking advantage of the opportunities of offshoring exploit the 9–12 hour time difference with the USA, giving Indian clients back-office processing work that can be done while American workers and customers are asleep. Wages and office rental costs are currently around one-fifth of the costs in US cities (Friedman 2006: 18). Over time, many Indian remote processing centres have moved up the value chain, embedding themselves into 'global value chains' by moving into higher-value work such as software coding and design, and consulting (Gereffi et al. 2005).

[12] 'India's Age of the Scooter Is Sputtering to a Halt', *The Times*, 11 December 2009.

Former communists became free market rightists. Guha quotes one such journalist who decried 'the smothering of free enterprise, a famine of consumer goods, and the tying down of millions of workers to ... soul-deadening techniques' in the Gandhi era and who now advocates reforms to stimulate 'a forward march by private enterprise' (Guha 2007: 693–694). It is here that analysts start to redefine India as globalized, marketized and 'open for business'. Examples of the mainstream, positive, business school or media line on India take on a similar narrative to those of the early years of post-communist Russia; of McDonald's outlets springing up and 'mom and pop' salesmen hawking Twix and Snickers bars on the street (Khanna 2007: 130). The next section will provide an overview of the emerging Indian 'variety of capitalism'.

'The India way'? An assessment of the contemporary Indian economy

In a real sign of the growing international profile of India, Thomas Friedman's multi-million selling *The World is Flat* (2006: 3-50) opens with a long chapter about the booming services economy of Bangalore. In a development that mirrors similar changes in China, sections of the USA look on India's growth with both admiration and trepidation, as the outsourcing of white-collar services and professional jobs to India mirrors the loss of blue-collar manufacturing jobs to China (see Chapter 10). In the USA in the mid-2000s there were several widely discussed presidential and congressional reports into offshoring (GAO 2005; Mankiw 2004), and offshoring briefly became a campaign issue in the 2004 Bush vs. Kerry presidential election. Much of the debate has circulated around predictions of how vulnerable the OECD nations are to widespread loss of well-paying middle-class jobs to low-cost countries via offshoring (Blinder 2006).[13] These debates reveal just how far India has come in a short space of time.

Despite India's dramatic progress, even the unashamedly pro-gloablization text *The Commanding Heights* by Yergin and Stanislaw admits that Bangalore 'remains an enclave amid an ocean of poverty and illiteracy' (2002: 229). The outsourcing or Information Technology Enabled Service (ITES) environment captures the extreme variation in India's emerging economy. Analysis of work cultures in Indian contact centres and back office service processing providers reveals high-technology connections to Western global clients, but also

[13] Blinder made a rough prediction that between 28–42 million US jobs are potentially offshorable (Blinder 2006).

monotony, an inauthentic and scripted environment, and low trust and near-zero formal discretion. Phil Taylor and Peter Bain's research on Indian call centres depicts an unpleasant working culture, characterized by a punishing regime of performance targets, incessant call demand, and a high burnout and turnover rate (see Exhibit 9.3).

Exhibit 9.3 'Assembly lines in the head' in Indian call centres

UK academics Phil Taylor and Peter Bain have researched the realities of working life in customer contact centres for a considerable time, and they expanded their focus from British to Indian workplaces. They coined the term 'an assembly line in the head' when referring to British call centres, and it would appear from their more recent work that Indian versions are similar or worse. Below are some excerpts from their 2005 paper on the Indian remote services sector which provide background context and a flavour of working conditions in this booming sector.

'The Indian industry originated in the mid-1990s when American Express, British Airways, and GE Capital established customer support operations and transaction processing services [...]'

'Policies stemming from successive Indian governments' commitment to economic reform and the tenets of the Washington consensus – liberalization, privatization, and globalization – have facilitated migration. Key initiatives include the provision of tax incentives and telecoms deregulation. In the neo-liberalist climate in which labour market deregulation is regarded as a prerequisite for growth in the 'new economy', states have legislated to benefit the industry. For example, lobbied by Nasscom, the Labour Department of Maharashtra relaxed regulations for forbidding women working at night [...]'

'The types of calls handled tend to be highly standardized, simple in content, tightly scripted, and of short duration. [...]'

'One experienced manager understood that 'taking 150 different calls a night is very difficult and there is high burnout, responsible even in "good" centres for 30–35 percent attrition. [...]'

A worker leaves home at 2pm, starts work at 5.30pm and after work reaches home at 5am. This is not a good thing, but a sure recipe for health problems.

'India largely hosts an extreme version of the mass production model.'

(Taylor and Bain 2005: 267–9, 271–2, 277)

Kiran Mirchandani (2012) wrote an important book based on 100 in-depth interviews with customer service agents working in India's ITES sector in New Delhi, Bangalore and Pune. Her interviewees reveal regimes of heavy standardization and intense workloads, with some staff complaining, for example, of feeling 'like a donkey' (2012: 80). Despite being tiring, emotionally draining and taking place during long and often very anti-social hours, the jobs are nevertheless attractive and comparatively well paid (2012: 77). She cites figures suggesting that the ITES sector employs 2.5 million workers in India across various fields such as back office processing, customer contact centres, software development and consulting. 'Total revenue from the sector has grown from five billion U.S. dollars in 1997 to seventy-two billion in 2009' (Mirchandani 2012: 2). The official body of the ITES sector suggests that the sector has recently been growing by around 24% annually (NASSCOM 2012: 16).

Parts of Indian industry have also developed rapidly in recent years, with several companies recently becoming internationally recognized. Perhaps most prominent is the Tata conglomerate (steel, automotive, IT). Another major player worldwide is Lakshmi Mittal, who left India for Indonesia in 1976 (Murphy 2008: 721) and eventually transformed the middle-sized Indian company Ispat into a global empire through acquiring steel producers around the world (Mexico, Trinidad and Tobago, Afghanistan) culminating in the purchase of the US giant Arcelor in 2006. This made Arcelor-Mittal the largest steel producer in the world (Pota 2010: 6). Registered in the Netherlands Antilles and in the Netherlands for tax purposes, and with its head office in London, it can perhaps hardly be called an Indian company at all (Murphy 2008). Although much less well-known, the Reliance petrochemistry and textiles giant is another major Indian company, which exports to over 100 countries in the world (Pota 2010: 4). Emblematic of the growth and sophistication of Indian multinationals is (ironically) a domestic development, namely the emergence of the Tata Nano (Witzel 2010). Launched in 2009, the Nano was envisaged as a 'one lakh car' or costing around US$1,800. This makes it significantly more expensive than a scooter, but affordable to millions of Indians. Clearly the manufacturers have economized (there is just one wing mirror and no air bags), but the car has been a success, with around 70,000 units sold by the end of 2010.[14] Bajaj Auto has also entered a joint venture with Renault-Nissan to build a competitor vehicle on sale for around US$2,500.[15]

At the upper end of the spectrum in 2008 Tata bought Jaguar-Land Rover from Ford when it ran into distress amid the subprime crisis. Along with many examples in China (see Chapter 10) this is another example of a firm from an emerging economy purchasing a struggling Western multinational in order to acquire technology, distribution chains and brand value. Ssangyong (a struggling Korean auto manufacturer) was purchased by Mahindra in 2011. The professional competence of Indian

[14] 'Tata Nano Car Sales Sink by 85%', *BBC News*, 1 December 2010.

[15] 'India's Age of the Scooter Is Sputtering to a Halt', *The Times*, 11 December 2009.

engineers is predicted to grow. Currently the UK produces 20,000 engineering graduates per year, whereas India produces 170,000.[16] India's cultural economy is also relatively high-profile, especially the so-called 'Bollywood' Indian movie industry which today not only makes films for domestic consumption but is increasingly linked into the value chains of Western products (such as cartoon animation, commercials and television programme production).

It is not surprising, therefore, that commentators in recession-hit Western nations are starting to heap praise on India in a way similar to how 'the Japanese model' was 'hyped' in the 1980s (see Chapter 11). A high-profile example of this trend is the work of Cappelli et al. (2010) on what they call 'The India Way', a management philosophy that combines high growth, corporate dynamism, enlightened forms of employment, and corporate social responsibility. The India Way appears similar to the measured and cautious pre-1980s managerial capitalism as exhibited in various historical forms in the USA, the UK or France (see Chapters 3–5). Shareholder value is a long way from being the core priority of Indian companies and top management. Instead, a broader range of stakeholders are considered amid a much wider contribution to society. Sizeable investments are made in human capital, with Cappelli and his colleagues writing approvingly of in-depth and lengthy training programmes for employees and paternalistic employment practices. At one point the authors even make a direct connection to Japanese practices (Cappelli et al. 2010: 15–16) as they provide examples of Indian companies that are reluctant to make redundancies unless they have absolutely no choice.

Contradictions emerge, however, in their analysis. As the article moves on, elements of cutting-edge Anglo-Saxon management and organizational forms are described as widespread in India, developments in keeping with what Boltanski and Chiapello (2005) would describe as the 'third spirit of capitalism'. At the Sasken Corporation, the organizational hierarchy is radically flat and status differentials between managers and workers are supposedly eliminated. At HCL '"command and control" is giving way to "collaborative management"' (Cappelli et al. 2010: 16–17). But critical research into the workplaces where such changes have been made some time ago (such as in the USA and UK) has often shown such developments to be problematic. When hierarchies are dissolved, spans of control for middle management grow to unsustainable levels, often causing stress, burnout and a collapse in morale (Hassard et al. 2009). Many employees are deeply cynical about the top management sloganeering that Cappelli et al. are so positive about in their article. Cappelli et al. focus only on senior

[16] 'Filling the Vacuum', *Guardian*, 24 July 2010.

executives and their official public announcements, and do not supplement their analysis with any voices from middle management and below, unlike Taylor and Bain (2005) or Mirchandani (2012). We are left in the dark as to what employees really feel about the realities of their work. Moreover, how can the 'second spirit of capitalism'-style paternalism of the India Way be squared with the neoliberal reform agenda launched by Rao and Singh? Will the much-praised managerial paternalism of Indian firms be able to survive when further demands for labour market flexibility and restructuring for shareholder value arise as they have in all advanced economies?

Although research into the ITES sector suggests that Indian labour–management relations are dominated by a low-trust culture, studies on industrial sectors provide complex and contradictory results, with no obvious trends about a general Indian labour and management systems. Instead there appears to be a wide range of managerial–labour relations in India. Joginder Singh (1990) argues that 'national culture' analyses in the mould of Hofstede's 'Values Survey Module' do not adequately capture the complexity and diversity of Indian forms of managerial behaviour, which ranges from consultative to authoritarian according to context, seniority, background and organizational form. Pro-business texts such as Pota (2010) and Witzel (2010) promote a picture of Indian managers and entrepreneurs who do nothing wrong, commercially or morally. Witzel's book is almost cultish in its promotion of the Tata company, family and brand. The reader learns that Tata provides a 'sense of emotional warmth and connection' in its service to the community; that it is an employer 'who will keep its promises', and has a 'halo' effect in which 'goodness rubs off on the employee' (Witzel 2010: 186–187). Such a picture is difficult to reconcile with the regular announcements of difficult restructurings that a company of Tata's size has had to make. Layoffs in its steel operations located in regions hit hard by decades of industrial decline are regularly reported in the British media, for example.[17]

Despite the claims of much of the free-market, pro-business literature, Indian society has not embraced capitalism in an unproblematic way. The legacy of Nehruvian socialism has probably had some influence in the reportedly high degree of attention paid to corporate social responsibility among Indian firms. Cappelli et al. (2010) claim that it is common for Indian companies to believe that the needs of money and profit should be subordinate to the needs of human beings. Indian unions are a reasonably powerful pressure group; they are certainly

[17] 'Tata Steel: 600 Welsh Jobs Cut, Mainly at Port Talbot'; 'Tata Steel to Cut 156 jobs in Yorkshire', *BBC News*, 23 November 2012; 'Tata Steel to Cut 1,500 Jobs in Scunthorpe and Teeside', *BBC News*, 20 May 2011.

genuinely independent from the state and are often vociferous (Ratnam and Verma 2011). However they represent a 'tiny fraction' of India's industrial workforce (Bardhan 2010: 33), with industrial sectors dominated by extremely small enterprises. Of manufacturing employment 87% is in 'microenterprises of fewer than ten employees' (Bardhan 2010: 35).

Indian infrastructure remains a problem: underpricing and theft of electrical power is rampant, leading to power cuts (Bardhan 2010: 56). The extent of highway building in India is very small in relation to China (Bardhan 2010: 63). Building projects often involve kickbacks and other forms of bribery: 'Foundation stones once laid with elaborate ceremony and etched with the name of now forgotten politicians litter the countryside in splendid isolation' (Bardhan 2010: 64).

Outside of the more economically developed regions, security is also a concern. Several armed separatist and revolutionary groups are active in India, such as in Kashmir and eastern regions sometimes labelled the 'Red Corridor'. The most notorious is the Communist Party of India (Maxist-Leninist), which has been responsible for numerous acts of violence (Gupta 2012: 286), but appears to have some support among deeply impoverished and isolated tribal groups. This Maoist insurgency is rarely, if ever, reported in pro-business works which looks to promote India as a vibrant, dynamic, and Westernizing economy. [18]

It is therefore important not to get carried away with the 'change is good' story that is so strongly promoted by free-market Western authors such as Friedman (2006) and Witzel (2010) or by Western-looking texts by Indian writers such as Das (2000) and Khanna (2007). For example, Khanna (2007: 130) suggests that in the decades of reform 'everyone had an uncle who was supplying bedspreads and linens to Macy's and a cousin who was a software engineer at Infosys'. Well, not everyone, obviously. There is no supplying to iconic New York department stores or 'symbolic analyst' jobs at Infosys for the millions trapped in chronic poverty. India has not experienced anything on the scale of China's labour-intensive rural industrialization, or rural reform. Growth is patchy and very unevenly distributed. Some have suggested that India's success in ITES suggests that the country may be able to leap over industrialization altogether and land in a new world of high-end IT services. But this sounds fanciful. Much of the Indian remote services sector involves labour-intensive, basic processing. The more cutting-edge services require expert

[18] 'India "Maoist" Bomb Blast Kills 15 Police', *BBC News*, 27 March 2012.

labour that is well paid and in short supply. Quite simply, India needs to find an industrial (and services) growth model that employs more people, rather like China's labour-intensive rural industrialization that seems to be the main driver of China's dramatic growth (Bardhan 2010: 13–14).

Child labour – although officially illegal in many forms (see Ratnam and Verma 2011: 352) – remains a notoriously persistent problem in India (Cigno and Rosati 2002). Campaigners estimate that as many as 11 million children are forced to work in India, many in potentially hazardous industries, such as the manufacturing of carpets, matchsticks and fireworks.[19] Bonded labour is also known to exist. This is where workers are forced to work to release them from some sort of a debt bond, often passed down through generations. This has also been illegal since 1976, but remains culturally entrenched in many regions (Srivastava 2005).

Although rates of poverty have been declining at increasing pace since the 1980s, around one in four of the entire Indian population exists on an income of less than one dollar per day (Gupta 2012: 4). The dysfunctional bureaucracy captured so vividly in Gupta's anthropological research into 'Block offices' in rural India perpetuates 'structural violence' on the poor; resources cannot reach impoverished families due to corruption, organizational failure and 'barely controlled chaos' (Gupta 2012: 14). This 'violence' causes perhaps 2 million unnecessary deaths per year (Gupta 2012: 5). The effectiveness, efficiency and fairness of welfare provision are indeed 'dismal' (Bardhan 2010: 16). Around 46% of children aged under three are underweight, as compared with 30% in sub-Saharan Africa and 8% in China (Bardhan 2010: 94). Educational opportunities are distributed extremely unfairly, to an extent comparable with the worst in the world (Bardhan 2010: 95–96). Around one-third of the residents of Kolkata and about half the population of Mumbai reside in slums (Gupta 2012: 3). 'An Indian's life expectancy is sixty-three years, lower than that in many poor countries. As many as sixty-five out of a thousand infants die ... Seventy-one percent cannot access sanitation. Four out of ten Indians are illiterate' (Das 2000: xiii).

Texts on India circulating the media and US-influenced business schools are divorced from these realities. They instead tend to focus on the 'dynamism' and 'entrepreneurialism' of Indian elites (Pota 2010; Witzel 2010). In reality the high cost of capital in India makes it hard to secure loans for small businesses, meaning a very large informal

---

[19] 'Child Labour – India's "Cheap Commodity"', *BBC News*, 13 June 2006.

sector.[20] India's financial sector is characterized by high levels of domestic savings but low levels of financial intermediation; Indians try to keep money aside because of economic uncertainty, but have few options extended to them by the underdeveloped banking industry that might help them become entrepreneurs, such as loans and mortgages (Bardhan 2010: 66). Government investment is also relatively low, contributing to infrastructure inadequacies. This is partly due to the long-term existence of government subsidies to industry and agriculture that are politically near-impossible to revoke and redirect into other projects (Bardhan 2010: 69–70).

According to Bardhan (2010: 91–2) China has a considerably better record than India of lifting its population above the poverty line. In 1981 around 73% of the Chinese population and 42% of the population of India lived in poverty, whereas in 2005 the figure for China was just 8.1% and in India 24.3%.

Media coverage of India often reports spectacular, elite, global-level features (such as the lavish spending of business leaders, or developments in sports and entertainment industries) reinforcing the impression of India's rapid growth and globalization. Examples include the formation of the Indian Premier League in cricket, and the development of an Indian Formula One team and racing circuit. In a seeming mimicry of the Russian oligarchs, Laksmi Mittal (along with Formula One tycoons Bernie Ecclestone and Flavio Briatore) purchased a major stake in the London football club Queen's Park Rangers in 2007. Top Indian elites are now comparable to those of the other BRICs in terms of their wealth and behaviour, disembedding themselves from their nation of origin, operating around the world and physically residing in London (perhaps to make use of the 'world class' opportunities it provides in the legal, financial and real estate worlds [Murphy 2008]). Some of these elites have been drawn into crises and/or scandals, especially as global (and Indian) growth slowed in the late 2000s. Vijay Mallya, billionaire chairman of Kingfisher Airlines and United Breweries (Holdings), is a good example. 'His troubles have coincided this year with India's own slow growth, high inflation, and corruption scandals that threaten the entrepreneurial self-confidence of an Asian economic juggernaut that likes to see itself taking on the world', reports *The Times of India.*[21] Often described as 'India's Richard Branson', and known for his

[20] The informal sector has been estimated at a stunning figure of 94% of the total workforce (Bardhan 2010: 78).

[21] 'Kingfisher Airlines Crisis: I Will Bounce Back, Says Vijay Mallya', *The Times of India*, 15 November 2011.

publicity-hungry and lavish lifestyle, Mallya owns cricket and Formula One teams, and a 312-foot yacht. But his Kingfisher Airlines ran into deep financial troubles in 2011, mirroring troubles in the rest of the industry. Air India has been effectively bankrupt almost in perpetuity (it is perhaps US$6 billion in debt), but the state has continued to supported it. A strike by airline pilots in 2012 was said to have cost the company more than £100 million.[22]

A major accounting scandal emerged at the Satyam software services firm (often reported as 'India's Enron'). In January 2009, its founder confessed to fraud and wrongdoing, admitting to accounting irregularities and the hiding of losses that went back years. In a now-famous statement, he wrote of 'riding a tiger, not knowing how to get off without getting eaten'.[23] In a perverse kind of way, corporate malfeasance on such a scale reveals how globalized and liberalized Indian global services has become, especially when global media make comparisons to Enron.

India has made considerable progress down the road to liberalism, but to some extent the imagery of globalization is projected onto India by globalized media. Fundamentally India remains a low-middle income economy. Important regulations and restrictions remain present in the Indian economy, including caps on totals of foreign direct investment (FDI) allowed into certain sectors, such as civil aviation, pensions and insurance.[24] Its position on the human development index is very weak in global terms: 134th among 182 nation-states (Gupta 2012: 3), and the dramatic unevenness and inequality of the economy's development is plain to see. Indian income distribution appears to be becoming unequal at a relatively slower rate than in many of the other rapidly developing societies. Gini figures (where available) suggest a still relatively egalitarian society (at 33.4 in 2005, up from 31.1 in 1983).[25] But such figures may be misleading. Bardhan (2010: 12), for example, claims rather convincingly that India is considerably less egalitarian than China when it comes to access to land, to educational and job opportunities, and to public services. His (2010: 159) analysis is somewhat pessimistic, signalling just how far India still has to go before it can genuinely be considered a major world economic power.

---

[22] 'Air India Pilots Call Off Strike', *BBC News*, 4 July 2012.

[23] 'Satyam Chief Raju Freed on Bail', *BBC News*, 19 August 2010.

[24] 'Economic Measures Will Help Reduce Fiscal Deficit: President Pranab Mukherjee', *The Times of India*, 14 November 2012.

[25] Gini coefficients taken from World Bank website: http://data.worldbank.org.

Conclusion

There is some value in placing an analysis of India alongside that of China. But in the final reckoning, India lags a considerable distance behind. There are undoubtedly some 'world class' developments in India (such as the ITES sector), but the persistently poor performance of human development indices arguably overshadow this (Gupta 2012). The Indian 'variety of capitalism' is weak as a 'model'. The Nehruvian system became ever more prone to crisis and stagnation, and after the Gandhi era the Indian government largely threw out the socialist model. In keeping with world trends, India embraced globalization, 'disorganized capitalism' and neoliberalism. Measured by the blunt instrument of GDP, India is now the fourth largest economy in the world (Gupta 2012: 3). Annual growth rates of 6–9% have been posted during the 2000s (Panagariya 2008: 3). But enormous problems with poverty and regional inequality persist. We perhaps need to have more patience in our analysis of timeframes of Indian growth; the insistence that India is now imagined as a globalized, 'open for business' model seems premature. Perhaps in time this will change. Das, for example, provides figures to suggest that annual growth since the 1991 reforms has been in the region of 5–7% annually, which has 'tripled the size of the middle class. Although the middle class is still only 18 per cent of India's one billion population, it is expected to become 50 percent within a generation' (2000: x). This appears somewhat optimistic, but as we've seen in other countries, economic 'miracles' can happen. In the meantime, India's emergent capitalism demonstrates dramatic unevenness – without denying the important strides made in much of the economy and in IT services in particular, overall the 'India Way' is perhaps less 'Shining' and 'Incredible' than its portrayal by certain political parties and in much of the business school literature.

Further reading

Chibber, V., (2003) *Locked in Place: State-Building and Late Industrialization in India*, Princeton, NJ: Princeton University Press.

This is a beautifully written and extremely useful book. It explains why India was unable to build an effective developmental state and compares this failure with the successful establishment of state-directed development in Korea. It is very detailed but also tightly focused, and provides a compelling and original account of Indian development and state dysfunction. It makes the vital point that industrial policy and state direction of the economy are not necessarily wrong in all circumstances as neoliberals often claim. Instead, Chibber explains why some countries possess the government capacity to manage and direct their economies and firms effectively (Korea, China) while others do not (India, the UK).

Bardhan, P., (2010) *Awakening Giants, Feet of Clay: Assessing the Economic Rise of China and India*, Princeton, NJ: Princeton University Press.

This is a very up-to-date and fresh account of Indian growth which also contains important comparative elements. It is refreshing to read less hysterical coverage of India (and China for that matter), as Bardhan is careful not to repeat the stereotypical and excited claims about 'astonishing' growth rates in India. The metaphor of 'feet of clay' is most useful in that it points to important enduring weaknesses in both China and India. His work is also interesting for refusing to follow the usual neoliberal line that India and China only started growing once they abandoned the 'failed experiments' of state planning, and notes the onset of growth in these economics began before significant liberalization. A useful book filled with interesting data and thoughtful interpretation.

Das, G., (2000) *India Unbound*, New York: Alfred A. Knopf.

The author is a playwright, novelist, public commentator and former senior executive, and the style of writing of this text is extremely attractive. It takes an orthodox neoliberal view on India's development and provides a damning critique of the restraints and controls of the Congress Party's socialism (especially the Indira and Rajiv eras). Das covers a huge amount of ground, and his recollections of Nehru's growth strategy and Manmohan Singh's reforms are very detailed and useful. His discussions of the need for Indian businesses to become lean and focused on one 'core competence' (based on his own experiences as an executive in Proctor and Gamble), are perhaps less original, and seem to mimic the 'throwaway' style of North American 'business guru' literatures.

TEN China: Multiple Models Amid Growth and Change

Chapter objectives

- To provide an historical overview of the economic and technological achievements of Chinese civilization before its puzzling stagnation and slowdown
- To show how China endured terrible hardship following partial colonization in the 19th century, which seriously retarded its prospects for economic growth
- To explore the emergence of the Maoist state-driven heavy industrialization strategy, and to note its successes, its failures, and its divergence from the Soviet model upon which it was based
- To describe the social organization of Chinese industry, especially the role that state-owned enterprises played in the construction of Chinese socialist society based on guaranteed lifetime employment for urban workers
- The deviation of the model, however, from the USSR was most important in that China was never able to fully replicate USSR-style modernization. Ultimately this set the course for China's abandonment of a planned economy and the move to market-led economic growth in the 1980s until today
- The chapter moves on to explore China's dramatic recent economic growth, pointing to both its strengths and prospects but also the often profound social costs and risks of marketization. In so doing, the chapter suggests that the Chinese 'variety of capitalism' is complex, distinct and significantly dissimilar to both Anglo-Saxon and CME models

Introduction

China's recent economic growth has been so remarkable that its labelling as a 'phenomenon' or 'miracle' is now a well-worn cliché (Knight and Ding 2012; Lin et al. 2003). In sheer scale (that is, measured by GDP) China overtook Japan as the world's number two economy in 2011 and it is widely predicted to overtake the USA as number one, perhaps as early as 2025.[1] Other measures are equally notable. In 2012, China moved above Japan in the number of companies listed in the *Fortune* Global 500, having 73 firms featured in the top 500 compared to Japan's 68 (and USA's 132).[2] China's rapid growth has long been one of the world's largest business news stories.

It is much less well known that China had already gained and lost world economic leadership in a prior age. In the 8th to the 12th centuries China was far ahead of Western nations in many aspects of technological and scientific development. Yet for complex reasons Chinese civilization lost developmental impetus in the 1400s–1700s, right about the time of the European Renaissance. The technology and sophistication gap between China and Europe was eventually closed over the 18th and 19th centuries, and China found itself rapidly overtaken by European powers and by Japan. China suffered many decades of political and military turmoil that severely hampered its chances of restoring some sort of economic and technical parity with the industrialized nations. It endured partial colonization by European powers and by Japan, and was engulfed in a prolonged civil war between the years 1927–50. What eventually emerged from these decades of struggle was a communist political and economic model, based around a Soviet-style 'big push industrialization' (see Chapter 8), as a desperate gambit to finally catch up and overtake the advanced powers. This 'New China' – the Peoples' Republic of China (PRC) – achieved some major economic and social successes, but was blighted by political and cultural authoritarianism and some disastrous policies that resulted in economic catastrophe and widespread misery.

Interestingly for this book's discussions of world variety in models and systems the Chinese model of communism diverged significantly from that of the USSR and a major political rift eventually opened up between Moscow and Beijing. China seemed to recognize the limitations

[1] 'China Overtakes Japan as World's Second-Biggest Economy', *BBC News*, 14 February 2011.

[2] 'China Overtakes Japan in Fortune Global 500 Companies for First Time', *CNBC*, 9 July 2012.

of state socialist economics and engaged in deep-seated and protracted reforms starting in 1978 and continuing to this day. While China remains a one-party state dominated by the Chinese Communist Party, its economic reforms have triggered rapid growth. The general movement of reform has been away from regulation and planning and towards markets and 'disorganized capitalism' (Lash and Urry 1987). This transition has broadly been a tremendous success, although huge problems continue to beset China, such as severe poverty, regional isolation and economic disparity, lack of democracy and adequate political representation, widespread economic informality, worker exploitation, political corruption and unfair forms of trading and governance (such as endemic violation of intellectual property rights).

The degree of change and disruption experienced is severe and in some ways similar to that endured by Russia, especially in China's chaotic first half of the 20th century. However, since the late 1970s the leadership of the PRC has somehow managed to oversee growth and change amid reasonable stability. China did not experience a horrendous political and social collapse as in Russia and most of the other former Soviet states. Instead, China has undertaken reform within the broad institutional contours of Chinese state socialism, managing to reform and partially preserve the system rather than overseeing a collapse that necessitated the painful and extremely difficult building of a totally new socio-economic model.

Some describe the contemporary Chinese model as one of 'state capitalism'[3] or 'local state corporatism' (Oi 1995), or even 'market socialism' (Garrick 2012) – a mixed economy in which the state plays a dominant, but far from exclusive role. Although in many ways similar to other East Asian growth trajectories (Chang 2006; Johnson 2002; Wade 2003), China's growth strategy has featured multiple tactics and 'models'. Its growth has been sustained since the late 1970s, involving privatization of state-owned enterprises and the general 'transition' away from state socialist planning, alongside a massive influx of foreign investment and very significant levels of overseas trade and exports to Western nations. But alongside all of these moves towards greater marketization and global openness, China has maintained important forms of state governance and planning over the economy (including capital controls which, in the eyes of America at least, constitute unfair forms of currency manipulation). The broader communist political and cultural system has not collapsed, inviting critique from Western democracies about human rights violations

[3] *The Economist* magazine (very much a neoliberal, business-friendly publication), produced a lengthy special report on 'State Capitalism'. 'The Visible Hand', *The Economist*, 21 January 2012.

(when the political timing suits them). Many believe there is a lot more economic development still to come with this mixture of models, even as the Chinese state continues to dominate 'the commanding heights' of the economy. China falls outside of the scope of the early classics on industrial structure or comparative management systems. Its development came far too late for it to appear in, for example, Shonfield's (1965) *Modern Capitalism*, Chandler's (1990) *Scale and Scope* or even McCraw's (1997a) *Creating Modern Capitalism*. This exclusion is coming to an end, it seems, as academic and popular writings on China have mushroomed in recent years.

The literature is often contradictory. Some claim that China has made massive progress towards an open and globalized capitalist system (such as Brandt and Rawski 2008: 14) while others (notably Huang 2008, 2010) maintain that China remains a totalitarian state that resents and suppresses free markets and entrepreneurialism. This chapter will chart a path through these complex debates, by outlining the various historical stages that Chinese economy, government and firms went through, including its rapid growth in ancient times before its period of stagnation and subjugation by richer powers, to its dramatic attempt to break out of 'backwardness' through a Soviet-style crash industrialization programme, to the reforms and eventual emergence of today's multiple models. Ultimately it suggests that China's restructuring and growth strategy is very much an unfinished project that continues to evolve. The reader may note that the tone of this chapter is not as optimistic as many current 'miracle'-style writings on China. It notes in detail the currently severe problems that China confronts, especially those of poverty-level wages and exploitation, and of endemic political corruption.

In general the recent story of China is one of very impressive growth, especially when considered in the light of some of the horrors it endured in prior periods. Its model is hard to pinpoint accurately. There are obvious parallels with the USSR command economy, but more general, perhaps less precise, comparisons can be made with a range of other economic models and development strategies, especially the Asian 'tigers'. Protectionist 'infant industry protection programmes' (as seen in prior American history) were also used, and recent tactics designed to protect strategic Chinese firms have echoes of French-style 'national champion' policies. Since the late 1970s into this complex mix is added massive overseas foreign direct investment, economic liberalization and the growth of domestic private corporations. Some of the major overseas entrants have brought in US-style corporate governance and market-oriented approaches, which some leading-edge domestic Chinese corporations are also claiming to adopt and emulate. There are some clear problems facing China and some commentators point to ominous signs of property asset price bubbles,[4] widespread non-performing loans (Allen et al. 2008: 507), excess industrial capacity and deflation (Lin et al. 2003: 257–275). It seems likely, however, that China will continue to grow in importance and influence. With a population of around 1.4 billion, a GDP of US$7.318 trillion[5] and the world's third largest landmass after Russia and Canada (Naughton 2007: 1) it shows all the signs of being a very major - and growing - force in the global politico-economic area.

From early leadership to stagnation and decline

Chinese civilization is one of the oldest and most influential in the world, boasting rich traditions in literature, philosophy, political theory and law, medicine, and the arts and sciences (Needham 1965; Witzel 2012). Throughout long spells of history China was economically far ahead of Europe. The first Chinese empire, the Qin dynasty, was formed in 221 BCE and there were arguably signs of a 'market economy' of sorts as early as 300 BCE (Lin 1995: 269). Chinese population was considerably larger than that of Europe during this time (Lin 1995: 273) and has consistently remained larger ever since. China in ancient and early modern times developed a huge array of sophisticated technological innovations. Huge advances were made in agricultural techniques to maximize crop yields, using methods perhaps 500 years in advance of Europe (Lin 1995: 270). China also lead the Europeans in iron-making capacity 'by a millennium and a half' (Mokyr 1990: 210), becoming the world's earliest adopter of blast furnaces to create cast iron and wrought iron. Water power was harnessed to drive bellows to assist the ironworking process. The spinning wheel appears to have been developed at about the same time as in the West, but China surpassed Europe in many other technologies vital for economic development, such as paper, printing, gunpowder and the compass (Lin 1995: 270). Chinese inventors also famously developed extraordinarily complex items such as astronomical clocks (Needham 1965: 446). China's shipbuilding capacity was also highly advanced (Needham 1965: 418). China was a world leader in the manufacturing of porcelain, explosives, kites and various chemical compounds (Mokyr 1990: 218).

[4] 'China Bubble in "Danger Zone" Warns Bank of Japan', *Daily Telegraph*, 28 September 2012.

[5] 2011 World Bank estimates of GDP and population, http://data.worldbank.org/country/china.

Joseph Needham's (1965) monumental multi-volume study *Science and Civilization in China* overflows with mind-boggling detail on China's scientific and industrial achievements. He writes that China seems to have been the earliest inventor of trip hammers (third and fourth centuries CE) the use of which became central to British and European industrialization until the 18th century (Needham 1965: 390–392). China seems also to have developed a kind of proto-Bessemer process in the 11th century, about 800 years before the process was developed (and named) in the UK (and simultaneously in the USA) (Mokyr 1990: 220). The economic historian Joel Mokyr suggests, therefore, that China was 'about to undergo a process eerily similar to the great British Industrial Revolution' (1990: 213).

All of the above begs the question as to why China did not continue to grow at such a pace, and why the explosive growth of mass industrialization instead occurred in the UK and Europe. A full explanation is well beyond the scope of this book. One reason is probably that China did not pursue the kind of aggressive expansion of overseas trade (often backed by military force or its threat) carried out by many European powers. It lacked Europe's large demand for foreign goods, developing nothing like an East India Company sent overseas to forcibly establish trade relations. This kind of freezing-out of international economic activity probably could not have occurred in Europe as no one nation or power structure controlled the whole continent. To a degree, it was a demand problem – the need to develop further labour-saving technology declined due to China's huge population. Cheap labour costs obviated the need for China to 'move up the value chain' – an issue with future echoes to today's China, perhaps.

Lin (1995), however, believes that the answer was really one of supply; for a complex set of reasons Chinese society in the 14th–18th centuries lost the ability or will to continue developing and applying new technologies. One reason may be that the dominant Chinese bureaucratic authorities stifled competition and the development of new ideas that may threaten political stability and the status quo (Mokyr 1990: 231). Chinese society seemed to 'forget' how to make use of some of the inventions it had developed centuries before. Chinese elites in 1583 were reportedly astounded by the modernity of Western mechanical clocks brought to the mainland from Macao by Jesuit missionaries (Needham 1965: 436). Once again the importance of institutions in shaping and constraining the range of available options for economic action comes to the fore. A similar situation seems to pertain in modern Chinese history, specifically when the Communist Party elite engages in radical shifts of policy which change the *motivations and incentives* surrounding the purpose and nature of economic action (Oi 1995: 1136). Mao's 'Great Leap

Forward' in the 1960s and the various reform processes initiated by Deng in the 1980s are particularly important examples.

While this is, of course, true of all political economies, Chinese history seems to indicate a particular importance of state authority in structuring what is possible, economically and politically. Mokyr (1990: 238) argues that there were 'no substitutes for the state' in that state authority sponsored and legitimized economic and scientific developments. This meant that economic growth was dangerously dependent on the whims of political elites. Support could be withdrawn by the political mandarins, which could stymie growth and inventiveness.[6] By contrast, states seemed to play a more arms-length role in Europe, as buyers, sellers and as the setters of economic rules. In China the state was a much more dominant force in culture, society and economy, meaning that markets, entrepreneurialism and competition were less developed than in other contexts (Mokyr 1990: 235). This criticism of China is very much applied to China today, especially by economists who are critical of the communist state (such as Huang 2008, 2010). Mokyr even states that 'China has always been a one party state', a phrase he attributes to Needham (Mokyr 1990: 236). Thus, according to Knight and Ding, 'Europe had developed arrangements in which capitalism and innovation could flourish but China had not' (2012: 5).

Even with the economic and scientific advances noted above, the Chinese economy and society remained overwhelmingly rural, with over 90% of the population living in the countryside throughout this period (Naughton 2007: 34). Historians such as Needham and Mokyr emphasize the role of sophisticated technologies, but their operation also necessitated the application of 'massive human labor to small plots of farmland' (Naughton 2007: 35), meaning very low standards of living. China experienced huge population growth – from around 72 million in 1400 to 381 million by 1820 (Naughton 2007: 36). Living standards seemed stable but the kind of explosive, self-sustaining industrial growth seen in Europe as (explored by authors such as Landes [2003], Mathias [1969] and Mokyr [2009]) failed to emerge in China. Naughton characterizes the economy as 'small-scale, bottom-heavy' (2007: 37–38), largely a household-based economy with little capital and no large-scale operations either in agriculture or industry. Tea export was lucrative, but small-scale and diffuse and unable to compete with Japanese and Indian standardized and high-quality 'bulk'

[6] Interestingly, the term 'mandarins' is also used in contemporary Britain, often in a pejorative way, to describe senior civil service bureaucrats. Critics describe 'mandarins' as unaccountable and accuse them of trying to 'pick winners', or for generally interfering in and micromanaging economic activity to the detriment of free market competition.

exports (Naughton 2007: 38). Cotton was spun across much of China, but large-scale, industrialized and factory-organized cotton mills did not emerge until the 20th century, considerably later than the emergence of the factory system in the UK (Naughton 2007: 38).

As in other developing nations (see Chapter 8 on Russia, for example) economic modernization was dependent to a great extent on state authority to approve and diffuse new technologies. See the passage in Exhibit 10.1 from Mokyr.

Exhibit 10.1 Long-term path-dependency in Chinese development

Joel Mokyr is one of the world's authorities on economic history, especially the roles played by science, technology and education in economic growth. Here he describes early Chinese modernization and points to signs of path-dependency that may be of relevance to contemporary China. While some might regard this passage as somewhat patronising towards China, it is likely to contain at least a kernel of truth:

'The difference between China and Europe was that in Europe the power of any social group to sabotage an innovation it deemed detrimental to its interests was far smaller. First, in Europe technological change was essentially a matter of private initiative; the role of rulers was usually secondary and passive. Few significant contributions to nonmilitary technology were initiated by the state in Europe before (or during) the Industrial Revolution. There was a market for ideas, and the government entered these markets as just another customer or, more rarely, another supplier. Second, whenever a European government chose to take an actively hostile attitude toward innovation and the nonconformism that bred it, it had to face the consequences in terms of its relative status in the economic (and thus, eventually, political) hierarchy. Moreover, the possibilities of migration within Europe allowed creative and original thinkers to find a haven if their place of birth was insufficiently tolerant, so that in the long run, reactionary societies lost out in the competition for wealth and power.'

(Mokyr 1990: 233)

Having made some progress however, China seemed to withdraw from the kind of state-sponsored process of infrastructure-building (roads, railroads) and systems (standardized systems of weights and measures, commercial law, tax-collection, law enforcement, education strategies), that all seemed central to European (and latterly Russian) development (see Chapters 4, 5, 6 and 8). Mokyr's (1990) rather gloomy prognosis of Chinese stagnation is disputed by some economists who were more optimistic about the institutional foundations of pre-revolutionary China's economy (Naughton 2007: 36), pointing to the existence of paper money, written contracts, legal and customary institutions, and even banks. China's comparative economic stasis lasted throughout the Qing Dynasty (1644–1911), the latter half of this period exactly when

Europe, USA, then belatedly Japan, industrialized and in many cases established and ran international empires or at least international trading routes and overseas financial relationships. The Chinese state's attempts to modernize were weakened from near constant political strife such as the Taiping Rebellion (civil war) of 1850–64. The Chinese state did try to bring in and learn from advanced Western science and technology, but seemed to lack the capacity to fully carry out an effective technology transfer policy (Hu and Henderson 2008: 290–291). It is not wrong for the state to be involved in economic growth *per se*, but involvement needs to come in a form that supports the economy and does not dominate or distort it to such a degree that self-sustaining economic development becomes impossible (Ohno 2012; Oi 1995; Wade 2003). State-led economic growth is 'a tricky strategy to execute and has many hidden consequences' (Johnson 2002: 150).

China was eventually forced out of isolation and stagnation by exogenous shocks. It found itself economically, militarily and strategically behind the rising powers. China appeared to experience its own version of Japan's famous 'black ships' episode as British 'gunboat diplomacy' forcibly open the so-called Treaty Ports in China following the end of the first Opium War in 1842 (Mokyr 1990: 219; Naughton 2007: 41–42). Very harsh terms of trade were imposed on China backed up by military force or its threat – Britain's steam-powered vessels had the ability to sail upstream and use powerful weaponry. Unlike Japan, however, China seemed unable to respond effectively to this form of hostile globalization. Japan responded to its forced opening up to European and American trade by bringing in Western European technology 'lock, stock and barrel' (Mokyr 1990: 231), rapidly borrowing from and improving on Western standards of science, technology and education (see Chapter 11). Japan's growth and its own imperialist expansion eventually lead it to replace China as the dominant power in Asia (Naughton 2007: 42).

Formerly the world's premier economic and scientific power, China had been humiliated by European powers. China was repeatedly defeated in trade disputes and wars, such as the Opium War of 1839–42 in which it was forced to cede the island of Hong Kong to the UK (Johnson 2002: 44, 164). (It later lost territory to Russia after the Second Opium War of 1856–60.) Moreover, economic and social change was, as in other late industrializing nations, leading to revolutionary pressures. Revolutionary leader Sun Yat-Sen declared a republic in 1911, and the last Chinese emperor abdicated in 1912. Education was becoming more widely available and more radical political and economic literature was being published as part of the New Culture Movement (Benton and Chun 2010: 7). A teenaged Mao Zedong came across the writings of Zheng Guanying, for example, who wrote of the urgent need for China to emulate Western industrial and political modernization or face national catastrophe (Spence 1999: 6). In 1913, he began to read the giants of European philosophical, economic and political theory, such as Adam Smith and Karl Marx (Spence 1999: 22).

Major political turbulence continued throughout this region. In 1931, Japanese forces invaded Manchuria, establishing the puppet regime of Manchukuo. The Japanese oversaw rapid industrialization of the region. The Yangtze River Delta (a large region around Shanghai) was another major growth pole (Brandt and Rawski 2008: 4). China was modernizing and liberalizing between the 1910s and the 1930s. Growth was afoot (Rawski 1989), but China's share of world GDP fell relative to other nations (Naughton 2007: 42–43) partially because China was held back during this period by near-continual political strife, violence and the threat of colonization right through the years 1839–1945. A Nationalist government based at Nanjing existed between the years 1927–37. Throughout this period there were on–off hostilities with the Communists (Naughton 2007: 43). Both nationalists and communists fought against the Japanese in the Second Sino-Japanese war (1937), a conflict that merged into the broader Pacific Theatre of the Second World War. Throughout this period of conflict, China suffered around 20 million deaths (Bullock 1991: 1087). After Japan's defeat in the Second World War the two political factions could not coexist. The US tried to broker an alliance and encourage a unified government, but it was not to be. Eventually it was the Communist Party of China (CPC) led by Mao Zedong (1893–1976) that emerged victorious from the civil war, ushering in a dramatic new era for Chinese history. In American foreign policy circles China was regarded as having been 'lost' to communism.

Vigour and chaos: the planned economy of the People's Republic of China

The new communist leadership established a political system similar to the USSR – a one-party state featuring bureaucratic ministries and commissions to control all manner of social and economic affairs, with the Politburu and Central Committee of the Party 'at the heart of power in China' (Mastel 1997: 44). The Party was determined to rapidly close the gap with the foreign powers. The overall size of the economy was slightly smaller than that of India (Naughton 2007: 50). Agriculture made up around 70% of the PRC's economy, and of the 30% made up by industry, just 7.9% was classified as the kind of 'heavy' industry needed for major industrial expansion and military build-up. Much like Stalin's industrialization drive in the USSR (Chapter 8), Mao and the CPC leadership focused on this specific area of the economy (heavy industry) in a desperate attempt to rapidly emulate Western powers. Like the USSR, China felt encircled and threatened by capitalist powers, and it was intent on arming itself. It entered the Korean war, leading it to a stalemate, and remained at war with the vestiges of the Nationalist regime that had fled to Taiwan.

'Big push industrialization' involved the forcible investment of a huge percentage of national wealth, similar to the strategies used in the USSR.[7] A planning apparatus was set up to oversee the development of Five Year Plans. A ministerial system was adopted for the oversight of industrial and agricultural sectors of the economy and for the enterprises and collectives charged with 'realizing' the plans. The officially stated goal of the Party was for China to overtake the UK and catch up with the USA (Lin et al. 2003: 39). It had to radically distort the economic system to do so. It could not extract much wealth from the peasantry in the form of taxation, so the PRC leadership decided to lower the cost of developing industry by setting the lowest possible interest rates, paying the lowest possible wages for labour and the lowest possible prices for inputs, such as electric power and raw materials (Lin et al. 2003: 40–42). Under the plan targets, domestic consumption was kept extremely low, perpetuating low living standards (Naughton 2007: 56). All industrial workers were placed on a national income scale of 8 bands, with average wages estimated as equivalent to around US$200 per year (Lin et al. 2003: 43). Prices were fixed for all goods at very low levels, which resulted in high demand for these products but little incentive to produce them. Demand outpaced supply and shortage was constant for many goods, a problem common to state socialist models (Lin et al. 2003: 46). Under a market economy shortage would be expected to push prices back up, but this cannot be allowed to happen under state socialism where the 'immiserating' capitalist system had been supposedly abolished. In other words, markets cannot be allowed to set prices and distribute goods because this would constitute profiteering and exploitation. Instead, the command-administrative system or planned economy is introduced to act *in place of* markets.

Despite some dreadful inefficiencies the system did achieve impressive growth, averaging annual growth rates of around 4.2% GNP per capita between 1950–75 (Brandt and Rawski 2008: 5).

[7] Soviet technical advisors were invited to China and played a significant role in building China's emulation of the Stalinist growth model and the transfer of technology (Brandt and Rawski 2008: 4; Naughton 2007: 354).

Macro-level improvements in life expectancy and living standards were significant (Brandt and Rawski 2008: 5) even when taking into account the disasters of the 'Great Leap Forward' (see below).[8] Banks were nationalized between 1949–52 and the People's Bank of China was formed as a 'monobanking' system that controlled all major financial flows in the economy but acted in a 'passive' fashion, with finance part of a system of control embedded within the goals of realizing the plan, 'rather than to independently influence resource allocation flows' (Knight and Ding 2012: 41; Naughton 2007: 61).

The system, however, was not as strongly centralized as the USSR version it was modelled on. This meant a more significant role for local planning administrators and comparatively less power for central planning and the economic ministries (a feature that became important as the system started to reform, see below). Small industrial enterprises were also more important than in the USSR. The PRC lacked the major transport and communication infrastructure of the USSR and the nation was economically less developed than the Soviet Union. The PRC launched many Stalinist-type 'showpiece' industrial projects, but these were implanted on top of a largely agrarian and fragmented economy. Industrial enterprises were given very little managerial autonomy (Naughton 2007: 61). Maoism was also associated with rigid political and cultural controls, including heavily ideologically-driven policies such as the 'sending down' of party cadres from cities 'to the countryside' for little economic purpose (Brandt and Rawski 2008: 7). There were no real labour markets in Mao's China – instead citizens were appointed to jobs through the *nomenklatura* system.

In spite of its obvious weaknesses the system did lead to major improvements for several social strata. Urban dwellers had access to a form of Soviet-style industrial modernity, including guaranteed employment security (often given the epithet 'the iron rice bowl') in a rather extreme form of paternalistic employment found in SOEs. Industrial enterprises were known as *danwei* or 'work unit', and employment was less a selling of labour in a business organization, and more a membership of a society. The industrial enterprise (as *danwei*) was envisaged as the microcosm of socialist society, where all workers had jobs for life and received important fringe benefits for themselves and their dependents, such as cheap or free healthcare, childcare, housing, schooling and vacations (again clearly modelled on the *sotskultbyt* of the Soviet enterprise, see Chapter 8). There were no independent trade unions to

[8] A famous policy that highlights the populist, pragmatic, cheap but sometimes effective approach of Maoism was the introduction of rural paramedics known as 'barefoot doctors' (Naughton 2007: 244–245).

represent workers. Although in theory able to protest and even go on strike, unions were administered by the Party and had little power to resist enterprise management. In theory they should never have the need to. Instead the unions' role was to act as the 'transmission belt' of cultural and political values from the Party to the workers, and to administer and distribute fringe benefits to workers. Walder (1986) famously described employment relations in China as 'communist neo-traditionalism' suggesting that the Chinese version of state socialism was quite well matched with the traditional cultural values of patrimonialism, 'harmony', communitarian relations and paternalism that are emphasized by many writers on China (Hwang 1987; Redding and Witt 2007: 86–87). While most studies of China portray the mass of industrial workers in a completely passive or even invisible role, others point to widespread opposition and conflict between the interests of workers and the state that was supposed to represent them (Sheehan 1998).

In any case contradictions were built into the system that limited its prospects for sustained growth without reform. According to critics such as Lin et al. (2003: 29) the policy of capital-intensive, heavy industrial growth clashed with the reality of the low levels of capital available for investment. Everything was subordinated to a bold vision of state socialism; with 'crash' industrialization and militarization placed top of the agenda. Management of enterprises was often conducted in military fashion and in some cases actually run by military commanders (Naughton 2007: 76). 'Realizing the plan' was the number one target and managerial discretion was minimal.

The replication of much of the Stalinist strategies meant that output grew hugely but at tremendous personal cost to workers and citizens. Living standards rose slowly as wages were kept low and consumer products were largely unavailable as the building of heavy industry was set as the regime's prime objective. Meanwhile the economies of Hong Kong, Singapore and Taiwan pressed ahead, causing much consternation. (In some way these much smaller Asian regions became the model for China's reforms at the end of the 1970s.) There were many complex power struggles at central and local levels of China's political leadership. Mao is often described as unpredictable and 'eccentric' (Spence 1999). Policy changes were common, leading to a 'surge and slump' pattern of industrial output as norms and inputs fluctuated according to political manoeuvrings (see Figure 10.1). Lin et al. (2003: xxxi) name this the 'vigour/chaos cycle' – a volatile and irrational situation that made effective planning for sustainable economic development very difficult. Policymaking procedures were shrouded in secrecy, corruption and a lack of clarity (problems that persist to a large extent to this day).

The opening years of the first Five Year Plan (up to 1953) were broadly successful and – not unlike Lenin's New Economic Policy in

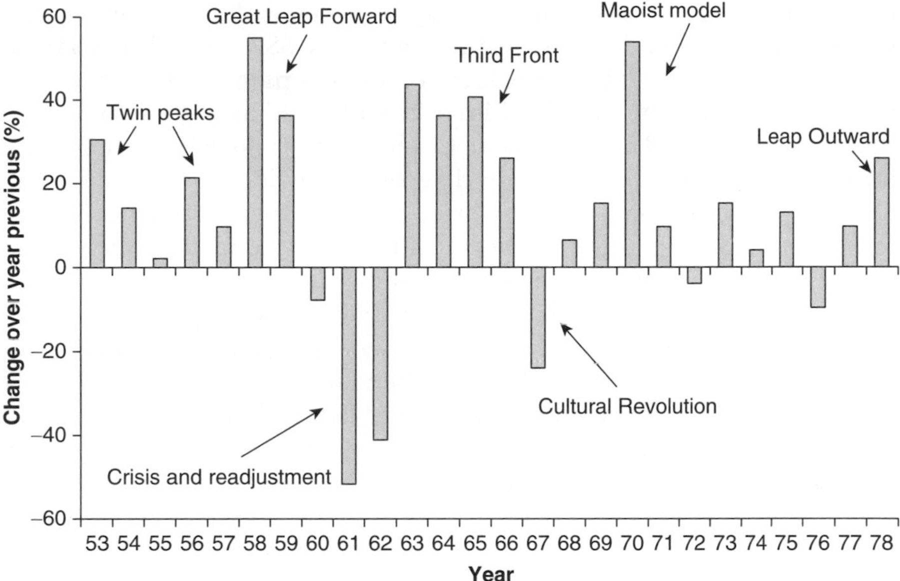

Figure 10.1 'Leaps' and crises in Chinese Growth

Source: Naughton 2007: 63. By permission of the MIT Press.

the early days of the Soviet economy - involved private business and a mixed economy. In its later period, however, the first Five Year Plan took a more totalitarian turn, with the period officially labelled as 'the high tide of socialism' (Naughton 2007: 67). During this time Mao pressed on with agricultural collectivization and private ownership of business became 'extinguished'.

The level of state control over the economy waned again in 1956–7 with some elements of markets again tolerated under the so-called 'Hundred Flowers' movement, a development that perhaps prefigured some of the reforms initiated in 1978 (Naughton 2007: 68). Then disaster struck. Apparently frustrated by what he perceived to be slow progress, Mao initiated a sudden change of policy, known as the 'Great Leap Forward' designed to further accelerate the crash industrialization programme and result in a quantum leap towards 'full' communism. This involved curtailing agricultural land use in order to produce cotton crops for export to fund further industrialization. The tragic result was a mass famine in the years 1959–61. Estimates often put the sum total of people killed by famine at 30 million (Johnson 2002: 151; Lin et al. 2003: 58).

Political repression became more severe. Around 800,000 citizens were condemned for their support for the 'Hundred Flowers' era and were imprisoned, accused of being 'Rightists', that is, too sympathetic to capitalism. This ugly episode is similar to the worst kinds of Stalinist paranoia and self-destructiveness. The leadership of the USSR appeared to be concerned. Soviet industrial experts were withdrawn during the period and relations between China and the USSR started to worsen, culminating in the 'Sino-Soviet split'. Mao, upset by Khrushchev's criticism of Stalinism, labelled him a 'deviationist' and came to believe that the USSR would not support China if the Cold War degenerated into an actual war. It did not help that the USSR sided with India in the (luckily very brief) Sino-Indian war of 1962. Further turbulence was to follow as Mao opened the so-called 'Third Front' to try to enhance the industrial capacity of China's more inland regions, partly out of fear of worsening international relations given the USA's deepening involvement in the Vietnam conflict. Another grave episode of political disruption occurred known as the 'Cultural Revolution' of 1967–9, an era of political purges, again involving mass denunciations and arrests. Historical analyses differ on the extent and importance of this episode, with most of the mainstream Western literature regarding it as a violent attempt by Mao to re-assert his power after the failures of the 'Great Leap', marginalizing criticism by surrounding himself with obsequious supporters – a typical 'totalitarian' power move. Others see the period more as a brief era where control was loosened to such a degree that dissent and discussion in the authoritarian system was finally allowed to appear, with much of the conflict surrounding the critical issue of who has the power to organize and run industrial enterprises (an issue that again survives in some form today [Sheehan 1998]).

In common with state socialist systems, Maoism generated considerable industrial growth at macro-level at the expense of instituting severe distortion and lack of efficiency at the micro-level (Lin et al 2003: 69). As in Five Year Plan USSR there are numerous fables of inappropriate incentives and perverse outcomes, such as factory directors deliberately turning out extremely heavy road vehicles because they were being monitored to hit output targets based on tonnage rather than quality (Kotkin 1997: 63, 64–65). There was widespread falsification and 'gaming' of the target system. As quality was sacrificed in the race to hit output targets, the 'output' was often defective meaning the target-driven planning system was actually counterproductive for the goal of rapid industrialization. The 'customer' (in reality other parts of the command economy) could not return the items, withhold payment or look elsewhere if it was unhappy with the product as supplied, so producers had insufficient incentive to focus on quality. It was quite common for defects to arise, such as cracks in steel production, but the order would be shipped regardless. Chinese and Soviet systems of industrial target-setting are often cited as prominent examples of 'goals gone wild' (Ordonez et al. 2009); in that the targets themselves (rather than the production outcomes that the targets are supposed to encourage) become the goal for action. Managers resolve to hit the targets at any cost, even if doing so perverts, distorts and defeats the broader principles.

Many extend this argument to the nature of the state socialist employment relation. Lin et al. (2003: 70) argue that the planning apparatus not only gave enterprises no incentive to work efficiently but in addition the rigid national wage structure gave workers no incentive to work hard. They note 'widespread free-riding' (Lin et al. 2003: 88). Brandt and Rawski use the term 'shirking' (2008: 6). While there are clear elements of truth to this picture, it ignores the real and symbolic importance of the *danwei* for its members. The provision of meaningful and secure employment gave people something to believe in and created (at least in urban areas) secure and improving socio-economic status for urban workers and very low levels of income inequality. Today one can obviously criticise the deep unpleasantness of Maoist political intrigue, the totalitarian cultural control, violence, and sidelining of dissent, but Mao also oversaw a major socio-economic development of his nation, which clearly engendered solidarity and a strong national mission for some. Annual investment in industrial development hit a rate of around 25% of GDP with 11% widely understood as the minimum required for self-sustaining growth (Lin 1995: 275). As Table 10.1 indicates, even with the dysfunctionality of the system and the horrors of the Great Leap Forward, Chinese economy grew substantially during the first series of Five Year Plans.

Table 10.1 Economic results of the Five Year Plans

	Output value of industry and agriculture	GDP	National income
First FYP	10.9	9.1	8.9
Second FYP	0.6	–2.2	–3.1
1963–5	15.7	14.9	14.7
Third FYP	9.6	6.9	8.3
Fourth FYP	7.8	5.5	5.5
1976–8	8.0	5.8	5.6
1953–78	8.2	6.0	6.0

Source: National Bureua of Statistics of China, as quoted in Lin et al (2003: 71)

The Maoist system eventually matured. Recovering from the turbulence of the Great Leap and the Cultural Revolution, from 1953–78 the economy continued to grow swiftly, posting average GDP growth rates of 6%, higher than world average and slightly lower than South Korean and Taiwanese rates (Lin et al. 2003: 70). Brandt and Rawski (2008: 5) put the average figure for GDP per capita growth around this period at 4.2% per annum, outpacing nations such as Brazil, Egypt,

India, Indonesia, and Mexico. After some horrific errors, China, like the USSR, had eventually laid the basis for an industrialized society. Life expectancy at birth had risen from perhaps as low as 30 in the early 20th century to approximately 50 in 1957 and then 60 in the mid-1960s and 1970s (Naughton 2007: 82). School enrolments increased dramatically. By 1978, the proportion of the population that had not completed primary school fell to 40%, down from 74% in 1952 (Brandt and Rawski 2008: 5). By 1978, industry accounted for 46.8% of total national income, up from just 12.6% in 1949 (Lin et al. 2003: 70–71). One major weakness - as with the USSR - was extremely low levels of GDP per capita - in other words the working class were largely impoverished in the so-called workers' state. While basic provisions were increasingly provided for under the modernization drive (free education and health, guaranteed employment and fixed wages for urban citizens) (Knight and Ding 2012: 43) general living standards were low, and wages were very low meaning few domestic savings and no broader base for further growth. Estimates of Chinese GDP per capita in 1977 were US$220 *per year* (Lin et al. 2003: 72). Household consumption grew only 2.3% annually between 1952–78 (Naughton 2007: 80).

Another problem common to state socialist systems was the chronic underutilization of labour. Even as the structure of the whole economy moved rapidly towards industry, as much as 73.3% of the labour force continued to work in agriculture by 1978 (Lin et al. 2003: 76). Even given the very inefficient overstaffing of SOEs, the Chinese planned economy could not provide enough industrial capacity for full employment. In retrospect the Maoist system's enthusiasm for heavy industry made for a lopsided and unsustainable macroeconomy. There were insufficient places to allocate the industrial labour force, which remained small. Complex, and advanced, industrial plants were underused meaning a very limited return on the large amounts of capital outlaid to build them. Moreover, Mao's autarkic approach and the Cold War hostility between communist and capitalist systems left few opportunities for international trade. At this stage the PRC was an inward-looking economy of broadly Soviet-type, but was considerably weaker than that of the USSR.

Interestingly, however, by being a weaker version of the USSR the country was perhaps less committed to Soviet industrial ideology and ultimately it proved to be more pragmatic and adaptable. It moved towards major reforms in 1978 - much earlier than in the USSR when the system there had by that time stagnated and seemed incapable of reform. (While Chinese reforms have proven to be hugely successful, Gorbachev's attempts to reform the USSR came too late to save it from collapse, see Chapter 8.) Ironically, the wider and deeper success of the

USSR led to the entrenchment of a system that went on to fail. China's inability to pursue this model as successfully as it aimed to perhaps ultimately turned out to be a blessing in disguise.

Mao died in September 1976. He is often vilified in Western nations, with some writers portraying him as a totalitarian dictator fond of political terror and forced labour camps, a 'monster' to be compared to Stalin and Hitler (Chang and Halliday 2005: 338). This view is very much disputed, with Chang and Halliday's portrayal of Mao particularly hysterical and often inaccurate (Benton and Chun 2010). He remains 'a revered figure for many' in China for the central role he played in the restoration of China's international status (Redding and Witt 2007: 47). Today 'Mao is inseparable from China's national and social progress, with which most Chinese identify, and with China's delivery from semicolonialism and backwardness' (Benton and Chun 2010: 2). But upon Mao's death in 1976 there was also widespread understanding that the system he was instrumental in building contained severe weaknesses and was in need of reform.

Experimenting with markets and globalization: Deng Xiaoping's 'reform and opening-up'

With the benefit of hindsight the Third Plenum of the Eleventh Communist Part of China Central Committee, held in December 1978, appears as significant for China's future as the revolutions of 1911 and 1949 (Goodman 1994: 90). It marks the beginning of the substantial (and largely very successful) economic reforms that continue to shape China to this day. At first gradual, then increasingly radical, reform affected almost all areas of Chinese society: the domestic political system, foreign affairs and critically the economy.

The changes were spearheaded by the new General Secretary of the Communist Party Central Committee, Deng Xiaoping (1904–97). A former Cultural Revolution victim, he eventually provided a 'final rejection' of such policies, rehabilitating other political figures who had also been cast out (Goodman 1994: 91, 97). He advocated more open and less wilful governance of the Party. Famously pragmatic, many idioms have been attributed to Deng, such as 'crossing the river by groping for stones'. Deng and other members of the senior CPC leadership were instrumental in beginning what became known as the 'Open Door' or 'reform and opening-up' policies.

This entailed much better international relations, including negotiating the eventual return of Hong Kong from UK to China in 1997, improving relations with the rapidly growing east Asian powers, and repairing some of the damage to the relationship with the (soon to collapse) USSR. The CPC nevertheless persisted with authoritarian political and cultural controls, insisting that a state-driven technocratic approach was appropriate and more effective than markets. The official line was pro-reform (including opening to international trade and inward investment) but also broadly against political and cultural 'pollution' that may come from overseas interactions (Goodman 1994: 101). Face-saving slogans emerged such as 'socialism with Chinese characteristics' to refer to the new socio-economic order, or, in relation to the reincorporation of a free-market, globalized Hong Kong into socialist China 'one country, two systems' (Goodman 1994: 100–101).

The first major economic changes took place in the countryside (Brandt and Rawski 2008: 9; Naughton 2007). Farmers had long borne the brunt of the Big Push industrialization policy in that the state purchased from collective farms at extremely low prices in order to divert funds into urban industrialization. New policies were experimented with that gradually introduced market elements into the countryside. Initial results were encouraging and fairly soon the radical policy of contracting agricultural land to farm households – effectively a form of partial privatization – took hold. To save face ideologically, the new contracts also stipulated that collectives had to continue to provide a certain amount of grain very cheaply or free to the state. While politically controversial, it was difficult to question their economic success. Rural efficiency grew, leading to massively increased grain output and even improved rural nutrition levels. Rural industry also recovered, as the increasingly efficient use of work time allowed parts of the agrarian population to turn their attentions to industrial development (Naughton 2007: 90). Township and village enterprises (TVEs) emerged rapidly in the years 1978–96 (Naughton 2007: 271–275). TVEs, originally rural communes with little scope for engaging in non-plan activity in earlier years of the command economy, after 1979 evolved into competitive small enterprises although technically still classed as 'collectives'. Up until 1988 it was still illegal for private firms to employ more than eight persons (Bardhan 2010: 80).

A system of 'dual pricing' was introduced which allowed markets and plan to awkwardly coexist; market prices and incentives existed for production over and above the plan quota, while the command economy still dictated prices, output and behaviour for the majority of the enterprise's activity (Brandt and Rawski 2008: 10; Knight and Ding 2012: 47). The process of post-Mao consolidation and readjustment was 'spectacularly successful' up until 1984 (Goodman 1994: 90), suggesting that it is possible for reforms that 'muddle along' to be successful, and that radical or wrenching change is not always appropriate or likely to succeed. This view is consistent with concepts of institutional theory and path-dependence, in that reforms have to work with the pre-existing institutional and cultural formations that structure what is possible for economic action. Over time China was 'growing out of the plan' (Naughton 2007: 92–93) without recourse to 'shock therapy' or other forms of radical change associated (rather tragically) with the former Soviet territories and Eastern Europe.

The CPC leadership believed that strategies similar to those used in the countryside could be applied to industry and services (Naughton 2007: 90). In policy switches that to some extent prefigured Gorbachev's *glasnost* and *perestroika* reforms in the USSR (see Chapter 8), directors of state-owned enterprises were given more autonomy, and incentives were gradually changed in the direction of allowing enterprises to make and retain profits (Lin et al. 2003: 215). The planning system became less prominent. Deng's government realized that the 'over-bureaucratized state machinery was simply not up to running the production process in a modernizing economy in a flexible way' (Goodman 1994: 93). Other forms of macroeconomic reform dramatically opened up China to world trade, in a controlled fashion at first, then in increasingly liberal ways. 'Special economic zones' (SEZs) were established in Guangdong and Fujian provinces (close to the dynamic international markets of Hong Kong and Taiwan), where low tax regimes were established to encourage domestic and international manufacturers.[9]

Deng's reforms led to economic growth at large and set the tone for further liberalization and market-driven change. But they also created conflict and pressures for retrenchment, particularly from urban workers hitherto protected by the institutions of the *danwei*. The Party was concerned about urban labour unrest, especially in light of the emergence of Solidarity, the genuinely independent workers' movement in state socialist Poland. Deng even removed workers' right to strike from the constitution in 1982 (Sheehan 1998: 155). The opening stages of reform were cautious, but from the mid-1990s onwards the reforms picked up pace, became more dynamic and more likely to produce obvious winners and losers (Naughton 2007: 90–91). In 1992, at the 14th Congress of the Party, the phrase 'socialist market economy' was officially adopted as formal policy (Naughton 2007: 100). Deng retired from the scene at this point, and more recent reforms have tended to be bolder and more obviously market-driven, including dramatic downsizing of state-owned industry (Knight and Ding 2012: 38).

Although many authors claim that China had no real 'model' in mind and was instead 'groping' along pragmatically, as time goes on it appears

[9] Further SEZs were later established on Hainan island and in Xianjiang.

that certain elements of Chinese reforms do appear 'modelled' on the East Asian nations that grew rapidly in the 1970s and 1980s, such as Singapore under Lee Kuan Yew, or even on 'Japanese-style state-guided capitalism' (Johnson 2002: 149). As the various polices evolved, parts of the Chinese economy began to look not dissimilar from those resulting from South Korean 'late industrialization' or 'developmental state' practices, as large group company structures were formed in China with very close ties to the (non-democratic) government (Amsden 1989). As China grows and marketizes there seems to be a tacit stress on development as nationalism – as a renewed Chinese developmental mission – in place of the prior Maoist rhetoric of development as part of the project of world communism (Johnson 2002: 151).

China's reforms also feature massive expansion of international economic activity. Inward investment into the PRC has been very considerable since the late 1970s. Annual flows of FDI into China have grown from around US$72 billion in 2005 to over US$100 billion in 2010, and the total stock of FDI to date reached US$578.8 billion in 2011, massively exceeding the flows into former Soviet regions (UNCTAD 2011: 193). FDI has come in the form of joint ventures of Chinese enterprises with international capital, the setting up of wholly owned subsidiaries of overseas corporations, or (largest of all) investment into mainland China from the population of approximately 55 million overseas Chinese (from Taiwan, Singapore, Macao and elsewhere). As in Russia, foreign investment in the form of joint ventures with foreign partners has often failed due to insufficient trust and lack of clarity, and the absence of adequate protection for overseas investors who often lose out in complex political games (Huang 2005). Wholly owned subsidiaries have tended to perform much better. Many of the factories set up in SEZs are wholly owned by overseas Chinese entrepreneurs who are not concerned with entering any 'partnership' or joint operation with Chinese businesses or authorities. Instead they are attracted to Guangdong and Fujian provinces by low tax rates and a cheap and docile labour force which they control tightly under strict labour-management principles.

China has internationalized, but it has done it to a large extent on its own terms (McCann and Schwartz 2006: 1348). It has been very careful about removing currency controls, and has maintained many forms of import barriers (although these have been progressively reduced from around 38% in 1993 to 9% in 2001 [Knight and Ding 2012: 288]). China has emerged as the low-cost export 'factory of the world', with items 'made in China' dominating consumer products from electronics, automotive parts, furniture, clothing and thousands of everyday household items. China now accounts for about 20% of total world manufacturing output,[10] although its focus on ruthless cost-cutting to secure contracts has tended to keep Chinese manufacturing locked in to only the simplest and cheapest forms of production with near-zero innovation or research-led input (Steinfeld 2004).

Johnson suggests (2002: 154) that the Chinese leadership views authoritarian rule as 'indispensible' to the project of national growth. Most Chinese citizens seem to accept this, or at least accommodate

Exhibit 10.2 Chalmers Johnson on 'soft authoritarianism' and 'soft totalitarianism'

Political scientist and former CIA analyst Chalmers Johnson wrote prolifically and often provocatively on East Asian economic models and on US military and diplomatic power. His writings tend to emphasize the importance of state power in economic matters, and here he provides his own interpretation of the Chinese economic model, explaining why China has managed to generate economic growth while at the same time refusing to give up on the one-party state political model.

In some ways this approach has some connection to Putin's Russia after the extreme turbulence of the Yeltsin era (see Chapter 8). Such an authoritarian model has many obvious limitations, but has a proven track record in purely economic and infrastructural terms (see South Korea, Japan, Singapore). How long such a model will persist perhaps depends on the speed at which wealth is distributed among the population; there is a strong expectation (especially held by Western writers) that a wealthier population will want a more open society, with a genuinely democratic political system, much less narrow forms of education, less censorship and control, and in general more scope for individuals to exercise their own choices.

'All of the Asian capitalist developmental states have been characterized by what I call "soft authoritarian" governments. Democracy – understood as a political system in which the force of public opinion makes a difference, a balance of powers exists within the government [...], and free elections can actually remove unsatisfactory officials – exists only partially in Japan, South Korea, and Taiwan, thanks to the pervasive, potent influence of unelected bureaucrats. [...] If the government of Japan and its emulator states – South Korea, Taiwan, and even Singapore – can be characterized as soft authoritarian, at least during their decades of high-speed economic growth, then China may be an example of 'soft totalitarianism', on a par with governments like Suharto's in Indonesia or Chiang Kai-Shek's in Taiwan, and considerably softer than the truly totalitarian worlds of Hitler, Stalin, and Mao.'

'A soft totalitarian regime directly restricts freedoms of speech and press, thereby curbing the effect of public opinion on the government. Under soft authoritarianism

(Continued)

[10] 'The End of Cheap China', *The Economist*, 10 March 2012.

Exhibit 10.2 (Continued)

(as in Japan, for example), such freedoms exist on paper but are attenuated in part by cartelization of the news media [...]. The public is better informed in soft authoritarian countries [...] but public opinion remains only a mild constraint on the government. Whereas a soft totalitarian state will employ direct suppression of offending books, imprisonment of authors, state control of Internet servers, and dismissal or imprisonment of dissidents, soft authoritarianism achieves its ends through peer pressure, bullying, fear of ostracism, giving priority to group norms, and eliciting conformity through social sanctions of various kinds. Under both kinds of regimes, elections are usually to one degree or another only formalities, behind which permanent state officialdoms actually govern.'

Source: Johnson 2002: 155–6. By permission of Little, Brown Book Group

themselves to this in a 'grand but unspoken bargain' between the CPC and the vast majority of its citizens (Brandt and Rawski 2008: 17). Once again it appears that simplistic claims of the 'superiority' or 'necessity' of Western-style globalization are not plausible. It appears that democracy, free markets, globalization and growth do not all have to exist together in order for development to take place.

Given the above, the Deng era appears as an 'unbalanced combination of vigorous economic reforms and relative political stagnation' (Naughton 2007: 100). A cautious, pragmatic, and gradual approach to reform is therefore understandable. Although this typical characterization of China's reforms as 'gradual' (Knight and Ding 2012: 45; Naughton 2007: 86–88) is broadly correct at a macro-level, the word 'gradual' does not sensibly capture the magnitude and velocity of change as felt by ordinary people. More subjective, more sociological accounts of China capture this reality more appropriately. Hsing (2010) writes very persuasively about China's cities as the new battlegrounds where the current contests about citizenship and representation, wealth and prosperity will be played out. Hsu (2007) discusses the enormous social changes associated with the rise of market socialism, especially the steady collapse of old state socialist status hierarchies such as solidarity and party discipline and their replacement with new forms of social legitimacy for markets and commerce. A significant stratum of 'new rich' has emerged (although probably amounting to less than 4% of the population [Goodman and Zang 2008: 12]). While at the meso/macro-level the authoritarian (or even 'soft totalitarian') Communist Party administers a rigid set of institutions designed to manage and control the movement of China towards 'state capitalism', all kinds of reactions and changes are taking place at more micro-levels. This remains very much true today, as the development of China's capitalism continues to gather pace.

China today: winners and losers in 'market socialism'

From the mid-1990s 'gradualism' and experimentation gave way to faster and more explicit moves towards markets and capitalism (but still not multi-party democracy). The most dramatic forms of economic growth appeared in China's coastal regions due to their rapid incorporation into overseas trade and investment. These cities have attracted migrant workers from across the Chinese landmass to work in export-oriented factories. Although the hours are long and the work exhausting, the pay is considerably better than that available in the less-developed interior. A proportion of these wages are sent back to workers' families in the countryside. Internal migrants are often employed according to seasonal demand and have to be housed in company-owned dormitories.

TVEs were effectively privatized in 1995–6 and most are now private SMEs in all but name (Huang 2008, 2010). The terms of state credit extended to them were toughened and many TVEs went bankrupt or changed ownership. Their exposure to market forces encouraged them to behave more aggressively, in turn pushing SOEs into competition that they were ill-prepared for. TVEs became highly cost-competitive, paying very low wages, often undercutting and outperforming SOEs (Naughton 2007: 275). In 1994, the Party announced the policy of 'seizing the large and letting go the small' (Cai et al. 2008: 17) meaning that the state would no longer promise to support the vast majority of SOEs which from then on would also be left to sink or swim in marketized waters.

Much of the SOE sector had been wading into financial trouble for years, using favourable state loans and informal political connections to help them tread water. But the planning mechanism was becoming less central to the economy, and many industrial enterprises found their debts to state banks increasingly unpayable (constituting the major part of China's very large non-performing loans problem). The biggest dilemma concerned what to do with the 'surplus labour problem' (Hassard et al. 2006). The Maoist approach to labour management was to overstaff SOEs in order to contribute to full employment, but as the command system was being overwhelmed by markets, this situation was no longer tenable. With a narrow product mix of low-grade, inefficiently produced goods, yet relatively higher wages and better terms and conditions of employment, the worst performing SOEs were in a false and precarious position – a kind of 'labour aristocracy' lacking the sales income or profits to support their traditionally high status. Dealing with this delicate political issue had been put off for decades as SOE closure or downsizing was expected to cause major unemployment and to totally undermine the Party's collectivist ideology (Cai et al. 2008: 208). Nevertheless, SOE restructuring has continued at a brisk pace since the mid 1990s, with annual *danwei* job losses amounting to an estimated ten million *per year* and an estimated total surplus of 54 million jobs (Johnson 2002: 159; Sheehan et al. 2000: 487–488).

Fortunately for China and the Party, growth of the private sector has been so far sufficient to provide jobs for millions of laid-off former SOE workers. The command economy was becoming irrelevant or non-existent by the mid 1990s and much of the SOE sector became exhausted 'zombie enterprises' propped up by soft government loans and acting as a drain on public funds. The rate at which jobs were shed in the once-proud SOE sector accelerated rapidly in the mid 1990s onwards.

While many SOEs fell into bankruptcy, others were reformed to become 'Modern Enterprises' and eventually sold off to new investors (Hassard et al. 2006). The state has kept ownership and control over the more fortunate firms (those of strategic importance such as steel, energy, arms and banks). Through the 'Group Company System' reforms, the Party aimed to merge the most viable state owned enterprises into major group companies, possibly with the model of Korean chaebols or Japanese-style corporate groups in mind. 'China hopes to forge its own versions of Mitsubishi, Sumitomo, Daewoo and Samsung' (Johnson 2002: 160–161). This is effectively a 'national champions' policy. The next logical step for these companies is to operate them along the lines of major multinationals operating 'world best practice' corporate forms. Firms of this nature are starting to become visible in international ranking lists such as the *Fortune* Global 500. So far all of these are government-owned 'crown jewels' such as Sinopec (5th largest corporation in the world), China National Petroleum (6th) and State Grid (7th).[11]

Although these developments are eye-catching, perhaps more important is the growth of private domestic start-ups, which constitute an ever-greater proportion of Chinese GDP (Yergin and Stanislaw 2002: 209). There are now a number of famous examples, such as the soft drinks company Wahaha, whose founder Zong Qinghou is reportedly China's richest man.[12] In the 19th-century West it was industrialists such as Arkwright and Carnegie who became household names. In post-Mao China major private business empires are starting to be built around consumer goods because steel, railways and investment banking are still largely state-only concerns. Many private start-ups are located in or around the SEZs, to take advantage of cheap labour costs and the

[11] *Forbes* Global 500, 2012, available at: http://money.cnn.com/magazines/fortune/global500/2012/full_list/.

[12] 'From Popsicle Maker to Beverage Billionaire, China's Richest Man', *International Herald Tribune*, 1 October 2012.

sheer scale of the distribution chains established in this region (Midler 2009). Chinese mainland entrepreneur-owned firms compete for business with the overseas Chinese-owned export production companies.

The rise in entrepreneurial activity and the opening of markets represent obvious and fundamental changes to the political economy of China. To what extent do ordinary people accept the changes? There is some research claiming that a new social discourse is emerging in which the traditions of the state-driven approach is being subtly delegitimized, being replaced by notions of private enterprise and the generation of family wealth. Hsu (2007) and Hanser (2008) have both conducted similar anthropological research in the city of Harbin, once a heartland of Maoist industrialism, but now occupying an uncertain role as the reforms advance. With state-run industry being replaced by private services and consumption, citizens were 'negotiating a world in flux, with few stable institutions' (Hsu 2007: 80). Social solidarity seems to be disappearing and the social safety net of the *danwei* seems a thing of the past. People were worried about instability, but also described the reforms as a largely popular and inevitable process. Things have broadly improved and there is no turning back. The Maoist model of state socialism thus becomes delegitimized by its association with poverty and exhaustion (Hanser 2008: 4), even replicating post-industrial trends in the USA, in which blue-collar, unionized, heavy industry are 'characterized as possessing an "obsolete" set of cultural values' (Hanser 2008: 15; see also Chapter 3).

A government official interviewed by Hsu describes it this way:

> After going through this short time of pain, things can get better. But if everyone just eats out of that big pot of rice, nothing ever gets better, everyone stays poor, that's long-term pain. ... In the past, in our work-units, it would be like this.

And a college professor suggests:

> Now whatever you're thinking of, you're thinking of how to make yourself wealthier, not caring about what the policies are. And this includes those who are supposed to be policy makers. Like if you ask people now, what is the policy about this or that, even if you ask professors, they'll say, I don't care. It's none of my business. My deal is to figure out how to make a little more money. (Hsu 2007: 120)

Such views may be common among middle-class professionals in China. For rural to urban migrants, or for former SOE workers in 'third front' industrial heartlands who have lost jobs and benefits that were promised to them for life (Hassard et al. 2006) the picture is likely to be bleaker.

A New Labour Law came into effect on 1 January 1995, giving further impetus to these radical changes. On one level the law was designed to speed up SOE restructuring, as it contains 'no fault dismissal' provisions making it legal for employers to fire workers for purely economic reasons (Cai et al. 2008: 173–174). Employee rights were also enshrined in the new law (such as a 40-hour work week, and an 8-hour work day) but such regulations are systematically ignored in practice (see below). As the *danwei* is downsized or 'corporatized' according to the policy aims of the Modern Enterprise System or the Group Company System (Hassard et al. 2006), the very promise of social welfare is threatened. There is little identifiable 'socialism' remaining (Naughton 2007: 202–206) as the SOE-based welfare system unravels. The government officially scrapped its guarantee of employment for urban state workers in 2003 – at the time it applied to around 30 million employees, who would have to adjust to the risks and uncertainties of market-driven employment relations.[13] Citizens have few forms of welfare to fall back on, as government spending on public services is low by OECD standards, for example just 1.8% of GDP on healthcare in 2004 (Lo 2009: 111). Efforts are afoot to encourage the liberalization of private insurance plans. The risks and burdens of social security are therefore progressively forced from the enterprise to local government, then eventually onto the shoulders of citizens themselves (Hassard et al. 2006). Most of the available welfare in China (especially in rural areas) is now user-charge financed (Bardhan 2010: 16).

Meanwhile the cost of urban labour is undercut by the millions of internal migrants 'floating' in China, many of whom work in a 'shadow' economy, which is semi-registered, semi-legal and very vulnerable to exploitation (Cai et al. 2008: 208; Knight and Ding 2012: 38). Parts of every Chinese city now feature capitalism operating in 'raw' and unregulated form. This poorly paid, poorly trained and under-protected labour force includes factory workers in special economic zones manufacturing items for export, or 'shadow economy' low-paid, low-skill service work such as domestic housekeepers (*baomu*) for richer urban inhabitants (Cooke 2006). Under such conditions the Gini coefficient for urban workers 'rose from 0.24 in 1988, to 0.33 in 1995 and to 0.37 in 2002' (Knight and Ding 2012: 38). Nationally, in 1978 on the eve of reforms Gini in the PRC was estimated at 0.22. By 2007, it had increased to 0.496 (Goodman and Zang 2008: 2).

The reforms have unleashed market forces but the Party continues to try to control them where possible. An important manifestation of this is the maintenance of the *hukou* system of permanent residential registrations, a clear restraint on the free movement of labour. Initially an

[13] 'China Scraps Jobs Guarantee', *BBC News*, 7 January 2003.

instrument of the command economy to administer the centralized allocation of employment, it officially inscribes citizens as either 'urban' or 'rural' workers (Cai et al. 2008: 173). Its use has adjusted to the slow demise of the command economy – today it limits the prospects of mass, uncontrolled migration to the cities and the predicted rise of overpopulated, 'slum' accommodation.

Contemporary China is a combination of many 'models' and 'systems', a mixed economy of state, private and semi-state (such as collectives and TVEs) actors. Competition for policy models plays out at senior levels of the Party apparatus, as local Party bosses hope to promote their status in the hierarchy by demonstrating the success of political-economic systems operating in each of their regions (Brandt and Rawski 2008: 17). Among the most high profile is 'the Shanghai model' (based around the growth of powerful 'group company' SOEs). This is set against the equally important example of 'the Guangdong model' (of SEZs and expansive market globalism) (Redding and Witt 2007: 222).

Meanwhile another famous example is the so-called 'Chongqing model', which is often portrayed as something of a Maoist throwback. Chongqing is a large inland city of around 30 million inhabitants, some distance from the high-growth coastal regions and from the CPC centre of gravity. Its high-profile former party boss, Bo Xilai, developed a conservative model of cheap housing and an 'anti-corruption' programme harnessing the slogan 'sing red, smash black' (where red refers to the traditions of communism and 'black' the criminal economy [Ho 2012]). In a development perhaps redolent of Putinism in Russia, it was hard to disentangle the official 'security forces' from the 'gangsters' they were supposed to be targeting. Bo was touted for a time as a possible Central Committee member, but in 2012 he dramatically fell from grace in a shocking scandal involving allegations of corruption and conspiracy to murder.

Such high-profile 'local heroes' (and their children in particular) are now often referred to as 'the princelings' by Western media.[14] Some estimates, for example, suggest that nine of the ten largest property companies in Shanghai are owned by the children of CPC members (Goodman and Zang 2008: 12). Such analysis implies favouritism, cronyism and clientalism at senior levels of Chinese economy and society, and thereby re-asserts the informal yet critical importance of favourable Party connections (and the Party at large) amid the seemingly inexorable growth of globalization and marketization in China. As Goodman and Zang persuasively argue, 'China's new rich are not readily separable from the Party-state as a social, political, or

[14] 'Children of the Revolution', *Wall Street Journal*, 26 November 2011.

even economic force' (2008: 6). Large segments of the new rich in China are both Party members and businesspeople. Goodman and Zang (2008: 5) mention the role of 'cadre families'; families which have leveraged Party political influence to gain wealth partly through *guanxi* (China's complex, informal code of social relations and exchange networks, see Hwang 1987). A significant segment of China's new rich have benefited from 'insider privatization' that took place as SOEs were corporatized. The Party has also broadened its membership to include those who in many other contexts could be regarded as capitalists, namely China's rapidly growing class segment of professionals, financial investors and firm executives. Given the widespread turbulence of markets in the West since 2008, some Western authors have begun to defend China's so-called 'state capitalism'[15] and have even used the term 'Beijing Consensus' when praising its stability and power (for a discussion and critique of this phrase, see Huang [2010]).

Whatever one makes of phrases such as 'Beijing Consensus' or 'state capitalism' it is important to note that they accurately describe only the 'commanding heights' of the economy (Yergin and Stanislaw 2002), such as strategic industries dominated by the national champion 'Group Company System' enterprises and the political jostling in the upper echelons of the Party. The base of the economy is now broadly driven by private companies operating according to market norms, and this seems to be widely accepted, legitimized and reproduced by ordinary people in their economic behaviour (Hanser 2008; Hsu 2007). China now operates multiple models. There is the China of the profitable remnants of the Maoist command economy that are strategically safe in government hands. There is the China of Party intrigue and the competition between regional and ideological policy models. But – overwhelmingly – there is now the China of rapidly liberalizing commerce: the TVEs and SMEs, the explosion in inward foreign investment and overseas trade, even the growth of a service economy and of international finance, including the Shanghai and Shenzhen stock markets, Hong Kong's historic role as a major financial market in East Asia, the 'special economic zones' and their sweatshop workforce of migrant youth.

Similar diversity exists at workplace level. There are remnants of the protected 'labour aristocracy' in the powerful state-controlled 'group companies'. But elsewhere there are strong signs of ruthless and exploitative labour management, involving poor safety levels, exhausting work and aggressive forms of management, with few avenues for employee involvement or representation. Accidents in heavy industry such as shipping and in extraction industries (especially

[15] 'Special Report: State Capitalism', *The Economist*, 21 January 2012.

coalmining) are tragically common. Officially there were nearly 2,000 deaths in Chinese coalmines in 2011, a figure that is probably a substantial underestimate.[16] Routine mistreatment of workers and the avoidance of and non-compliance of labour laws are well-known problems (Cooney 2007).

There is little role for employee voice and a distinct lack of workplace democracy and representation. Echoing the post-Soviet Russian experience, official unions are vestigial and newer forms of worker representation are underdeveloped, semi-legal and vulnerable. There have been some major worker protests in China, which is mostly unlike Russia where there was much less organized opposition because of the total collapse of the entire socio-economic system. Protests about illegal or undemocratic seizure of land for developers have been widespread. Hsing's research on urban China argues that cities are the new battlegrounds upon which the conflicts and power games of the next phases of China's restructuring will be played out. Given China's extremely rapid urbanization since the reforms Hsing (2010: 2–3) argues that China's reforms do not look 'gradual' to people on the ground, especially when social security has been cut back. Bitter protests in rural regions are also common.[17] Many of these conflicts are near-intractable because the institutions regulating exchanges of land, property and assets are fuzzy, untrusted and poorly enforced. Much day-to-day 'business' in China is informal and non-transparent. The stock markets of Shanghai and Shenzhen are mired by insider trading. Intellectual property rights are widely disrespected meaning rampant piracy (of products such as software and film, but also industrial patents and designs or branding, logos and clothing designs, see Midler 2009).

Perhaps no element of China's recent transformation better captures this sense of flux and turmoil than China's so-called 'floating population' or internal migrants. 'An estimated one hundred million – more than the entire population of Mexico – are now adrift in China, largely migrants from the interior looking for work in rich coastal areas' (Johnson 2002: 158). Chang (2008: 24) suggests a figure of 130 million. The population is described as 'floating' as its members are not allowed to reside in cities permanently without a *hukou*, and they tend to periodically return to their families when time and money allows. Their 'floating' nature makes them very vulnerable to intimidation and exploitation.

[16] 'China Coal Mine Gas Explosion Kills 19 Miners and Traps Dozens', *Guardian*, 30 August 2012.

[17] 'Chinese Villagers Clash with Police in Land-Grab Protests', *Guardian* 3 April 2012.

There have been major protests over factory closures all over China (especially in the 'core' Maoist industrial regions of the Northeast), with Morris et al. (2001) suggesting that the traditional pattern on workers' 'dependence' on the traditional paternalism of the 'Shanghai model' has turned to 'defiance' as promises of secure employment and benefits are torn up. In 'Guangdong model' China, there have also been significant and widespread labour protests. A new labour law was developed in Shenzhen in 2010 in order to respond to a wave of strikes and stoppages in 2009 and 2010. The new code aims to improve industrial relations in the SEZ, stipulating an increased minimum wage of ¥1100 per month. This move was almost certainly influenced by the international outcry over the Foxconn suicides.[18]

Foxconn is a trading name of Hon Hai Precision Industry, a company that employs 1.3 million workers making it possibly the tenth largest employer in the world.[19] Taiwanese-owned and Shenzhen-based Foxconn is one of the world's most important electronics assemblers and suppliers, acting as a subcontractor to major global brands such as Apple and Sony. The company became notorious for allegations of worker mistreatment after 14 worker suicides took place in 2010.[20] In a development that seems scarcely believable, Foxconn management decided to erect 'suicide nets' around its buildings to deter any further jump attempts.

This has created intense media interest, with the company eventually allowing inspections by international labour pressure groups and visits by US media corporations.[21] The work is demanding, exhausting and extremely monotonous, and the living conditions in the company dormitories are cramped and unpleasant. But the pay is attractive to migrant workers (even after the cost of company accommodation and meals in the company canteens), with thousands of young workers appearing at recruitment days.

Smith and Pun's (2006: 1463) research into an overseas Chinese-owned electronics factory reveals a picture very similar to that at Foxconn. Dormitory-housed migrants working 84-hour weeks (12-hour shifts, 7 days per week) earning around ¥900–1000 per month (approximately US$160, an average hourly wage of around 1.9 dollars). This was considered decent pay for the work and the region, and

---

[18] 'Shenzhen Drafts New Drafts New Labor Law', *China Daily*, 1 September 2010.

[19] 'Which Is the World's Biggest Employer', *Guardian*, 20 March 2012.

[20] 'Foxconn Worker Plunges to Death at China Plant: Report', Reuters, 5 November 2010.

[21] 'A Trip to The iFactory: "Nightline" Gets an Unprecedented Glimpse Inside Apple's Chinese Core', *ABC News*, 20 February, 2012.

Exhibit 10.3 'China Wonder Electronics': working life in the Special Economic Zones

The following text is a brief extract from some important primary research into the daily reality of life and work in one of China's export-oriented Special Economic Zones. Smith and Pun gained access to 'China Wonder Electronics', a major organization that carries out subcontracted assembly work for global electronics multinationals. Many of the workers are internal migrants that are housed in nearby company dormitories, and Smith and Pun provide one of the very few available studies on this 'dormitory labour system'. A particularly notable part of their paper is the inclusion of text from posters that are prominently displayed around the living areas:

'The Management of the Dormitory

1. Dormitory conditions shall be kept clean and sanitary. A dorm room found dirty would mean a fine of RMB 10.
2. Spitting will incur a fine of RMB 10 if found in the dormitory compound.
3. No noise is allowed after midnight. Everybody has to keep quiet once they enter the dormitory rooms. Those caught being noisy after midnight will be penalized.
4. No argument or fighting is allowed. Those found fighting in the compound would be dismissed at once.
5. Dormitory facilities shall be protected. Anyone found to have made malicious damage will be penalized and dismissed.
6. Stealing dormitory property or residents' property will incur dismissal.
7. No visitors are allowed to stay overnight. If overnight visitors are caught, a fine of RMB 100 will be imposed.
8. Unless on night shift, or in times of emergency, nobody is allowed to enter or leave the compound after 12am.
9. Living identity cards have to be carried all the time in the compound. If lost, the person will be charged RMB 20.
10. No cooking or eating is allowed in the rooms. Secretly using cooking machines in the dorm will mean a penalty of RMB 20.
11. Nobody is allowed to independently change his or her bunk. If they do so a penalty of RMB 50 will be incurred.'

(Smith and Pun 2006: 1464)

'China Wonder' recruited only skilled, reliable, and experienced workers.

Protests about working conditions are rarely effective in China and are often met with employer and police hostility. According to Johnson: 'Part of the unholy alliance between China's domestic autocrats and its foreign investors is that both hate unions and any movement toward workers' rights, even if for different reasons' (Johnson 2002: 159). Although technically a workers' state, with – on paper – progressive labour laws, post-socialist China appears to be adopting a 'low-road' employment model (McCann and Schwartz 2006). Chinese workers lack proper institutional forms of support, as official unions are company-controlled and must be affiliated to the government-run All-China Federation of Trade Unions, which is not an independent workers' organization. Genuinely independent, worker-run unions that try to protest about poor working conditions or go on strike are illegal, meaning that many of the protests against management are informal, and therefore much riskier for workers to engage in or support. Chan (2009) even describes workers being beaten and intimidated if any dared to raise concerns about grievances or unfair treatment in a Taiwanese-owned factory on the Chinese mainland.

The country seems unready - as of yet - to develop a German-style high voice, high-quality export model, and it will probably retain the low trust, no unions, no voice model with little employee involvement. Strongly authoritarian management styles are the norm, even in services. Gamble (2010), for example, describes working conditions in Chinese branches of a major Japanese department store in which managers use football referee-style 'yellow cards' and 'red cards' to discipline workers. Nevertheless, there has been upward pressure on wages, particularly in the SEZs. To keep up with very demanding delivery targets, firms involved in export processing need reliable and effective workforces with high productivity and few quality errors.[22] Labour laws were toughened in 2008 in an attempt by the Party to tighten up on private sector companies that have not signed contracts with their workforces. There are some signs of improvement in job security and pay, with mainstream Western business media suggesting that China needs to 'take a leaf out of Germany's book ... to make products with higher margins and offer services to complement them'.[23]

Overall, however, China seems 'likely to remain for the foreseeable future the assembly workshop of the world' (Redding and Witt 2007: 227). OEM assembly remains its focus, where the informality, low wages, low skill and fast pace of production, and the possibilities for quick ramp up of scale are China's strengths, especially in the SEZs, but also elsewhere (Midler 2009). The prospect for genuinely global Chinese multinationals to emerge, competing head to head with the brand name products supplied on international markets by major European, American, Japanese or Korean global corporations are 'remote' (Redding and Witt 2007). One of the reasons is that the state-defended group company SOEs still tend to feature opaque and 'low trust' management regimes, and lack the experience and capacity for handling the complexity required in the design and conception of world class products. In any

[22] 'The End of Cheap China', *The Economist*, 10 March 2012.

[23] 'The End of Cheap China', *The Economist*, 10 March 2012.

case, the global shift towards dismembering large corporations to take advantage of cheap production networks suits the lower-level insertion of China into global production networks or 'value chains' (Gereffi et al. 2005). For now, Chinese manufacturers overwhelmingly operate as assemblers of other companies' products rather than as innovators in their own right (Redding and Witt 2007: 229; Steinfeld 2004). Time will tell if China's group companies are able to keep up with cutting-edge European and US employment and organizational practices and to move up the value chain in ways that Japan and (to a lesser extent) Korea managed in the 1970s and 1980s (Redding and Witt 2007: 229). An even bigger problem is the need to expand growth to China's huge hinterland, much of which has been left behind by the explosive growth and change in China's more dynamic regions.

Conclusion

Few can deny the massive achievements of China's economy in the last 30 years. Perhaps as many as 600 million people have been lifted out of poverty by the reforms in China (Bardhan 2010: 91). However, China is also beset with difficulties and contradictions. Post-Mao China seems to encapsulate many of the controversies, ironies and feedback loops of globalization itself. A key reason why working conditions in the SEZ have such a high profile in the West, is that USA and European consumers may be shocked to learn about the labour exploitation that goes into assembling pieces of Apple's iPhones or Sony's PlayStations. Even as Chinese workers are increasingly drawn into a globalized division of labour, there is no chance that their meagre earnings from this labour could stretch to buying any of these supposedly 'global' products. Not unrelated is the (much less well-known) controversy about China's political authoritarianism and use of prison labour. This subject is a massive taboo in China, and the whole history of the labour camps of the Mao era and beyond is far less widely appreciated than their Soviet equivalents upon which they were at least partially based (Applebaum 2003: 412). Some émigré critics of China describe a network of 'correctional' labour camps known as *laogai* that are comparable in scale and cruelty to the Soviet ones (see Wu 1992; and for a useful overview, Chan 1993). Even today several activists claim that certain items for overseas export are assembled under duress using prison labour. But like the Tiananmen crackdown in 1989 this issue is so controversial as to be not openly discussed. Chinese authorities block access to sensitive internet content and divert users to 'official' versions of events (Khanna 2009: 40). Print, broadcast and internet media remains extensively controlled and censored.

Western democracies sometimes deplore China's limited human rights and democratic freedoms, but at the same time voraciously consume cheap Chinese exports, which have helped to keep inflation low in OECD nations. Families with squeezed household budgets benefit from this in one way, and it is hard to imagine the Wal-Mart, Aldi or Carrefour retail models without Chinese exports to fill their shelves. On the other hand, China as 'the workshop of the world' also accelerates manufacturing job loss in OECD nations, destroying working class jobs. Western politicians and businesspersons champion China's move towards freer markets, and Western citizens happily consume cheap Chinese-made goods. But they also fret about jobs lost to China and complain (at times) about Chinese labour and human rights abuses. Such are the double-edged connections of today's globalized product markets. At the same time, China's orientation towards export growth has meant a neglect of the skills and income development of its own workforce, suppressing domestic consumption and clustering its industrial firms towards the lower end of the value stream (Lo 2009).

To some extent China's low-cost export model may be endangered if quality levels fall too far. Many argue that China needs to move up value chain in future, and progress into the higher value export markets. One way of doing this is to buy distressed assets which gives the purchaser quick access to technology and brands. This has happened regularly in the car industry, with, for example, London Taxis International (20% owned by Shanghai's Geely International) and MG Rover (purchased by Nanjing Automotive). In 2010 Geely purchased Volvo from Ford for US$1.8 billion following the latter's desperate financial struggle after the subprime collapse. Another Chinese automotive company made a move for GM's Hummer brand, but this was eventually blocked by the Chinese government. It is not easy to jump straight into global product markets; it takes a lot of time and learning, but some Chinese firms are already making the move.

One weakness of the Chinese political economy is its financial system, especially the issue of widespread non-performing loans, which may amount to US$500 billion and constitute between 23% and 43% of total loan value in the system (Redding and Witt 2007: 83, 88). Embattled SOEs are the worst culprits here, as they are unable to pay back the soft loans provided by the state to postpone factory closure. China has been relatively unaffected by the subprime collapse as its financial system was not really exposed to toxic loans. However, the economy's skewing towards export trade resulted in a slowdown in China as orders from the OECD economies contracted. In 2008–9, China deployed a major government stimulus package, which critics regard as a step away from globalization, free markets and liberalization and a populist return to the CPC's traditional comfort zone of state-driven industrial policy (Huang 2010; Lo 2009).

Much has been made of China's 2001 admission into the World Trade Organization, but the official strategy espoused by World Trade Organization members is basically at odds with the strategy that China is really following (Johnson 2002: 180). Protection of intellectual property rights seem minimal, with piracy remaining rampant (Midler 2009). The USA frequently criticizes the People's Bank of China for refusing to fully float its currency, claiming that the Party indulges in currency manipulation to artificially keep Chinese exports competitive. It is worth bearing in mind, however, that the US government faced similar trade conflicts with Korea and Japan during their rapid growth phases (Mastel 1997: 75, 125–137).

On a more positive side, China's trade boom has meant the amassing of colossal foreign exchange reserves and a trade surplus of around US$38 billion (Lo 2009: 117). The widespread growth of economic risk, coupled with the very limited provision of social security such as health services, encourages China's very high domestic savings rate which suppresses domestic consumption (Bardhan 2010: 65). The CPC's traditional preference for large-scale investment projects may look impressive as new science parts, apartment blocks and retail parks continue to fly up, with new highways and railways to serve them (Bardhan 2010; Lo 2009). Cautious voices, however, warn of industrial overcapacity, an economy unbalanced towards export rather than domestic consumption, and the potential for a real estate bubble. Given the subprime fallout, China's authorities are understandably reluctant to continue liberalizing financial services and this means a continued impetus to invest in high-profile construction projects rather than stimulating broader economic consumption around the wider population (Lo 2009).

Income inequalities are huge across China. Although the overall record of poverty alleviation in China since the reforms is impressive, many interior regions feature little more than a subsistence-level economy (Yergin and Stanislaw 2002: 209). There is no way of knowing where the political winds will blow – liberalization might eventually be political, as well as economic (Redding and Witt 2007: 233). At this current historical point, it seems as if policymakers in China fail to see how democracy would make the growth model run more effectively. Redding and Witt similarly suggest that '[t]he assumption that only a single central government was appropriate was implanted from the beginning and has survived to the present day' (2007: 43), implying that ordinary Chinese also see little of value in Western notions of democracy.

Brandt and Rawski (2008: 13) suggest that Chinese growth proves the value of globalization, markets and free trade for ordinary people. Neoliberal arguments point to the effectiveness of 'price signals' (Brandt and Rawski 2008: 15) in education markets and how an effective 'labour market' now exists in China. But what happens to those citizens without capital to spend on education, or ageing former SOE workers lacking up-to-date skills with no prospect of decent employment? Although the Communist Party leadership talks of developing policies to promote a 'Harmonious Society', this seems to ring hollow as the Gini coefficient edges ever upwards and as millions are left behind to face poverty and exclusion.

Further reading

Brandt, L., and Rawski, T.G., eds, (2008) *China's Great Economic Transformation*, Cambridge: Cambridge University Press.

This gigantic volume is a mine of information on the contemporary Chinese economy, containing chapters on practically all imaginable angles, from political economy overviews to detailed discussions of employment and legal reforms. Mostly the chapters take a rather mainstream and neoliberal economic viewpoint, but there is a very wide variety of authors and perspectives. Any reader looking to learn more detail about China - particularly at an 'overview' level - will find plenty of value in this text.

Naughton, B., (2007) *The Chinese Economy: Transitions and Growth*, Cambridge, MA: MIT Press.

This is another excellent overview textbook that provides a very accessible and even-handed account of China's economy and society. Written by a solo author, it offers a useful alternative to Brandt and Rawski in that it is somewhat more readable and integrated. This is one of the best places to look to provide a detailed historical overview of China and its changing structures. It is highly lucid and hugely authoritative.

Pun, N., (2005) *Made in China: Women Factory Workers in a Global Marketplace*, Durham, NC: Duke University Press.

This fascinating book provides a wealth of details of the realities of working life in a segment of the Chinese population that now plays such a major role in the world economy – internal migrants working in the special economic zones. This is a powerful and vital book for any reader interested in the intense labour struggles involved in producing the everyday items (socks, laptops, children's toys) that customers in economically advanced nations take for granted, and the ways in which contemporary factory labour attempts to discipline and shape the bodies and minds of workers. Importantly, various forms of worker resistance (albeit limited) are also meticulously documented.

Hsu, C.L. (2007) *Creating Market Socialism: How Ordinary People are Shaping Class and Status in China*, Durham, NC: Duke University Press.

This book is a useful alternative to the often rather dry literature on China that is content to provide 'run-downs' of policy changes over the years. This anthropological study takes the reader right into the daily lives of Chinese capitalism, but this time as viewed through the eyes of the emerging Chinese middle class – as consumers rather than as producers, and as service workers rather than manufacturers. It provides huge detail on the work regimes of retail workers, showing how everyday actions serve to create the new reality of 'market socialism.' In doing so it tries to explain why ordinary Chinese tolerate and support the authoritarian growth model of the Communist Party.

ELEVEN Japan: Still the World's Second Most Prominent Model?

Chapter objectives

- To introduce the history of Japanese economic growth
- To describe and account for the massive influence of Japanese firms and management/manufacturing systems throughout the world
- To describe the key features of Japan, as a key example of a CME
- To explain and account for the bubble economy and the 'lost decades' as Japan experiences a boom, a bust and a long recession
- To provides an analysis of the undoubted strengths of the Japanese model, but also to critique the 'darker' elements of Japanese organizational life, such as its sexism, bullying, exploitation and authoritarianism

Introduction

Japan's influence on debates around economic growth, financial systems, working life, labour and technology management, and corporate governance has been enormous. Japan is one of the most obvious examples of a successful CME. Its direct, non-academic, impact on many advanced nations across the world has also been huge in terms of the widespread dissemination, imitation and uptake of Japanese-style management, work and production systems (Milkman 1997).

Concepts such as total quality management, lean and just-in-time production, have for many years been central in large and small Japanese companies, and these ideas have been widely promulgated in many countries as potential 'solutions' or 'best practice' (Liker and Hoseus 2007; Womack et al. 1990/2007). Many ideas widely used in Japanese firms have become staple parts of management consulting initiatives and business education. No MBA course would be complete without coverage of lean production. There is even now a *Lean for Dummies* book (Sayer and Williams 2007). Even if it did not solely originate from Japan, Japanese firms are the undisputed masters of the practical usage and philosophical development of lean. More recent Western management systems such as Six Sigma borrow heavily from Japanese ideas. The rapid rise of the Japanese economy in the 1970s and 1980s, and the reputation Japanese companies have developed for the quality and reliability of their products ever since, fundamentally challenged the traditional ethnocentric idea that the USA has all the answers when it comes to business and management.

Indeed, Japan's rise to economic prominence in the 1970s and 1980s was accompanied by a whole publishing industry around the coming crises of the US economy and its seemingly outdated management ideas (Best 1990; Byrne 1993; Halberstam 1987; Peters and Waterman 1982). All of a sudden, well-known and widely accepted ideas of the dominant US version of organized capitalism (Lash and Urry 1987) – multi-divisional, publically listed firms based on tall, rigid structures of managerial authority, command and control, arms-length contracting and 'rational' numerical analysis – were thrown into turmoil. Instead, theorists looked to Japan for USA's way out of stagnation. Clearly this model seemed central in explaining the growth of Japan itself, but its influence can also be widely viewed in Japanese-owned factories overseas (the 'transplants' [Delbridge 1998; Graham 1995; Millkman 1991, 1997]), and in Anglo-Saxon and other contexts (notably in Germany and Nordic Europe) where the emulation of Japanese-style systems have been attempted. Even as Japan's economy fell into recession in the 1990s, its systems (and underlying philosophies) remained admired by many observers. As Japan seemed to emerge from stagnation in the mid-2000s, lean once again become flavour of the month for consultants and 'performance improvement' gurus. For example the UK's NHS and HM Revenue and Customs service have recently taken on lean systems with mixed results (Carter et al. 2013; Fillingham 2007; Waring and Bishop 2010). Perhaps more than any other country covered in this book, Japan's economic systems have been widely discussed, not just in their own terms, as analysts look to explain the success of the Japanese nation, but also as techniques for firms to adopt, and new paths for businesses to take, wherever they are located.

However, Japan has also faced numerous severe problems since the 1990s, and its economy faces immense pressure for reform. The subprime crisis also hit Japan failing hard and, once again, the weaknesses of the Japanese model started to come under scrutiny from 2009 onwards, just as they were in the long period of deflation in Japan (1991–2004).

This chapter begins by outlining the country's remarkable recovery from the disasters of the Second World War, covering in detail the particular economic institutions (notably the Japanese state itself) which supported, fuelled and framed this growth. It goes on to describe Japan in the post-war period, in which it will mention several of Japan's mighty multinational firms and business groups, and will describe the powerful and influential work, management and manufacturing systems for which Japan became famous. The following section describes the 'era of high growth' or the so-called 'Japanese miracle', when its economy rapidly caught up with the leading Western industrialized nations. The chapter will then go on to discuss the deterioration of the Japanese model in the 1990s, and the so-called 'lost decade' when the Japanese economy unexpectedly lost its way. During this section, there will be considerable discussion of how the Japanese government and large Japanese firms approached the thorny issue of *risutora* – restructuring. The chapter then goes on to discuss some more recent developments, including Japan's apparent recovery from around 2004 onwards and the sudden and once again unexpected fall into recession amid the subprime collapse, a recession horribly compounded by the devastating Tōhoku earthquake and tsunami of 2011. The chapter concludes with a final summary of what could be considered the central concepts of Japanese capitalism, and provides some ideas about where Japan might be going, how connected it is to global capitalism, and its further influence on the rest of the world.

Japan's phenomenal growth: an historical overview

Japan's dramatic rise to economic prominence is all the more unusual given the high level of exclusion of the country from Europe for many generations. Only relatively recently did Japan become a united, industrial power and a modern nation state. For a long period of history, the country was a collection of disunited feudal entities, involved in frequent and bloody civil wars. Under the dictatorial regime of the Tokugawa era (or Edo period) of 1600–1868, the country deliberately cut itself off from European outside influences, regarding them as barbaric, exploitative, immoral and disruptive. During this period China was the dominant power in Asia, and Japan had virtually no contact with Europe or America. Limited trade with the Portuguese, English and Spanish was ended in the 1620s as their trading representatives were expelled from the country. Japan eventually became united under the Tokugawa rulers, who brought the civil wars to an end and laid the groundwork for the establishment of Japan as the recognizable nation it is today. Economic growth was considerable during this period and Edo (now Tokyo), with around a million residents, became at this time the largest city in the world (Gordon 2003: 23). The Tokugawa ruling elite essentially pursued an isolationist, domestic growth strategy, with foreign relations limited to trade with Korea and Okinawa (Gordon 2003: 18). Repeated attempts at trade missions from European nations and the USA were resisted, at times violently.

However, the Japanese nation was eventually forced into participation with Western powers, which were rapidly industrializing during this time. In 1853 the famous 'Black Ships' from USA under Commodore Perry sailed into Edo bay, demanding that the rulers of Japan open the nation to trade or face a war it could not win (Gordon 2003: 48–49). Japan reluctantly submitted and signed unequal trade agreements with Western powers. In doing so forces were set in motion that were to eventually overpower the inward-looking Tokugawa rulers. Following widespread political unrest the Tokugawa regime was overthrown by a *coup d'état* and a new period, the Meiji era, began. The Meiji government saw the value in Western technology and Western social systems (such as education and political structures), and eradicated many traditional Japanese social structures from history (such as the samurai). With hindsight the 'Black Ships' episode can be interpreted as an excellent example of the pressures and conflicts that can be opened up by processes of globalization.

From the Meiji era onwards, Japanese government policy was to import technology, techniques and systems almost wholesale from the West. Trade missions to major industrial centres such as the mid-west USA and the northwest UK took place at the end of the 19th century. These involved purchases of equipment and technology licenses from such places as the Manchester cotton mills, securing access to technologies that were to become central to Japan's future economic growth. The general strategy was to begin with the importation of skills, under strict state guidance, use, develop and learn from them, and then basically force the Westerners back out once they had served their purpose. The number of overseas technical advisors in Japan 'peaked at 527 in 1875 but fell quickly to 155 in 1885, suggesting a rapid absorption of knowledge on the part of the Japanese' (Chang 2003: 47–48). The strategy involved adapting foreign technology for Japan's own ends without allowing Western actors much of a foothold.

The Japanese were very effective in learning from, adapting and very rapidly improving on, Western technology and ideas.[1]

During this period Japan became a major industrial and imperial power. It developed all of the engineering innovations associated with the industrial revolution in Europe and America, such as railways and textile manufacturing. Powerful families rose to prominence through their ownership and control of major conglomerates. These family-run business groups were known as the *zaibatsu.* Some have survived in some form until today such as Sumitomo and Mitsubishi (Gordon 2003: 97–105; Mouer and Kawanishi 2005: 233–234). The Meiji era also saw the rise of modern politics in Japan including labour unrest among the newly formed class of industrial, urban workers. Like many Western nations it experienced bank failures during the 1920s (Gordon 2003: 141–144). By this time Japan was essentially the only modern power outside Europe or the USA.

As Japan joined the elite group of world imperial powers it, like the European powers of the time, built up considerable military power with which to intimidate its neighbours. It invaded Taiwan in 1874. It employed gunboat diplomacy to force unfair trade treaties upon Korea in 1876. It embarked on several military expeditions, including victory in a war with China (1894–5), and some major gains in a brief war with Russia (1904). It invaded and occupied Korea (1910) and Manchuria (a large part of China). By 1937, it was involved in full-scale war with China, where some horrendous acts of violence were committed by Japanese troops, incidents which remain very controversial and are often described as war crimes. Japanese forces overstretched themselves and became deadlocked in the Chinese mainland 'unwilling to retreat, but unable to overcome their foes' (Gordon 2003: 207). Tensions were building with the USA, which broadly supported Chinese independence at this time, and had a powerful naval presence in Asia.

A diplomatic solution to this crisis appeared impossible and Japan eventually attacked and destroyed a large proportion of the US Pacific Fleet stationed at Pearl Harbor, Hawaii on 7 December 1941. In addition Singapore and Burma were captured from the British, the Philippines from the USA and Japan also took the Dutch East Indies and the Pacific islands. Although a dramatic military success, the attack on Pearl Harbor brought the USA into the Second World War with eventually catastrophic results for Japan. By 1945, the growth phase of unification, industrialization, economic growth and militarism had eventually led Japan to ruin.

---

[1] The Japanese enthusiasm for the process improvement ideas of W. Edwards Deming from 1950 onwards is an excellent example of this, see Exhibit 11.1 (page 313).

Japan in the post-war period

Japan at the end of the Second World War was in a state of utter destruction. Most of its large cities had been devastated by US saturation bombing, and Hiroshima and Nagasaki were destroyed by atomic weapons, with the deaths of many thousands of civilians (estimates suggest 140,000 killed in Hiroshima and 70,000 in Nagasaki, out of a total of over 393,000 killed in air raids [Duus 1998: 249]).

Partly under the force of occupation and partly out of internal rejection of the ultimately disastrous imperialist project and the aggressive foreign policy, Japan established a new constitution in 1947 which removed its right to wage war or own nuclear weapons, and restricted it to a small, technically speaking civilian, Self-Defence Force (Choucri et al 1992: 228). Since its defeat Japan has shown a clear rejection of its colonial policy towards Asia, even when the issue of apologizing to its neighbours for the invasion and subjugation of their citizens remains a highly controversial and largely unresolved issue.

After the war Japan lost all of its colonial gains and was occupied by the Allied Powers (1945–52). At the summit of the chain of command sat General MacArthur, who was given the title SCAP (Supreme Commander of the Allied Powers), a title which also served as a shorthand term for the occupation headquarters in Tokyo (today the offices of Dai-Ichi Mutual Life). SCAP (pretty much completely a US-run operation) pushed through numerous socio-economic reforms that were designed to prevent the kind of militaristic economic build-up that facilitated Japan's imperialist adventures. The relationship between the USA and Japan has remained complex and ambiguous ever since. The 1951 Security Treaty and then the later 1960 Mutual Cooperation and Security Pact were highly controversial agreements signed between the nations. These agreements continue to be disputed by Japanese nationalists, as well as those on the political left, especially Japan's independent trade unions and by students who engaged in mass protests, especially in the 1960s, against these policies (Kumazawa 1996). The post-war security infrastructure involved the establishment of many US military bases on Japanese soil, especially on Okinawa, but indeed all over the Japanese islands. There are around 50,000 active, uniformed US personnel, plus 6,400 US Department of Defense civilians and 50,0000 US dependents based over 123 installations across Japan. (There were also 37,000 uniformed personnel in Korea [Johnson 2004: 158].[2]) The Japan Self-Defence

[2] US Department of Defense, *Base Structure Report* 2009, p. 7; 'Okinawa Deal between US and Japan to Move Marines', *BBC News*, 27 April 2012.

Forces (JSDF) amounts to just 140,000 personnel across its army, navy and air force services.[3]

The strong US political, economic and military investment in Japan was a central part of the US foreign policy agenda. The USA envisaged Japan (and later South Korea) as its bulwark against the spread of communism across Asia, and the USA was determined to ensure that market capitalism and democracy would be firmly established in Japan, much as the other victorious Allied powers at the end of the Second World War were eager to contain and develop West Germany. It is one of history's ironies that, while these policies were hugely successful in turning these two nations into rich, democratic and largely peaceful nations, they also failed to shape them into free-market economic models in the image of the UK and USA (Djelic 1998). Germany and Japan are key exemplars of CMEs, and they have stubbornly remained different from the Anglo-Saxon model.

In the aftermath of war Japanese businesses and economic planners had massive tasks ahead of them. Most of Japan was suffering from acute poverty to the extent of mass starvation and widespread disease epidemics. About a third of the population was homeless (Duus 1998: 254). The economy was shattered and reduced to a barter system, there was almost no transportation network or infrastructure, and almost no industry. It all had to be made anew. Whole cities needed to be rebuilt, almost literally out of nothing (Gordon 2003). With this devastation in mind, Japan's successful rise to becoming the second-largest economy in the world is all the more astonishing. What Japan did was to follow a similar path to that taken in its pre-war era. The Japanese government protected infant domestic industry and used active stimulus policies to get the economy moving (Chang 2003: 46–49). Japan became a great example of the possible successes of a 'developmental state' growth strategy (Bernstein 1997a; Chang 2006; Johnson 1992), even as state-led models are now largely rejected as outdated and illegitimate by mainstream economists (who seem to conveniently forget that similar policies have been used in all countries at certain times including the USA and UK [Chang 2003: 1–9]).

Although the general thrust of SCAP's reforms was adhered to, the detail was not. Reforms were implemented partially. One of the goals of the new policies was to break up the large financial-industrial conglomerates thereby reducing the power of a number of important families which had established these cartelized relationships with the political power structure. The idea was to break these *zaibatsu* relationships down and establish a more liberal economy with widespread and diffused stock ownership so that these monopolistic, oligarchic firms

[3] Japanese Ministry of Defence, 'Defence of Japan 2012', p. 4.

Exhibit 11.1 W. Edwards Deming – ignored by the Anglo-Saxons, embraced by the Japanese?

W. Edwards Deming (1900–1993) is a good example of the trend whereby Japanese growth was to some extent built on clever adoption of, and improvement on, Western ideas. Deming was a physicist who became a pioneer of statistical process techniques for engineering and manufacturing. In some sense he was almost a latter-day Frederick W. Taylor, who, in 1950 went to work as an expert consultant to Japanese firms during the SCAP occupation. It is widely noted that his ideas became much more influential in Japan than they did in the US. At the heart of his methodology lies a form of Statistical Process Control, which rests on a very methodical and calculated approach to manufacturing, emphasising quality control far above quantity of output. His approach was enthusiastically adopted by many leading Japanese firms. Deming's most famous book *Out of the Crisis* (1982) suggests that if US companies are to emerge from stagnation they need to look towards long-term planning (1982: 25), total quality control (1982: 167–182), and the elimination of 'seven deadly diseases' (1982: 97–148), concepts which sound very Japanese. These seven deadly diseases refer specifically to poor practices common in the States, but they are similar in tone to Toyota's famous 'seven wastes' associated with Taiichi Ohno (see Womack et al. 1990/2007).

Deming's work was heavily influenced by another American statistical process engineer Walter A. Shewhart (1891–1967). The Shewhart Cycle of 'Plan Do Check Act' (PDCA) has become mixed up over time to such an extent that the terms 'Deming Wheel', or 'Shewhart Cycle' seem to have become interchangeable. More recent developments on this theme include the massively influential Six Sigma methodology (originally developed by the US firm Motorola and widely adopted by GE, General Motors, Ford and many other large multinationals).

Japanese 'lean' systems depend heavily on standardization and statistical process control methods, often using visible methods such as flow charts and histograms (Liker and Morgan 2006). The influence of Deming is clear in Japanese approaches to manufacturing. The Deming Prize, awarded by the Japan Union of Scientists and Engineers to companies that have demonstrated major developments in quality improvement in Japan, is testament to the enduring respect the American has been granted in Japan. While clearly a powerful approach, critics have said that it works well for perfecting existing technology over time, but that it inhibits drastic new ideas and radical innovation – a criticism regularly made of Japanese firms. The irony here is that the limitations of 'number-crunching' approaches (such as those of Deming and of others in the US) also became a central explanation for why the US economy fell behind Japan in the 1980s! (Byrne 1993; Starkey and McKinlay 1994). Moreover, lean is also widely criticized for being extremely demanding on workers, who face very fast line speeds and in reality have no say in determining work practices (Berggren 1992; Delbridge 1998; Graham 1995; Mehri 2005, 2006; Milkman 1997).

Again the problem arises of convenient mythologies becoming established in political economy and sociology – depending on how one spins the argument Deming's statistical process techniques can be depicted either as strengths or as weaknesses.

would be weakened. That never happened to the extent MacArthur and his occupational government wished. In fact, no sooner had the USA left and power was restored to Tokyo, did the *zaibatsu* business groups start to recollect, but in modified form.

After the end of the occupation, the Japanese 'developmental state' enacted some powerful policies. Central to this was the marginalization of the socialist and communist trade unions that were potentially an important source of power after the war (just as they were in Western Europe). Similarly to the situation in Germany, a powerful post-war compromise was eventually struck after prolonged conflict between management and labour across Japanese industry. The compromise is still of massive importance today. The essence of the Japanese industrial relations system has remained remarkably stable over the years. The Japanese post-war settlement granted significant rights to working people at the cost of subordinating them to very strict controls within the workplace. Workers were given good pay and conditions and the security of so-called 'lifetime employment' but in return for this they were compelled to give up a great deal of their autonomy over work tasks and the independence of their unions. Trade unions in large firms typically became firm-based rather than occupancy or craft-based. What this meant was the establishment of, for example, Toyota and Nissan unions rather than an independent union of auto workers. Company unions are not independent of company management, and in many ways are simply an extension of managerial control. Job security became a central feature of large Japanese firms, and staff hired from school or university tended to stay with the one company for life; being promoted and rewarded according to seniority-based payment systems.

So it was that large Japanese firms' employment policies became dominated by the notions of tall hierarchies of 'company men', and jobs for life for white-collar managers and for unionized blue-collar skilled workforces. This system has proved very durable and Japan has remained largely free of industrial relations strife except for periods in the 1960s and 1970s. Lifetime employment, seniority-based payment systems and company unions are often described as the 'three sacred treasures' of Japanese management. The system of lifetime employment is a key part of the socio-cultural phenomenon of the 'salaryman', a core employee of a Japanese firm or a government agency who has been with the company for life and slavishly follows the company line, devoting countless hours and years to the job (Matanle et al. 2008). The word salary*man* here is no accident – women in Japan were almost totally excluded from this core employment track, had massively lower employment status, pay and benefits, were barred from climbing the company hierarchy, and were expected to leave employment when starting a family (Ogasawara 1998; and see Exhibit 11.2).

Exhibit 11.2 Sexism in the Japanese office

Yuki Ogasawara's book *Office Ladies and Salaried Men* is a fascinating study of the myriad forms of sexism and ostracism that women face in traditional Japanese organizations. Usefully, it also draws attention to the subtle forms of resistance that women engage in as they attempt to survive and gain 'small victories'. Here, Ogasawara describes the menial work that 'Office Ladies' (OLs) were expected to perform in their usually truncated careers at her case study company, which she calls 'Tōzai Bank'.

'The OLS on the bank floor were assigned all kinds of miscellaneous jobs. They picked up mail from the basement mail room, sorted it, and distributed it to the appropriate addresses. They sorted and distributed various memoranda and notifications. They stored important materials by putting them in order, punching holes in the margins, and filing them in binders. They addressed envelopes. They copied documents and sent them by fax or by air-shooter. They printed out deposit balances. They typed letters and documents. They sent telegrams of condolence and congratulations. They bought gifts for customers. They served tea when customers came. They constantly picked up telephones and transferred calls to the appropriate people.'

'The OLS were also often summoned to fix paper jams and add paper to copiers and fax machines. They were sometimes even asked to paste together papers that had mistakenly been torn apart by men. A woman would, upon being called, jump up from her desk and scurry over to a general manager's desk, only to be asked to fetch him an eraser or refill his stapler. One OL sewed a button back on a general manager's suit.'

Source: Ogasawara 1998: 39. By Permission of University of California Press.

While heavily hierarchical, the gaps between the rungs in the ladder are relatively small in terms of wages and other benefits in Japan. The gap in salaries between top management and new recruits is far smaller than that in the USA (Dore 2000: 29–30). Symbolically at least, all (male) employees are treated much more equally in the Japanese context than they are in the Anglo-Saxon tradition; all staff wear the same company uniform (usually company-branded T-shirts, combat pants and running shoes in manufacturing companies). All employees eat in the same cafeteria and there is much less of an obvious white collar/blue collar divide in Japanese firms (Pfeffer 2005). The layout of a Japanese workplace is typically open-plan, which inhibits individual privacy and enforces a code of 'company-first' communitarianism (Graham 2003; Mehri 2005).

At a more general level, Japan is extremely egalitarian. It has the smallest income gap in the world (Wilkinson and Pickett 2009: 17). The Gini coefficient in Japan is very low – at just 24.9 it is slightly lower than the Nordic nations.[4]

[4] 'In Praise of Inequality', *Forbes*, 17 March 2003.

Exhibit 11.3 The traditional organization of corporate Japanese offices and departments

Fiona Graham (2003) wrote a very useful book on a highly traditional Japanese corporation she identifies as 'C-Life'. A former employee of the company, she writes with great clarity and detail about the everyday working realities of such a company. Below she describes the strict, military-style management hierarchy and the physical layout of the international department where she worked:

'The section was headed, in descending order of seniority, by the Buchō (department head) Fukubuchō (vice department head), and Kachō (section head). The section head did most of the practical work of the department as a liason with other departments throughout the company. There were 24 employees altogether in the international department at that time [...] housed in the main C-Life building: a large rectangular building with a passage down the middle of each floor. On either side of the passage were two enormous open-plan spaces. [...] The only subdivisions of the room were a small office for one of the directors at one end of the room and small rooms for conferences and holding meetings with guests to the company. The other sections ran the entire length of the room. Thus, one's every action was visible to everyone else for every minute of the day. The desks were placed close together and there was no room for files, so the desks were piled sometimes two feet high with documents.'

(Graham 2003: 23–4)

With the collapse of the bubble economy and the onset of recession in the 1990s, lifetime employment and seniority-based pay became subject to reforms (Ogoshi 2006), but the extent of change is vigorously debated in the literature (Jacoby et al. 2005). Most analysts suggest that both have been limited somewhat in recent years, but that both are likely to remain important (Mouer and Kawanishi 2005: 260). Dore (1973: 314–315) noted that pressures to dispose of lifetime employment and seniority-based pay systems go back as far as the 1950s, yet still they exist today.

Japanese growth pre-war and post-war possessed a substantial role for state intervention. A number of important Japanese firms were given financial support and direction from the government. A great example of this is Toyota Motors. This 'world class' firm started out as Toyoda Automatic Looms, a manufacturer of textile-making machinery. The owners were persuaded to move into auto manufacturing following strong direction from the government, which offered soft loans in support of what was at the time a very risky strategy (Bernstein 1997b). Sakichi Toyoda was so successful in his policy of emulating and improving upon Western technologies that in 1929, English firm Platts of Oldham signed a licensing agreement with Toyoda to allow it to manufacture copies of Toyoda's superior 'G-type' automatic looms. This represents a reversal of the former direction of technology transfer (Bernstein 1997b: 398). 'Directed credit programmes' such as these have formed important parts of state-led development models in several countries (Chang 2003: 16). In Japan the state coordinated many such policies, especially through the Ministry of International Trade and Investment (MITI) (Johnson 1992).

Under the stewardship of a state that protected Japanese industry, large firms grew rapidly in size and scope. They tended to grow within the context of establishing and maintaining many important relationships, many of which became highly traditional, long-term and mutually responsive. This long-term approach is demonstrated in the traditional relationships between large firms and hundreds or even thousands of their suppliers. Japanese companies are famous for the ways in which the set up long-term relationship with their subcontractors, in a long chain of trusted companies known as the vertical *keiretsu*. Large firms will tend to work with the same suppliers for decades, and will work closely with them, often transferring staff from the core firm to the supplier for the purposes of product development, quality control and even education and training of the supply chain staff. It is traditionally considered bad practice for large firms to cut these ties for any reason, especially on the grounds of seeking cheaper suppliers from elsewhere.

Another key part of these long-term relationships are the defensive mutual shareholdings between 'friendly' firms. Firms that have become related over time often bought blocks of shares in each other, thereby blocking any potential aggressive takeovers. While this situation is common throughout Japan, it is most commonly discussed in relation to the largest business groups, especially the so-called 'big six', the successors to the *zaibatsu*. With the maturing of the economy and the pressures for globalization, many of these long-term linkages have faded into little more than symbolic usage (Dore 2000: 141).[5] In other ways, however, the group structure remains important, as it allows financially weaker firms to be cross-subsidized by stronger members. All members are expected to operate closely with the 'main bank', which dominates the group. The six main Japanese enterprise groups are displayed in Table 11.1 overleaf.

Many of these relationships have complicated historical roots which cannot be explained very well with reference to neoliberal notions of free markets and selfish profit-maximizing activities. Many of the linkages make little obvious economic sense, involving

---

[5] For example, a commonly used anecdote refers to which beer someone should buy when out drinking with Japanese executives. If you are with Mitsubishi group salarymen then make sure you order Kirin beer as Kirin Brewery is part of the Mitsubishi keiretsu - do not order Asahi as that company is part of the Sumitomo empire!

Table 11.1 Traditional Business Groups in Japan in 1995

Grouping	Number of companies in the grouping	Main bank	Main trading company
Mitsui	27	Sakura	Mitsui Bussan
Mitsubishi	28	Mitsubishi	Mitsubishi Shoji
Sumitomo	20	Sumitomo	Sumitomo Shoji
Fuyo	29	Fuji	Marubeni
Sanwa	44	Sanwa	Nichimen Nissho Iwai
Ichikan	48	Daiichi Kangyo	Itochu Nissho Iwai

Source: Adapted from Mouer and Kawanishi (2005: 234). By permission of Cambridge University Press.

relationships between firms involved in unrelated product markets. For example, the car manufacturer Mazda is associated with Sumitomo group, a group that goes back to 17th century as one of the original *zaibatsu*. Other major Sumitomo-owned or Sumitomo-related firms include Sumitomo Heavy Industries, NEC electronics, Sumitomo Metals, Nippon Sheet Glass (although this merged in 2007 with UK's Pilkington) and Presidio Ventures, a wholly owned subsidiary of Sumitomo Corporation, which provides venture capital investments in US start-ups.

Sumitomo Corporation (along with many other venerable Japanese firms) makes great play of its prestigious history. Its website proudly displays the 'Business Principles' of the company which were originally formulated in 1891:[6]

> Article 1: Sumitomo shall achieve strength and prosperity by placing prime importance on integrity and sound management in the conduct of its business.
>
> Article 2: Sumitomo shall manage its activities with foresight and flexibility in order to cope effectively with the changing times. Under no circumstances, however, shall it pursue easy gains or act imprudently.

The concept of path-dependence is clearly visible here, in that Sumitomo deliberately refers to the pre-war, *zaibatsu* era on its current website. Reading the Principles one could be forgiven for thinking that the US occupation never happened. Major conglomerates such as Sumitomo clearly played a large role in the rapid growth of Japan since 1945, as did the various institutions of the Japanese state itself. The next section explores how this happened.

[6] http://www.sumitomocorp.co.jp/english/company/principles/index.html.

The era of high-growth

The 'era of high growth' or the 'Japanese miracle' is one of the most significant and widely discussed phenomena in the economic history of the 20th century. During the period of 1950–73 Japan demonstrated the most rapid and sustained growth rates of any OECD country, breaking records for year on year growth. This 'era of high growth' was no utopia. Japan's shattered economy was rebuilt post-war on the exploitation of workers and families, as working hours were extremely long and work tasks arduous. Industrial accidents were common and employees often worked in very unpleasant environments. The economy was structured around the low-cost, labour-intensive industries associated with industrialization; chemicals, steel, iron, coal. An important role was played by state spending, including major public works infrastructure projects such as railway lines and airports, and widespread use of infant industry protection policies in a similar vein to what went on before the war. Prime Minister Ikeda famously announced the 'income-doubling plan' in the early 1960s, where he declared the aim of a 7.2% annual GDP growth rate, thereby doubling per capita income over 10 years. Incredibly, this was actually achieved. GDP growth rates soared to over 11% per annum in the latter half of the 1960s, and stayed at an average of around 8% per annum across the whole period of post-war growth of 1950–73 (Chang 2003: 49). Much of this economic growth was enabled by investment from generous lending by banks on relatively soft terms. Low-interest lending was underwritten by the Japanese government (Johnson 1992). The institutional mix of the country strongly favoured and mutually reinforced Japan's fast growth, based partially on a strategy of domestic infant industry protection and subsequently on export growth.

Japan really started to move, and it started to raise alarm bells in the rest of the developed world, in the 1970s and 1980s. Japan's large firms developed capital-intensive industries, driving up the quality and value of their products, and expanding into highly lucrative export streams. Firms such as Sony and Matsushita (trading globally under the Panasonic brandname) in electronics, and Toyota and Honda in automotive, became the household names they are today. Japan built a highly successful export-driven economy, generating huge budget surpluses. Japan is still today by far the world's biggest creditor nation. Japan's hardworking families also generated massive levels of domestic savings – Japan Post became the largest postal savings account in the world. In Japan itself real incomes were growing fast. Japanese families tended to place their money into low-risk savings accounts. Personal credit lines were hard to establish, but Japanese citizens were often tied into very long-term mortgages (sometimes on 100 year terms, which would be passed on to the next generation!). This lent further weight to the impetus of the mission of national rebuilding. Citizens almost had a duty to work hard and to generate domestic savings in the construction of Japan's model of 'organized capitalism' (Lash and Urry 1987).

The 1964 Olympics in Tokyo were highly symbolic of this rebuilding mission. Hosting the Olympics symbolized that the country had 'made it' into the fold of developed, advanced nations.[7] The government made sure that the first Shinkansen high-speed railway line was open for business before the Games began, so that visitors to the country would be impressed by its technological advances. The Shinkansen thus became a powerful symbol of modern Japan (Hood 2006). The first stages of Japan's post-war rebuilding were complete – Japan was on a stable footing, and the groundwork had been laid for the next phase of development.

Analysts scrambled to find the answers as to how Japan went from utter devastation in 1945 to a major challenger to the USA and Europe by the 1980s, Some commentators looked for explanations in Japan's work culture, developing the notion of a culturally unique 'Nihonjinron' or Japanesesness, which emphasizes worker loyalty and servitude (Graham 2003: 10). As the USA and other Western economies struggled with cycles of stagnation, inflation and recession in the 1970s and 1980s, Japan just seemed to continue growing. A number of important books claimed that Japan would overtake the USA in the near future as the world's foremost economic power (Vogel 1979). Japan's threat to US economic hegemony was even reflected in popular culture. For example the wildly successful Hollywood action movie *Die Hard* (director John McTiernan, 1988) was set in the Los Angeles office towers of the American branch of a fictional Japanese firm 'The Nakatomi Corporation'. Early in the film one of the US executives jokes with Mr Takagi, the senior Japanese expatriate manager in charge of US operations. Tagaki quips: 'Pearl Harbor didn't work, so we got you with tape decks!'

It was widely argued that the focus on longevity and genuine quality production was the cornerstone of Japan's success, and that this focus had been lost by US companies as they become slaves to the whims of short-term stock market performance. The traditional Japanese model was all about stability and reliability, and long-term relationships governed and supported the whole business culture (Abbeglen and Stalk 1988; Dore 1987). Given the focus on lifetime employment, Japanese companies would be extremely careful about their recruitment processes for new hires (Graham 2003) and would put new graduate entrants

[7] A very similar situation surrounded the 2008 Olympic Games in China.

through very prolonged systems of training, orientation and indoctrination in company 'ways' (Dasgupta 2013: 58–79), even in some cases involving new graduates having to live together in company dormitories during weeks of orientation (Graham 2003: 53–64). Although such conservatism and caution is sometimes criticized as excessive, myopic and cronyist (Katz 2006), taking an ultra-long-term view for strategy and staff development can be beneficial in many ways.

However, in what is a recurring theme in this book across all the societies discussed, steady conservative, organized capitalism mutated into a hectic, credit-fuelled rush as 'irrational exuberance' came to Japan in a big way.

The 1980s: Japan triumphant; but hubris sets in

The Japanese economy seemed to sweep all before it in the 1980s. A whole string of Western electronics firms were snapped up by Japanese competitors, such as the UK's ICL which was purchased by Fujitsu in 1990. Other companies in the sector simply collapsed under the competitive strain such as the venerable RCA (Chandler 2006: 23–36). Equally famous companies such as IBM changed tack completely, selling off its production sites and moving into software development and consultancy. Worse, the car industry, one of the spiritual touchstones of America's economy, was being devastated by Japanese competition. GM, Ford and Chrysler seemed to have no answer to the Japanese challenge, as Toyota, Honda, Nissan and the smaller Japanese firms managed to take more and more market share away from the Big Three, mostly by building cheap, reliable, economical and safe cars, at a fraction of the US production costs (Halberstam 1987). But it did not stop there. Japan proved itself remarkably adept at 'moving up the value chain'. For example, Japanese carmakers were able to develop highly successful luxury products such as Toyota's Lexus badge (advertising slogan 'the Pursuit of Perfection') as well as 'economy boxes' such as the Suzuki Carry or the Daihatsu Charade. And the world's biggest selling motor vehicle of all time? The Honda Super Cub, a 49cc moped, whose simple, cheap, robust, reliable and enormously fuel-efficient design proved to be a phenomenon in Europe and Asia since its introduction in 1958.[8] The world's biggest selling car is the Toyota Corolla, with more than 35 million sales and counting. Japanese firms have proved themselves to be adept at high-, medium- and low-cost sectors. Japan's macroeconomic performance has been very impressive, and its rapid rise to world economic prominence

[8] 'Japan Sells Its 60 Millionth – Yes, Millionth – Super Cub', *Wired*, 23 May 2008.

still has not been replicated, not even yet by China (which has yet to develop a high-quality export sector, see Chapter 10).

Japan's success in export product markets is widely attributed to Japanese firms' genuine focus on quality improvement. The patience of the Japanese financial system allows difficult technology to be persisted with when firms in other countries (perhaps under greater short-term financial pressure) have abandoned them. One example is the Wankel rotary engine that was written off as too fuel-hungry by almost all car manufacturers in the 1980s. However, Mazda, having originally been almost bankrupted by its adoption of the Wankel in some of its car lines in the 1970s and 1980s (Fucini and Fucini 1992), dramatically resurrected the technology in the early 2000s after having vastly improved its efficiency. A rotary engine powers the RX-8 sports coupe which has won several international awards. The rotary, widely dismissed as a great feat of engineering but a commercial failure, has been made to work (arguably) by the persistence of Japanese engineering.[9]

However, patience is not always a virtue. Japanese firms are criticized for spending too long on high-tech but non-profitable products, and their firms are dominated by the engineering 'geeks' who are not commercially savvy. One example is the Sony MiniDisc, which was a technological marvel but never caught on (certainly not in the West anyway), mostly because it was let down by poorly designed and very limiting software developed by Sony, the lack of a clear marketing message and Sony's conservatism as regards the problem of music piracy. MiniDisc was ultimately killed by MP3, and especially by the (very well marketed) Apple iPod, which is inferior to MiniDisc in terms of technical sophistication. Based just on technological qualities, MiniDisc 'should' have replaced CDs. But in part due to Sony's conservatism the technology never got close to replacing the 'locked-in' format of CDs despite years of Sony persisting with the technology. The engineering dominance of Japanese firms at the expense of commercial nous has often been costly. Japanese firms can be too slow to get out of failing markets. MiniDisc was one of several lines of business cancelled by the new (Western) CEO of Sony, Sir Howard Stringer in the early 2000s.

Japan as a CME is renowned for incremental innovation over time, but there are dangers in simplifying this issue. There have been dozens of important, genuinely new and radical ideas generated by Japanese firms and engineers. There are elements of xenophobia in the argument that somehow 'the Japanese' are unable to think creatively and come up with

---

[9] It is highly debatable whether the RX-8 has been a commercial success or not. Is it always necessary for something to be a commercial success for it to be considered a success more generally? Engineering-led firms in Japan (and Germany) are often more tolerant of engineering successes but commercial failures.

genuinely new ideas of their own, preferring instead they rip off 'Western' ideas. Some very successful product innovations by Japanese firms include the Toyota Prius (the first commercially successful petrol-electric hybrid car), or the Nintendo Wii and DS games consoles (that significantly changed the video gaming market by bringing it in to new market segments, such as women and older players). The Sony Walkman was launched in 1979. Many thought that none of the above would catch on. Sony's Blu-ray format has also turned into a huge success. The technique of 'soft laser desorption' which was a major breakthrough in the field of mass spectrometry was also partially a Japanese invention for which a Nobel Prize for chemistry was awarded. Instant noodles was another massively influential Japanese invention, developed by Nissin Foods Inc.[10] The same is true of a wide range of entertainment and household products that have sold in huge number around the world such as Pokémon trading cards, karaoke machines, electric rice cookers (brought to market by Mitsubishi), manga and anime brands as Godzilla, Dragonball and Yu-Gi-Oh!, or multi-million selling video games such as the Metal Gear Solid series published by Konami. The top two – and five of the world's top 10 – video games publishers are Japanese (Storz 2008: 1480). So-called 'J-Cool' – the fad whereby very distinctly Japanese cultural products have been massively successful globally – has recently brought huge financial gains for Japan (Allison 2006). Japan has also long been at the forefront of robotics technologies, such as those used in manufacturing and for medical applications. While incremental innovation is clearly a part of Japanese economic success, it is wrong to argue that Japanese firms cannot come up with radical new products of their own (Storz 2008).

Deep problems, however, lurked below the shiny surface of the Japanese boom. Even as the economy continued to grow strongly other parts of the society were much less fortunate. The Japanese construction industry, for example, relied on the exploitation of poorly paid day labourers (Fowler 1996) and was renowned for bribery, 'pork-barrel' projects and links to organized crime (the *yakuza*). All across the labour market employees were forced to deal with extremely heavy workloads and an absence of workplace democracy. The labour historian Makoto Kumazawa has written widely on this subject, but as the Japanese model was so in favour in English-speaking parts of the world, critical research such as his were ignored or sidelined. He describes the frantic pace of work as 'working like mad to stay in place' (1996: 249–254). Moreover, bullying, secrecy, ostracism, sexism, authoritarianism and excessive workloads are very widespread in Japanese companies.

[10] A survey in 2000 found that Japanese citizens regard instant noodles as the country's most important invention, beating CDs, video games and karaoke machines, 'Japan Votes Noodles the Tops', *BBC News*, 12 December 2000.

Japan suffered a horrible shock which jolted it out of the complacency associated with the boom years. On 17 January 1995, the Great Hanshin Earthquake devastated the city of Kobe, causing around 6,400 deaths and terrible destruction of buildings and infrastructure. The arguably slow response of the regional and central government to the disaster was interpreted by many as symbolizing Japanese leadership's inability to predict and to deal with crises. The earthquake caused a lengthy shutdown of the region's economy, which was compounded by the lack of flexibility in a Japanese work culture that traditionally places great emphasis on presenteeism rather than teleworking or homeworking. Sato and Spinks (1998: 236) showed that more than half of the firms in Japan at the time had no disaster management plan in place. The earthquake was a shocking indication of the vulnerability of such a seemingly advanced nation.

A different kind of disaster was also looming just over the horizon.

The 1990s: 'the lost decade'

In the year 2000 Michael Porter and colleagues published the book *Can Japan Compete*? Such a title would have looked ludicrous in the 1980s when the story was all about runaway Japanese success and Anglo-Saxon stagnation. However, Porter et al.'s was simply one of many texts that emerged since the mid to late 1990s, once it had become clear that the hitherto massively successful Japan had run into severe trouble. The years 1997–99 were the worst of all, when it looked as if bankruptcies, scandals and plant shutdowns were running out of control (Matanle et al. 2008: 643).

What on earth had happened to cause such a turnaround? For some time, a major problem had been brewing in the world of Japanese finance. This problem became known as the 'bubble economy', and it was a pivotal event in Japanese economic history. It was a time of 'irrational exuberance' of the highest order. It also shows that bubbles can, and do, build up in co-ordinated market economies. The yen appreciated rapidly in the 1980s, hurting Japan's export economy. The Bank of Japan decided to reduce interest rates in response which caused a speculative boom. In the 1980s there seemed to be more money sloshing around the economy than people knew what to do with. The iconic Rockefeller Center complex in New York City was purchased by Mitsubishi Estate in 1989. The major Hollywood film studio Columbia Pictures was sold to Sony in 1989. All through the latter half of the 1980s prime US and European real estate was being bought up by cash-rich Japanese speculators, who were looking beyond the ridiculously inflated land prices of Tokyo or Osaka. Eventually the real-estate boom turned into bust as it became clear that an enormous asset-price bubble had been inflating in real estate and in stocks. This boom pushed up land and stock prices until the Bank doubled interest rates which put an end to bubble. The Nikkei index crashed on 31 December 1989, as the so-called 'bubble economy' burst.

The bursting of the bubble ushered in a major period of retrenchment in the 1990s and beyond. Japanese banks were overloaded with bad debts and non-performing loans. Confidence in the system plummeted. Companies and consumers were unwilling to spend and unwilling take on the risk of new loans. Banks, in any case, were refusing to offer them the opportunity of borrowing any more. The value of the Japanese stock price index almost halved. The unemployment rate soared. The collapse of Japan's bubble economy has got a lot in common with the subprime crisis of 2007 onwards in the West, and it was the key driver of the 1990s 'lost decade'. The longevity of the slowdown in Japan following their asset price bubble collapse is a sobering lesson for Western economies today.[11]

Mainstream authors such as Porter et al. (2000: 2) also blame the government for 'meddlesome' policics and 'over-regulation', as it clung on too long to its export-oriented policy and suppressed innovation and growth by over-controlling the economy. It is a somewhat perverse feature of so much literature on Japan that the very things said to be the drivers of Japanese growth (strong government, export excellence), suddenly appeared to be part of the problem once the bubble burst. The lost decade stimulated all kinds of authors to note that the sacred treasures of the Japanese system had become worthless. Lifetime employment and seniority-based pay had to be reformed, as they were products of the high-growth, organized capitalism era, and are now inhibiting growth. Carlos Ghosn, the new non-Japanese CEO of Renault-Nissan, announced plans to close some Nissan plants and scale back on its use of traditional keiretsu suppliers. Western authors such as Porter also criticized Japanese firms for having no identifiable strategy; instead, large Japanese firms continued to produce very wide ranges of essentially the same goods. Nobody was specializing and offering genuine alternatives, and they were refusing to make the tough decisions to downsize, outsource, streamline and focus their

[11] Several commentators have made direct links between the Japanese lost decade in the 1990s and the subprime recession of 2007 onwards, arguing that a similarly long period of stagnation and deflation is the likely outcome for the US and Europe. For example, 'An Awesome Warning', *Guardian*, 21 May 2009. The phrase 'a lost decade' was also used in reference to the UK in a front-page article in 2012. 'Pay Freeze to Last Until 2020 for Millions', *Guardian*, 23 January 2012.

operations, just as US firms have been doing since the 1980s (Porter et al. 2000: 82–85). Japanese firms were also criticized for being overly conservative and failing to develop strategies for going global. Porter and colleagues (2000: 86–89) provide the examples of Japanese clothes and chocolate manufacturers who were reluctant to push overseas. The only way out of crisis, according to Porter and so many other commentators of the time (and since) was for Japan to become more Westernized and liberalized, no matter how painful this might be in the short term. Japan needed to move to disorganized capitalism, investor capitalism, or the third spirit of capitalism, but seemed unwilling to do this.

Research into the effects of the slowdown on Japanese firms shows a mixed picture, but most of it points to a powerful new focus on cost-control throughout Japanese management (Hassard et al. 2009: 175–227; Jacoby 2005). While it would be wrong to assert that lifetime employment and seniority-based pay have disappeared, they have certainly been reformed and limited (Ogoshi 2006). Yuji Genda (2006) makes the interesting point that the slowdown actually hit Japanese youth the hardest of all, although the question of youth unemployment and under-employment remains largely hidden from view. The 'problem' of restructuring in Japan has been constructed around the job insecurities of the salaryman – the middle-aged, white-collar worker in a large firm (Dasgupta 2013; Matanle et al. 2008). While of course the salaryman is the most subsumed into the system and would have the most to lose from job loss, the fact is that few have actually become unemployed during the lost decade. According to Genda (2006: 53), out of a total of around 3 million unemployed in Japan, only 50,000 are college graduates aged between 45 and 54, not enough to fill all the seats in the International Stadium in Yokohama (2005: 12–13). The strength of the lifetime employment system has protected older workers from job loss, pushing the risks and penalties of unemployment onto the young. Many younger workers became so-called 'freeters', job-hoppers with no prospect of finding enduring employment (Mouer and Kawanishi 2005: 258). Younger Japanese have often been attacked by traditional sections of the media as showing no ambition, having no sense of commitment and becoming over-dependent on their hardworking parents. The rather nasty phrase sometimes used is 'parasite singles'.

Although young people have certainly had a hard time in the lost decade and since, salarymen have by no means had it all their own way. Substantial organizational changes have taken place in large Japanese firms as they have attempted to meet the pressures of the economic slowdown and the increase in international competitiveness. Early retirements have been widely used as firms have attempted to control their personnel costs (Hassard et al. 2009: 175–227). Tragically, the pressures of work and the threat of redundancy have driven some salarymen to suicide (Hassard et al. 2009: 231; Hood 2006: 182–3). Japan also has a rapidly ageing population. Much like other OECD nations, Japan is said to be facing a pensions 'time bomb' in the future as the demographics of the nation change. With a much larger percentage of pensioners relative to employees, and with all citizens tending to live longer lives, the Japanese state will face growing social security expenses. The median age of the population is expected to rise from 41.5 in 2000 to 51.1 in 2025 (Mouer and Kawanishi 2005: 256). Companies in Japan are rapidly closing the more generous defined-benefit (DB) pension schemes to new entrants which is exactly what has been going on in Anglo-Saxon nations for some time. 'Globalization appears to encourage firms to freeze or close their DB pensions despite the existence of different laws, customs, norms, histories, and, indeed varieties of capitalism' (Monk 2009: 54).

It is no surprise then that Genda writes of a 'vague uneasiness about the future' (2006: 2), and Dasgupta describes an 'intensifying collected socio-cultural anxiety' (2013: 41). Japan seems to be suffering from a kind of generalized anxiety disorder, which sounds very similar to a malaise that many authors claim is affecting Western nations. What Genda describes appears to be a very postmodern loss of confidence about the direction the society is going, or the very concept of 'progress' itself. In the UK, James (2007) coined the term 'affluenza' whereby citizens in rich societies nonetheless feel dissatisfied. Furedi (2004) describes a recent decline in confidence in experts and technology, replaced by widespread fear, panic, irrationality and a 'therapy culture'. Layard's work on happiness (2006) has been mentioned previously (see Chapter 1). It is interesting that similar discussions are also circulating in Japan. Perhaps this is because it is a mature OECD economy and it too is facing up to the question of what the point of all this prosperity might be (Mouer and Kawanishi 2005: 261–263). At least in the era of high growth people were clear on what was meant by the sacrifices they were making; it was for the good of the firm and the nation. Nowadays, in an era of stagnation, freeters, layoffs and parasite singles, what does it all mean?

Mid-2000s and beyond: Has Japan finally emerged from recession?

Even in the depths of despair there is hope. Following endless delay and several false dawns, eventually Japan seemed to emerge from recession. From around 2004 onwards, some much more upbeat assessments of the Japanese economy started to appear. Unemployment went back to its more usual, internationally very low, level. Companies reported higher profits once again. After over a decade in the doldrums, Japan was back in vogue, and so was Toyota and lean management (Liker and Hoseus 2007). Authors such as Katz (2006) and Vogel (2006) spoke of an updated Japanese model that had reformed slowly but successfully. Although it took far too long to finally recognize some of its weaknesses, these were duly noted by reformers in business and government, who liberalized certain areas but without ditching all of the traditional sources of Japanese strength. This slow, cautious response to the bubble recession was described as sensible and effective, even if it looked overly slow and conservative to reform-minded Westerners. *The Economist*, for example, noted in November 2007 a more effective, 'hybrid' Japan that had certainly changed and taken on certain elements of the 'more dynamic' Anglo-Saxon model, but probably had not gone far enough to satisfy the neoliberal bent of that particular journal.[12]

One year on, this positive message lay in ruins. Just as it looked as if Japan had finally emerged from the 1990s recession with the four good years of 2004–7, it was hit very hard by the subprime crisis that swept through the world economy in 2007 onwards. Although Japanese banks were mostly quite conservative and were not heavily exposed to the 'toxic' subprime loans that brought the Anglo-Saxon and Icelandic banking systems to the verge of collapse, the export-led model of Japan proved very vulnerable to the downturns in USA and Europe. Compared to January 2008 figures, the volume of all exports from Japan was down 45.7% in January 2009. Car exports were down 69% on the previous year.[13] Layoffs have been announced in a string of high-profile Japanese companies, especially in consumer electronics and cars as households scale back on their spending. Panasonic and NEC announced major cuts, and the carmakers Honda, Nissan and Toyota all stopped production for months as order books dried up. In May 2009, Toyota announced its first ever annual loss, of around US$4.3 billion. It predicted it would make bigger losses in the following financial year.[14]

On top of this, a devastating earthquake and tsunami – a far worse disaster than that of 1995 – hit the Tōhoku region in March 2011. This horrendous event took over 15,000 lives and came at a terrible time for Japan, compounding the economic misery. Politically, the country has been in turmoil since the late 2000s, with senior politicians frequently resigning amid a seemingly total collapse of public support and confidence.

[12] 'Japan's Hybrid Model of Capitalism', *The Economist*, 29 November 2007.

[13] 'Japan Exports Drop 46% in January', *BBC News*, 25 February 2009.

[14] 'Toyota Reports Record Loss and Predicts Worse to Come', *Guardian*, 8 May 2009.

The bubble-induced slowdown coupled with subprime seems to be pushing Japan even further towards the fragmentation of its employment system. Recent years have seen Japanese firms increase their use of part-timers and non-regular employees who are the first to be cut during downturns (Keizer 2008). Although Japanese institutions of lifetime employment, seniority-based pay and patient capital definitely still exist, they continue to be strongly threatened and need to adapt to survive. Hassard et al. (2009) report widespread use of Anglo-Saxon style reform measures in Japanese firms, such as the flattening of organizational hierarchies, the expansion of spans of control, expanded workloads and increased work intensity.

This is not to say that somehow Japan now resembles a Western, investor-driven economy. Japanese institutions still seem incompatible with the most liberal forms of US-style economic behaviour. For example, the Long-Term Credit Bank of Japan, a highly conservative Japanese financial company was on the verge of bankruptcy in the late 1990s. After nationalization it was eventually purchased by the US firm Ripplewood Holdings in 2000, with considerable financial input from US private equity group JC Flowers. Flowers attempted to convert it into a US-style commercial bank with the highly symbolic new name of Shinsei Bank (meaning 'Reborn'). Although JC Flowers benefited financially from the floatation of the new bank, the new company has so far been a rather dismal commercial failure. The US private equity involvement was very unpopular among the Japanese public, especially as the company was protected by government loans. According to Yorozu et al. (2013), employees of Shinsei have been dismayed by the 'aggressive' new direction of the company, and many have quit.

Arguably, the degree of Japanese financial innovation is underplayed in most of the literature on Japan which is fixated on the idea of the Japanese financial system being 'bank based'. Japanese financial companies are indeed more heavily regulated than Anglo-Saxon companies, but foreign operators in Tokyo are subject to considerably weaker regulation and control (Partnoy 2003: 231–232). There were several scandals in the mid-1990s involving venerable Japanese companies such as Sumitomo Corporation and Daiwa Bank (Partnoy 2003: 44–6). More recently, some major Japanese investment houses, such as Nomura, lost out heavily in the subprime fallout. Nomura had to write down almost US$1.6 billion in subprime-related losses in 2008. It also lost over US$300 million in losses relating to exposure to the Bernard Madoff scandal.[15] Despite their image as conservative and cautious, some Japanese companies have become embroiled in malpractice and in 'irrational exuberance' as they seek to make profits amid ever-greater levels

[15] 'Nomura Could Lose Millions in Madoff Affair', *France 24*, 15 December 2008.

of competition (just as firms do in LMEs and other CMEs such as France and Germany [Bruff and Horn 2012]). Ronald Dore's most recent writings portray Japan moving inexorably towards investor capitalism (2009; see Exhibit 11.5).

Exhibit 11.4 Ronald Dore on the ambivalent restructuring of Sony

Dore takes seriously the idea that the *rhetoric* of US-style shareholder value logic is becoming far more pronounced in Japan. But he also notes that actual change at the level of firms can often appear limited 'on the ground'. Here Dore describes Sony's recent corporate restructuring as a deliberate attempt to prove to outside investors that the company is now modelling itself on US 'best practice'. Although symbolic and somewhat superficial, this does not mean it is irrelevant.

'There is no clearer sign of the "cultural hegemony" exercised by the American business school than the frequency with which the word 'restructuring' occurs in the Japanese business press and the speeches of business leaders. In 1998 and at the beginning of 1999, the major electronics firms – Toshiba, Sony, and Hitachi – all announced what sounded like extensive plans for internal reorganization, always accompanied by announcements of substantial cutbacks in their employee headcount – the feature which made the headlines in the foreign business press.'

'Sony's restructuring is worth looking at closely since it has long been regarded as the leader, and is certainly the biggest, of the handful of Japanese manufacturing firms which have explicitly adopted American business practices – declaring decades ago that it was abolishing the seniority system [...], having an outside director on the board [...], adopting stock options for 200 senior managers as soon as the law was changed, and so on. [...] It does a great deal of business in the United States, of course, and the New York Stock Market is as important to it as Tokyo's; already 40 per cent of the firm's shares are owned outside Japan.'

'So it is not surprising that the first paragraph of the English-language press release announcing the restructuring ran: 'Sony corporation today announced plans to realign and strengthen its Group architecture. The objective of this change is to enhance shareholder value through what it calls "Value Creation Management"." [...]

'There are enough arbitrary elements in the calculation to make it entirely possible that bonus differentials will depend on much the same assessment by organizational superiors as before; but even if the change is only symbolic, symbols can have long-range effects on attitudes and practice.'

Source: Dore 2000: 116–118 By permission of Oxford University Press.

While subprime has certainly caused a slowdown in Japan, the country it is still unlikely to change the core features of its version of capitalism, just as the earlier Asian crisis of 1998 and the wider issue of the bubble economy did not fundamentally alter the system (Dore 1998).

Japanese firms still tend not to value the downsizing and focusing on core competencies approach put forward by Porter and other Western experts. While Japanese firms often appear overly conservative and risk-averse, Porter and others have tended to judge Japan by the US standards and trends that were prevalent at the time. Even in the USA, the ruthless cost-cutting and re-focusing strategies adopted by large firms do not always bear fruit, but they certainly cause a lot of pain (Cascio 2002). US firms often do not have the patience to stick with certain lines of business that are struggling. Instead they typically go for restructuring at the first signs of slowdown, and certain technologies or lines of business are never given the chance to work (Hassard et al. 2009: 72–73). Japanese-style stability and patience can be virtues (Katz 2006, Vogel 2006).

It is important to also note that there are plenty of critics from within Japan. Authors such as Kumazawa and Kamata have produced devastating critiques of the uncompromising work demands and the dishonesty of Japanese 'company as family' rhetoric. Kamata's (1983) critique of Toyota as a harsher form of Taylorism is compelling. Another very interesting, highly personal discussion of the harsh realities and disquieting contradictions of Japanese labour management comes from Kumazawa (1996). He provides a vivid account of a white-collar bank worker who was also a committed socialist. He mentions in great detail the ostracism of non-conformist staff including the blocking of promotion of active members of the non-mainstream union. Some were even shadowed by private detectives on their way home from work (Kumazawa 1996: 220). So much for the Japanese culture of workplace camaraderie or the 'employee favouring' firm! The 'office politics' were so severe that at one stage the bank officer writes in his diary: 'A dark pall hangs over the office, like smog' (Kumazawa 1996: 218).

More broadly Coates (2000: 237) mentions the 'appalling' exploitation of workers and marginalization of women in Japanese workplaces. He also notes the very low job satisfaction rates given in employee surveys in Japanese workplaces, which challenges the notion that Japanese work systems are based on trust and teamwork (Coates 2000: 237). Political cronyism is also a problem in Japan, which has erupted into scandals when the economy turned bad in the 1990s (Coates 2000: 238). Japanese firms have also been guilty of exploitation of cheaper labour regions in Asia, such as Taiwan (Coates 2000: 238–239). While some Japanese companies are at the cutting edge of new green technology development, others are also widely accused of major environmental destruction and resource depletion, such as Sumitomo's mining operations in Brazil.

The restructuring literature often displays a patronizing approach on the part of the Western 'business gurus'. Clearly Japan is suffering but does Japan really need to change so radically? For large parts of its economic history it has performed extremely well. It should be sufficient for Japan's pre-eminent economic status to speak for itself. Japan's government and firms have probably done enough not to be patronized, exoticized or belittled by Western writers. This was essentially the argument of a popular and controversial book *The Japan That*

Can Say No, written in 1989 by Akio Morita (co-founder of Sony) and Shintaro Isihara (governor of Tokyo). Japan is likely to remain a powerful and influential economy. Although weakened by subprime it has not been so directly exposed in terms of banking crises and government renationalization of the banks as we've seen in the USA and UK. Taking into consideration the enormous strides made since the devastation of war, Japan still surely ranks as a powerful economic success story. Relatively speaking Japan has very low levels of income inequality and of violent crime. Japanese society consistently outperforms many other OECD nations on general measures of quality of life and well-being (Wilkinson and Pickett 2009).

Conclusion: a troubled, yet powerful and influential model

This final section summarizes the Japanese CME and forms the conclusion to the chapter. Although some believe it has made significant moves towards 'investor capitalism' (Dore 2009), most regard Japan as conservative when it comes to change. Much of its traditional system of organized capitalism or managerial capitalism remains intact. There is a general sense in Japan that important, traditional linkages need to be treated with respect, and should not be allowed to wither on the vine. These relationships might be between commercial firms and their banks, with local and central government and bureaucracies, and with suppliers and other long-term trading partners. This kind of thinking tends to extend into the realm of employment relations; while there is often a core–periphery system at work, the central, core employees (especially at *kachō* level and above) are regarded as important stakeholders in the firm, not simply as 'human resources' that can be treated like any other kind of asset. Japanese firms, even during difficult times, are extraordinarily reluctant to part company with core employees.

Related closely to the above, a Japanese firm is more than something that can be bought, repackaged, and then sold like a US or British firm. It is not a purely economic tool for delivering shareholder value. It is genuinely considered by Japanese society to be much more serious than this; as part of the social fabric of Japan (Dore 2000). The close relationships between Japanese firms, especially the defensive blockholdings, serve to sustain this long term, mutual 'feel' of Japanese business. Japanese managers tend to lack interest in the kind of financial engineering that goes on so regularly in Anglo-Saxon countries. The value in it is not generally seen. There are some signs of a slow unravelling of mutual shareholdings (Witt 2006: 44–45), but these relationships still appear to be quite important, especially if one looks below the surface at the 'heart' of these companies' cultures.

Quarterly profits and share price movements are clearly a lot less important to Japanese firms than they are to US firms, which have increasingly embraced the notion of 'shareholder value' since the 1980s. This central difference, of patient capital in 'coordinated' Japan versus flighty capital in 'liberal' Anglo-Saxon countries, is recognized by practically all authors writing on Japan and/or VoC. This idea can be traced back at least as far as Dore (1973) and Deming (1982).

The bank-based financial system creates considerable pressures for continuity, rather than disruption in product development. Concepts such as lean and *kaizen* rest on the assumption of stability and steady improvement over time (indeed this is a frequent criticism made of lean, in that it inhibits radical creativity). Nevertheless, stability, regularity and incremental innovation can be very successful strategies, leading to cost savings and massive quality improvements, which can be seen clearly in Japanese automotive and electronics industries (see Coffey [2006] on the prolonged success of Toyota models that are improved over time without abandoning the basic formula or getting distracted by offering too many product lines and regular new product launches).

The wage structure is also traditionally very flat in Japan; there is little discretion available in the wage system to award higher salaries in order to recruit and retain 'high fliers'. The dominance of internal career structures in large Japanese firms pretty much eliminates the need for this anyway; traditionally speaking there is no real external labour market for management 'talent'. Instead, managers and senior experts such as engineers or designers are recruited from university and work their way up the company hierarchy. Core employees in Japanese firms tend to receive generous pay and benefits, especially defined benefit (DB) pensions (which also serve to lock employees in for 'life'). (The same is not true for 'periphery' employees who have little job security and greatly reduced pay and conditions.) Firms take training of their employees very seriously, and circulate them around the firm. While much of this might appear very attractive, there is a darker edge to this. In return for high pay and job security, Japanese workers are expected to pour in total devotion to their companies – excessive workloads, so-called 'service overtime' (for which staff are not paid!) and bullying are very commonplace. The personnel division holds a huge amount of power over the core employees, and workers in Japan have little choice but to directly follow what is demanded of them. Employees are quite strictly controlled and this can easily become a cause for resentment.

Behind the scenes Japanese political and economic power can be opaque and its ethics questionable. Favourable connections with local and central government can be important in Japan's somewhat conservative, insider business culture. Mehri (2005: 176–178) describes some very shady politicking involving rigged bidding for contracts (*dango*) and other forms of corruption in local government. The *yakuza* (Japanese organized crime gangs) have also been involved in corporate scandals in Japan, being used to disrupt AGMs and to intimidate opponents in disputes (Dore 2000: 78, 80). The notion of core and periphery also clearly extends into the area of gender relations in Japan; men are overwhelmingly the holders of formal organizational power, and women continue to be excluded from managerial positions. Toyota's first ever female *buchō* (division chief) was appointed in 2006.[16] At the time she was the only woman among 528 division chiefs in the firm. Mehri (2006: 78–79, 101–103) also mentions racist attitudes among some core Japanese employees towards agency staff from Africa and South America.

Japanese capitalism will always have its supporters and its detractors. The Indian author Gurcharan Das claims that '[T]he Japanese, despite their current troubles, can teach us many things' (2000: 152). It is easy to see the attraction of a less flighty, less marketing-obsessed version of the firm, one that really does value quality over a flashy sales pitch. The commitment to long-term employment and high skills are also laudable parts of the Japanese system. However, Japan also has a very limited state welfare system and its large firms tend to suffer from undemocratic, intensive working environments.[17] Sexism, bullying and ostracism are rife. While Japanese firms might not be pleasant places to work, they are part of a very impressive, and mostly very successful, business model, one that is likely to maintain its powerful influence over much of the world. In some sense Japan 'punches above its weight,' in that it has achieved so much from humble beginnings in a very short time. However it is important not to patronize Japan as so much Western literature does. This is a nation with a large population (over 120 million) that has been a major economic player for several generations. It will stand and fall by its own standards, and no amount of critique or

[16] 'Toyota Names 1st-ever Woman "Bucho" General Manager', *Kyodo News International*, 26 December 2006.

[17] One of the harshest elements of Japanese working life is the long hours and expectation of total commitment. Japan is infamous for the excessive work hours of its employees, and there is even a word for death from overwork – *karoshi*. Tragically, this problem rears its head fairly regularly, with over 315 requests for compensation from bereaved families in 2005-6. In 2002, a Toyota employee developed heart arrhythmia triggered by excessive overtime hours, and died after passing out at the factory at around 4am. In 2006, a senior Toyota engineer collapsed and died after returning from work. He had been working to tight deadlines on a petrol–electric hybrid version of Toyota's Camry range, a hugely successful model in the USA. 'Court Rules Toyota Employee Worked to Death', *Reuters*, 30 November 2007; 'Senior Toyota Engineer Died from Overwork', *Guardian*, 10 July 2008.

dismissal from Anglo-Saxon authors is likely to change this fact. Why should Japan change? Japan's economic system has, in general, been a massive success story, and one that is likely to continue. While it will probably always differ from Anglo-Saxon economies in many ways, Japan is a mature, rich country which is suffering from similar problems to those of Western nations and the USA, including some significant anxiety about the value and future of the mature capitalist system.

Further reading

Dore, R. (1973) *British Factory–Japanese Factory: The Origins of Diversity in Industrial Relations*, London: George Allen & Unwin.

This is a superb book that has dramatically stood the test of time. Although much has changed in the business world since the 1970s (especially in the UK), this book still captures the differences in approach to almost all areas of work in Japanese and British manufacturing firms. The detail in this book is phenomenal, and anyone interested in the traditions (and especially the strengths) of Japanese management should read it.

Mehri, D., (2005) *Notes From Toyota-Land: An American Engineer in Japan*, Ithaca, NY: Cornell University Press.

This hugely readable book takes the form of a personal diary of the author's experiences working in a Toyota subsidiary. Basically he hated it. The book is a brilliant critique of some of the boosterism around Japan, although his jaded judgments on Japan appear to be strongly influenced by his own negative experiences.

Mouer, K., and Kawanishi, H., (2005) *A Sociology of Work in Japan*, Cambridge: Cambridge University Press.

This is a complex but rewarding book to read. The authors provide a very detailed and thought-provoking coverage of a very wide range of features of the Japanese economy, focusing mostly on work and organization at meso level. It is essentially a neo-Marxist account, which provides a lot of coverage of the intense pressures and demands of Japanese organizations, and the different types of power that circulate Japanese work and society. Mouer and Kawanishi are critical of some of the mainstream assumptions on Japan, and are strong on the changes in recent years.

TWELVE Conclusion

Chapter objectives

- To recap one of the key arguments of the book; that various national economic models, while remaining distinct in important ways, have all gone through significant and fairly common forms of change. All have proceeded through liberal, organized and disorganized forms of capitalism
- To discuss the problem of institutional change in contemporary varietles of capitalism and to consider various approaches to interpreting institutional transformation which may be useful to students of VoC
- To briefly discuss the direction of contemporary world capitalism and to note a number of disturbing developments as regards the growth of instability and inequality amid economic growth
- To consider whether a 'more moral capitalism' is ever likely to arise

Understanding continuity and change, both in institutions and in capitalism

This book has covered a lot of ground and this will be a short conclusion. Previous chapters have provided historical accounts of the development, structuring and change of a range of national models of capitalism. The narrative has tracked the ways in which national models have all undergone change from liberal, organized to disorganized capitalism (Lash and Urry 1987), or through the first, second and third 'spirits of capitalism' (Boltanski and Chiapello 2005). Yet in doing so it is clear that each country remains significantly divergent; each nation progresses through these changes within the context of their own organizational, political and cultural norms. In other words, action and change are structured by various national institutions which govern and shape economic action (DiMaggio and Powell 1983; North 1991; Scott 2008a, 2008b; Whitley 1999).

In developing these chapters I have turned away from discussing or asserting abstract models and axes around which to compare the various subsystems of national business systems as they develop and change. I have found the presentation of such technical and abstract comparisons to be somewhat formulaic and their tendency towards 'idcal types' not always helpful. Instead I have tried to describe the more 'real world' features of these societies in turn, by relying on the findings and arguments of regional experts. The approach has been to focus on country details first then to shift the focus 'up' from the micro to the meso and macro where possible. Athough the VoC school typically explores a wider range of subsystems (such as innovation systems, or cultural systems) I have concentrated mostly on issues of finance and corporate governance, labour management and organizational change, and governmental policies and ideologies.

Many (perhaps all) nations have developed their own ideas about their supposed 'uniqueness', as expressed in such terms as *l'exception française*, American Exceptionalism, the *Sonderweg*; the 'British Disease', Japan's *Nihonjinron*. But on a broad level, I have tried to show that all of these nations have travelled through similar stages, towards increased integration and convergence on a neoliberal agenda, at least to some degree. Globalization is mythologized, propagandized and exaggerated, but increasing international integration and exposure is surely happening in certain important ways (Beaud 2001). It is harder than ever for OECD nations and their firms to remain isolated from each other. Globalization is an extension and intensification of trends that are inherent in capitalism, a capitalism that 'batters down all Chinese Walls' (Marx and Engels 2004/1848: 224).

Important similarities are, therefore, apparent in the broad development of nations through liberal, organized and disorganized capitalism. Classic literature reflects international trends in the achievements and setbacks of industrializing capitalism, such as Emil Zola's novel *Germinal* about striking French mineworkers, Charles Dickens' *Oliver Twist* on British workhouses and industrial poverty, John Steinbeck's *The Grapes of Wrath* on America's Great Depression. All the nations surveyed in this book have also exhibited periods of incalculable cruelty and violence: slavery and aggressive foreign policy in the USA, British imperialism, the Nazi holocaust, Japanese colonialism, Russia's serfdom and the Soviet Gulag, China's *laogai*. Thankfully, economic development has broadly broken out of its connection to such outright forms of barbarism. The problems facing people today in advanced societies are less about clear repression and control; their struggles are more around economic security and the prospects for stability and dignity in life and work.

While each country has taken different paths in their journey to the third spirit of capitalism, the overall directions of travel and even the timings of the changes, are similar. The major exceptions are the state socialist experiments in USSR and China (and partially in India). But even here it makes some sense to think of these periods as 'organized'. If not organized *capitalism*, they were at least organized *economies*. They also attempted reform, or gave up on command economies and planning at roughly the same points in time (1978 in China; perestroika in the 1980s in the USSR and the subsequent collapse in 1991; the abandonment of Congress Party economic planning after India's 1991 crisis).

National workforces are thus thrown into the same broad context of change and turbulence associated with the third spirit or disorganized capitalism. This entails near-constant organizational change, cutbacks to welfare state provisions, the rise of unemployment and uncertainty for all workers, perhaps especially the youth. Those fortunate to be in paid employment typically find work pressures mounting everywhere, despite the persistence of national distinctions in corporate governance and employment regimes (Green 2006; Hassard et al. 2009). As the world economy has matured it appears to have become much more competitive, and much more unequal in its rewards. Beaud reports massive global inequalities in income: 'On a worldwide level, the poorest 20 percent of the world's population possessed 2.3 percent of world resources in 1969, and 1.1 percent in 1994. The richest 20 percent possessed 69 percent of the resources in 1969, and 86 percent in 1994' (2001: 282). If Wilkinson and Pickett (2009) are correct about what inequality means for socio-economic outcomes, then this is a worrying development indeed.

Are there any alternatives to the globalization of this neoliberal, restless, ruthless, finance-driven capitalism? Lash and Urry's theory of the break from organized to disorganized capitalism is a binary change. But Boltanski and Chiapello's three 'spirits' of capitalism leave open the opportunity for a fourth 'spirit'. The second spirit was an attempt to rein in and regulate capitalism and markets. Perhaps after the subprime disaster we have made a return to the conditions that necessitated greater state involvement and an attempt to reformat capitalism as more stable, more subject to government control, and more fair in its opportunities and outcomes? Perhaps today's turbulent third spirit could develop into a fourth, as governments or social movements could find some way to rein capitalism in, make it more civilized, to do something about the runaway growth of inequality and the persistence of chronic poverty, precarious employment, unemployment and underemployment, and financial instability (Bourdieu 1999). But how? Who can do this? And with what means?

Many suggest that governments and states are the only possible counterbalance to market forces. For the USA critical sociologists Perrucci and Perrucci (2009: 136–139) suggest policies of public works, using public money to improve schools, housing, infrastructure and broadband cabling, creating thousands of jobs in the process. However, governments tend to be 'bought' by industry lobbies, and policy instruments have been blunted by years of neoliberal deregulation. Even with (arguably) the most liberal US President all time in Barack Obama, real 'change' has been limited, foundering on narrow, sectional, partisan interests which are hard to reconcile. Moreover these interests are often simply invisible to ordinary people unconnected to the machinations of Beltway politicians, bureaucrats and lobbyists. The result? Citizens back away from political involvement; understandably they become cynical and disenchanted (McCann 2013a). Surely we can imagine better ways to live than this (Granter 2009: 1–2)? How can we build a 'good society?' We are still waiting for an answer, and we probably have to look outside of the often rather technical field of VoC to find it.

I have been avoiding this question throughout the book, so maybe I should provide some notional answer here at the end. What is the 'best' model? Is there one? Throughout the book there are elements of the various country models that appear to be more morally defensible than others. These include the French traditions of refusing to work excessive hours, its traditionally strong regulation of capital markets, and publicly funded welfare state based on the principles of solidarity. The 'firm as community of fate' idea in Japan is attractive to some, but the abusive work practices hidden behind this paternalism are most unpleasant. German works councils and employee democracy seem both ethically and practically attractive. The USA will always be a powerful model because of its culture of openness and flexibility. Minimal government interference (arguably) may be necessary for the development of creative and knowledge industries, such as the media, IT and entertainment industries where the USA is now so strong. But on the flipside the USA for too long has pursued deregulation that has allowed reckless lending, mis-selling of financial products, 'off balance sheet' accounting and widespread corporate malfeasance. Free market fundamentalism does not work well for natural monopolies where markets tend to perform badly, where public spending and borrowing are often the most practical source of funding for healthcare systems, for transport infrastructure, green energy generation, or high-speed rail networks and fibre-optic broadband cabling. Workers probably deserve to have secure and stable forms of employment in order to plan for their future and the future of their children. All economies have elements of the above in different proportions: Anglo-Saxon openness in creative industries, German and Japanese expertise in engineering quality and reliability, Nordic work dignity and gender equality, French regulation of working hours and a strong welfare state. Is it realistic to pluck out one's 'favourite' parts of a model and propose them as parts of a new model for another country to emulate?

Institutional theory and VoC approaches (which often emphasize path-dependency, embeddedness and complementarity) would suggest that the answer is 'no' due to the importance of pre-existing institutional forms. No actor or group of actors is really in a position to make changes in such a deliberate and planned fashion; attempts at change are usually slow and incomplete, and often generate unintended consequences. Yet we've seen all the nations covered in this book go through significant forms of change. Firms, nations and institutions do change – they are not 'locked' in to path-dependent forms indefinitely, and change can be significant enough to disrupt national patterns to such an extent that their coherence as 'models' are called into question (Perraton and Clift 2004: 258).

How, then, can institutional change be explained? This is an important issue for VoC, and there can be many ways to go about answering this question. Here I highlight three related approaches that may be most relevant to our purposes:

- The first is to explore institutional change in terms of *evolution and adaption* in that institutions go through complex processes of redefinition, expansion, or collapse as the general circumstances under which they operate (such as political compromises) also undergo change (Steinmo 2010; Streeck 2011; Thelen 2004; Thelen and Streeck 2005).
- Second, and not dissimilar from the above, is the recently emerged stream of writing around so-called 'institutional work' (Lawrence et al. 2009). This concept tries to engage in a more serious discussion of the role of *agency* in changing institutions, as individuals and groups dissatisfied with the status quo engage in 'institutional work' which aims at the construction, maintenance, and disruption of institutions. To some extent, this work builds on the concepts of legitimacy as developed in new institutional theory (see for example DiMaggio and Powell 1983; Greenwood et al. 2002; Scott 2008a, 2008b) in that the construction, maintenance, and disruption of institutions engages with and potentially transforms discourses and narratives about what is acceptable and unacceptable across various socio-economic contexts (Schmidt 2002).

- Last, there are viewpoints that place more emphasis on various forms of political *power* in essentially forcing change to occur (Clegg 2010, Steger 2005; Steger and Roy 2010). Such views are often adopted by authors contributing from the discipline of political economy (Bruff and Horn 2012; Perraton and Clift 2004). Power may relate to senior-level political and business decision making and agenda setting, particularly forms of ideology that purport to be 'world best practice' (Callinicos 2001; Krause-Jensen 2006; Lazonick and O'Sullivan 2000; McCann et al. 2004; Ryner 2002). Such a view would, for example, take seriously the role of ideologies such as neoliberalism and shareholder value and the delicate political games of 'framing' change as 'desirable, necessary', or unavoidable (Bevir and Rhodes 2010; McCann 2013a; Vogel 2012) in order to make it more acceptable or tractable across various institutional contexts. Nevertheless these are essentially power games enacted by those with unequal access to the resources of power.

Accounting for how institutions change is one of the foremost challenges for students of VoC, because the prospect of institutional change can dislodge institutions from the centre of the analysis as concepts such as path-dependency, complementarity and embeddedness seem to make less sense. What levels of power does one attribute to traditional national institutions? Even amid the turbulence of globalization there definitely remain identifiably Japanese, British, American, India and Chinese ways of working and being. Through processes of *translation*, even as new ideologies and systems filter across national boundaries, there will never be 'full' convergence as if one model can simply map onto or even replace another. Change will always have to accommodate in some way to norms of legitimacy and acceptability that emerge from national institutional traditions, and 'best practice' changes as it is adopted elsewhere (Schmidt 2002).

However, VoC's language of innovation *system*, of complementarity, of institutional *interlock* doesn't really provide us with adequate tools for understanding critically the effects of versions of capitalism on human society – the balance between markets and regulation or state provision, the degree of competition, the ideas of a good society, a fair society, of decent work, of sustainable employment, ethics, justice, environmental protection. It contains nothing really on the *politics* of the way we understand and grapple with our perceptions of reality, of ideology, and of alternatives. We need to bring people back in to our analysis of economy, society and politics (Bevir and Rhodes 2010). We need to better understand their belief systems and motivations in an attempt to understand Varieties of Capitalism in a more normative sense (Steinmo 2010: 228).

Throughout the book I have tried to offer a fair analysis of a very wide and diverse literature. Just as Dore suggests in his classic work *British Factory–Japanese Factory* (1973: 9), the reader can probably detect where I am more favourable to some concepts and features of societies than others. But in a textbook of this kind it is probably not appropriate to make explicit political judgements. Having presented a very wide range of opinions, arguments, evidence and rhetoric in the book, I will leave it for the reader to decide which political interpretations he or she wishes to make about the complexity, the variety and the directions of change in contemporary capitalism.

References

Abbeglen, J.C., and Stalk, G. Jr, (1988) *Kaisha: The Japanese Corporation*, New York: Basic Books.

Abrams, F., (2002) *Below the Breadline: Living on the Minimum Wage*, London: Profile.

Ackryod, S., (2002) *The Organization of Business: Applying Organizational Theory to Contemporary Change*, Oxford: Oxford University Press.

Ackroyd, S., and Procter, S., (1998) 'Are the British Bad at Flexible Manufacturing?', in Delbridge, R., and Lowe, J., eds, (1998) *Manufacturing in Transition*, London: Routledge.

Adachi, Y., (2010) *Building Big Business in Russia: The Impact of Informal Corporate Governance Practices*, Abingdon: Routledge.

Adams, W.J., (1989) *Restructuring the French Economy*, Washington, DC: Brookings Institution.

Adler, P.S., (1992) 'The "Learning" Bureaucracy: New United Motor Manufacturing, Inc.', in Straw, B.M., and Cummings, L.L., eds, *Research on Industrial Behaviour*, Greenwich, CT: JAI Press.

Agnblad, J., Berglöf, E., Högfelt, P., and Svancar, H., (2001) 'Ownership and Control in Sweden: Strong Owners, Weak Minorities, and Social Control', in Barca, F., and Becht, M., eds, *The Control of Corporate Europe*, Oxford: Oxford University Press.

Albert, M., (1993) *Capitalism Against Capitalism*, London: Whurr.

Allen, F., Qian, J., and Qian, M., (2008) 'China's Financial System: Past, Present and Future', in Brandt, L., and Rawski, T.G., eds, *China's Great Economic Transformation*, Cambridge: Cambridge University Press.

Allen, M.M.C., (2004) 'The Varieties of Capitalism Paradigm: Not Enough Variety?', *Socio-Economic Review*, 2, 1: 87–108.

Allen, M.M.C., (2006) *The Varieties of Capitalism Paradigm: Explaining Germany's Comparative Advantage?*, Basingstoke: Palgrave.

Allen, R.C., (2011) *Global Economic History: A Very Short Introduction*, Oxford: Oxford University Press.

Allison, A., (2006) 'The Japan Fad in Global Youth Culture and Millennial Capitalism', in Lunning, F., ed., *Mechademia 1: Emerging Worlds of Anime and Manga*, Minneapolis: University of Minnesota Press.

Almond, P., and Ferner, A., (2006) *American Multinationals in Europe: Managing Employment Relations Across National Borders*, Oxford: Oxford University Press.

Amable, B., (2003) *The Diversity of Modern Capitalism*, Oxford: Oxford University Press.

Amatori, F., and Colli, A., (2011) *Business History: Complexities and Comparisons*, Abingdon: Routledge.

Ambler, J.S., (1985) 'French Socialism in Comparative Perspective', in Ambler, J.S., ed., *The French Socialist Experiment*, Philadelphia, PA: Institute for the Study of Human Issues.

Amsden, A., (1989) *Asia's Next Giant, South Korea and Late Industrialization*, Oxford: Oxford University Press.

Andreev-Khomiakov, G., (1997) *Bitter Waters: Life and Work in Stalin's Russia*, Boulder, CO: Westview Press.

Appay, B., (1998) 'Economic Concentration and the Externalization of Labour', *Economic and Industrial Democracy*, 19, 1: 161–184.

Applebaum, A., (2003) *Gulag: A History of the Soviet Camps*, London: Allen Lane.

Appelbaum, E., Bailey, T., Berg, P., and Kalleberg, A.L., (2000) *Manufacturing Advantage: Why High-Performance Work Systems Pay Off*, Ithaca, NY: Cornell University Press.

Appelbaum, E., Bernhardt, A.D., and Murmane, R.J., eds, (2003) *Low-Wage America: How Employers are Reshaping Opportunity in the Workplace*, New York: Russell Sage Foundation.

Arthur, B.W., (1989) 'Competing Technologies, Increasing Returns, and Lock-in by Historical Events', *Economic Journal*, 99: 116–131.

Ashwin, S., (1999) *Russian Workers: The Anatomy of Patience*, Manchester: University of Manchester Press.

Auboyer, J., (1965) *Daily Life in Ancient India: From 200 BC to AD 700*, London: Weidenfeld and Nicolson.

Augar, P., (2000) *The Death of Gentlemanly Capitalism: The Rise and Fall of London's Investment Banks*, London: Penguin.

Bacon, R.W., and Eltis, W.A., (1978) *Britain's Economic Problem: Too Few Producers*, London: Macmillan.

Bardhan, P., (2010) *Awakening Giants, Feet of Clay: Assessing the Economic Rise of China and India*, Princeton, NJ: Princeton University Press.

Barley, S.R., and Kunda, G., (2004) *Gurus, Hired Guns, and Warm Bodies: Itinerant Experts in a Knowledge Economy*, Princeton, NJ: Princeton University Press.

Barnes, J., (2005) 'Capitalism's Long Hot Winter has Begun', *New International*, 12: 99–204.

Barnett, C., (1987) 'Long-Term Industrial Performance in the UK: The Role of Education and Research, 1850–1939', in Morris, D., ed., *The Economic System in the UK*, 3rd edn, Oxford: Oxford University Press.

Bauman, Z., (1991) *Modernity and the Holocaust*, Ithaca, NY: Cornell University Press.

Baumol, W.J., Litan, R.E., and Schramm, C.J., (2007) *Good Capitalism, Bad Capitalism, and the Economics of Growth and Prosperity*, New Haven, CT: Yale University Press.

Beaud, M., (2001) *A History of Capitalism, 1500–2000*, New York: Monthly Review Press.

Becht, M., and Böhmer, E., (2001) 'Ownership and Voting Power in Germany', in Barca, F., and Becht, M., eds, *The Control of Corporate Europe*, Oxford: Oxford University Press.

Beck, H., (1992) 'The Social Policies of Prussian Officials: The Bureaucracy in a New Light', *The Journal of Modern History*, 64, 2: 263–298.

Bendix, R., (1956) *Work and Authority in Industry*, New York: John Wiley.

Benton, G., and Chun, L., eds, (2010) *Was Mao Really a Monster? The Academic Response to Chang and Halliday's* Mao: The Unknown Story, Abingdon: Routledge.

Berggren, C., (1992) *The Volvo Experience: Alternatives to Lean Production in the Swedish Auto Industry*, Basingstoke: Macmillan.

Berghahn, V.R., (1986) *The Americanisation of West German Industry 1945–1973*, New York: Berg.

Berman, M., (1982) *All That is Solid Melts into Air: The Experience of Modernity*, London: Verso.

Bernstein, J., (1997a) 'Japanese Capitalism', in McCraw, T., ed., *Creating Modern Capitalism: How Entrepreneurs, Companies, and Countries Triumphed in Three Industrial Revolutions*, Cambridge, MA: Harvard University Press.

Bernstein, J., (1997b) 'Toyoda Automatic Looms and Toyota Automobiles', in McCraw, T., ed., *Creating Modern Capitalism: How Entrepreneurs, Companies, and Countries Triumphed in Three Industrial Revolutions*, Cambridge, MA: Harvard University Press.

Bertero, E., (1994) 'The Banking System, Financial Markets, and Capital Structure: Some New Evidence from France', *Oxford Review of Economic Policy*, 10, 4: 68–78.

Best, M.H., (1990) *The New Competition: Institutions of Industrial Restructuring*, Cambridge: Polity.

Best, M.H., (2001) *The New Competitive Advantage: The Renewal of American Industry*, Oxford: Oxford University Press.

Bevir, M., and Rhodes, R.A.W., (2010) *The State as Cultural Practice*, Oxford: Oxford University Press.

Beyer, J., and Höpner, M., (2003) 'The Disintegration of Organised Capitalism: German Corporate Governance in the 1990s', *West European Politics*, 26, 4: 179–198.

Beynon, H., (1984) *Working for Ford*, Harmondsworth: Penguin.

Bissell, R.M., (1951) 'The Impact of Rearmament on the World Economy', *Foreign Affairs*, April.

Bjorn-Andersen, N., and Hedberg, B., (1977) 'Designing Information Systems in Organizational Perspective', in Nystrum, P., and Starbuck, W., eds, *Prescriptive Models of Organizations*, Amsterdam: North Holland, TIMS Studies Management Association.

Blackler, F.H.M., and Brown, C.A., (1978) *Job Redesign and Management Control: Studies in British Leyland and Volvo*, Farnborough: Saxon House.

Blackwell, W.L., (1974) *Russian Economic Development From Peter the Great to Stalin*, New York: New Viewpoints.

Blinder, A.S., (2006) 'Offshoring: The Next Industrial Revolution?', *Foreign Affairs*, March/April.

Bluestone, B., and Harrison, B., (1982) *The Deindustrialization of America: Plant Closings, Community Abandonment and the Dismantling of Basic Industry*, New York: Basic Books.

Boltanski, L., and Chiapello, E., (2005) *The New Spirit of Capitalism*, London: Verso.

Booth, C., and Rowlinson, M., (2006) 'Management and Organizational History: Prospects', *Management & Organizational History*, 1, 1: 5–30.

Bonefeld, W., (2012) 'Freedom and the Strong State: On German Ordoliberalism', *New Political Economy*, 17, 5: 633–656.

Borchardt, K., (1991) *Perspectives on Modern German Economic History and Policy*, Cambridge: Cambridge University Press.

Botticelli, P., (1997) 'British Capitalism and the Three Industrial Revolutions', in McCraw, T., ed., *Creating Modern Capitalism: How Entrepreneurs, Companies, and Countries Triumphed in Three Industrial Revolutions*, Cambridge, MA: Harvard University Press.

Bourdieu, P., ed., (1999) *The Weight of the World: Social Suffering in Contemporary Society*, Stanford, CA: Stanford University Press.

Brandt, L., and Rawski, T.G., eds, (2008) *China's Great Economic Transformation*, Cambridge: Cambridge University Press.

Brewer, M., Sibieta, L., and Wren-Lewis, L., (2008) 'Racing Away? Income Inequality and the Evolution of High Incomes', Institute for Fiscal Studies Briefing Note BN76, London: Institute for Fiscal Studies, avaiable at: http://www.ifs.org.uk/publications/4108.

Brown, W., Bryson, A., Forth, J., and Whitfield, K., eds, (2009) *The Evolution of the Modern Workplace*, Oxford: Oxford University Press.

Browning, C.R., (2001) *Ordinary Men: Reserve Police Battalion 101 and the Final Solution in Poland*, London: Penguin.

Bruff, I., and Horn, L., (2012) 'Varieties of Capitalism in Crisis?', *Competition & Change*, 16, 3: 161–168.

Buchanan, J., Dymski, G., Froud, J., Johal, S., Leaver, A., and Williams, K., (2013) 'Unsustainable employment portfolios', *Work, Employment and Society*, 27, 3: 396–413.

Bullock, A., (1991) *Hitler and Stalin: Parallel Lives*, London: HarperCollins.

Burleigh, M., (2001) *The Third Reich: A New History*, London: Pan.

Buxton, T., Chapman, P., and Temple, P., eds, (1998) *Britain's Economic Performance*, 2nd edn, London: Routledge.

Byrne, J.A., (1993) *The Whiz Kids: Ten Founding Fathers of American Business – And the Legacy They Left Us*, New York: Doubleday.

Byrne, J.A., (1999) *Chainsaw: The Notorious Career of Al Dunlap in the Era of Profit-at-any-Price*, New York: HarperBusiness.

Cai, F., Park, A., and Zhao, Y., (2008) 'The Chinese Labour Market in the Reform Era', in Brandt, L., and Rawski, T.G., eds, *China's Great Economic Transformation*, Cambridge: Cambridge University Press.

Callinicos, A., (2001) *Against the Third Way*, Cambridge: Polity.

Campbell, J.L., and Pedersen, O.K., (2007) 'The Varieties of Capitalism and Hybrid Success: Denmark in the Global Economy', *Comparative Political Studies*, 40, 3: 307–332.

Cappelli, P., Singh, H., Singh, J., and Useem, M., (2010) 'The India Way: Lessons for the U.S.', *Academy of Management Perspectives*, 24, 2: 6–24.

Carlzon, J., (1989) *Moments of Truth*, New York: HarperPaperbacks.

Caron, F., (1979) *An Economic History of Modern France*, London: Methuen.

Carr, W., (1972) *Arms, Autarky and Aggression: A Study in German Foreign Policy, 1933–1939*, London: Edward Arnold.

Carter, B., Danford, A., Howcroft, D., Richardson, H., Smith, A., and Taylor, P., (2013) 'Taxing Times: Lean Working and the Creation of (In)Efficiencies in HM Revenue and Customs', *Public Administration,* 91, 1: 83–97.

Cascio, W.F., (2002) 'Strategies for Responsible Restructuring', *Academy of Management Executive*, 16: 80–91.

Castells, M., (2000) *The Rise of the Network Society*, 2nd edn, Oxford: Blackwell.

Chan, A., (1993) 'Book reviews of Wu's "Laogai: The Chinese Gulag" and Shinqing's "A March of No Regret"', *The Australian Journal of Chinese Affairs*, 29: 172–175.

Chan, C., K-C., (2009) 'Strike and Changing Workplace Relations in a Chinese Global Factory', *Industrial Relations Journal*, 40, 1: 60–77.

Chandler, A.D., (1977) *The Visible Hand: The Managerial Revolution in American Business*, Cambridge, MA: Harvard University Press.

Chandler, A.D., (1990) *Scale and Scope: The Dynamics of Industrial Capitalism*, Cambridge, MA: Harvard University Press.

Chandler, A.D. (2006) 'How High Technology Industries Transformed Work and Life Worldwide from the 1880s to the 1990s', *Capitalism & Society*, 1, 2.

Chandler, G., (1998) 'The Political Framework: The Political Roller Coaster', in Buxton, T., Chapman, P., and Temple, P., eds, *Britain's Economic Performance*, 2nd edn, London: Routledge.

Chang, H-J., (2003) *Kicking Away the Ladder: Policies and Institutions of Economic Development in Historical Perspective*, London: Anthem Press.

Chang, H-J., (2006) *The East Asian Development Experience: The Miracle, the Crisis, and the Future*, London: Zed Books.

Chang, L.T., (2008) *Factory Girls: Voices from the Heart of Modern China*, London: Picador.

Chang, J., and Halliday, J., (2005) *Mao: The Unknown Story*, London: Jonathan Cape.

Chapman, P., and Temple, P., (1998) 'Overview: The Performance of the UK Labour Market', in Buxton, T., Chapman, P., and Temple, P., eds, *Britain's Economic Performance*, 2nd edn, London: Routledge.

Chernow, R., (2004) *Titan: The Life of John D. Rockefeller, Sr.,* New York: Vintage.

Chernow, R., (2010) *The House of Morgan: An American Banking Dynasty and the Rise of Modern Finance*, New York: Grove Press.

Chibber, V., (2003) *Locked in Place: State-Building and Late Industrialization in India*, Princeton, NJ: Princeton University Press.

Choucri, N., North, R.C., and Yamakage, S., (1992) *The Challenge of Japan Before World War II and After*, London: Routledge.

Christian, D., (1997) *Imperial and Soviet Russia: Power, Privilege and the Challenge of Modernity*, Basingstoke: Macmillan.

Cigno, A., and Rosati, F.C., (2002) 'Child Labour, Education, and Nutriotion in Rural India', *Pacific Economic Review*, 7, 1: 65–83

Clark, I., (2009) 'Owners and Managers: Disconnecting Managerial Capitalism? Understanding the Private-Equity Business Model', *Work, Employment and Society* 23, 4: 775–786.

Clarke, S., (2004) 'A Very Soviet Form of Capitalism? The Management of Holding Companies in Russia', *Post-Communist Economies*, 16, 4: 405–422.

Clegg, S., (2010) 'The State, Power, and Agency: Missing in Action in Institutional Theory?', *Management Inquiry*, 19, 1: 4–13.

Clift, B., (2007) 'French Corporate Governance in the New Global Economy: Mechanisms of Change and Hybridisation within Models of Capitalism', *Political Studies*, 55, 3: 546–567.

Clift, B., (2012) 'Comparative Capitalisms, Ideational Political Economy and French Post-Dirigiste Responses to the Global Financial Crisis', *New Political Economy*, 17, 5: 565–590.

Coates, D., (2000) *Models of Capitalism: Growth and Stagnation in the Modern Era*, Cambridge: Polity.

Coates, D., ed., (2002) *Models of Capitalism: Debating Strengths and Weaknesses*, Cheltenham, Edward Elgar.

Coates, D., ed., (2005) *Varieties of Capitalism, Varieties of Approaches*, Basingstoke: Palgrave.

Coffey, D., (2006) *The Myth of Japanese Efficiency*, Cheltenham: Edward Elgar.

Coggan, P., (2002) *The Money Machine: How the City Works*, London: Penguin.

Cohen, Y., (1991) 'The Modernization of Production in French Automobile Industry Between the Wars: A Photographic Essay', *The Business History Review*, 65, 4: 754–780.

Cohn, S.H., (1968) 'The Soviet Economy: Performance and Growth', in Treml, V.G., ed., *The Development of the Soviet Economy*, New York: Praeger

Cole, G.D.H., Bevan, A., Griffiths, J., Easterbrook, L.F., Beveridge, W., and Laski, H.J., (1943) *Plan for Britain: A Collection of Essays Prepared for the Fabian Society*, London: Routledge.

Collins, J., (2001) *Good to Great: How Some Companies Make the Leap ... and Others Don't*, New York: Random House.

Cooke, F.L., (2006) 'Informal Employment and Gender Implications in China: The Nature of Work and Employment in the Community Services Sector', *International Journal of Human Resource Management*, 17, 8: 1471–1487.

Cooke, W., (2003) 'The Denial of Slavery in Management Studies', *Journal of Management Studies*, 40, 8: 1895–1918.

Cooney, S., (2007) 'China's Labour Law, Compliance and Flaws in Implementing Institutions', *Journal of Industrial Relations*, 49, 5: 673–686.

Covey, S., (2004) *The 7 Habits of Highly Effective People*, London: Simon & Schuster.

Crafts, N.F.R., and Woodward, N.W.C., (1991) 'The British Economy Since 1945: Introduction and Overview', in Crafts, N.F.R., and Woodward, N.W.C., eds, *The British Economy Since 1945*, Oxford: Oxford University Press.

Crawford, R., Emmerson, C., and Tetlow, G., (2009) 'A Survey of Public Spending in the UK', Institute for Fiscal Studies Briefing Note BN43, London: Institute for Fiscal Studies, available at: http://www.ifs.org.uk/bns/bn43.pdf.

Cressey, P., Eldridge, J., and MacInnes, J., eds, (1985) *'Just Managing': Authority and Democracy in Industry*, Milton Keynes: Open University Press.

Culpepper, P.D., (1999) 'The Future of the High-Skill Equilibrium in Germany', *Oxford Review of Economic Policy*, 15, 1: 43–59.

Dalton, M., (1959) *Men Who Manage: Fusions of Feeling and Theory in Administration*, New York: Wiley.

Das, G., (2000) *India Unbound*, New York: Alfred A. Knopf.

Das, A.B., and Chatterji, M.N., (1967) *The Indian Economy: Its Growth and Problems*, Calcutta: Bookland Private Limited.

Dasgupta, R., (2013) *Re-Reading the Salaryman in Japan: Crafting Masculinities*, Abingdon: Routledge.

David, P.A., (1986) 'Understanding the Economics of QWERTY: The Necessity of History', in Parker, W.N., ed., *Economic History and the Modern Economist*, Oxford: Oxford University Press.

Davies, N., (1998) *Dark Heart: The Shocking Truth About Hidden Britain*, London: Vintage.

Davis, L.E., and Huttenbuck, R.A., (1986) *Mammon and the Pursuit of Empire: The Political Economy of British Imperialism, 1860–1912*, Cambridge: Cambridge University Press.

Deeg, R., and Jackson, G., (2007) 'Towards a More Dynamic Theory of Capitalist Diversity', *Socio-Economic Review*, 5, 1: 149–179.

Delbridge, R., (1998) *Life on the Line in Contemporary Manufacturing: The Workplace Experience of Lean Production and the 'Japanese' Model*, Oxford: Oxford University Press.

Deming, J.E., (1982) *Out of the Crisis*, Cambridge, MA: MIT Press.

Dicken, P., (2007) *Global Shift: Mapping the Changing Contours of the World Economy*, 5th edn, London: Sage.

DiMaggio, P.J., and Powell, W.W., (1983) 'The Iron Cage Revisited: Institutional Isomorphism and Collective Rationality in Organizational Fields', *American Sociological Review*, 48, 1: 147–160.

DiTomasso, M.R., and Schweitzer, S.O., (2013) *Industrial Policy in America: Breaking the Taboo*, Cheltenham: Edward Elgar.

Djelic, M-L., (1998) *Exporting the American Model: The Postwar Transformation of European Business*, Oxford: Oxford University Press.

Dobbin, F., and Boychuk, T., (1999) 'National Employment Systems and Job Autonomy: Why Job Autonomy is High in the Nordic Countries and Low in the United States, Canada, and Australia', *Organization Studies*, 20, 2: 257–291.

Doellgast, V., (2012) *Disintegrating Democracy at Work: Labor Unions and the Future of Good Jobs in the Service Industry*, Ithaca, NY: Cornell University Press.

Doellgast, V., and Greer, I., (2007) 'Vertical Disintegration and the Disorganization of German Unions', *British Journal of Industrial Relations*, 45, 1: 55–76.

Donaldson, P., and Farquhar, J., (1988) *Understanding the British Economy*, London: Pelican.

Dore, R., (1973) *British Factory–Japanese Factory: The Origins of Diversity in Industrial Relations*, London: Allen & Unwin.

Dore, R., (1987) *Taking Japan Seriously*, London: Athlone.

Dore, R., (1998) 'Asian Crisis and the Future of the Japanese Model', *Cambridge Journal of Economics*, 22, 773–787.

Dore, R., (2000) *Stock Market Capitalism: Welfare Capitalism: Japan and Germany Versus the Anglo-Saxons*, Oxford: Oxford University Press.

Dore, R., (2008) 'Financialization of the Global Economy', *Industrial and Corporate Change*, 17, 6: 1097–1112.

Dore, R., (2009) 'Japan's Conversion to Investor Capitalism', in Whittaker, D.H., and Deakin, S., eds, *Corporate Governance and Managerial Reform in Japan*, Oxford: Oxford University Press.

Dormois, J.-P., (2004) *The French Economy in the Twentieth Century*, Cambridge: Cambridge University Press.

Drees, B., and Pazarbasioglu, C., (1998) 'The Nordic Banking Crises: Pitfalls in Financial Liberalization?', International Monetary Fund Occasional Paper 161, Washington, DC: IMF.

Dudley, K.M., (1994) *The End of the Line: Lost Jobs, New Lives in Postindustrial America*, Chicago, IL: University of Chicago Press.

Duus, P., (1998) *Modern Japan*, Boston: Houghton Mifflin.

Eckes, A.E., (1995) *Opening America's Market: U.S. Foreign Trade Policy Since 1776*, Chapel Hill, NC: University of North Carolina Press.

Edwardes, M., (1971) *Nehru: A Political Biography*, London: Allen Lane.

Ehrenreich, B., (2002) *Nickel and Dimed: Undercover in Low-wage USA*, London: Granta.

Eichengreen, B., (2007) *The European Economy Since 1945: Coordinated Capitalism and Beyond*, Princeton, NJ: Princeton University Press.

Elbaum, B., and Lazonick, W., (1984) 'The Decline of the British Economy: An Institutional Perspective', *Journal of Economic History*, 44, 2: 567–583. [Reproduced in Coates, D., ed., (2002) *Models of Capitalism: Debating Strengths and Weaknesses*, Cheltenham, Edward Elgar, vol. 3: 205–221.]

Ellsberg, D., (2002) *Secrets: A Memoir of Vietnam and the Pentagon Papers*, London: Penguin.

Ellwood, D.W., (2012) *The Shock of America: Europe and the Challenge of the Century*, Oxford: Oxford University Press.

Elster, J., Preuss, U.K., and Offe, C., eds, (1998) *Institutional Design in Post-Communist Societies: Rebuilding the Ship at Sea*, Cambridge: Cambridge University Press.

Engels, F., (1887/1993) *The Condition of the Working Class in England*, Oxford: Oxford University Press.

Erturk, I., Froud, J., Johal, S., Leaver, A., and Williams, K., (2008) 'General Introduction: Financialization, Coupon Pool, and Conjecture', in Erturk, I., Froud, J., Johal, S., Leaver, A., and Williams, K., eds, *Financialization at Work: Key Texts and Commentary*, Abingdon: Routledge.

Esping-Andersen, G., (1990) *The Three Worlds of Welfare Capitalism*, Princeton, NJ: Princeton University Press.

Farrell, D., Laboissiere, M.A., and Rosenfeld, J., (2006) 'Sizing the Emerging Global Labor Market: Rational Behavior from Both Companies and Countries Can Help It Work More Efficiently', *Academy of Management Perspectives*, 20, 4: 23–34.

Fayol, H., (1949) *General and Industrial Management*, London: Sir Isaac Pitman & Sons, Ltd.

Fear, J., (1997) 'German Capitalism', in McCraw, T., ed., *Creating Modern Capitalism: How Entrepreneurs, Companies, and Countries Triumphed in Three Industrial Revolutions*, Boston, MA: Harvard University Press.

Feldenkirchen, W., (1991) 'Banking and Economic Growth: Banks and Industry in Germany in the Nineteenth-Century and their Changing Relationship During Industrialization', in Lee, W.R., ed., *German Industry and German Industrialization*, London: Routledge.

Fellman, S., (2008) 'Growth and Investment: Finnish Capitalism, 1850-2005', in Fellman, S., Iversen, M.J., Sjögren, H., and Thue, L., eds, *Creating Nordic Capitalism: The Business History of a Competitive Periphery*, Basingstoke: Palgrave Macmillan.

Figes, O., (1997) *A People's Tragedy: The Russian Revolution 1891–1924*, London: Pimlico.

Fillingham, D., (2007) 'Can Lean Save Lives?', *Leadership in Health Services*, 20: 231–241.

Finegold, D., and Soskice, D., (1988) 'The Failure of Training in Britain: Analysis and Prescription', *Oxford Review of Economic Policy*, 4, 3: 21–53. [Reproduced in Coates, D., ed., (2002) *Models of Capitalism: Debating Strengths and Weaknesses*, Cheltenham: Edward Elgar, volume 3: 222–254.]

Flanagan, R.J., (1987) 'Efficient and Equality in Swedish Labor Markets', in Bosworth, B.P., and Rivlin, A.M., eds, *The Swedish Economy*, Washington, DC: The Brookings Institution.

Fougère, D., Pouget, J., and Kramarz, F., (2009) 'Youth Unemployment and Crime in France', *Journal of the European Economic Association*, 7, 5: 909–938.

Fowler, E., (1996) *Sanya Blues: Laboring Life in Contemporary Tokyo*, Ithaca, NY: Cornell University Press.

Frank, T., (2000) *One Market Under God: Extreme Capitalism, Market Populism, and the End of Economic Democracy*, New York: Doubleday.

Frankel, F.R., (1978) *India's Political Economy, 1947–1977: The Gradual Revolution*, Princeton, NJ: Princeton University Press.

Freeland, C., (2000) *Sale of the Century: The Inside Story of the Second Russian Revolution*, London: Little, Brown.

Frick, B., and Lehmann, E., (2005) 'Corporate Governance in Germany: Ownership, Codetermination, and Firm Performance in a Stakeholder Economy', in Gospel, H., and Pendleton, A., eds, *Corporate Governance and Labour Management: An International Comparison*, Oxford: Oxford University Press.

Friedman, T.L., (2006) *The World is Flat: The Globalized World in the Twenty-First Century*, London: Penguin.

Froud, J., Johal, S., Leaver, A., and Williams, K., (2006) *Financialization and Strategy: Narrative and Numbers*, Abingdon: Routledge.

Froud, J., Johal, S., Law, J., Leaver, A., and Williams, K., (2011) 'Knowing What to Do? How Not to Build Trains', CRESC Research Briefing, avaiable at: http://www.cresc.ac.uk/sites/default/files/Knowing%20what%20to%20do.pdf.

Fucini, J.J., and Fucini, S., (1992) *Working for the Japanese: Inside Mazda's American Auto Plant*, New York: Free Press.

Fulbrook, M., (2005) *The People's State: East German Society from Hitler to Honecker*, New Haven, CT: Yale University Press.

Fulcher, J., (2004) *Capitalism: A Very Short Introduction*, Oxford: Oxford University Press.

Furedi, F., (2004) *Therapy Culture: Cultivating Vulnerability in an Uncertain Age*, London: Routledge.

Galbraith, J.K., (1958) *The Affluent Society*, Boston, MA: Houghton Mifflin.

Gallie, D., (1978) *In Search of the New Working Class*, Cambridge: Cambridge University Press.

Gamble, A., (1994a) *Britain in Decline: Economic Policy, Political Strategy, and the British State*, 4th edn, Basingstoke: Macmillan.

Gamble, A., (1994b) *The Free Economy and the Strong State: The Politics of Thatcherism*, 2nd edn, Basingstoke: Macmillan.

Gamble, J., (2010) 'Transferring Organizational Practices and the Dynamics of Hybridization: Japanese Retail Multinationals in China', *Journal of Management Studies*, 47, 4: 705–732.

Gandhi, I., (1975) *India: The Speeches and Reminiscences of Indira Gandhi, Prime Minister of India*, London: Hodder and Stoughton.

Ganesh, S., (2008) '"It's Time to Fly!" An Assessment of Optimism in Contemporary India', *Organization*, 15, 2: 293–298.

Garrick, J., ed., (2012) *Law and Policy for China's Market Socialism*, Abingdon: Routledge.

Gatrell, P., (1986) *The Tsarist Economy 1850–1917*, London: BT Batsford.

GAO, (2005) *Offshoring of Services: An Overview of the Issues*, Washington, DC: US Government Accountability Office.

Genda, Y., (2006) *A Nagging Sense of Job Insecurity: The New Reality Facing Japanese Youth*, Tokyo: International House of Japan Press.

Gennard, J., (2008) 'Editorial: Vaxholm/Laval Case: Its Implementations for Trade Unions', *Empoyee Relations*, 30, 5: 473–478.

Gereffi, G., Humphrey, J., and Sturgeon, T., (2005) 'The Governance of Global Value Chains', *Review of International Political Economy*, 12, 1: 78–104.

Gerschenkron, A., (1962) *Economic Backwardness in Historical Perspective: A Book of Essays*, Cambridge, MA: Harvard University Press.

Gerstner, L.V., (2003) *Who Says Elephants Can't Dance? How I Turned Around IBM*, New York: HarperCollins.

Giddens, A., (1998) *The Third Way: The Renewal of Social Democracy*, Cambridge: Polity.

Golding, T., (2003) *The City: Inside the Great Expectation Machine*, London: FT Prentice Hall.

Goldman M., (2003) *The Piratization of Russia: Russian Reform Goes Awry*, Abingdon: Routledge.

Goldman, M., (2010) *Petrostate: Putin, Power, and the New Russia*, Oxford: Oxford University Press.

Goodman, D.S.G., (1994) *Deng Xiapoing and the Chinese Revolution: A Political Biography*, London: Routledge.

Goodman, D.S.G., ed., (2008) *The New Rich in China: Future Rulers, Present Lives*, Abingdon: Routledge.

Goodman, D.S.G., and Zang, X., (2008) 'The new rich in China: the dimensions of social change', in Goodman, D.S.G., ed., *The New Rich in China: Future Rulers, Present Lives*, Abingdon: Routledge.

Gordon, A., (2003) *A Modern History of Japan, From Tokugawa to the Present*, Oxford: Oxford University Press.

Gordon, C., (1996) *The Business Culture in France*, Oxford: Butterworth-Heinemann.

Goscilo, H., and Strukov, V., eds, (2010) *Celebrity and Glamour in Contemporary Russia: Shocking Chic*, Abingdon: Routledge.

Government of India Planning Commission (1961) *Third Five Year Plan*, Delhi: Government of India Press.

Graham, L., (1995) *On the Line at Subaru-Isuzu*, Ithaca, NY: Cornell University Press.

Graham, F., (2003) *Inside the Japanese Company*, London: RoutledgeCurzon.

Grahl, J., and Teague, P., (1997) 'Is the European Social Model Fragmenting', *New Political Economy*, 2, 3: 405–426.

Gramlich, E.M., (1987) 'Rethinking the Role of the Public Sector', in Bosworth, B.P., and Rivlin, A.M., eds, *The Swedish Economy*, Washington, DC: The Brookings Institution.

Grandin, G., (2010) *Fordlandia: The Rise and Fall of Henry Ford's Forgotten Jungle City*, London: Icon Books.

Granovetter, M., (1985) 'Economic Action and Social Structure: The Problem of Embeddedness', *American Journal of Sociology*, 91, 3: 481–510.

Granter, E., (2009) *Critical Social Theory and the End of Work*, Farnham: Ashgate.

Green, F., (2006) *Demanding Work: The Paradox of Job Quality in Advanced Economies*, Princeton, NJ: Princeton University Press.

Greenwood, R., Suddaby, R., and Hinings, C.R., (2002) 'Theorizing Change: The Role of Professional Associations in the Transformation of Institutionalized Fields', *Academy of Management Journal*, 45, 1: 58–80.

Griffiths, J., (1943) 'Plan for the Key Industries', in Cole, G.D.H., Bevan, A., Griffiths, J., Easterbrook, L.F., Beveridge, W., and Laski, H.J., eds, *Plan for Britain: A Collection of Essays Prepared for the Fabian Society*, London: George Routledge and Sons.

Grugulis, I, Bozkurt, O., and Clegg, J., (2010) ''No Place to Hide?' The Realities of Leadership in UK Supermarkets', SKOPE Research Paper No. 91, available at: http://www.skope.ox.ac.uk.

Guha, R., (2007) *India after Gandhi: The History of the World's Largest Democracy*, Basingstoke: Pan Macmillan.

Guillen, M., (1994) *Models of Management*, Chicago, IL: University of Chicago Press.

Gupta, A., (2012) *Red Tape: Bureaucracy, Structural Violence, and Poverty in India*, Durham, NC: Duke University Press.

Gustafson, T., (1999) *Capitalism Russian-Style*, Cambridge: Cambridge University Press.

Habib, I., (1999) *The Agrarian System of Mughal India, 1556–1707*, 2nd edn, Oxford University Press.

Halberstam, D., (1987) *The Reckoning: How Japan Beat the United States in the Auto Industry War and Rewrote the Rules of International Business Competition*, London: Bantam.

Halberstam, D., (1992) *The Best and the Brightest*, New York: Ballantine Books.

Hall, P.A., (2008) 'The Evolution of Varieties of Capitalism in Europe', in Hancké, B., Rhodes, M., and Thatcher, M., eds, *Beyond Varieties of Capitalism: Conflict, Contradictions, and Complementarities in the European Economy*, Oxford: Oxford University Press.

Hall, P.A., and Soskice, D., (2001) 'An Introduction to Varieties of Capitalism', in Hall, P.A., and Soskice, D., eds, (2001) *Varieties of*

Capitalism: The Institutional Foundations of Comparative Advantage, Oxford: Oxford University Press.

Hamper, B., (1992) *Rivethead: Tales from the Assembly Line*, London: Fourth Estate.

Hancké, B., (2002) *Large Firms and Institutional Change: Industrial Renewal and Economic Restructuring in France*, Oxford: Oxford University Press.

Hancké, B., ed., (2009) *Debating Varieties of Capitalism: A Reader*, Oxford: Oxford University Press.

Hancké, B., Rhodes, M., and Thatcher, M., eds, (2008) *Beyond Varieties of Capitalism: Conflict, Contradictions, and Complementarities in the European Economy*, Oxford: Oxford University Press.

Hanser, A., (2008) *Service Encounters: Class, Gender, and the Market for Social Distinction in Urban China*, Stanford, CA: Stanford University Press.

Hanson, A.H., (1966) *The Process of Planning: A Study of India's Five-Year Plans, 1950–1964*, Oxford: Oxford University Press.

Harcave, S., (2004) *Count Sergei Witte and the Twilight of Imperial Russia: A Biography*, New York: M.E. Sharpe.

Harding, R., and Paterson, W.E., eds, (2000) *The Future of the German Economy: An End to the Miracle?* Manchester: University of Manchester Press.

Harrison, B., and Bluestone, B., (1988) *The Great U-Turn: Corporate Restructuring and the Polarizing of America*, New York: Basic Books.

Hassard, J., Morris, J., Sheehan, J., and Xiao, Y., (2006) 'Downsizing the Danwei: Chinese State-Enterprise Reform and the Surplus Labour Question', *International Journal of Human Resource Management*, 17, 8: 1441–1455.

Hassard, J., McCann, L., and Morris, J., (2009) *Managing in the Modern Corporation: The Intensification of Managerial Work in USA, UK and Japan*, Cambridge: Cambridge University Press.

Hassel, A., (1999) 'The Erosion of the German System of Industrial Relations', *British Journal of Industrial Relations*, 37, 3: 483–505. [Reproduced in Coates, D., ed., (2002) *Models of Capitalism: Debating Strengths and Weaknesses*, Cheltenham: Edward Elgar, vol. 2: 323–345.]

Hibbs, D.A., and Locking, H., (1995) 'Solidarity Wage Policies and Industrial Productivity in Sweden', *Nordic Journal of Political Economy*, 22: 95–108

Hikino, T., and Amsden, A.H., (1994) 'Staying Behind, Stumbling Back, Sneaking Up, Soaring Ahead: Late Industrialization in Historical Perspective', in Baumol, W.J., Nelson, R.R., and Wolff, E.N., eds, *Convergence of Productivity: Cross-National Studies and Historical Evidence*, Oxford: Oxford University Press.

Hildebrand, K.-G., (1978) 'Labour and Capital in the Scandinavian Countries in the Nineteenth and Twentieth Centuries', in Mathias, P., and Postan, M.M., eds, *The Cambridge Economic History of Europe*, volume VII, *The Industrial Economies: Capital, Labour, and Enterprise*, Cambridge: Cambridge University Press.

Hill, C., (2008) *International Business,* Maidenhead: McGraw-Hill.

Ho, N.P., (2012) 'Organized Crime in China: the Chongqing Crackdown', in Garrick, J., ed., *Law and Policy for China's Market Socialism*, Abingdon: Routledge.

Hoffman, D.E., (2002) *The Oligarchs: Wealth and Power in the New Russia*, Oxford: PublicAffairs.

Holtferich, C.L., (1991) 'Germany and the International Economy: The Role of the German Inflation in Overcoming the 1920/1 United States and World Depression', in Lee, W.R., ed., *German Industry and German Industrialization*, London: Routledge.

Hood, C.P., (2006) *Shinkansen: From Bullet Train to Symbol of Modern Japan*, Abingdon: Routledge.

Höpner, M., and Jackson, G., (2001) 'An Emerging Market for Corporate Control? The Mannesmann Takeover and German Corporate Governance', Max-Planck-Institute fur Gesellschaftsforschung, Discussion Paper 01/04, September.

Höpner, M., and Krempel (2004) 'The Politics of the German Company Network', *Competition & Change*, 8, 4: 339–356.

Hsing, Y., (2010) *The Great Urban Transformation: Politics of Land and Property in China*, Oxford: Oxford University Press.

Hsu, C.L., (2007) *Creating Market Socialism: How Ordinary People are Shaping Class and Status in China*, Durham, NC: Duke University Press.

Hu, A.G.Z., and Henderson, G.H., (2008) 'Science and Technology in China', in Brandt, L., and Rawski, T.G., eds, *China's Great Economic Transformation*, Cambridge: Cambridge University Press.

Huang, Y., (2005) *Selling China: Foreign Direct Investment During the Reform Era*, Cambridge: Cambridge University Press.

Huang, Y., (2008) *Capitalism with Chinese Characteristics: Entrepreneurship and the State*, Cambridge: Cambridge University Press.

Huang, Y., (2010) 'Debating China's Economic Growth: The Beijing Consensus or the Washington Consensus?', *Academy of Management Perspectives* , 24, 2: 31–47.

Hutton, W., (1995) *The State We're In*, London: Jonathan Cape. Chapter 10. [Reproduced in Coates, D., ed., (2002) *Models of Capitalism: Debating Strengths and Weaknesses*, vol. 1, Cheltenham: Edward Elgar.]

Hutton, W., (2002) *The World We're In*, London: Little, Brown.

Hwang, K.K., (1987) 'Face and Favor: The Chinese Power Game', *American Journal of Sociology*, 92, 4: 944–974.

Ishihara, S., (1991) *The Japan that Can Say No: Why Japan will be First Among Equals*, London: Simon & Schuster.

Jackson, G., Höpner, M., and Kurdelbusch, (2005) 'Corporate Governance and Employees in Germany: Changing Linkages, Complementarities, and Tensions', in Gospel, H., and Pendleton, A., eds, *Corporate Governance and Labour Management: An International Comparison*, Oxford: Oxford University Press.

Jacoby, S.M., (1997) *Modern Manors: Welfare Capitalism Since the New Deal*, Princeton, NJ: Princeton University Press.

Jacoby, S.M., (2005) *The Embedded Corporation: Corporate Governance and Employment Relations in Japan and the United States*, Princeton, NJ: Princeton University Press.

Jacoby, S.M., Nason, E.M., and Kazuro, S., (2005) 'Corporate Organization in Japan and the United States - Is there Evidence of Convergence?', *Social Science Japan Journal*, 8, 1: 43–68.

James, O., (2007) *Affluenza*, London: Vermilion.

Jasny, N., (1974) 'The Great Industrialization Drive', in Blackwell, W.L., ed., *Russian Economic Development from Peter the Great to Stalin*, New York: New Viewpoints.

Johal, S., and Leaver, A., (2007) 'Is the Stock Market a Disciplinary Institution? French Giant Firms and the Regime of Accumulation', *New Political Economy,* 12, 3: 349–368.

Johnson, C., (1982) *MITI and the Japanese Miracle*, Palo Alto, CA: Stanford University Press.

Johnson, C., (1991) *The Economy Under Mrs Thatcher, 1979–1990*, London: Penguin.

Johnson, C., (2002) *Blowback: The Costs and Consequences of American Empire*, London: Little, Brown.

Johnson, C., (2004) *The Sorrows of Empire: Militarism, Secrecy and the End of the Republic*, London: Verso.

Johnson, M., (1996) *French Resistance: Individuals Versus the Company in French Corporate Life*, London: Cassell.

Johnson, J., and Orange, M., (2003) *The Man Who Tried to Buy the World: Jean-Marie Messier and Vivendi Universal*, New York: Viking.

Jonung, L., Kiander, J., and Vartia, P., eds, (2009) *The Great Financial Crash in Finland and Sweden: The Nordic Experience of Financial Liberalization*, Cheltenham: Edward Elgar.

Kahan, A., (1989) *Russian Economic History: The Nineteenth Century*, Chicago, IL: University of Chicago Press.

Kamata, S., (1983) *Japan in the Passing Lane: An Insider's Account of Life in a Japanese Auto Factory*, London: Allen & Unwin.

Katz, R., (2006) *Japanese Phoenix: The Long Road to Economic Revival*, London: M.E. Sharpe.

Katz, H.C., and Colvin, A.J.S., (2011) 'Employment Relations in the United States', in Bamber, G.J., Lansbury, R.D., and Wailes, N., eds, *International & Comparative Employment Relations: Globalisation and Change*, 5th edn, London: Sage.

Kaysen, C., (1957) 'The Social Significance of the Modern Corporation', *American Economic Review* 47, 2: 311–319.

Keep, E., and Mayhew, K., (1999) 'The Assessment: Knowledge, Skills and Competitiveness', *Oxford Review of Economic Policy*, 15, 1: 1–15.

Keizer, A., (2008) 'Non-Regular Employment in Japan: Continued and Renewed Dualities', *Work, Employment & Society*, 22, 3: 407–425.

Keller, B.K., and Kirsch, A., (2011) 'Employment relations in Germany', in Bamber, G.J., Lansbury, R.D., and Wailes, N., eds, *International & Comparative Employment Relations: Globalisation and Change*, 5th edn, London: Sage.

Kerr, C., Dunlop, J.T., Harbison, F., and Meyers, C., (1960) *Industrial Society and Industrial Man: The Problems of Labor and Management in Economic Growth*, Cambridge, MA: Harvard University Press.

Kets de Vries, M., (1996) 'Leaders Who Make a Difference', *European Management Journal*, 14, 5: 486–493.

Khanna, T., (2007) *Billions of Entrepreneurs: How China and India are Reshaping Their Futures, and Yours*, Cambridge, MA: Harvard Business School Press.

Khanna, T., (2009) 'Learning from Experiments in China and India', *Academy of Management Perspectives*, 23, 2: 36–43.

Khurana, R., (2004) *Searching for a Corporate Savior: The Irrational Quest for Charismatic CEOs*, Princeton, NJ: Princeton University Press.

Kinderman, D., (2005) 'Pressure from Without, Subversion from Within: The Two-Pronged German Employer Offensive', *Comparative European Politics*, 3, 4: 432–463.

Klein, N., (2000) *No Logo,* London: Fourth Estate.

Klein, N., (2007) *The Shock Doctrine: The Rise of Disaster Capitalism*, London: Penguin.

Knight, J., and Ding, S., (2012) *China's Remarkable Economic Growth*, Oxford: Oxford University Press.

Kocka, J., (1978) 'Entrepreneurs and Managers in German Industrialization' in Mathias, P., and Postan, M.M., eds, *The Cambridge Economic History of Europe*, volume VII, *The Industrial Economies: Capital, Labour, and Enterprise*, Cambridge: Cambridge University Press.

Koehn, N.F., (1997) 'Josiah Wedgewood and the First Industrial Revolution', in McCraw, T., ed., *Creating Modern Capitalism: How Entrepreneurs, Companies, and Countries Triumphed in Three Industrial Revolutions*, Cambridge, MA: Harvard University Press.

Kotkin, S., (1997) *Magnetic Mountain: Stalinism as a Civilization*, Berkeley, CA: University of California Press.

Krause-Jensen, J., (2006) 'Ideology at Work: Ambiguity and Irony of Value-Based Management at Bang and Olufson', *Ethnography*, 12, 2: 266–289.

Kravchenko, V.A., (1947 /1988) *I Chose Freedom: The Personal and Political Life of a Soviet Official*, New York: Garden City Publishing.

Kristensen, P.H., (2011a) 'The Co-Evolution of Experimentalist Business Systems and Enabling Welfare States: Nordic Countries in Transition', in Kristensen, P.H., and Lilja, K., eds, *Nordic Capitalisms and Globalization: New Forms of Economic Organization and Welfare Institutions*, Oxford: Oxford University Press.

Kristensen, P.H., (2011b) 'Developing Comprehensive, Enabling Welfare States for Offensive Experimentalist Business Practices', in Kristensen, P.H., and Lilja, K., eds, *Nordic Capitalisms and Globalization: New Forms of Economic Organization and Welfare Institutions*, Oxford: Oxford University Press.

Krueger, G., (2004) *Enterprise Restructuring and the Role of Managers in Russia*, London: M.E. Sharpe.

Kumazawa, M., (1996) *Portraits of the Japanese Workplace: Labor Movements, Workers, and Managers*, edited and translated by A. Gordon, Boulder, CO: Westview.

Kusnet, D., (2008) *Love the Work, Hate the Job: Why America's Best Workers Are More Unhappy Than Ever*, Hoboken, NJ: Wiley

Lala, R.M., (2004) *The Creation of Wealth: The Tatas from the 19th to the 21st Century*, New Delhi: Penguin Portfolio.

Landes, D.S., (2003) *The Unbound Prometheus: Technological Change and Industrial Development in Western Europe from 1750 to the Present*, Cambridge: Cambridge University Press.

Lane, C., (1992) 'European Business Systems: Britain and Germany Compared', in Whitley, R., ed., *European Business Systems: Firms and Markets in the National Contexts*, London: Sage. [Reproduced in Coates, D., ed., (2002) *Models of Capitalism: Debating Strengths and Weaknesses*, Cheltenham: Edward Elgar, vol. 3: 275–308.]

Lane, D., (2000) 'What Kind of Capitalism for Russia? A Comparative Analysis', *Communist and Post-Communist Studies*, 33, 4: 485-504.

Lane, D., (2008) 'From Chaotic to State-led Capitalism', *New Political Economy*, 13, 2: 177–184.

Lash, S., and Urry, J., (1987) *The End of Organized Capitalism*, Cambridge: Polity.

Law, J., and Mol, A., (2002) 'Local Entanglements or Utopian Moves: An Inquiry into Train Accidents', in Parker, M., ed., *Utopia and Organization*, Oxford: Blackwell.

Lawrence, T.B., Suddaby, R., and Leca, B., eds, (2009) *Institutional Work: Actors and Agency in Institutional Studies of Organizations*, Cambridge: Cambridge University Press.

Layard, R., et al (2006), *The Depression Report: A New Deal for Depression and Anxiety Disorders*, London: London School of Economics, Centre for Economic Performance, available at: http://cep.lse.ac.uk/textonly/research/mentalhealth/DEPRESSION_REPORT_LAYARD.pdf.

Lazonick, W., (2005) 'Coporate Restructuring', in Ackroyd, S., Batt, R., Thompson, P., and Tolbert, P.S., eds, *The Oxford Handbook of Work and Organization*, Oxford: Oxford University Press.

Lazonick, W., and O'Sullivan, M., (2000) 'Maximizing Shareholder Value: A New Ideology for Corporate Governance?', *Economy and Society*, 29, 1: 13–35.

Ledeneva, A.V., (1998) *Russia's Economy of Favours: Blat, Networking, and Informal Exchange*, Cambridge: Cambridge University Press.

Liker, J.K. and Morgan, J.M., (2006) 'The Toyota Way in Services: The Case of Lean Product Development', *Academy of Management Perspectives*, 20: 5–20.

Liker, J.K., and Hoseus, M., (2007) *Toyota Culture: The Heart and Soul of the Toyota Way*, New York: McGraw-Hill.

Lin, J.Y., (1995) 'The Needham Puzzle: Why the Industrial Revolution Did Not Originate in China', *Economic Development and Cultural Change*, 43, 2: 269–292.

Lin, J.Y., Cai, F., and Li, Z., (2003) *The China Miracle: Development Strategy and Economic Reform,* rev. edn, Hong Kong: Chinese University Press.
Lloyd, C., and Payne, J., (2006) 'Goodbye to All That? A Critical Re-Evaluation of the Role of the High Performance Work Organization Within the UK Skills Debate', *Work, Employment and Society*, 20, 1: 151–165.
Lo, C., (2009) *Asia and the Subprime Crisis: Lifting the Veil on the Financial Tsunami*, Basingstoke: Palgrave.
Mackenzie, D., (2008) *An Engine, Not a Camera: How Financial Models Shape Markets*, Cambridge, MA: MIT Press.
Mandel, E., (1975) *Late Capitalism*, London: New Left Books.
Mankiw, N.G., (2004) 'The Economic Report of the President', Washington, DC: Council of Economic Advisors.
March, J.G., and Simon, H.A., (1958) *Organizations*, New York: Wiley.
Marsden, D., and Belfield, R., (2010) 'Institutions and the Management of Human Resources: Incentive Pay Systems in France and Great Britain', *British Journal of Industrial Relations*, 48, 2: 235–283.
Marsh, D., (2000) 'A Pattern of Light and Shade for the Germany Economy', in Harding, R., and Paterson, W.E., eds, *The Future of the German Economy: An End to the Miracle?* Manchester: University of Manchester Press.
Martin, C., (1996) 'French Review Article: The Debate in France over "Social Exclusion"', *Social Policy and Administration*, 30, 4: 382–392.
Maunce, M., Sellier, F., and Silvestre, J. -J., (1986) *The Social Foundations of Industrial Power: A Comparision of France and Germany*, Cambridge, MA: MIT Press.
McCann, L., (2013a) 'Public Services after the Crash: The Roles of Framing and Hoping', *Public Administration,* 91, 1: 5–16.
McCann, L., (2013b) 'Managing from the Echo Chamber: Employee Dismay and Leadership Detachment in the British Banking and Insurance Crisis', *Critical Perspectives in International Business*, 9, 4.
McCann, L., and Schwartz, G., (2006) 'Terms and Conditions Apply: Management Restructuring and the Global Integration of Post-Socialist Societies', *International Journal of Human Resource Management*, 17, 8: 1344.
McCann, L., Hassard, J., and Morris, J., (2004) 'Middle Managers, the New Organizational Ideology, and Corporate Restructuring: Comparing Japanese and Anglo-American Management Systems', *Competition & Change*, 8, 1: 27–44.
McCormick, K., (2007) 'Sociologists and "the Japanese model" - A Passing Enthusiasm?', *Work, Employment & Society*, 21, 4: 751–771.
McCraw, T., ed., (1997a) *Creating Modern Capitalism: How Entrepreneurs, Companies, and Countries Triumphed in Three Industrial Revolutions*, Cambridge, MA: Harvard University Press.
McCraw, T., (1997b) 'American Capitalism', in McCraw, T., ed., *Creating Modern Capitalism: How Entrepreneurs, Companies, and Countries Triumphed in Three Industrial Revolutions*, Cambridge, MA: Harvard University Press.

McCraw, T., and Tedlow, R.S., (1997) 'Henry Ford, Alfred Sloan, and the Three Phases of Marketing', in McCraw, T., ed., *Creating Modern Capitalism: How Entrepreneurs, Companies, and Countries Triumphed in Three Industrial Revolutions*, Cambridge, MA: Harvard University Press.

McGovern, P., Smeaton, D., and Hill, S., (2004) 'Bad Jobs in Britain: Nonstandard Employment and Job Quality', *Work and Occupations*, 31, 2: 225–249.

McMahon, R.J., (2003) *The Cold War: A Very Short Introduction*, Oxford: Oxford University Press.

Madsen, J.S., Due, J., and Andersen, S.K., (2010) 'Employment relations in Denmark', in Bamber, G.J., Lansbury, R.D., and Wailes, N., eds, *International & Comparative Employment Relations: Globalisation and Change*, 5th edn, London: Sage.

Manning, S., Massini, S., and Lewin, A.Y., (2008) 'A Dynamic Perspective on Next-Generation Offshoring: The Global Sourcing of Science and Engineering Talent', *Academy of Management Perspectives*, 22, 3: 35–54.

Marchington, M., Waddington, J., and Timming, A., (2011) 'Employment Relations in Britain', in Bamber, G.J., Lansbury, R.D., and Wailes, N., eds, *International & Comparative Employment Relations: Globalisation and Change*, 5th edn, London: Sage.

Marx, K., (1867/1976) *Capital: A Critique of Political Economy*, Volume One, London: Pelican.

Marx, K., and Engels, F., (1848/2004) *The Communist Manifesto*, London: Penguin.

Mastel, G., (1997) *The Rise of the Chinese Economy: The Middle Kingdom Emerges*, New York: M.E. Sharpe.

Matanle, P., McCann, L., and Ashmore, D., (2008) 'Men Under Pressure: Representations of the "Salaryman" and his Organization in Japanese Manga', *Organization*, 15, 5: 639–664.

Mathias, P., (1969) *The First Industrial Nation: An Economic History of Britain 1700–1914*, London: Methuen.

Maxton, G.P., and Wormald, J., (2004) *Time for a Model Change: Re-Engineering the Global Automotive Industry*, Cambridge: Cambridge University Press.

Meardi, G., (2006) 'Multinationals' heaven? Uncovering and Understanding Worker Responses to Multinationa Companies in Postcommunist Central Europe', *International Journal of Human Resource Management*, 17, 8: 1366–1378.

Mehri, D., (2005) *Notes From Toyota-Land: An American Engineer in Japan*, Ithaca, NY: Cornell University Press.

Mehri, D., (2006) 'The Darker Side of Lean', *Academy of Management Perspectives*, 20, 2: 21–42.

Meidner, R., (1993) 'Why did the Swedish Model Fail?', in Panitch, L., ed., *The Socialist Register 1993*, London: Merlin Press. [Reproduced in Coates, D., ed., (2002) *Models of Capitalism: Debating Strengths and Weaknesses*, Cheltenham: Edward Elgar, vol. 2: 395–412.]

Meyerson, P.-M., (1982) *The Welfare State in Crisis – the Case of Sweden*, Stockholm: Federation of Swedish Industries.
Midler, P., (2009) *Poorly Made in China: An Insider's Account of the Tactics Behind China's Production Game*, New York: Wiley.
Milkman, R., (1991) *Japan's California Factories: Labor Relations and Economic Globalization*, Los Angeles, CA: Los Angeles Institute for Industrial Relations.
Milkman, R., (1997) *Farewell to the Factory: Auto Workers in the Late twentieth century*, Berkeley, CA: University of California Press.
Milkman, R., (2006) *L.A. Story: Immigrant Workers and the Future of the U.S. Labor Movement*, New York: Russell Sage Foundation.
Mills, C.W., (1953) *White Collar: The American Middle Classes*, Oxford: Oxford University Press.
Mills, C.W., (1959) *The Power Elite*, Oxford: Oxford University Press.
Mills, J.H., Dye, K., and Mills, A.J., (2009) *Understanding Organizational Change*, Abingdon: Routledge.
Mirchandani, K., (2012) *Phone Clones: Authenticity Work in the Transnational Service Economy*, Ithaca, NY: Cornell University Press.
Mokyr, J., (1990) *The Lever of Riches: Technological Creativity and Economic Progress*, Oxford: Oxford University Press.
Mokyr, J., (2009) *The Enlightened Economy: Britain and the Industrial Revolution, 1700–1850*, London: Penguin.
Monk, A.H.B., (2009) 'The Financial Thesis: Reconceptualizing Globalisation's Effect on Firms and Institutions', *Competition & Change*, 13, 1: 51–74.
Morgan, G., Campbell, J.L., Crouch, C., Pedersen, O.K., and Whitley, R., eds, (2010) *The Oxford Handbook of Comparative Institutional Analysis*, Oxford: Oxford University Press.
Morin, F., (2000) 'A Transformation in the French Model of Shareholding and Management', *Economy and Society* 29, 1: 36–53.
Morris, D., (1987) 'Introduction', in Morris, D., ed., (1987) *The Economic System in the UK*, 3rd edn, Oxford: Oxford University Press.
Morris, J., Sheehan, J., and Hassard, J., (2001) 'From Dependency to Defiance: Work Unit Relationships in China's State Enterprise Reforms', *Journal of Management Studies*, 38, 4: 5–22.
Morrison, C., (2008) *A Russian Factory Enters the Market Economy*, Abingdon: Routledge.
Moss, D.A., (1997) 'The Deutsche Bank', in McCraw, T., ed., *Creating Modern Capitalism: How Entrepreneurs, Companies, and Countries Triumphed in Three Industrial Revolutions*, Cambridge, MA: Harvard University Press.
Mouer, R., and Kawanishi, H., (2005) *A Sociology of Work in Japan*, Cambridge: Cambridge University Press.
Moynahan, B., (1997) *The Russian Century: A History of the Last Hundred Years*, London: Pimlico.

Murphy, J., (2008) 'International Financial Institutions and the New Global Managerial Order', *Critical Perspectives on Accounting*, 19, 714-740.

NASSCOM (2012) *Annual Report 2011–2012*, New Delhi: NASSCOM.

Naughton, B., (2007) *The Chinese Economy: Transitions and Growth*, Cambridge, MA: MIT Press.

Nee, V., and Swedberg, R., eds, (2005) *The Economic Sociology of Capitalism*, Princeton, NJ: Princeton University Press.

Needham, J., (1965) *Science and Civilization in China: Volume 4, Part II: Mechanical Engineering*, Cambridge: Cambridge University Press.

new economics foundation (2009) *National Accounts of Well-Being: Bringing Real Wealth onto the Balance Sheet*, London: new economics foundation.

Newman, K.S., (2000) *No Shame in My Game: The Working Poor in the Inner City*, New York: Vintage.

Nordström, K., and R. Ridderstråle, J., (2004) *Karaoke Capitalism: Managing for Mankind*, London: FT Prentince Hall.

Nordström, K., and R. Ridderstråle, J., (2007) *Funky Business Forever: How to Enjoy Capitalism*, London: FT Prentince Hall.

North, D.C., (1981) *Structure and Change in Economic History*, New York: Norton.

North, D.C., (1991) *Institutions, Institutional Change, and Economic Performance*, Cambridge: Cambridge University Press.

Nove, A., (1992) *An Economic History of the USSR, 1917–1991*, London: Penguin.

Obama, B.H., (2008) *The Audacity of Hope: Thoughts on Reclaiming the American Dream*, Edinburgh: Canongate.

Office of National Statistics, (2011) *Labour Force Survey*, London: ONS.

Ogasawara, Y., (1998) *Office Ladies and Salaried Men: Power, Gender and Work in Japanese Companies,* Berkeley, CA: University of California Press.

Ogoshi, Y., (2006) 'Current Japanese Employment Practices and Employment Relations: The Transformation of Permanent Employment and Seniority-Based Payment System', *Asian Business & Management* 5, 4: 469–485.

Oi, J.C., (1995) 'The Rise of the Local State in China's Transitional Economy', *The China Quarterly*, 144: 1132–1149.

Olegario, R., (1997) 'IBM and the To Thomas J. Watsons', in McCraw, T., ed., *Creating Modern Capitalism: How Entrepreneurs, Companies, and Countries Triumphed in Three Industrial Revolutions*, Cambridge, MA: Harvard University Press.

Ohno, K., (2012) *Learning to Industrialize: From Given Growth to Policy-Aided Value Creation*, Abingdon: Routledge.

Ordonez, L.D., Schweitzer, M.E., Galinsky, A.D., and Bazerman, M.H., (2009) 'Goals Gone Wild: The Systematic Side Effects of Overprescribing Goal Setting', *Academy of Management Perspectives*, 23, 1: 6–16.

Osterman P., (2008) *The Truth about Middle Managers: Who They Are, How They Work, Why They Matter*, Boston, MA: Harvard Business School Press.

Osterman, P., Kochan, T.A., Locke, R.M., and Piore, M.J., (2001) *Working in America: A Blueprint for a New Labor Market*, Cambridge, MA: MIT Press.

O'Sullivan, M., (2003) 'The Political Economy of Comparative Corporate Governance', *Review of International Political Economy*, 10, 1: 23–72.

Palm, G., (1977) *The Flight From Work*, Cambridge: Cambridge University Press.

Panagariya, A., (2008) *India: The Emerging Giant*, Oxford: Oxford University Press.

Partnoy, F., (2003) *Infectious Greed: How Deceit and Risk Corrupted the Financial Markets*, London: Profile.

Payne, C., (2001) '"You duh Man!" African Americans in the Twentieth Century,' in Sitkoff, H., ed., *Perspectives on Modern America*, Oxford: Oxford University Press.

Perraton, J., and Clift, B., (2004) 'So Where are National Capitalisms Now?' in Perraton, J., and Clift, B., eds., *Where Are National Capitalisms Now?* Basingstoke: Palgrave.

Perrucci, R., and Perrucci, C.C., (2009) *America at Risk: The Crisis of Hope, Trust and Caring*, Lanham, MD: Rowman & Littlefield.

Peters, T.J., and Waterman, R.H. Jr., (1982) *In Search of Excellence: Lesson's from America's Best-Run Companies*, New York: Harper & Row.

Pfeffer, J., (2005) 'Producing Sustainable Competitive Advantage Through the Effective Management of People', *Academy of Management Perspectives* 19, 4: 95–106.

Piketty, T., (2003) 'Income Inequality in France, 1901–1998', *Journal of Political Economy*, 111, 5: 1004–1042.

Piore, M.J., and Sabel, C.F., (1984) *The Second Industrial Divide*, New York: Basic Books.

Polanyi, K., (1944) *The Great Transformation*, New York: Rinehart.

Pontusson, J., (1992) 'At the End of the Third Road: Swedish Social Democracy in Crisis', *Politics and Society*, 20, 3: 305–32. [Reproduced in Coates, D., ed., (2002) *Models of Capitalism: Debating Strengths and Weaknesses*, Cheltenham: Edward Elgar, vol. 2: 413–440.]

Pontusson, J., (2005) 'Varieties and Communalities of Capitalism', in Coates, D., ed., *Varieties of Capitalism, Varieties of Approaches*, Basingstoke: Palgrave.

Porter, M.E., (1990) *The Competitive Advantage of Nations*, Basingstoke: Macmillan.

Porter, M.E., Takeuchi, H., and Sakakibara, M., (2000) *Can Japan Compete?* Basingstoke: Palgrave Macmillan.

Pota, V., (2010) *India Inc.: How India's Top Ten Entrepreneurs are Winning Globally*, London: Nicholas Brealey.

Prahalad, C.K., and Hamel, G., (1990) 'The Core Competence of the Corporation', *Harvard Business Review*, May.

Presthus, R., (1979) *The Organizational Society*, New York: St Martin's Press.

Puffer, S.M., and McCarthy, D.J., (2007) 'Can Russia's State-Managed, Network Capitalism be Competitive? Institutional Pull Versus Institutional Push', *Journal of World Business*, 42, 1: 1–13.

Pun, N., (2005) *Made in China: Women Factory Workers in a Global Workplace*, Durham, NC: Duke University Press.

Randlesome, C., (1994) *The Business Culture in Germany*, Oxford: Butterworth-Heinemann.

Ratnam, C.S.V., and Verma, A., (2011) 'Employment Relations in India', in Bamber, G.J., Lansbury, R.D., and Wailes, N., eds, *International & Comparative Employment Relations: Globalisation and Change*, 5th edn, London: Sage.

Rauchway, E., (2008) *The Great Depression and the New Deal: A Very Short Introduction*, Oxford: Oxford University Press.

Rawski T.G., (1989) *Economic Growth in Prewar China*, Berkeley, CA: University of California Press.

Reddaway, P., and Glinski, D., (2001) *The Tragedy of Russia's Reforms: Market Bolshevism Against Democracy*, Washington, DC: United States Institute for Peace Press.

Redding, G., and Witt, M.A., (2007) *The Future of Chinese Capitalism: Choices and Chances*, Oxford: Oxford University Press.

Reich, R.P., (1991) *The Work of Nations: A Blueprint for the Future*, New York: Simon & Schuster.

Robins, N., (2006) *The Corporation That Changed the World: How the East India Company Shaped the Modern Multinational*, London: Pluto Press.

Roethlisberger, F.J., and Dickson, W.J., (1939) *Management and the Worker*, Cambridge, MA: Harvard University Press.

Rubery, J., (1994) 'The British Production Regime: A Societal-Specific Model?', *Economy and Society*, 23, 3: 335–354.

Ryner, J.M., (2002) *Capitalist Restructuring, Globalisation, and the Third Way: Lessons from the Swedish Model*, Abingdon: Routledge.

Sakwa, R., (2008) *Putin: Russia's Choice*, 2nd edn, Abingdon: Routledge.

Sandberg, Å., (1995) *Enriching Production: Perspectives on Volvo's Uddevalla Plant as an Alternative to Lean Production*, Aldershot: Avebury.

Sato, H., and Spinks, W.A., (1998) 'Telework and Crisis Management in Japan', in Jackson, P.J., and van der Wielen, J.M., eds, *Teleworking: International Perspectives: From Telecommuting to the Virtual Organisation*, London: Routledge.

Sayer, N., and Williams, B., (2007) *Lean for Dummies*, Indianapolis: Wiley Publishing.

Schmidt, V.A., (2002) *The Futures of European Capitalism*, Oxford: Oxford University Press.

Schultz, K.S., (1990) 'Building the "Soviet Detroit": The Construction of the Nizhnii-Novgorod Automobile Factory, 1927–1932', *Slavic Review*, 49, 2: 200–212.

Schwartz, G., (2003) 'Employment Restructuring in Russian Industrial Enterprises: Confronting a "Paradox"', *Work, Employment and Society*, 17, 1: 49–72.

Schwartz, G., (2004) 'The Social Organisation of the Russian Industrial Enterprise in the Period of Transition', in McCann, L. ed., (2004) *Russian Transformations: Challenging the Global Narrative*, London: Routledge.
Scott, J., (1941/1989) *Behind the Urals: An American Worker in Russia's City of Steel*, Bloomington, IN: University of Indiana Press.
Scott, W.R., (2008a) *Institutions and Organizations*, 3rd edn, Thousand Oaks, CA: Sage.
Scott, W.R., (2008b) 'Lords of the Dance: Professionals as Institutional Agents', *Organization Studies*, 29, 1: 219–238.
Sennett, R., (1998) *The Corrosion of Character: The Personal Consequences of Work in the New Capitalism*, London: W.W. Norton.
Sennett, R., (2007) *The Culture of the New Capitalism*, New Haven, CT: Yale University Press.
Sentance, A., (1998) 'UK Macroeconomic Policy and Economic Performance', in Buxton, T., Chapman, P., and Temple, P., eds, (1998) *Britain's Economic Performance*, 2nd edn, London: Routledge.
Sereny, G., (1996) *Albert Speer: His Battle With Truth*, London: Picador.
Sheehan, J., (1998) *Chinese Workers: A New History*, London: Routledge.
Sherman, S.G., and Latkin, C.A., (2002) 'Drug Users' Involvement in the Drug Economy: Implications for Harm Reduction and HIV Prevention Programs', *Journal of Urban Health*, 79, 2: 266–277.
Shonfield, A., (1965) *Modern Capitalism: The Changing Balance of Public and Private Power*, Oxford: Oxford University Press.
Shostak, A.B., (2006) 'Finding Meaning in Labor's "Perfect Storm": Lessons From the 1981 PATCO Strike', *Employee Responsibilities and Rights Journal*, 18, 3: 223–229.
Siebert, H., (2005) *The German Economy: Beyond the Social Market*, Princeton, NJ: Princeton University Press.
Simon, D., and Burns, E., (2009) *The Corner: A Year in the Life of an Inner-City Neighbourhood*, Edinburgh: Canongate.
Singh, J.P., (1990) 'Managerial Culture and Work-Related Values in India', *Organization Studies*, 11, 1: 75–101.
Sixsmith, M., (2011) *Russia: A 1000 Year Chronicle of the Wild East*, London: BBC Books.
Sjögren, H., (2008) 'Welfare Capitalism: The Swedish Economy 1850–2005', in Fellman, S., Iversen, M.J., Sjögren, H., and Thue, L., eds, *Creating Nordic Capitalism: The Business History of a Competitive Periphery*, Basingstoke: Palgrave Macmillan.
Smith, C., (2005) 'Beyond Convergence and Divergence: Explaining Variations in Organizational Practices and Forms', in Ackroyd, S., Batt, R., Thompson, P., and Tolbert, P.S., eds, *The Oxford Handbook of Work and Organization*, Oxford: Oxford University Press.
Smith, C., and Pun, N., (2006) 'The Dormitory Labour Regime in China as a Site for Control and Resistance', *International Journal of Human Resource Management*, 17, 8: 1456–1470.

Smith, R.C., and Walter, I. (2006) *Governing the Modern Corporation: Capital Markets, Corporate Control, and Economic Performance*, Oxford: Oxford University Press.

Smyser, W.R., (1993) *The German Economy: Colossus at the Crossroads*, New York: St Martin's Press.

Sorman, G., (2009) *Economics Does Not Lie: A Defense of the Free Market in a Time of Crisis*, New York: Encounter.

Spence, J., (1999) *Mao*, London: Weidenfeld and Nicholson.

Southworth, C., (2004) 'The Development of Post-Soviet neo-Paternalism in Two Enterprises in Bashkortostan: How Familial-Type Management Moves Firms and Workers Away From Labor Markets', in McCann, L., ed., *Russian Transformations*, Abingdon: Routledge.

Srivastava, R.S., (2005) 'Bonded Labor in India: Its Incidence and Pattern', Working paper, Cornell University ILR School, available at: http://digitalcommons.ilr.cornell.edu/forcedlabor.

Stark, D., (1995) 'Not by Design: The Myth of Designer Capitalism in Eastern Europe', in Hausner, J., Jessop, B., and Neilson, K., eds, *Strategic Choice and Path-Dependency in Post-Socialism*, Aldershot: Edward Elgar.

Starkey, K., and McKinlay, A., (1994) 'Managing for Ford', *Sociology*, 28, 4: 975–990.

Steger, M., (2005) *Globalism: Market Ideology Meets Terrorism*, Lanham, MD: Rowman and Littlefield.

Steger, M., and Roy, R.K., (2010) *Neoliberalism: A Very Short Introduction*, Oxford: Oxford University Press.

Steinfeld, E.S., (2004) 'China's Shallow Integration: Networked Production and the New Challenges for Late Industrialization', *World Development*, 32, 11: 1971–1987.

Steinmo, S., (2010) *The Evolution of Modern States: Sweden, Japan and the United States*, Cambridge: Cambridge University Press.

Storz, C., (2008) 'Dynamics in Innovation Systems: Evidence from Japan's Game Software Industry', *Research Policy*, 37, 9: 1480–1491.

Streeck, W., (1997) 'German Capitalism: Does it Exist? Can it Survive?', *New Political Economy*, 2, 2: 237–256. [Reproduced in Coates, D., ed., (2002) *Models of Capitalism: Debating Strengths and Weaknesses*, Cheltenham: Edward Elgar, vol. 2: 283–302.]

Streeck, W., (2011) 'Taking Capitalism Seriously: Towards an Institutionalist Approach to Contemporary Political Economy', *Socio-Economic Review*, 8, 1: 137–167.

Streeck, W., and Yamamura, K., (2001) *The Origins of Nonliberal Capitalism: Germany and Japan in Comparison*, Ithaca, NY: Cornell University Press.

Swamy, S., (1971) *Indian Economic Planning*, Delhi: Vikas Publications.

Swann, G., (1998) 'Quality and Competetiveness', in Buxton, T., Chapman, P., and Temple, P., eds, *Britain's Economic Performance*, 2nd edn, London: Routledge.

Swenson, P.A., (2002) *Capitalists Against Markets: The Making of Labor Markets and Welfare States in the United States and Sweden*, Oxford: Oxford University Press.

Swianiewicz, S., (1974) 'The Main Features of Soviet Forced Labor', in Blackwell, W.L., ed., *Russian Economic Development from Peter the Great to Stalin*, New York: New Viewpoints.

Tamura, Y., (2006) 'Japanese Production Management and Improvements in Standard Operations: Taylorism, Corrected Taylorism, or Otherwise?', *Asian Business & Management*, 5, 4: 507–527.

Taylor, P., and Bain, P., (2005) '"India Calling to the Far Away Towns": The Call Centre Labour Process and Globalization', *Work, Employment and Society*, 19, 2: 261–282.

Templar, R., (2005) *The Rules of Management,* Harlow: Pearson Education.

Thelen, K., (2004) *How Institutions Evolve: The Political Economy of Skills in Germany, Britain, the United States, and Japan*, Cambridge: Cambridge University Press.

Thelen, K., and Streeck, W., eds, (2005) *Beyond Continuity: Institutional Change in Advanced Poltiical Economies*, Oxford: Oxford University Press.

Thurow, L., (1992) *Head to Head: The Coming Economic Battle Among Japan, Europe, and America*, New York: Morrow.

Tillman, R.H., and Indergaard, M.L., (2005) *Pump & Dump: The Rancid Rules of the New Economy*, New Brunswick, NJ: Rutgers University Press.

Toynbee, P., (2003) *Hard Work: Life in Low-Pay Britain*, London: Bloomsbury.

Turner, G., (1971) *Business in Britain*, Harmondsworth: Penguin.

UNCTAD (2011) *World Investment Report*, Geneva: UNCTAD.

US Department of Health, Education, and Welfare (1973) *Work In America: Report of a Special Task Force to the Secretary of Health, Education and Welfare*, Boston, MA: MIT Press.

Useem, M., (1999) *Investor Capitalism: How Money Managers are Rewriting the Rules of Corporate America*, New York: Basic Books.

Varese, F., (2001) *The Russian Mafia: Private Protection in a New Market Economy*, Oxford: Oxford University Press.

Vatiero, (2010) 'The Ordoliberal Notion of Market Power: An Institutionalist Reassessment', *European Competition Journal*, 6, 3: 689–707.

Vitols, S., (2001) 'The Origins of Bank-Based and Market-Based Financial Systems: Germany, Japan, and the United States', in Streeck, W. and Yamamura, K., eds, *The Origins of Nonliberal Capitalism: Germany and Japan*, Ithaca, NY: Cornell University Press.

Vitols, S., (2004a) 'Continuity and Change: Making Sense of the German Model', *Competition & Change*, 8, 4: 331–337.

Vitols, S., (2004b) 'Negotiated Shareholder Value: the German Variant of an Anglo-American Practice', *Competition & Change*, 8, 4: 357–374.

Vitols, S., (2005) 'Changes in Germany's Bank-Based Financial System: Implications for Corporate Governance', *Corporate Governance*, 13, 3: 386–396.

Vogel, E.F., (1979) *Japan as Number One*, New York: HarperCollins.

Vogel, R., (2012) 'Framing and Counter-Framing New Public Management: The Case of Germany', *Public Administration*, 90, 2: 370–392.

Vogel, S., (2006) *Japan Remodeled: How Government and Industry are Reforming Japanese Capitalism*, Ithaca, NY: Cornell University Press.

von Laue, T., (1974) 'The State and the Economy', in Blackwell, W.L., ed., *Russian Economic Development from Peter the Great to Stalin*, New York: New Viewpoints.

Wacquant, L., (2004) *Body & Soul: Notebooks of an Apprentice Boxer*, Oxford: Oxford University Press.

Waddington, J., and Hoffmann, J., (2000) 'The German Union Movement in Structural Transition: Defensive Adjustment or Setting a New Agenda?', in Hoffmann, R., Jacoby, O., Keller, K., and Weiss, M., eds, *Transnational Industrial Relations in Europe*, Düsseldorf: Hans-Böckler-Stiftung.

Wade, R., (2003) *Governing the Market: Economic Theory and the Role of Government in East Asian Industrialization*, Princeton, NJ: Princeton University Press.

Walder, A.G., (1986) *Communist Neo-Traditionalism: Work and Authority in Chinese Industry*, Berkeley, CA: University of California Press.

Walker, C., (2011) *Learning to Labour in Post-Soviet Russia*, Abingdon: Routledge.

Wallace, T., (2008) 'Cycles of Production: From Assembly Lines to Cells to Assembly Lines in the Volvo Cab Plant', *New Technology, Work, and Employment*, 23, 1–2: 111–124.

Waring, J.J., and Bishop, S., (2010) 'Lean Healthcare: Rhetoric, Ritual and Resistance', *Social Science & Medicine*, 71, 7: 1332–1340.

Weber, M., (1905/1962) *Protestant Ethic and the Spirit of Capitalism*, London: Allen & Unwin.

Wedderburn, D., (1977) 'Introduction', in Palm, G., ed., *The Flight From Work*, Cambridge: Cambridge University Press.

Weitz, J., (1997) *Hitler's Banker*, London: Little, Brown.

Whitley, R., (1999) *Divergent Capitalisms: The Social Structuring and Change of Business Systems*, Oxford: Oxford University Press.

Whitley, R., ed., (2002) *Competing Capitalisms: Institutions and Economies*, Cheltenham: Edward Elgar.

Whitley, R., (2007) *Business Systems and Organizational Capabilities: The Institutional Structuring of Competitive Competences*, Oxford: Oxford University Press.

Whitley, R., (2009) 'U.S. Capitalism: A Tarnished Model?', *Academy of Management Perspectives*, 23, 2: 11–22.

Whyte, W.H., (1960) *The Organization Man*, London: Penguin.

WHO, (2000) *The World Health Report 2000 – Health Systems: Improving Performace*, Geneva: World Health Organisation.

Wilkinson, A., and Pickett, K., (2009) *The Spirit Level: Why More Equal Societies Almost Always Do Better*, London: Allen Lane.

Wilks, S., (1996) 'Class Compromise and the International Economy: The Rise and Fall of Swedish Social Democracy', *Capital and Class*, 58, Spring, 89–111. [Reproduced in Coates, D., ed., (2002) *Models of Capitalism: Debating Strengths and Weaknesses*, Cheltenham: Edward Elgar, vol. 2: 441–463.]

Williams, H., (1985) *APT: A Promise Unfulfilled*, London: Ian Allen.

Williams, K., Williams, J., and Haslam, C., (1990) 'The Hollowing Out of British Manufacturing and its Implications for Policy', *Economy and Society*, 19, 4: 456–90. [Reproduced in Coates, D., ed., (2002) *Models of Capitalism: Debating Strengths and Weaknesses*, Cheltenham: Edward Elgar, vol. 3: 331–365.]

Williams, K., Williams, J., and Thomas, D., (1983) *Why are the British Bad at Manufacturing?* London: Routledge and Kegan Paul.

Willmott, H., (1993) 'Strength is Ignorance; Slavery is Freedom: Managing Culture in Modern Organizations', *Journal of Management Studies*, 30, 4: 515–552.

Wilson, J.F., (1992) *The Manchester Experiment: A History of Manchester Business School, 1965–1990*, London: Paul Chapman.

Wilson, J.F., (1995) *British Business History, 1720–1994*, Manchester: Manchester University Press.

Wilson, S., (1955/2005) *The Man in the Gray Flannel Suit*, London: Penguin Classics.

Witzel, M., (2010) *Tata: The Evolution of a Corporate Brand*, New Delhi: Penguin Portfolio.

Witzel, M., (2012) 'The leadership philosophy of Han Fei', *Asia Pacific Business Review*, 18, 4: 489–503.

Witt, M.A., (2006) *Changing Japanese Capitalism: Societal Coordination and Institutional Adjustment*, Cambridge: Cambridge University Press.

Womack, J.P., Jones, D.T., and Roos, D., (1990/2007) *The Machine That Changed the World: How Lean Production Revolutionized the Global Car Wars*, London: Simon & Schuster.

Wood, G., and Demirbag, M., eds, (2012) *Handbook of Institutional Approaches to International Business*, Cheltenham: Edward Elgar.

Wortmann, M., (2004) 'Aldi and the German Model', *Competition & Change*, 8, 4: 425–441.

Wu, H.H., (1992) *Laogai: The Chinese Gulag*, Boulder, CO: Westview Press.

Xiang, B., (2007) *Global 'Body-Shopping': An Indian Labor System in the Information Technology Industry*, Princeton, NJ: Princeton University Press.

Yamamura, K., and Streeck, W., eds, (2003) *The End of Diversity? Prospects for German and Japanese Capitalism*, Ithaca: Cornell University Press.

Yergin, D., and Stanislaw, J., (2002) *The Commanding Heights: The Battle for the World Economy*, New York: Simon & Schuster.

Yorozu, C., McCann, L., Hassard, J., and Morris, J., (2013) 'Japan, Corporate Organizational Reform, and the Global Financial Crisis: The Case of Shinsei Bank', *Asia-Pacific Business Review*, 19, 2: 200–216.

Zhou, J., (2007) 'Danish for All? Balancing Flexibility with Security: The Flexicurity Model', IMF Working Paper WP/07/36, Washington, DC: IMF.

Zinn, H., (2005) *A Peoples' History of the United States, 1492–Present*, New York: Harper Perennial.

Zysman, J., (1983) *Governments, Markets, and Growth: Financial Systems and the Politics of Industrial Change*, Ithaca, NY: Cornell University Press.

Index